THE RISE OF THE MILITARY ENTREPRENEUR

THE RISE OF THE MILITARY ENTREPRENEUR

WAR, DIPLOMACY, AND KNOWLEDGE IN HABSBURG EUROPE

SUZANNE SUTHERLAND

CORNELL UNIVERSITY PRESS

Ithaca and London

First published 2022 by Cornell University Press

Librarians: A CIP catalog record for this book is available from the Library of Congress.

ISBN 978-1-5017-5100-4 (hardcover)
ISBN 978-1-5017-6500-1 (pdf)
ISBN 978-1-5017-6499-8 (epub)

Contents

ACKNOWLEDGMENTS

This book evolved considerably over the ten years it took to write. Those years were bursting with exciting interactions at conferences and workshops as well as informal conversations, other publication projects, summer trips to archives and libraries, and stimulating discussions with university students. A ten-year project is challenging to sustain alongside full-time teaching, service, and family obligations. For that reason, I am deeply grateful to the scholarly community that provided inspiration, camaraderie, and support. Above all, I am indebted to Paula Findlen, who shaped this book at every turn, journeying with me into the fascinating world of early modern military entrepreneurs. Without Paula's sharp guidance, amiable mentorship, and unflagging support, this publication would not have been possible.

Many others shaped this book. I would like to thank Daniel Riches and Gregory Hanlon for their close, careful readings of my manuscript, their advice, and their collegiality over the course of several years. Corey Tazzara and Jeff Miner, who were always willing to look at the roughest of drafts and respond to urgent calls for feedback, read and commented on nearly every page. Those who read the entire manuscript and provided critical direction and support include Nancy Kollmann, Laura Stokes, Tamar Herzog, Lydia Barnett, Noah Millstone, Liz Thornberry, and Nick Valvo. Still others read chapters or offered advice and feedback on different aspects of the book, including Philippe Buc, Molly Taylor-Poleskey, Filippo de Vivo, William Caferro, Becky McIntyre, and Andrew Fialka. Members of the Early Modern Mobility group at Stanford University—Leo Barleta, Iva Lelková, Katie McDonough, Rachel Midura, and Luca Scholz—provided fresh stimulus in the book's final stages. I fondly recall those who played roles early in the research, such as David Como, Michael Silber, and Jaroslav Čechura, and those who provided other tips and conversations, including Petr Mat'a, Thomas Winkelbauer, Renata Schreiber, Katrin Keller, Jeroen Duindam, Giampiero Brunelli, and Tryntje Helferrich. I am extremely grateful to György Domokos, who shares a fascination in Montecuccoli and has been uncommonly generous with information, especially sources and maps. I must also acknowledge the indefatigable efforts of archivists and librarians. Special thanks to Sarah Sussman and Nathalie Auerbach at Stanford and Pam Middleton and Ken Middleton at Middle Tennessee State University (MTSU), as well as the many wonderful archivists of the Austrian State Archives and Library in Vienna; the Moravian Provincial Archive in Brno; the National Archives in Prague; the State Regional Archives in Zámrsk and Litoměřice-Žitenice; the State Archives in Florence, Modena, Mantua, and Siena; the Este Library in Modena; the University Library in Bologna; and the Vatican Secret Archive, Vatican Library, and National Library in Rome. The Lobkowicz family and their staff kindly granted me special access to the family's personal papers in Žitenice. Finally, thank you to the editorial team at Cornell University Press, especially Emily Andrew and Bethany Wasik.

The research and writing of this book were supported by funding from MTSU, the Stanford University History Department, the William J. Fulbright Commission, the National Endowment for the Humanities, the Mabelle McLeod Lewis Memorial Fund, the UPS Endowment Fund at Stanford University, the Suppes Center for the History and Philosophy of Science at Stanford University, two Faculty Research and Creative Activity Committee grants from MTSU, and the Foreign Language and Area Studies Fellowships program. I am so grateful for this financial support.

Portions of chapter 2 were previously published as "War, Mobility, and Letters at the Start of the Thirty Years War, 1621–23," in *The Renaissance of Letters: Knowledge and Community in Italy, 1300–1650*, ed. Paula Findlen and Suzanne Sutherland (New York: Routledge, 2019), 272–92.

Portions of chapters 2 and 3 were previously published as "Warfare, Entrepreneurship, and Politics," in *The Routledge History of the Renaissance*, ed. William Caferro (New York: Routledge, 2017), 302–18. A portion of chapter 4 was previously published as "From Battlefield to Court: Raimondo Montecuccoli's Diplomatic Mission to Queen Christina of Sweden after the Thirty Years War," *Sixteenth Century Journal* 47 (2016), 4 (Winter): 915–38.

Over the course of the ten years I spent writing this book, my husband and I raised two children, and we all experienced a global pandemic. I would like to thank the caretakers, especially Joan and Pat Sutherland and Eva Ducháčková, as well as the daycare, preschool, and elementary school teachers who make it possible for parents to write books. I am especially grateful to Karel.

This book is dedicated to Karel, Lukáš, and Veronika.

NOTE ON TERMS

During the seventeenth century, "Austria" referred to the House of Austria and included both the Spanish and Central European Habsburgs. However, historians overwhelmingly use the phrase "Austrian Habsburgs" to denote the Central European branch of the family, with its base in Vienna. I follow standard practice and use "Austrian Habsburgs" in the same manner. I also at times refer to "Austria," which connotes the Austrian Habsburg monarchy. I often call the Austrian Habsburg ruler the "emperor" because contemporaries referred to him this way, reflecting the most prestigious title he held, "Holy Roman emperor."

The decision to use German, Czech, Slovak, Polish, Croatian, or Hungarian place names was a difficult one. I have attempted to use the historical versions of place names, especially when the German name is the clear convention in English-language historiography. In many cases, I have also indicated in parentheses what the place name is in another language to help orient the reader.

THE RISE OF THE MILITARY ENTREPRENEUR

Introduction

A Warrior's Life

In the summer of 1644, after taking over temporary command of the imperial army in Bavaria, Raimondo Montecuccoli (1609–80) grew extremely frustrated. It was the final decade of the Thirty Years' War (16–48), and both France and Sweden were on the verge of invading parts of the Holy Roman Empire and the Habsburg lands. Habsburg emperor Ferdinand III (r. 1637–57) had chosen Montecuccoli to take over command from Field Marshal Melchior Hatzfeld, who had fallen ill, but soon revised those orders and demanded that Montecuccoli travel north to support the main army campaigning in Denmark. In a letter to a friend—the Modenese ambassador in Vienna, Ottavio Bolognesi—Montecuccoli complained bitterly about the disorganization he encountered and the sacrifices he had made.[1] The continuous travels, Montecuccoli declared, "drive me crazy," and he was tired of "orders that make me begin many things without finishing anything."[2] Due to unreliable communications and poor administration, the court center reacted slowly and often ineffectively to developments on campaign. The inherent uncertainty of war—Clausewitz's "fog of war"—meant that even the best-informed and most capably administered early modern governments improvised in the face of rapidly developing military realities.

Montecuccoli had a lot on his shoulders. Originally from the Duchy of Modena, he had been fighting in the imperial army for nearly two decades, during which time he recruited, financed, and commanded his own regiments

1

for the emperor. He was in debt and had been injured and imprisoned (he was captured twice in battle and arrested once by the elector of Brandenburg on suspicion of wartime excesses). He complained that his imprisonments and arrest had hindered his advancement and he had not received any repayments or rewards for his service. Turning to a sympathetic fellow countryman, Montecuccoli asked Bolognesi to imagine "the journeys and the roads that I have taken since joining the army." He especially wanted Bolognesi to reflect on logistical challenges, emphasizing the geographic space he had traversed and what long journeys with soldiers entailed. Montecuccoli continued, "and then you will be able to imagine for yourself how many horses I have ruined and what expense I have had to make and whether I am in debt or not." Montecuccoli often skirmished with enemy forces while traveling, leading him to muse that "if in so many trips some disgrace does not befall me, it will be a miracle."[3] Winning battles remained important, but figuring out how to supply, encamp, quarter, and coordinate the movements of large numbers of soldiers across both enemy and friendly territories—logistics—was the central problem early modern officers faced. Montecuccoli's letters remind us of the personal nature of these campaign experiences: managing logistics drove Montecuccoli into debt and jeopardized his hard-won reputation. The burdens of campaigning during the Thirty Years' War were borne not by the imperial court, but rather by officers like Montecuccoli, their soldiers, and the peasants they subjugated.

During the period in which Montecuccoli served in the imperial army, the scale, scope, and complexity of warfare expanded dramatically. Firepower was broadly integrated into battle, and larger armies began operating in multiple theaters, pushing the long-standing problem of logistics to a breaking point. These and other developments constitute what some scholars argue was a military revolution that ultimately reshaped armies, governments, and societies.[4] The expenses required to meet these challenges were crushing, and Emperor Ferdinand III (and Ferdinand II before him) was chronically short of cash and had poor credit, making it impossible to raise an army on his own, let alone maintain a professional standing army. Like most early modern rulers, he lacked a centralized bureaucratic apparatus to oversee and administer warfare in a systematic manner. Figures like Montecuccoli—noblemen who believed they had a natural military calling and who had access to wealth, credit, and transregional aristocratic networks—emerged to serve his needs and raise the troops who filled the imperial armies. These noblemen were military entrepreneurs. Historians distinguish seventeenth-century military entrepreneurs from military contractors of other periods (including mercenary captains) by the multitude of functions they performed under contract to rulers—recruitment, training, and provisioning, as well as command—and by their increased use of credit. Successful military entrepreneurs were not only investors in regiments but also became creditors to one another and even extended credit to rulers.[5] Since rulers were usually unable to pay military entrepreneurs back for their services in cash, these noblemen gained unprecedented political power, receiving court offices, honors, and property in lieu of monetary reimbursements.[6] The minor Bohemian nobleman Albrecht Wallenstein (1583–1634), who recruited and commanded an army of more than fifty thousand men for Emperor Ferdinand II (r. 1619–37) in the mid-1620s, attained a status equivalent to the most important princes of the empire before he was suspected of treason and assassinated in 1634.[7] Military historians often view Wallenstein as the quintessential example of an early modern military entrepreneur, but his career was one of extremes. As Montecuccoli's complaints show, other military entrepreneurs labored for smaller-scale rewards and were not always successful.

As they responded to the challenges of near-continuous war, military entrepreneurs became pervasive figures in early modern politics and society, yet we lack a coherent picture of who they were, what motivated them, how they operated, and what influence they held both on and off the battlefield. Despite the difficulties he faced in 1644, Montecuccoli persevered, eventually becoming one of the most consequential figures in the Austrian Habsburg monarchy. In the 1660s, he was lieutenant general of the imperial army (the highest command, directly subordinate to a member of the Habsburg family), the president of the Aulic War Council (Hofkriegsrat Präsident), a close advisor to Emperor Leopold I, and the writer of scientific treatises on warfare that laid the foundations for a new discipline: military science.[8] When his treatises were published after his death, they became some of Europe's most popular writings on warfare—key works that transmitted military knowledge from the era of Machiavelli to that of Napoleon and Clausewitz.[9]

Montecuccoli was exemplary in many ways, but a broader group of Italian noblemen who served in the imperial army and court from the late sixteenth through the end of the seventeenth centuries shared similar experiences.[10] Although they have never been systematically studied, this group was particularly successful, holding a disproportionate number of command positions in the imperial army. During the Thirty Years' War, 43 out of 196 imperial infantry regiments were commanded by Italians. Italians also represented four out of twelve lieutenants general and ten out of forty-three field marshals.[11] Many of these same noblemen served on the Aulic War Council in Vienna. Two of the Italian noblemen who served as lieutenant general, Matteo Galasso (1584–1647) and Ottavio Piccolomini (1599–1656), had been leading conspirators in the plot to murder Wallenstein. Friedrich Schiller later immortalized this event in one of the greatest German dramas of all time, *The Wallenstein Trilogy*, a complex depiction that contributed to the notoriety of Italian noblemen in imperial service in Central European literature and historiography.[12]

Through a close analysis of Montecuccoli's life within the context of several generations of Italian noblemen in imperial service, this book analyzes the motivations, methods, ideas, and broader influence of military entrepreneurs in seventeenth-century Habsburg Europe. Rather than assume the perspectives of rulers and ministers, it adopts a ground-level view of these fascinating entrepreneurial noblemen as they confronted and attempted to solve problems, often far from the court center. It uses a variety of formal and informal writings—official documents and military treatises, as well as letters, diaries, poetry, fiction, and notes—to examine these figures in all of their many contours. Italian noblemen in imperial service usually operated as contractors (*condottieri*), but not always. Sometimes they were adventurers (*avventurieri*) who requested to join armies with their own retinues and without formal office. They passed fluidly in and out of office and in and out of military service. They also served as diplomats and courtiers, and some became scholars. Above all, they identified and acted as members of aristocratic clans: they were heads of households, vassals, patrons, and clients, rather than mere contractors. Their experiences show that early modern warfare was more of a family business than an official activity of the state.[13] Examining this dynamic picture demands an approach that not only takes military entrepreneurs and their methods seriously but also integrates military history—a field that is often still isolated from other fields of historical inquiry—with social and cultural history, as well as with the history of science. The study of multifaceted individuals and their relationships illuminates the ways warfare was inseparably interconnected with other spheres of early modern life, including the court and the world of scholarship.

War, Loyalty, and Expertise

The insights into battlefield, court, and scholarship that emerge from the following chapters can be organized into three key themes: war, loyalty, and expertise. For many noblemen, warfare became a new kind of occupation starting in the late sixteenth century, because of its continuous nature and its increasing tactical, strategic, and technological complexity. War was often ideological, with high stakes: Reformation tensions between Catholics and Protestants combined explosively with long-standing disputes about how to govern and who should govern, as well as with competition among leading dynasties. Like other Italian noblemen, who were almost all uniformly Catholic by the seventeenth century, Montecuccoli joined the imperial army in the 1620s in order to support the Austrian Habsburg monarch/Holy Roman emperor, Ferdinand II, in the fight against the Protestant estates that had rebelled against his rule and their international allies.[14] This conflict had triggered the outbreak of the Thirty Years' War. Even after the Thirty Years' War ended with the Peace of Westphalia in 1648, Italian noblemen continued to serve in the imperial army during the Second Northern War (1655–60) and in multiple conflicts against Louis XIV's France, as well as against the Ottoman Empire. Montecuccoli reached the peak of his career in the 1660s and 1670s. After winning a surprise victory over the Ottomans at the Battle of St. Gotthard (Mogersdorf) in 1664, he was proclaimed lieutenant general of the imperial army. After his death in 1680, other noblemen from the Italian peninsula, including Antonio Carafa (1642–92), Luigi Ferdinando Marsigli (1658–1730), and Eugene of Savoy (1663–1736), helped conquer vast stretches of Eastern Europe from the Ottomans, following the harrowing 1683 Siege of Vienna.[15] By the end of the seventeenth century, Austria had laid the foundations for becoming a great power. Further acquisitions at the start of the eighteenth century would make the Habsburg lands second only to Russia in size and to France in population.[16] A remarkable fact that emerges from this narrative is that during its impressive expansion, Austria lacked an adequate standing army and powerful centralized military institutions. One of the main arguments of this book is that although military entrepreneurs have been misleadingly considered "nonstate actors" in international relations theory, they played an essential role in Austria's growth as a great power by providing the means to wage war.

While war was important in the consolidation and expansion of Austrian Habsburg power, this book is more concerned with exploring the integral nature of war to aristocratic society and identity. For noblemen capable of financing and leading regiments on behalf of rulers, war provided numerous opportunities for advancement, including entryways into other lines of service such as diplomacy, court careers, and scholarship. Diplomatic missions—which often concerned war and similarly required long-distance travel and the commitment of private resources to financing trips—were often part of military careers. Montecuccoli, Piccolomini, and Galasso maintained far-reaching correspondence networks in which they exchanged information and intelligence with officers and spies in armies and at courts across Europe. Montecuccoli was also involved in wars of words, creating and disseminating propaganda about military events. Finally, during breaks from campaigning, Montecuccoli composed treatises that addressed the major problems of warfare, emphasizing logistics, discipline, provisions, finance, and training. In the dedicatory letter of his final treatise, *On the War against the Turks in Hungary* (*Della guerra col Turco in Ungheria*, 1670), Montecuccoli claimed he had spent forty-three years in imperial service, most of which would have involved campaigning or preparing for campaigns.[17]

Intense, demanding experiences of war shaped political loyalties as well as expertise. Through repeated military service, several generations of Italian noblemen developed a vibrant loyalty to the Habsburg dynasty—the second major theme of this book—while juggling loyalties to local Italian lords as well as to other Catholic rulers. Many of the Italian officers of the Thirty Years' War had fathers and grandfathers who had established these patterns by intermittently fighting abroad in late sixteenth- and early seventeenth-century Habsburg wars in Flanders and Hungary. Over the course of his career, Montecuccoli served a series of Austrian Habsburg emperors, his "natural lord" Francesco I d'Este, duke of Modena (r. 1629–58), and Queen Christina of Sweden (r. 1632–54). Throughout these experiences, Montecuccoli maintained strong ties to the Modena-based Montecuccoli family, whose support helped fuel his career and whose interests remained at the forefront of his mind. Later, his marriage into the Central European magnate clan the Dietrichsteins sealed his ascent in Vienna.[18]

Multiple loyalties were common in early modern Europe and especially within the setting of Habsburg Europe. Geographically, the two branches of the House of Habsburg, the Spanish and the Austrian, controlled or maintained substantial influence over the Italian and Iberian peninsulas, the Netherlands, much of Central Europe, and parts of Hungary. The Austrian Habsburg ruler was the elected head of both the Holy Roman Empire and the Kingdom of Hungary, and held the right of permanent succession in the Austrian Habsburg hereditary lands (*Erblande*) of Upper and Lower Austria, Styria, Carinthia, Carniola, and the Tyrol, as well as Bohemia, Silesia, and Moravia (Map 0.1).[19] Spain also presided over a global empire with claims to the Americas and parts of Asia and North Africa. Finally, because the Austrian Habsburg monarch held the position of Holy Roman emperor, he had a unique (though mostly informal) power in the regions of northern Italy that had once been part of the medieval Holy Roman Empire. These realms were composite political communities: loose collections of diverse territories and peoples acquired over time in piecemeal fashion through conquest, marriage alliance, and inheritance. They were subordinated to ruling dynasties but lacked strong unity. Each community held its own distinctive rights, privileges, and obligations in a contractual relationship to the ruler, while borders were flexible and contested. Italian military entrepreneurs in the imperial army found opportunities to move through this landscape with relative ease, because the era of the Protestant and Catholic reformations had created transregional ideologi-

MAP 0.1. The Holy Roman Empire and Austrian Habsburg lands. Cartography by Bill Nelson.

cal alliances that encouraged formerly distant or separate communities to seek unity, engaging in politics and war on an international level.[20]

The wide, nebulous sphere of Catholic Habsburg influence permitted Italian military and governing elites to pledge fealty to the Habsburg dynasty, while maintaining relationships to a wide variety of rulers and other governing elites.[21] For instance, the Montecuccoli family identified as vassals of the Este dukes of Modena and of the Holy Roman emperor (the Montecuccoli had occupied an imperial fief long before the Este governed Modena), and cultivated clientage relationships to powerful dynasties such as the nearby Tuscan Medici family. Beyond their purported loyalty to the Habsburgs, the Montecuccoli and their various patrons were unified in their Catholicism, which was especially meaningful when the Habsburgs fought Protestants and Muslims. A major argument that emerges from this theme is that multiple loyalties were not necessarily damaging to political consolidation and the conduct of warfare—especially when they occurred among coreligionists within composite political communities. For the Montecuccoli family, maintaining multiple loyalties was a rational strategy, while rulers ranging from the dukes of Modena to the Austrian Habsburg emperors sought to exploit their vassals' connections to other rulers and courts for political and military purposes.

The final theme examined in this book is expertise. Starting in the late sixteenth century, military entrepreneurs who served for many years as officers in armies across Europe began to identify strongly as experts and contributed to the professionalization of armies. Montecuccoli's works, beginning with *Treatise on War* (*Trattato della guerra*, 1641) and culminating in his magnum opus, *On the War against the Turks in Hungary* (1670), exemplify broader trends, while also standing apart from others on account of their systematic, encyclopedic methods. My research sets his works in the context of a large, evolving body of ideas that flowered after 1560 within the context of near-continuous warfare and ideological divisions between Catholics and Protestants.[22] It argues that some of the most effective military entrepreneurs, like Montecuccoli, can fruitfully be seen as scientific theorists and practitioners who created a fusion between experience, technical know-how, and abstract knowledge, contributing to a shift from the *art* to the *science* of war.[23] By using scientific methods in war, military entrepreneurs hoped to control war.

While he admired the Roman army, Montecuccoli was acutely aware of the need to experience warfare himself, due to changes since Roman times, including the use of firepower. Experiencing war firsthand required frequent travel to different battlegrounds over the course of many years and the ability to manage daunting logistical operations. Military entrepreneurs were the only figures who had extensive experience of this kind, as well as the educational backgrounds to analyze and codify it. Another key argument of this book is that military expertise that was later absorbed by the state originally emerged from decisions military entrepreneurs made as they encountered problems far beyond the oversight of rulers and ministers. To understand the military revolution as an international phenomenon involving the participation of diverse actors from different regions, we must walk alongside figures like Montecuccoli, contemplating the meaning of their words in the context of what they did, who they knew, and how they perceived the world around them.[24]

War, loyalty, and expertise are all interconnected and together provide a coherent view of military entrepreneurs that includes the military, political/social, and cultural/intellectual aspects of their lives. War remained the essential activity that consumed the time, energy, and resources of military entrepreneurs, fundamentally reshaping the way they perceived and acted in the world. Loyalty, though at times slippery, was a central ingredient of personal, familial, and confessional relationships shaped and exploited to meet the demands of war. Expertise, finally, was the way in which these figures reflected on war, created new identities as professional soldiers, and argued for the broader relevance of military experience and knowledge in a rapidly changing world. While this book focuses specifically on Italian military entrepreneurs in imperial service, its conclusions relate to other armies and to aristocratic experience more broadly. Even René Descartes, a contemporary of Montecuccoli's, pursued knowledge of war by studying military engineering in the Netherlands and joining the imperial army before he wrote his major philosophical treatises. In recounting his early years, Descartes explained, "I spent the remainder of my youth travelling, visiting courts and armies, meeting people of different temperaments and rank, acquiring different experiences, testing myself in meetings that came my way by chance, and everywhere reflecting on the things I observed so as to derive some benefit from them."[25] Some of Descartes's most radical thoughts occurred in military quarters during the Thirty Years' War while he awaited a period of campaigning that nearly took his life. His revelations belong to a broader military and diplomatic environment in which an international, interconnected group of cosmopolitan elites shared information, composed writings, and participated in intrigue, some of them serving as agents for multiple patrons.[26] Military entrepreneurs were significant figures within this environment but have been misunderstood, in part because military historians have failed to analyze them as multifaceted individuals, limiting our understanding of them to warfare. At the same time, social, cultural, and intellectual historians do not often examine military figures.[27]

In the nineteenth century, the cultural historian Jacob Burckhardt recognized the dynamism of military contractors when he made the Italian *condottiere* the model for his ideal Renaissance man. Rather than characterize military contractors as archaic, Burckhardt argued that they were the first self-made, individualistic men who innovated a modern culture of statecraft.[28] Italian military entrepreneurs in imperial service continued the *condottiere* traditions of the Renaissance in a wider world transformed by commerce, technological change, new scientific methods, Reformation divisions, and Habsburg dominance. I have adopted Burckhardt's inclination to study military contractors as figures who profoundly altered politics, society, and culture, but my conclusions emphasize the distinctively *early* modern features of these careers. Montecuccoli's life reveals details into how war as a family business worked as well as the personal (rather than formal institutional) nature of service to rulers in the age of state building. Rulers who succeeded in defending and expanding their realms depended upon the initiatives of an entrepreneurial aristocracy willing to commit their own wealth and credit to military activities, reliant upon transregional networks and multiple alliances, and unified by confessional and dynastic bonds. Military entrepreneurs were at times innovative—as

the development of military science reveals—but they could also be highly de-
structive figures who ravaged local economies, brutalized populations, and
abused common soldiers. Nonetheless, some of them were the first to diag-
nose systematically the problems presented by early modern warfare and propose solutions. Ultimately, understanding the complex roles played by military
entrepreneurs in war, diplomacy, and the development of knowledge forces us
to grapple with the diffuse nature of power on the eve of modernity.

War and State Building

Why would an Italian nobleman risk his life, health, reputation, and wealth in
the imperial army during the seventeenth century? How did he finance, recruit,
organize, and command his soldiers, managing demanding logistical operations
with minimal support from the imperial center? How did the experience of serving multiple rulers in contractual relationships influence the way he thought
and behaved? It seems remarkable that a nobleman would endure years of hard-
ship without apparent reward. In the midst of his 1644 litany of complaints to
Bolognesi, Montecuccoli provided a clue to his motivations: he wrote that he
needed to have patience "because this year I made a vow of obedience."[29] Although he took part in a military marketplace in which noblemen contracted
out their services to various rulers, this statement shows that Montecuccoli did
not understand his career in terms of impersonal forces. He identified as a vassal
and a Catholic for whom obedience remained a central virtue. He was also the
head of a line of counts who wielded his own authority. In difficult times, he
relied on his family and a range of friends and patrons. His service was personal
and familial: without institutions or a stable chain of command within the army,
he depended on the faith that others had in him personally and on a record of
service accumulated by members of the Montecuccoli family from the late sixteenth century onward.

Although he complained vociferously, Montecuccoli collected both tangi-
ble and intangible rewards through a lifetime of commitment to a series of
emperors. His example affirms David Parrott's insight that successful military
entrepreneurs from the Thirty Years' War onward made "modest but incremental levels of return" through the careful management of soldiers, contributions (war taxes imposed on a local populace by an army), plunder, and other
income sources, a topic I reflect upon in the Epilogue.[30] Even if the Habsburgs
never provided the desired rewards, military entrepreneurs gained advantages
from the reputations they built and glory they attained. A strong reputation

and record of success led to good credit, since it generated the trust necessary to secure loans from merchants and other nobles in distant networks.[31] An aristocratic dynasty accumulated reputation in a collective, rather than purely individual, sense. A recitation of the services of multiple family members across generations often accompanied requests for rewards.[32] Even if they suffered setbacks as individuals, noblemen expected their families would benefit from their service, as long as they avoided disgrace.

The experiences of Italian military entrepreneurs in imperial service show that the relationships constructed to conduct war and wield power were interwoven within a latticework of aristocratic bonds, confessional allegiances, and feudal ties to the imperial dynasty, the Austrian Habsburgs, that stretched across territories and jurisdictions. This political vision contrasts to that of conventional military histories that have overwhelmingly focused on how the almost constant wars of the period related to the evolution of centralized, territorial states with impersonal institutions and standing armies. In these accounts, war plays an inexorable, mechanistic role in triggering, sustaining, and furthering this evolution because it created a demand for standing armies, regular systems of taxation to support those armies, and more efficient bureaucracies to oversee standing armies and taxation.[33] This book does not openly dispute this narrative, but rather seeks to engage with sociocultural studies of the state in order to reexamine early modern power as dispersed and pluralistic, created and deployed not only through institutions but also through patronage relationships and informal practices.[34] The analysis of military entrepreneurs is key to creating a more complex understanding of war and power in the early modern world, showing how a range of aristocratic families managed turbulent politics by forming advantageous alliances and establishing wealth and connections across distinct yet interconnected communities.

War played a critical role in reshaping a family's power, since it was the primary way to gain territory, plunder, and offices in other parts of Europe. Chapter 2 traces these patterns back to the late sixteenth century, when members of Italian aristocratic clans served in both the Spanish and imperial armies in the wars in Flanders and Hungary. I argue that the Thirty Years' War created an important shift in these patterns by fundamentally reorienting Italian aristocratic military service toward the Austrian Habsburg family for several decades. A new generation of Italian noblemen in imperial service emerged with the glorious Battle of White Mountain (1620) and its aftermath—the freewheeling 1620s, in which land grabs and exploitative behaviors were more common than later on. This "generation of White Mountain" assumed the war would end quickly in the Habsburgs' favor. However, expectations and the strategies for achieving those expectations evolved when hopes for a conclusive victory faded—especially after the invasion of the Holy Roman Empire by Gustavus Adolphus of Sweden in 1630.

Montecuccoli assumed his first major leadership roles during the 1630s and 1640s, when the Habsburgs faced a seemingly endless onslaught of threats from Sweden, France, and Transylvania, among others. The nature of conducting war changed as armies grew smaller, attempts were made at systematizing contributions, and the relationship between campaign maneuvers and diplomatic negotiations grew closer. Military entrepreneurs like Montecuccoli faced new pressures as they sought ways to improve operational effectiveness.[35] By viewing the Thirty Years' War through the eyes of different generations of ambitious aristocratic clans, we can see how the war was experienced as a series of conflicts with sudden, unexpected shifts that required frequent adaptation, a topic more fully explored in chapter 3. A close, personal view of Montecuccoli's activities reveals the importance of relying upon long-distance kin in facilitating political connections, managing wealth, and acquiring essential military resources such as horses. Montecuccoli found himself torn between the demands of family members, rulers, and patrons in the army, making conscious decisions about whom to be loyal to and how to advance family interests.

If the Thirty Years' War forced military entrepreneurs to make political choices and learn hard military lessons, how did their experiences and views evolve after the war ended? Furthermore, what did a military entrepreneur do when he was not campaigning? On a broader geopolitical level, the two decades following the Thirty Years' War were critical for Habsburg Austria and inaugurated major changes in Europe as a whole, but tend to be overshadowed in the historiography by military developments that portend the emergence of a new configuration of great powers. Austria transitioned from defensive to offensive warfare with the conquest of parts of Eastern Europe from the Ottomans from 1683 to 1699. By 1700, the Spanish Habsburgs had become extinct, while Bourbon France had emerged as the biggest threat to an uneasy balance of power still taking shape. Political history focused on the rise of Louis XIV's France tends to associate the period with a decline for the Habsburg family, despite Austria's incredible expansion. In reality, the late sixteenth-century incarnation of Habsburg Europe—a distinctively Spanish world—was supplanted by one that gravitated around the Austrian Habsburgs by the late seventeenth century.

Examining the experiences and worldviews of some of Austria's most ardent supporters in these decades—Italian noblemen in imperial service—helps fill in some of the missing contours of the development of Austrian Habsburg power and also humanizes geopolitical shifts usually conceived in broad, mechanistic terms. In his attempt to understand the seventeenth-century foundations of Austria's rise as a great power, R. J. W. Evans argued that the cultural and ideological coherence of the Habsburg monarchy, held together by the courts, generated unity among elites across the bewilderingly decentralized monarchy in these formative decades.[36] My study integrates war and foreign military entrepreneurs into this picture, arguing that Italian noblemen maintained serious ideological and dynastic allegiances to the Habsburgs throughout the seventeenth century, contributing to Austria's military strength and expertise, as well as a robust transregional loyalty to the dynasty that reached far beyond the hereditary lands. In the eyes of Montecuccoli and others, a unified Catholic Europe under Habsburg influence remained the only possible guarantor of peace as new threats loomed in the decades following the Peace of Westphalia.

After the Thirty Years' War ended, Montecuccoli served as an imperial diplomat on two major missions that provide insights into the world of aristocratic politics and culture at two sites of Habsburg influence: Antwerp and the Italian port of Finale. Chapter 4 analyzes these trips not only to understand the role played by diplomatic missions in military careers but also to take the temperature of Habsburg Europe at a critical transitional stage between the Thirty Years' War and Austria's wars with France and the Ottomans. Antwerp, which was part of the Spanish Netherlands, was the location of Queen Christina of Sweden's court in 1654 after the queen—Gustavus Adolphus's daughter—controversially abdicated her throne. During her stay in the Spanish Netherlands, Christina also converted to Catholicism. Montecuccoli reported on Christina's maneuvers, attended Christina's secret conversion in Brussels, and later escorted her to Rome, where she made a dramatic entrance as one of the most celebrated converts of the century. His second major diplomatic assignment occurred roughly a decade later, when Emperor Leopold I ordered him to greet the Spanish infanta and imperial bride, Margarita Teresa, at Finale as she made her journey to Vienna. Montecuccoli detailed both of these trips in diaries that offer insights into why a diverse group of cosmopolitan elites saw alliances to the Habsburg family as appealing political choices and how these elites, military men included, negotiated for status and position beyond Vienna or Madrid.[37] In Montecuccoli's case, serving as a diplomat provided him with a bridge to a career at court and opened the door to marriage into the powerful Dietrichstein clan.

One of the major themes that animated the thoughts and conversations of Habsburg allies in Antwerp and Finale was the threat presented by the Ottomans—the Austrian Habsburgs' eastern neighbor. Twenty years before the 1683 Siege of Vienna, the Ottomans attempted a large-scale invasion of the Habsburg hereditary lands that was halted at the Battle of St. Gotthard (Mogersdorf) in 1664 by troops Montecuccoli commanded. As chapter 5 argues, the 1663–64 war, although neglected by historians, was a major turning point for Montecuccoli and other Italian officers whose careers had initially taken shape during the Thirty Years' War. Fighting in Hungary and Transylvania was especially taxing for the imperial army's logistical capabilities. At the same time, Montecuccoli struggled politically with the powerful Hungarian magnate Miklós Zrínyi, whose family had long conducted warfare in a mostly autonomous manner along the frontier. The ideological differences between Montecuccoli and Zrínyi provide a striking contrast to the general ideological agreement among the cast of Habsburg allies he interacted with at Finale. Montecuccoli continued to see the Habsburgs as defenders of Christendom, whereas Zrínyi denounced imperial intervention on the frontier because the imperial army failed to protect Hungarian property. From 1664 to 1671, disaffected Hungarian noblemen plotted to throw off Habsburg rule—to Montecuccoli's horror—in the failed Wesselényi Conspiracy. Montecuccoli took a hard-line approach toward Hungary, advocating suppression of political and religious liberties. Chapter 5 reflects upon how the extremely dangerous Ottoman threat of the 1660s fundamentally reshaped the way members of the international Catholic aristocracy responded to Habsburg power long before the Siege of Vienna.

Throughout these decades, military entrepreneurs and transregional networks remained important. For the Austrian Habsburg emperor or the duke of Modena, it made sense to disband troops that were prohibitively expensive to maintain in both war and peace and permit officers to serve in other armies until they were needed again. This practice was widespread. As long as rulers had access to the transregional circulation of warriors, they could recruit military men and expertise in an emergency. Rather than impede the movements of their subjects and clients between courts and armies, they often assisted them with the intention of benefiting from increased access to information and resources. Meanwhile, aristocratic families pursued their own international objectives that only sometimes coincided with the aims of their traditional lords. My research as a whole provides a nuanced perspective on how early modern military contracting worked in interaction with the state-building efforts of rulers and aristocratic family strategies throughout the seventeenth century. Although contemporaries became acutely aware of its limitations, military entrepreneurship was not a shoddy substitute for standing armies but remained the preferred method of organized coercion.

Knowledge and Power

One of the main arguments of this book is that the development of modern military expertise or military science coincided with the activities of this international cast of elite warriors traveling between multiple battlefields across Europe from the sixteenth century onward. Michael Roberts's military revolution thesis posited that revolutionary military reforms started in the Dutch army and were transmitted to the Swedish army of Gustavus Adolphus in the first several decades of the seventeenth century.[38] Numerous scholars have debated this timeline and the priority granted to Sweden and the Dutch, but very few studies capture the truly international dimensions of military changes or the participation of a diverse range of actors.[39] Rather than view changes in the ideas and practices of warfare, including conceptions of the standing army, as indigenous to the state itself, this book argues instead that innovations were imported into governance at a critical moment of state development by military contractors.

My research shows that in order to understand the development of the science of war, we must begin from the viewpoints of the military entrepreneurs who invested their own wealth, credit, and reputations in warfare. They were among the first to experience and articulate the dramatic changes that accompanied the vast expansion of the scale and scope of war, including the disorganization and suffering caused by armies that lacked adequate provisions and discipline. As a result, military entrepreneurs argued that only an empirical, mathematical, and principled approach to war would allow rulers to control and direct war. The surge of a particularly popular genre of scientific writing—military treatises written by officers with experience of war—reflected the urgency of mastering the lessons of warfare from the late sixteenth century and on. Wars against the Ottomans and the French in the late seventeenth century further shaped understandings. A new discipline, military science, was born that reflected engagement in the debates of the Scientific Revolution, including those concerning the role of experience, mathematics, and instrument use. A model of the professional officer who boasted of a new kind of expertise materialized.

The emergence of military science, a topic that appears to some degree in each of the following chapters, provides a glimpse of how science became part of the toolkit of modern governance. Military science was useful to newcomers at courts who made arguments about personal merit based on knowledge and experience rather than traditional privileges. In the past few decades, historians of science have identified the ways that court patronage affected the careers of scientific practitioners, as well as the content of their knowledge and methods. New types of entrepreneurial figures claimed specialized expertise in appeals to patrons and shaped a court culture that welcomed innovation.[40] The conclusions of these historians parallel those of political, military, and economic historians who have similarly noted the rise of entrepreneurs, including military entrepreneurs, to meet the needs of expanding governments during this period.[41] My research intersects with both of these historiographical trends by addressing how officers—figures not generally categorized as scientific practitioners—developed a new kind of expertise in service to rulers that allowed them to transfer their skills to other arenas of political, social, and intellectual significance.

The military treatises of Italian officers and engineers in the imperial army can also be understood as a late transfer of the Renaissance across the Alps, composed by humanistically educated Italian elites who were encountering new problems in Central Europe. As chapter 1 outlines, Italian noblemen belonged to a rich genealogy of cultured aristocratic warriors that included some of the most renowned Italian Renaissance rulers.[42] The science of war they contributed to integrated studies of antiquity, empiricism, mathematics, and political philosophy, and was the result of ongoing communication between military men and court networks that included natural philosophers, mathematicians, artists, librarians, and other scholars. Chapter 4 helps illuminate the courtly sites at which a military entrepreneur encountered other learned elites and includes an analysis of Montecuccoli's *zibaldone*: an 850-page commonplace book containing notes on sixty-nine volumes he read at mid-career. The literature on his list, including political philosophy, duel manuals, and alchemical treatises, reveals the polymathic knowledge deemed necessary for a career spanning both court and army.

Montecuccoli's science of war ultimately centered upon the creation of a professional standing army supported by a robust fiscal system. It may strike the reader as odd that a military entrepreneur advised his then patron, Emperor Leopold I, to build a standing army and avoid using mercenaries, apparently excluding future careers like his own. Montecuccoli, however, distinguished himself from common mercenaries who served for pay alone. Rather, he saw himself as a noble servant of princes, fulfilling long-standing aristocratic expectations about leading men into battle and governing. At the same time, the nature of the work was grueling, and so Montecuccoli hoped to exchange it for a more secure position as a government minister or, at the very least, as a permanent, salaried *generalissimo* with supreme authority over a well-cared for, disciplined body of troops.

Montecuccoli's understanding of the importance of the standing army became much clearer during the 1660s, when he led troops against the Ottoman army—the imperial power with the largest standing army in Europe and most advanced logistical and administrative capabilities. Chapter 6 discusses his final major treatise, *On the War against the Turks in Hungary*, which offered recommendations on the standing army that were profoundly influenced by the Ottoman example. It also recounted the Habsburg-Ottoman conflicts and presented a proposal for a new conquest of Ottoman territories. One of the conclusions to emerge from my research is that, when we separate the history of the standing army from its nearly exclusive association with the development of the centralized institutions of Western nation-states, we can perceive the influence of the Ottoman Empire on European military development more clearly. The Habsburgs' greatest enemy was also their most important model. Montecuccoli died in 1680, but *On the War against the Turks in Hungary* provided the blueprint for the later Habsburg conquest of much of Eastern Europe, as the epilogue relates. This book ultimately concludes that Montecuccoli's science of war and vision of a standing army were the fruit of many generations of military contractors who studied war, identified with the Habsburg cause, and reflected on the military and political implications of what they did.

Sources and Methodology

In order to adopt the perspectives of military entrepreneurs rather than those of rulers and/or government ministers, this book focuses primarily on sources such as printed and manuscript treatises, correspondence, reports, diaries, notes, wills, and other private writings composed by military figures. Nothing is off limits, including a scrap of paper on which Montecuccoli jotted down the purchase price of a diamond ring for his wife, Margarethe.[43] These documents were gathered from sixteen different archives and libraries in three different countries: Italy, Austria, and the Czech Republic. The dispersal of sources itself reflects the geographical fluidity of a career in imperial service, and the fact that these regions were the hub of political and cultural life for seventeenth-century Austrian Habsburg governing elites. One of the reasons that military entrepreneurs have not been well studied is that documents on these figures were not always collected in central state archives. The highly scattered documents concerning military entrepreneurs are rarely examined together, if at all. Not only did the Iron Curtain long prevent easy access to Czech archives for Western scholars, but the Italian and Central European historians who have addressed these figures have often relied upon either exclusively Italian or exclusively Central European archival sources. The linguistic challenges of unifying these sources into a single project are formidable and frequently prohibitive.

Each type of source has its virtues, but the letters of military entrepreneurs can be particularly revealing. Letters were practical tools for moving men and resources across large distances, key pieces of infrastructure in a war fueled by transregional support networks. The correspondence of military entrepreneurs extended across regions, revealing the extent to which major military endeavors involved the summoning of resources and expertise from far beyond any single government's territorial or institutional reach. Letters also disseminated military intelligence, showing how information about war traveled faster and farther than ever, but also created a sense of chaos, especially when a correspondent received two or more letters with diverging information. Military entrepreneurs, for whom faulty intelligence could lead to disaster, used their own spies and worked tirelessly to determine fact from fiction, as well as to control what others knew. Often far from the court center, officers also relied on letters to maintain relationships with key court patrons. While Montecuccoli took a more formal approach to letters and reports to the emperors he served, his correspondence with Francesco I d'Este (with whom he had grown up at court in Modena) or to members of his own family reveals his motivations, hopes, and fears—information that is often hidden from view in formal or institutional sources. His more candid letters affirm the multifaceted nature of his experience, as he might report on a variety of topics—geopolitical events, campaign realities, the repayment of a loan, marriage plans, etc.—in a single letter. Considering the importance of letters and the large size of early modern officers' correspondence collections, it is clear that military leaders were constantly writing. They used secretaries, but many extant letters from Montecuccoli were written in his own hand. It would be fascinating to know how much time letter writing or dictating consumed in the life of an imperial general.

Other writings left behind by Montecuccoli point to a compulsion to collect and record information. Scattered through the Montecuccoli archive in Vienna are documents that include the seating arrangement of a banquet, the details of a miscarriage his wife suffered, and the jokes bandied about by Queen Christina of Sweden, in addition to analysis of military and diplomatic maneuvers. His formal military treatises emerged out of a flurry of drafts, shorter reports, pamphlets, and treatises on other topics. Montecuccoli was acutely self-aware: he composed an autobiographical love story, as well as chronologies of significant life events. The richness of this archive presents an opportunity to study an imperial general and military theorist not solely in terms of battlefield strategy and high politics but also as a complex individual for whom warfare, family life, diplomacy, the court, and scholarship were inextricably bound up with one another. Collectively, these sources expose the at times paradoxical realities for military figures whose careers transpired during a time of military, political, and epistemological turmoil.[44] The result of this analysis of a blend of formal and informal writings is a more flexible and capacious view of power and aristocratic identity.

The overarching goal of *The Rise of the Military Entrepreneur* is to reimagine critical military, political, and cultural changes of the seventeenth century from the perspectives of mobile, semiautonomous military figures who inhabited transregional communities. To understand these figures, we must take their mobility seriously, tracing them beyond the boundaries of particular territories to comprehend the exact nature of the problems they faced and how they viewed and reacted to those problems. In the process, we gain a more intimate understanding of the ideas, relationships, and activities of the figures who supplied early modern rulers with the means of coercion upon which their power and state-building enterprises largely depended. The early modern army appears to have been similar to missionary, scholarly, and mercantile networks in which people, knowledge, information, and goods circulated across territories. The regiments under the command of military entrepreneurs were diverse, unwieldy assemblages of soldiers—some native, some foreign, including other noblemen with their own family, friends, and followers—collected around a core of contracted troops.[45] They experienced minimal oversight from the court center, and their officers often provided services to multiple rulers at once. They were highly permeable, with a continuous stream of officers and common soldiers joining or abandoning service. These armies were structured more by courtly patronage networks than by impersonal hierarchies of command. The experiences of Italian noblemen in imperial service are a testament to the fact that early modern power derived from complex and contested sets of allegiances and resources that rulers and noblemen exploited across regions.

CHAPTER 1

The Order of War

War occupied a primary place in Montecuccoli's view of the world. In 1641, he wrote that the "art of war" "is above all the other arts and without it no one can have life" or "peaceful custom."[1] Later, he asserted that "statesmen cannot doubt that there can be no real peace between powerful competing states; one must suppress or be suppressed, one must either kill or perish."[2] War was unavoidable. Mastery of war permitted states to defend their subjects and territory from attack, creating the conditions of stability in which civilization prospered. This view of the centrality of war derived from Niccolò Machiavelli (1469–1527). In the preface to *Art of War* (*Arte della guerra*, 1521), Machiavelli wrote a passage that Montecuccoli and other writers would emulate in their own treatises: "For all the arts that are ordered in a city for the sake of the common good of men, all the orders made there for living in fear of the laws and of God, would be in vain if their defenses were not prepared. When these [defenses are] well ordered, they maintain the [arts and orders], even though the latter are not well ordered."[3] This passage placed war at the root of broader social, economic, political, and religious order. No other aspect of civilization took precedence over war, because war, when conducted well, was what permitted civilization to exist in the first place.

Starting in the late sixteenth century, army officers began writing treatises on war that reflected Machiavelli's canonical view that "well-ordered" war lent order far beyond the battlefield. However, while writers of Machiavelli's era wrote of the art of war, these officers began to differentiate their work as a science. The science of war that gradually emerged was a methodical, systematic, pedagogical genre that absorbed and diffused elements of the new science, especially empiricism, mathematics, and technical skill, as well as the political philosophy of the religious wars. The widespread participation of officers—many of whom had a decade or more of experience of war—in creating military science also distinguishes it from prior military theory.[4] After 1560, these officers grappled with major shifts in warfare, including the widespread integration of firepower, new styles of fortifications, larger armies, more complex field maneuvers, and near-continuous conflict. While they shared Machiavelli's vision of the importance of war, they knew that battlefield realities and knowledge had evolved since the early sixteenth century, creating an urgent demand for a new kind of mastery.

The educated officers who composed military science treatises were almost all military entrepreneurs: noblemen who used their own wealth and credit to raise companies or regiments under contract to a ruler.[5] The modern era inherited stereotypes about military contractors (a term that encompasses military entrepreneurs as well as mercenaries) as greedy and ineffective from a nationalistic literature with origins in a specific line of thinking that can be traced back through the Enlightenment to the Renaissance. Machiavelli famously opposed the use of any type of military contractor or military professional, a figure known as a *condottiere* in Italian. Influenced by republican ideology, he preferred the use of citizen militias. Central to Machiavelli's objections to *condottieri* were his concerns about their loyalties: he believed military contractors were only loyal to the master who paid the most, whereas subjects were naturally loyal to their homelands. Nevertheless, even Renaissance republican discourse offered multiple models of the military contractor. The mouthpiece of Machiavelli's own wisdom in *Art of War*, Fabrizio Colonna, was a virtuous character based on a real-life *condottiere* who commanded papal forces. Military contractors emerged from a complex legacy.

The military entrepreneurs who wrote treatises after 1560 can be likened to Colonna: noblemen who functioned as contractors but who saw themselves as more than mere mercenaries. We can assume that most were aware of Machiavelli's views, since *Art of War* was widely read in the seventeenth century, especially by the military elite. And while the new generation of military writers owed many of their ideas to patterns of thought and behavior that had originally developed in the Renaissance, their writings reflected new experiences. Many of them were newcomers attempting to gain status within foreign military and court hierarchies as they served different rulers across Europe.

They created identities as experts, governors, and advisors to princes who promised to bring order to war. Montecuccoli expanded upon their ideas in his own writings and became a shining example of what a newcomer might achieve through a military career, but he was also just one member of a rich genealogy of learned warrior elites.

Many-Sided Men

The careers of Italian military entrepreneurs in the seventeenth-century imperial army can be traced back to Renaissance Italy. Men who made war into a profession by contracting out their services to rulers—*condottieri*—had become far more common in the Italian peninsula with the late medieval expansion of banking and commerce, which provided copious amounts of money to pay wages. At the same time, the disintegration of the traditional authority of the Holy Roman emperor over the Italian peninsula led to the outbreak of near-continuous conflicts among the many small- and medium-sized states jockeying for power in the Italian peninsula. With political factionalism within city-states running high, it was difficult to build unified militias, while developing technologies and strategies (including the use of the crossbow and siege warfare) demanded a professional touch. War became big business as Italian city-states started to hire whole companies of soldiers headed by a captain. When men who had only ever known war as their calling suddenly found themselves unemployed after the end of the Hundred Years' War (1337–1453), many of them joined these autonomous associations of warriors.[6] They migrated to the wealthy, commercial, and politically fragmented regions of the Italian peninsula, where, William McNeill argues, conditions were ripe for "a remarkable merger of market and military behavior to take root and flourish."[7] They roved through the countryside offering military service to rulers and blackmailing towns by taking a position outside of a city and threatening to attack if not paid off. Citizens opted to pay taxes in order to hire *condottieri* who could protect them from other *condottieri*. The effects on small city-states like Siena were profound, eventually leading to bankruptcy and a decline that Siena's rival, Florence, exploited.[8]

An early case of military contracting providing the avenue for personal transformation was that of John Hawkwood, an Englishman who served in the Hundred Years' War and then led the notorious White Company through Southern France and into Italy, gaining extraordinary wealth along the way. At the end of his career, Hawkwood transitioned from leading a wholly autonomous company to offering his services under contract to Florence and winning a lordship. Many of the contemporaries he terrorized viewed him as ruthless, but over time his reputation morphed, until he became known as a loyal adopted son of the republic. His image was emblazoned upon the interior wall of Florence's Duomo, an early experiment in perspective painting by Paolo Uccello.[9]

In fifteenth-century Italy, the *condottieri*—most of whom were Italian—followed Hawkwood's example and started to receive contracts (*condotte*) from rulers. They gained permanent political positions through military service and married into ruling families. Many served more than one patron. Famous Renaissance Italian rulers rose to power as military contractors, including Francesco Sforza, duke of Milan (1401–66), and Federico da Montefeltro, duke of Urbino (1422–82), and some continued to offer to raise armies under contract to other rulers. These *condottieri* mastered new ways of waging war as the intensity of conflicts in the region generated innovation. Values shifted, and aristocratic warriors increasingly viewed caution, calculation, and faithfulness as central to their profession. Many also became patrons of art, investing the spoils of war in some of the greatest cultural achievements of the Renaissance.[10] Some of the leading figures of the Renaissance were military contractors.

Despite their contributions to the Renaissance, one of the reasons military contractors have a negative reputation is that, according to the established narrative, they are intimately associated with its demise. In conventional views of Italian history, the achievements of the Renaissance died out during the Italian Wars (1494–1559), a series of conflicts during which foreign powers intervened in the Italian peninsula, hiring *condottieri* to wage their battles. The end of the Italian Wars marked the beginning of Spanish Habsburg dominance in the Italian peninsula. In many ways, the later Thirty Years' War mimicked the Italian Wars: both sets of almost-constant conflict saw rapid military innovation. Many of the problems faced during the Thirty Years' War, including lack of provisions and rapacious looting by troops, were on display during the Italian Wars. Some of the most canonical writings on war—Machiavelli's *Art of War* and Niccolò Tartaglia's *A New Science* (1537)—were responses to the Italian Wars.[11]

One of the most traumatic events of the Italian Wars was the 1527 Sack of Rome by the undisciplined troops of Emperor Charles V. Many of the soldiers who ransacked the homes of cardinals and nobles were a type of common German mercenary known as *Landsknecht*. The *Landsknechte* were the fashion icons of their day who wore flamboyant costumes in bright colors with ripped sleeves and ostrich feathers in their hats. Their dress showed their desire to exempt themselves from the rules and customs of ordinary society, where clothing was usually regulated by sumptuary laws. Military careers brought certain liberties of which soldiers were acutely aware.[12] The *Landsknechte* are evidence that, a century before the Thirty Years' War, an increasingly international group of military contractors established new political, social, and economic significance within a European landscape plagued by warfare.[13]

As military careers evolved and men gained new advantages from serving in wars, the humanists who witnessed the Italian Wars consolidated their opinions against the roving warriors in their midst. Most notably, Machiavelli claimed that good men could not make a career of war because they "are necessitated either to plan that there not be peace or to succeed so much in times of war that they can nourish themselves in peace. And neither one of these two thoughts dwells in a good man. For from wanting to be able to nourish oneself in every time arise the robberies, the acts of violence, and the assassinations that such soldiers do to friends as well as to enemies. And from not wanting peace come the deceptions that the captains use on those who hire them so that war may last."[14] At the same time, Machiavelli criticized what he considered mercenary methods, complaining about the bloodless battles and chess-like maneuvers military contractors allegedly engaged in to avoid sacrificing their troops. Machiavelli, who had limited experience at the head of the Florentine militia from 1503 to 1506, thought that since citizen soldiers fought not for a wage but because they were loyal and committed to their homelands, they were virtuous and ferocious fighters. After a military crisis passed, these soldiers were disbanded in order to return to their regular work. This typical Renaissance humanist opinion was passed on to the Enlightenment and helped shape opinions about military men in the early American Republic. George Washington, a farmer who relinquished military command to return to pastoral life, represented the late eighteenth-century ideal.

Nonetheless, the humanist discourse about mercenaries that survived over time was over-simplified: even Machiavelli was capable of entertaining positive views of these figures if they brought order rather than disorder to the peninsula. In *The Art of War*, the model of the ideal military man was a military contractor himself, Fabrizio Colonna, who expressed Machiavelli's views on warfare in dialogue with Cosimo Rucellai in the sumptuous Rucellai gardens of Florence. In Machiavelli's text, Colonna argued that he had never made war his profession or "art." Rather, he asserted, "my art is to govern my subjects and to defend them, and, so as to be able to defend them, to love peace and know how to make war. And my king rewards and esteems me not so much because I understand war as because I know how to counsel him in peace."[15] This statement reveals military skill as part of a larger portfolio of abilities that a servant of princes required. Colonna provided a model of the military contractor as governor, an expert in stability rather than destruction. Italian noblemen in imperial service, many of whom read Machiavelli or were at least aware of his views, inherited complicated and ambivalent understandings of military contracting from the Renaissance.

The idea of the *condottiere* as a prudent, many-sided statesman who guided his prince through both war and peace matched the vision of the perfect courtier made famous by Machiavelli's contemporary Baldesar Castiglione in *The Book of the Courtier* (1528). Published just after the sack of Rome, the book grappled with concerns about the unstable politics of Castiglione's day and offered advice for those who served princes in volatile times. Castiglione delivered his analysis as a series of witty conversations between members of the court of Urbino, originally built by the *condottiere*-scholar Federico da Montefeltro. Castiglione, who had lived at Urbino for several years and who based his characters on real historical figures, lavished praise on Federico: an "unconquerable" military hero, prudent governor, and learned patron of the arts. Misfortune, however, had fallen upon Federico's heir, Guidobaldo, under whose auspices the playful investigation of the perfect courtier ostensibly took place.[16]

One of the key disagreements the characters in *The Book of the Courtier* deliberated over was whether it was better for a courtier to be well versed in arms or letters. Arms remained the traditional calling of the nobility, although fixation on warfare without regard for the arts turned a nobleman into an uncouth brute with no place at court. At the same time, as Giuliano de' Medici remarked, some believed that Italians had become connoisseurs of letters to the detriment of arms. Castiglione's character defended letters, arguing that respect for letters instilled a higher calling: glory. "Whereas," Castiglione wrote, "anyone who acts for gain or from any other motive not only fails to accomplish anything worthwhile but deserves to be called a miserable merchant rather than a gentleman." An education in letters and, even better, the ability to write literature was what made the difference between an honorable and dishonorable military career, between participating in the market for force as a lowly merchant and fulfilling the noble call to fight and govern. Furthermore, as the character modeled on Pietro Bembo pointed out, literature was more powerful than arms because it made the victories of the battlefield last far into the future, creating heroes for all time.[17] Over a century later, Montecuccoli's drive to account for his military experiences in formal treatises in part reflected his awareness of the role played by literature in creating and maintaining a military reputation beyond an officer's lifetime.

And yet, for all of these writers—Castiglione, Machiavelli, and later generations of officer-scholars, including Montecuccoli—personal glory was ultimately subsumed by a more important goal. By book 4, the final night of the conversation in Urbino, Ottaviano Fregoso observed that, when judging a courtier, one must keep in mind the courtier's ultimate purpose: "to win for himself the mind and favour of the prince he serves so that he can and always will tell him the truth about all he needs to know, without fear or risk of displeasing him."[18] Governance was the most difficult and yet most important art. Rulers were prey to self-aggrandizement, surrounded by the deceits of bad men. The perfect courtier's most perfect goal lay in being a virtuous guide for his prince at a time when "ignorance of how to govern peoples gives rise to so many evils, so much death, destruction, burning and ruination, that it may be said to be the deadliest plague of all."[19] Montecuccoli would face fierce opposition at court in the 1660s and 1670s as he competed with other powerful elites to influence the mind of Emperor Leopold I. The art of deception—behaving like a fox rather than a lion or demonstrating *sprezzatura* (studied nonchalance)—was critical, but the most widely read works of the Renaissance also taught that a reputation as a prudent, military man based on a record of virtuous deeds lent powerful credibility.[20]

The turmoil that inspired the pens of Machiavelli and Castiglione came to an end with the Spanish Habsburg domination of the peninsula in 1559, but war spread north of the Alps after 1560 as Reformation tensions exploded into open conflict. Although they are not often studied for their political insights, early modern military treatises were a part of Reformation political philosophy, related to works such as the writings of the Flemish humanist and Catholic convert Justus Lipsius (1547–1606) and the Italian Giovanni Botero (1544–1617). Lipsius was especially popular during the seventeenth century. Following Machiavelli, as well as Aquinas, Bodin, Seneca, and Tacitus, he became a leading figure in the revival of Stoicism, whose adherents were religiously nondogmatic and emphasized using reason, virtue, prudence, modesty, justice, clemency, and submission to rulers to solve the profound crises of their lifetimes.[21] Lipsius was concerned with how a prince should rule with peace as the overriding goal. Prudent behavior on the part of a ruler depended on wise counselors who embodied the virtue of constancy and were committed to educating their patron: "We educated citizens to bear up and to obey, so here [we educate] those who rule to govern."[22] Lipsius was also a military theorist whose studies of the Roman army inspired the reforms of Maurice of Nassau and Gustavus Adolphus. Montecuccoli cited Lipsius as a chief influence and adopted Lipsius's Ramist pedagogy, which involved a logical ordering of pithy maxims and was a far cry from Machiavelli's dialogue in a garden.[23] This kind of clear, concise writing also reflected the popularity of drill manuals.

Montecuccoli was part of a group of military men who had fully absorbed a message passed down from Machiavelli, Castiglione, Lipsius, and others that their highest purpose was neither profit nor the mere acquisition of power, but the education and advising of rulers. The best of these servants of princes accepted that their roles required a well-rounded education, prudence, charisma, subtlety, and a host of dynamic skills that would allow them to assist in the virtuous purposes of governance. They agreed that Rome provided the best model of an army, but rejected Machiavelli's republicanism in favor of an imperial humanism that sought to restore the achievements of the Roman Empire as an antidote to Reformation strife.[24] Italian noblemen, who were uniformly Catholic in the seventeenth century (a testament to the success of the Catholic Reformation in the peninsula), genuinely understood their goals to be virtuous, even if they also sought profit. However, in contrast to canonical political theorists like Lipsius, these warriors spent large chunks of their lives on campaigns or in garrisons—experiences that strongly shaped their writings.

Officer-Scholars in Habsburg Europe

Starting around 1560, the near-continuous Reformation wars produced a new wave of treatises written by officers that resembled the "mirror of Princes" genre, in which writers instructed rulers on how to rule.[25] This writing became a "surrogate for expertise" and was dominated by "the self-styled expert" who fused theory and practice.[26] These treatises provide insights into how military entrepreneurs understood their activities, while the dedications and prologues hint at career strategies, since they usually indicate which patrons a writer sought or received support from. Most significantly, these writings reveal the stages through which the science of war emerged. The meaning of "expert" is closely tied to experience, derived from the Latin *expertus sum*—"I have experienced."[27] Post-1560 warfare transformed Italian military entrepreneurs into new kinds of practitioners for whom experience and technical ability became essential. They crafted aristocratic identities as experts that reflected their engagement with broader political and scholarly trends, as well as campaign realities.

In his military revolution thesis, Michael Roberts credited the Dutch reformer Maurice of Nassau, prince of Orange (1567–1625), and the Swedish king Gustavus Adolphus (1594–1632), with initiating modern military reforms, including the creation of standing armies of trained, disciplined conscripts.[28] Geoffrey Parker offered a useful revision to Roberts's thesis when he pointed out how the reforms outlined by Roberts can be traced back to the Italian Wars (1494–1559) and the use of the bastioned fortification.[29] Parker also noted that the elements we identify with the military revolution—professionalism, organization, an evolution in tactics and strategy—have appeared, disappeared, and reappeared at different points in history, especially "wherever a situation of permanent or semi-permanent war existed."[30] Military science and innovation occurred across a wide expanse of time and space and involved piecemeal changes rather than a strictly linear progression.

Analyzing the writings of military entrepreneurs allows us to decenter military change from any single government or army and instead observe how practices and ideas evolved in the experiences of warriors who traveled between armies, battlefields, and courts. When we trace their ideas across multiple generations, we can make further connections between wars that served as the hotbeds of change: the Italian Wars, the War in Flanders, the Long War in Hungary, and the Thirty Years' War. Flanders may have been particularly fruitful in terms of generating printed treatises because of the proximity of printing houses in Antwerp. While this section deals with some of the more accessible printed materials, other writings circulated in manuscript form. Printed books are just one way of measuring and describing a new, shared military culture, which had Renaissance origins but bloomed across the continent in the late sixteenth and early seventeenth centuries.[31]

Early modern soldiers were active participants in both print and manuscript culture, composing poetry, treatises, histories, and letters.[32] Fernando Gonzalez de Leon's methodical study of late sixteenth-century Spanish "ideal-officer" treatises shows that commanders with experience fighting in Flanders developed foundational ideas and conventions of military science. These ideas included the wedding of technical and practical ability to theoretical knowledge and the promotion of a more meritocratic system in which officers systematically passed through a sequence of offices of increasing importance, also known as the *cursus honorum*.[33] Maurice of Nassau and Gustavus Adolphus studied the ideas of their opponents in the Spanish army, as well as the ancients.[34] It was not until later in the seventeenth century that Olivares began implementing military reforms anticipated by ideal-officer treatises, indicating that the works of soldiers preceded and probably influenced those of the minister.[35] In England, gentlemen who volunteered for service in the Low Countries were the first to write treatises in which they urged the discipline and training of English soldiers. In both the Elizabethan and Jacobean states, official court policy emerged in the wake of private initiatives.[36]

Italian officers in the Army of Flanders shared in the task of transforming and disseminating military expertise. During the Italian Wars, firepower had been integrated into military operations with greater effect than before, altering strategy and tactics. Engineers developed the bastion fort to withstand artillery. As a result, sieges, which could last for months, and attrition became central features of warfare. This kind of warfare required larger numbers of infantrymen spread out across territories, laying siege to fortresses and attempting to control resources. These features—larger armies fighting more continuously—inspired early professionalization, including a stronger push for discipline.[37] The star fortress spread to both Flanders and Hungary and, as a result, Habsburg rulers recruited larger armies to challenge enemy fortifications.[38] Italian engineers were employed across the continent, and treatises produced during the Italian Wars were widely read. In fact, Italian elites were often assumed to have military expertise. Despite his lack of practical experience, Jacopo Aconcio earned a reputation as a fortifications expert in England simply by virtue of being Italian and having written the treatise *Booke of Fortifyinge*.[39]

The treatises of Italian officers reflected their authors' humanist educations. They emulated Machiavelli's and Lipsius's direct study of the ancients, especially the works of Herodotus, Thucydides, Xenophon, Caesar, Polybius, and Vegetius, pursuing the much-vaunted mastery of both arms and letters.[40] After serving in Flanders, France, Transylvania, and Hungary, Imperiale Cinuzzi published *La vera militar disciplina antica e moderna* (1604), in which he claimed that he had been driven to write a treatise by "the desire to see the modern military on the level of excellence at which the ancient Roman military was now seen" as well as to assist the Christian Republic against enemies and to help his prince, the future grand duke Cosimo II.[41] The title page to the Neapolitan Lelio Brancaccio's (1560–1637) 1610 treatise, *I carichi militari*, is illustrative. Brancaccio served in Savoy, Burgundy, and Flanders before composing a book that systematically described every level of military rank—the increasingly important *cursus honorum*. The symbolism on the title page, which includes both a modern soldier with a pike and firearm and a Roman soldier equipped with bow and shield, as well as depictions of ancient and modern sieges, announces the fusion of knowledge Brancaccio sought. Between the images, an emblem depicting two visions of the universe—on the left, a formless space containing water, sun, moon, stars, and planets, and, on the right, an ordered Aristotelian cosmos with Earth in the center surrounded by the celestial spheres—reads, "Ex hoc, hunc efficit ordo" ("from this, order creates this"; essentially: "order out of chaos").[42] With the proper knowledge and training, disorderly multitudes of men could be transformed into coherent bodies of troops, a microcosm of the divine order established in the universe.[43] Other humanist captains joined their knowledge of ancient militaries to modern-day examples and experiences in order to create a new order of war, including Giorgio Basta (1540–1607) and Ludovico Melzi (1558–1617). Montecuccoli cited these writers in his first major treatise, *Treatise on War* (*Trattato della guerra*, 1641).

These writers made strong arguments about the role of experience or practice in developing military abilities, contributing to the emergence of a pan-European tradition in which theory was frequently paired with practice. In the dedication of *I carichi militari*, Brancaccio emphasized that he wrote "after some experience and practice acquired in matters of war in the space of many years."[44] Basta's 1612 *Il governo della cavalleria leggiera* boasted of "forty years of military experience in Flanders and in Hungary."[45] And while Cinuzzi explained that "all the rules and the teachings that are found in (this treatise) I based upon long and diligent observation made during a continuous reading of history," the primary foundation of his knowledge was "long experience of twelve continuous years which I spent serving, working, and commanding in Flanders, and in France, as soldier, ensign-bearer, and captain of arquebusiers in the Italian infantry under the most certain guide of the Great Alessandro Farnese, Duke of Parma, of most glorious memory, and under the excellent masters, my captains, Lord Camillo Capizucchi of happy memory and Lord Silvio Piccolomini, and then in Transylvania and finally in Hungary, enduring the greater battles of war which in our age came to pass."[46] Other similar works with international influence explicitly connecting theory and practice included Don Bernardino de Mendoza's *Theory and Practice of War* (*Theorica y Pratica de la Guerra*, 1595) and Henri, the duke of Rohan's *The Perfect Captain* (*Le parfait capitaine*, 1631). Rohan's work became one of the most popular books of the century. In it he asserted that the would-be captain should read treatises on fortification, but, "even better, [should learn] from the exercise of war, where every day experience adds something."[47] Reverence for experience dated as far back as the early humanists, who believed that learning should be put to practical use. However, the late sixteenth and seventeenth centuries saw a particularly fruitful interchange between theory and practice, which some historians of science posit provided the roots of the Scientific Revolution.[48]

Military men contributed to this change, but they did not necessarily need humanists or natural philosophers to teach them about the value of experience. Perhaps more than any other field, warfare was widely considered to be uniquely empirical. Commanders practiced science every day as they oversaw their responsibilities related to logistics, engineering, and troop maneuvers, all of which required a practical understanding of not only mathematics but also subjects like agronomy, botany, and forestry.[49] In fact, ideas often moved in the opposite direction, from the field of war to books. As early as Leonardo da Vinci's day, the greatest scientific minds had produced notable works in the military field in response to the demands of their patrons. Galileo, who taught a class on fortifications at Padua, affirmed the practical empiricism of war. His studies of ballistics produced insights into physics, and he argued for the military usefulness of his telescope to the Republic of Venice or the Grand Duchy of Tuscany.[50] Matteo Valleriani, who characterizes Galileo as a "scientific engineer," has shown that many of Galileo's innovations occurred in response to military needs.[51]

Contemporaries especially lauded experience in war, where victory or defeat was clear and consequential. As Cinuzzi wrote, "the governing of war is the most difficult matter there is among all other human actions, and requires greater experience and vigilance than all the others."[52] Challenges arose from new features of war. The continuous nature of conflicts meant that colonels preferred to retain veterans rather than disband troops at the end of each conflict, leading to early versions of standing armies. Experienced troops had usually already received training and developed discipline, both of which were required for increasingly complex field operations. Reformers strove to organize troops into thinner lines in order to make the army nimbler and firepower more effective, while troops performed particular tactical roles in coordination rather than operate as a herd.[53] Basta argued that the field marshal (maestro di campo) required two central qualities: "fear of God" and "experience." While fear of God was important for the mental state of the general, experience was necessary for "operations."[54] Cinuzzi viewed experience, in combination with science, as critical for practical war maneuvers such as quartering troops, marching, and fighting.[55] However, perhaps even more importantly, experience allowed a commander "to know wisely how to take advantage of opportunities."[56] Knowledge about the organization of armies and sieges could be acquired by reading books in the comfort of one's home. Experience enabled an officer to put these ideas into practice amid the chaos of actual combat.[57] Experience was strongly associated with action, grooming the sense of timing that was necessary for knowing when and how to direct troops.

In these new circumstances, officers became teachers, masters, and disciplinarians, and common soldiers became students in need of practice and drilling. Illustrated drill manuals emerged, quickly copied and translated into multiple languages.[58] Military writers called officers maestri—masters, teachers, instructors—who needed experience in order to model actions and educate and discipline soldiers. Cinuzzi had referred to his captains—Capizucchi and Piccolomini (Ottavio Piccolomini's father)—as maestri and emphasized that a commander should "instruct and exercise his soldiers well."[59] He should be master of all (maestro di tutti).[60] Brancaccio wrote, "the captain should know how to manage every kind of arms and to do every action customary in the army in order to be able to, conforming to his obligation, teach and discipline his soldiers."[61] Such discipline, for instance, consisted in using "great diligence that the soldiers whom he conducts always march in their lines and not disorder themselves, nor break apart, informing his sergeant who is marching in the train that he not let anyone tarry."[62] For the field marshal, Basta claimed that experience was "born, raised and for a long course of years confirmed in him by the continuous management of all the military offices."[63]

The need to gain experience at every military rank in order to know how to direct the soldiers under one's command produced a culture of meritocracy and encouraged the internationalization of armies. Experience was allegedly more important than social rank or country of origin.[64] Cinuzzi claimed that an "illustrious captain" did not succeed because of "the nobility of blood, but on account of the shining deeds performed by him."[65] By organizing his treatises according to which aptitudes one had to acquire in order to succeed at each level of military office, Brancaccio revealed a sense that advancement from the lowest to the highest levels of military rank was a possibility, especially if one exhibited "virtue."[66] Indeed, many lesser nobles, including Montecuccoli, claimed with pride that they had started out as simple pikemen and worked their way up the military hierarchy.

At the same time, we must take these statements about merit-based promotion in armies with a grain of salt, supplementing them with the iconic vision of military hierarchy provided by Grimmelshausen's *Simplicissimus*. In this tragicomic account of a peasant boy's Thirty Years' War adventures, written by an eyewitness to the war, the narrator imagined the military hierarchy as a tree, with vicious noblemen obstinately monopolizing its upper branches. They were separated from the lower branches by a bare section of tree trunk, "greased with all the lotions and soaps that malice could devise, so that no man, however good he was at climbing, could scale it, neither by courage, skill or knowledge, unless he came from the nobility."[67] While there are some examples of commoners achieving high military rank, they are very rare. Most of the flexibility regarding status involved lesser nobles ascending to top command—especially possible when frequent injury, illness, and death opened those positions up on a regular basis.[68] Early modern armies were not pure meritocracies (and certainly could never be meritocracies when war functioned as a family business), but they did provide many low-ranking noblemen with opportunities for social as well as geographic mobility.

The fact that many lesser nobles composed treatises as they crossed geographic, social, and political boundaries suggests that military science was initially the expertise of outsiders seeking ways to distinguish themselves as they pursued patronage. They may have seen treatises as a kind of résumé in which they could advertise experience, technical skill, and theoretical knowledge. Military science allowed these newcomers to distinguish themselves from commoners who had experience in war but lacked the cultural backgrounds and educations to become experts. In this way, military science was an ingre-

dient of the "grease" that Grimmelshausen complained prevented commoners from attaining higher rank. At the same time, new forms of expertise often
existed under a cloud of suspicion at early modern courts precisely because
they were associated with deceitful, *arriviste* men who used their wits to vio-
late carefully patrolled social and disciplinary categories.[69] Even the most ambitious noblemen faced opposition from rivals and might fail to achieve the
rewards they sought.

In the context of the court, military writers joined a crowd of other early
modern would-be experts whose claims of special knowledge and experience
buttressed patronage requests at a time when governments were expanding
and centralizing. Due to the importance of war, military books were studied
by a wide audience, including ministers, diplomats, and scholars.[70] Practitioners in other fields proposed their own practical military projects, elevating their
status at court and indicating that the military field offered truly unique opportunities for social advancement.[71] By studying this climate, historians of
expertise have concluded that the suppliers of patronage—the emerging
states—demanded expertise to serve their practical needs.[72] The explosion of
treatises on a broad range of purportedly useful topics reflected the desire of
rulers and their ministers to institutionalize and codify the knowledge of practitioners. For instance, Cosimo I de' Medici's founding of the Accademia del
Disegno in 1563 is an early example of a ruler attempting to take over practical training.[73] The early modern court is now seen as a site of science, and the
emergence of the Scientific Revolution appears to have been made possible in
the context of state building as clients proposed projects and codified knowledge in service to expansionist-minded rulers. This process is usually envi-
sioned from the vantage point of the court center and in the context of the
growth of individual states such as England or Tuscany.

Often overlooked, however, is the degree to which these authors appear to
have written their treatises for immediate, practical use by fellow officers.[74]
Demand for military treatises and manuals arose in large part from officers
aware of the need to comprehend an increasingly complicated subject.[75] In particular, treatises targeted junior officers—the "crucial links" who synchro-
nized the movements of smaller units with the orders of the commander—for
improvement.[76] In his preface to the reader, Melzi admitted that he used
technical terms when necessary under the assumption that his main audience
was composed of soldiers.[77] If garrisoned troops had manuals and treatises
available, they may have read them aloud in groups.[78] Officers often composed
treatises during breaks in fighting, when troops were garrisoned or disbanded.
Officers awaiting orders may have written their treatises elbow to elbow, so
to speak. Brancaccio, Melzi, and Pompeo Giustiniani all served in the Army

of Flanders, and all three wrote treatises shortly after the Twelve Years' Truce was declared in 1609. They knew one another because they referred to each other in their writings and used the same publisher: Joachim Trognaesius in Antwerp.[79] A "professional discourse" among officers emerged in which even those who did not write treatises participated.[80] Cristóbal Lechuga, an expert on artillery and fortification serving in Flanders apparently brought the manuscript of his treatise, *Treatise on the Rank of Infantry General* (*Discurso del Cargo de Maestro de Campo General*, 1603), on campaign to solicit feedback from other officers.[81] Armies had their own cultures of expertise that, while connected to courts, also developed according to their own reasons.

By decentering this process from single courts and observing military entrepreneurs formulating and disseminating ideas as they moved between battlefields, garrisons, prisons, and courts, we can better understand the complex context in which modern military expertise emerged. Military treatises were the products of a transregional culture in which an international cadre of military entrepreneurs were the first to recognize the need to explain and codify new ideas and practices of warfare. These writers trained rulers on military needs and instructed one another on how to be professional soldiers. Whether officer-scholars achieved their desired promotions or not, military writings allowed them to participate in a broader political discourse. The enlightened despots of the eighteenth century would eventually don officer uniforms and present themselves as disciplinarians in command of well-trained standing armies. The conversation about the centrality of military affairs to governments, however, started in the late sixteenth century among military contractors, explicitly codified in treatises they wrote and circulated. Military affairs became a gripping conversation and deeply studied topic long before rulers reimagined themselves as commanders-in-chief.

The decades in which officer-scholars wrote occurred during a rich moment of intersection between the legacies of Renaissance learning and the emergence of the mathematical and empirical sciences. War seemed to be particularly susceptible to improvisation as rulers, statesmen, and officers searched desperately for ways to dominate and win. Military entrepreneurs, who belonged to a longer tradition of learned warriors, became scientific practitioners. Military expertise and professionalism became core features of modern states, but it was individuals paradoxically classified today as nonstate actors who were the first to introduce these ideas and practices to states. The military entrepreneurs who fought in the Thirty Years' War, Montecuccoli included, absorbed and enriched the writings and conversations of the soldier-scholars of the late sixteenth and early seventeenth centuries.

The knowledge produced by early modern military entrepreneurs emerged from geographically wide-ranging careers that involved service to multiple rulers on battlefields across Europe. The treatises themselves reflect a kaleidoscope of possibility: the Sienese Cinuzzi fought in the Spanish and Imperial armies but dedicated his treatise to the grand duke of Tuscany. A particularly telling example is Giovanni Francesco Fiammelli, a Florentine mathematician-engineer who served under Farnese in Flanders and lived in Rome after Farnese's death. From 1602 to 1606, he published five treatises, each of which dealt with war in some way, and each of which was dedicated to a different patron. Perhaps Fiammelli attempted but failed to secure the patronage he desired, leading him to dedicate each subsequent treatise to a new possible employer. It was relatively ordinary after 1560 for Italian noblemen to attempt to forge ties to multiple patrons through the dedications of treatises. Italian military writers had attained the expertise they displayed in treatises—a fusion of theory, experience, and pedagogical method—precisely because they had traveled to different war zones and sometimes served in different armies.

As they led troops in conflicts across Europe, Italian noblemen invested their own families' wealth and credit and risked their reputations, health, and safety. What relationship did the military theory some officers wrote about bear to these realities? What were the contexts in which the ideas emerged and were subsequently applied? The vibrant literary traditions of learned aristocratic warriors must be set within a European landscape of interconnected battlefields, courts, confessional alliances, and patronage relationships. Furthermore, the Thirty Years' War played a special role in the evolution of these careers. While many Italian noblemen served in the Spanish Army of Flanders, the Thirty Years' War, which broke out in 1618 in Habsburg Central Europe, when the Protestant Bohemian estates defied Emperor Ferdinand II's rule over Bohemia, fundamentally reoriented many of them from Spanish to imperial service. The allied Catholic forces' glorious victory over the rebel

Table 1.1   Giovanni Francesco Fiammelli's treatises, 1602–6

TITLE	YEAR PUBLISHED	DEDICATED TO
Il principe cristiano guerriero	1602	Cardinal Alessandro de' Medici
Modo di ben mettere in ordinanza gli eserciti	1603	Cardinal Antonio Facchinetto
Il principe difeso [. . .] *nel quale si tratta di fortificazione, oppugnazione, espugnazione, o difesa*	1604	King Philip III of Spain
La riga mathematica	1605	Grand Duke Cosimo II de' Medici
I quesiti militari [. . .]	1606	Ferdinando Rucellai

army at the 1620 Battle of White Mountain generated enormous excitement among Catholic noblemen from across Europe, many of whom eagerly volunteered to fight in the imperial or Catholic League armies. As the war continued, it offered unprecedented opportunities for gaining experience, wealth, and status in a foreign army. At the same time, the realities of battlefield, garrison, and campaign in 1620s Central Europe quickly revealed the difficulty of implementing the vision of well-ordered war described in contemporary treatises. Nonetheless, the Italian military entrepreneurs who established prestigious positions in imperial service during the 1620s provided models that later noblemen, including Montecuccoli, attempted to follow.

CHAPTER 2

The Generation of White Mountain

On 8 November 1620, an allied Catholic army faced off against the Protestant forces of Frederick V, the elector palatine, on a low plateau that rose just west of Prague called White Mountain. Although not particularly high, the area was "uneven, strewn with hills, dales, and hollows" and was "everywhere sandy." Frederick's army had taken the most advantageous position, setting up camp at the peak. The Catholics hurried along with their plans, hoping to attack before "the enemy entrenched himself and fortified his camp such that neither could he be lured out of it, nor could it be taken from him by force."[1] With their troops in order—the imperial army on the right side and the Catholic League army on the left—the Catholics attacked. They routed the rebel army after only an hour. Frederick V, dubbed the "Winter King" for his brief reign, immediately fled Prague.[2]

The Battle of White Mountain was the first major battle of the Thirty Years' War (1618–48) and was instrumental in reestablishing the authority of the Austrian Habsburg ruler, Emperor Ferdinand II, in Bohemia. Two years earlier, the Protestant Bohemian estates, citing religious and political grievances, had rebelled against Ferdinand II when they unceremoniously threw his representatives out of a window at Prague Castle. After forming an estates government and building alliances to Protestant estates in the Habsburg hereditary lands (including Moravia, Austria, Silesia, and Hungary), the Bohemians had deposed Ferdinand II as king of Bohemia and elected the Calvinist Frederick V.[3] From afar, Italian rulers and nobles looked on in horror at what they saw as a brazen act of rebellion on the part of Protestants in the heart of Christendom. An international alliance featuring Spain, Bavaria, the papacy, and Tuscany quickly formed to help Ferdinand II quell the rebellions.[4]

As a result of this alliance, the decisive confrontation between Protestant and Catholic armies at White Mountain included soldiers from as far afield as Flanders and Friuli. Prominent Italian noblemen, including Ottavio Piccolomini of Tuscany, Torquato Conti of Rome, and Tommaso Caracciolo of Naples, were on the battlefield that day. Some of the participants swore that Teresa of Ávila had appeared to them just before battle, leading Pope Gregory XV to canonize her in 1622.[5] Enthusiasm about the victory at White Mountain spurred further recruitment to the imperial army as Catholics across Europe sought to share the glory of their coreligionists, imagining that the final victory over heresy was imminent. They were wrong: the war continued for nearly three more decades. By the end of the 1620s, a new Protestant alliance challenged Habsburg dominance, and the war reached into northern Italy with the War of the Mantuan Succession (1628–31).

The "generation of White Mountain" refers to members of a transregional military elite who fought at White Mountain or were inspired to join or otherwise support Catholic imperial forces in the aftermath of the battle. Historians of the eighteenth- and nineteenth-century Austro-Hungarian Empire have long noted the commitment of the Austro-Hungarian army's international officer corps to the Habsburg dynasty as one of the army's most distinctive features.[6] An examination of one especially successful cohort of officers in imperial service, Italian noblemen, indicates that the origins of these relationships can be traced back to the late sixteenth and early seventeenth centuries. The Battle of White Mountain and the ensuing Thirty Years' War were an especially critical turning point in Habsburg military culture.

The aftermath of Catholic victory at White Mountain included a decade of acquisitive behavior and inconclusive fighting that Montecuccoli's patrons, including Piccolomini, found ways to benefit from. Ferdinand II enacted heavy-handed punishments against Protestant nobles, including execution, forced conversions to Catholicism, and the confiscation and redistribution of properties, offices, and titles.[7] Many native nobles simply fled. As wealth and offices changed hands, incredible fortunes were made: Albrecht Wallenstein, who single-handedly raised an entire army for Ferdinand II, transformed from a middling nobleman to duke of Sagan and Mecklenberg, with vast estates valued at 9,280,000 florins before his death.[8] The stream of opportunities and rewards enticed Italian noblemen to pursue long-term careers in imperial service, during which they participated in exploitative behaviors to extract wealth from local populations. Harsh conditions meant that many Italian military entrepreneurs failed to achieve the glory they originally sought. Nonetheless, they remained loyal to the Habsburgs and developed an aristocratic identity revolving around service to the dynasty.

Cosmopolitan Careers

Italian noblemen in the imperial army during the Thirty Years' War nourished rich family traditions of service to the Spanish and Austrian branches of the Habsburg family dating back to Spanish domination of the Italian peninsula after the 1559 conclusion of the Italian Wars.[9] Despite historical stereotypes about the decline of Italian military traditions after the Renaissance, popular compendia of noble families written by contemporary historiographers reveal the widespread participation of Italian elites in conflicts spanning this period. Gregory Hanlon's analysis of one particularly comprehensive catalog for Siena, written by Antonio Sestigiani in 1696, reveals that 99 out of 143 of the old nobility listed in the manuscript had at least one family member in military service from 1560 on.[10] Although many military contractors formed social and political bonds in the countries where they obtained military positions, singular loyalty to a ruler was an impediment if better opportunities lay elsewhere. Beneath the umbrella of Spanish domination, a multitude of Italian actors pursued divergent interests.

Prior to the Thirty Years' War, the two most popular battlefield destinations were Flanders and Hungary, where Catholic supporters of the Spanish and Austrian Habsburgs were pitted against Protestants and Muslims. Of these conflicts, Italian participation in the War in Flanders has received the most attention. Benedetto Croce surmised that the "hearts, minds, and imaginations" of Italians were essentially "transported" to Flanders during the late sixteenth and early seventeenth centuries.[11] The greatest commanders of the Spanish Army of Flanders, Alessandro Farnese and Ambrogio Spinola, were from Parma and Genoa, respectively, while as much as 10–20 percent of the entire army was composed of Italians. Although rulers across Europe regularly employed foreigners in armies, the Spanish Army of Flanders took this practice to a new level, divided into six main "nations" (Spanish, Italian, Walloon, German, Burgundian, and British), with each nation valued differently. The Italian troops were second only to the highly revered Spanish soldiers.[12] Spain's strategies for securing service and loyalty included granting subsidies, revenues, titles, admission to military orders, and land as rewards.[13] The noblemen who followed Italian rulers like Farnese into foreign wars did so as clients of their lord hopeful for future rewards, rather than as career officers seeking promotions.[14]

Providing honors for military service was so pervasive and well understood that it amounted to a de facto system for eliciting and maintaining consensus for Spanish rule among peninsular elites.[15] In the Lombard Trotti and Visconti dynasties, military careers in Spanish service evolved across multiple generations, elevating the family's status.[16] Such strategies were common in territories directly controlled by Spain—Milan, Naples, Sicily, and Sardinia—and in the independent central and northern regions, as Farnese's example attests.[17] Many commanders with experience in the Army of Flanders, such as the Neapolitan Tommaso Caracciolo (b. 1572), went on to fight in Central Europe in the 1620s.[18] The two Italians who served as supreme commanders of the imperial army in the 1630s and 1640s, Matteo Galasso (1584–1647) and Ottavio Piccolomini (1599–1656), had fathers who had served under Farnese.[19] Galasso, who hailed from Trento, was a direct subject of the emperor's and established his career through connections to the powerful Madruzzo family.[20]

While some commanders in the Thirty Years' War started out in the War in Flanders, others served the Austrian branch of the Habsburg family in Hungary during the Long War against the Ottomans (1593–1606), including members of the Montecuccoli family. An important prelude to the Thirty Years' War, the Long War saw an extensive mobilization of imperial and Habsburg troops and activated transregional support networks. Emperor Rudolf II secured aid from Spain, the papacy, and northern Italian princes, and the pope rallied support by seeking to expand the conflict into a new crusade. Montecuccoli's father, Galeotto, led Tuscan troops in Hungary. Galeotto Montecuccoli's trajectory was not uncommon. Born the bastard son of Fabrizio Montecuccoli and Paola Stavoli, he relied on Emperor Rudolf II to legitimize his birth. He committed a murder in 1599 and fled to France, where a relative, Alfonso Montecuccoli, represented the grand duke of Tuscany as an ambassador. Alfonso arranged Galeotto's command of Tuscan troops in Hungary. After reinventing himself as an officer in the imperial army, Galeotto returned to Modena and led Este troops in the 1613 war over the Monferrato succession and again during hostilities against Lucca. He was also in charge of a feudal militia comprising seven hundred men from Montecuccolo and an additional four hundred from the Frignano region.[21]

Galeotto died before the Thirty Years' War broke out, but other veterans of the Long War, including Ernesto Montecuccoli (1582–1633)—Raimondo's "uncle"—and Rambaldo Collalto (1575–1630), continued their advancement in the first decade of the Thirty Years' War. Ernesto had fought in the regiment of Giorgio Basta alongside Wallenstein. He remained close to Wallenstein throughout the Bohemian general's meteoric rise, eventually filling in for Wallenstein as commander-in-chief when Wallenstein fell ill. When Ernesto died in 1633—just before Wallenstein's assassination—he was the general of artillery and commanded imperial forces in Alsace.[22] Collalto eventually commanded imperial troops in the War of the Mantuan Succession (1628–31) and became president of the Aulic War Council. Observing the many careers that overlapped the Long War and the Thirty Years' War, Peter Wilson has remarked that the list of Emperor Rudolf's officers from the earlier conflict amounts to a "roll-call of the senior generals of the first half of the Thirty Years' War."[23]

The service of Italian noblemen in the Long War reminds us of the importance of ties to the Holy Roman emperor, an elected office held by the Austrian Habsburgs, in the Italian peninsula. These ties dated back to the Middle Ages, when the Holy Roman emperor held lordship in Italy and grappled for influence with the papacy. The Italian states are not often included in historical analyses of the Holy Roman Empire because they were vassal states of the empire that lacked a deliberative body, compared to the German diets. Nonetheless, the relationship to the emperor appears to have been especially important to princes and nobles from the independent or semi-independent principalities in northern Italy, where no major political power had been able to establish overarching authority. For members of these states, it was acceptable to claim the protection of the Holy Roman emperor, the Spanish king, and a local Italian lord and to alternate between service to these various rulers. At the same time, the Austrian Habsburgs sought to use their position as Holy Roman emperors to maintain and extend their influence in northern Italy. Critical military corridors stretched from Milan to Central Europe and the Netherlands, allowing troops to pass between Spanish-controlled territories and between Spanish- and Austrian-controlled territories. As French power grew more menacing throughout the century, the Austrian Habsburgs saw the Italian peninsula as an essential buffer zone between their territories and those of Louis XIV (r. 1643–1715).[24]

While the power of the emperor in the Italian peninsula was largely symbolic by the seventeenth century, it is important to remember that it retained significant practical applications. Association with imperial power granted prestige: many northern Italian noble dynasties even claimed descent from invading Germanic warlords.[25] The ethereal status of the emperor, who ranked above all other rulers of Christendom, attracted marriage alliances. At the same time, the Holy Roman emperor continued to exercise significant real-world power in parts of the peninsula within his jurisdiction when he decided the fate of Italian states that fell into devolution due to the extinction of a dynasty (along with a handful of other possible legal reasons, including criminal activity on the part of the landowner).[26] For numerous Italian aristocratic families, the emperor also provided authority to legitimize births, confirm privileges, and mediate territorial disputes.[27] Finally, the Holy Roman emperor continued to collect—or attempted to collect—contributions from Italian states for war, including in 1618.[28]

The contested northeastern Friuli region—a mountainous territory at the crossroads of Venetian, Austrian, and Ottoman power—provides a case study for understanding one kind of Italian region that produced imperial servants. From 1560 to 1710, thirty-three officers in imperial service came from Friuli.[29] Friulian military families emerged from a borderland that had long suffered the depredations of armies and resulting economic stagnation. As the Republic of Venice increasingly asserted control over the region in an effort to build its land empire, Friuli was torn apart by rival clans bent on controlling its limited material resources. The Strassoldo family was oriented more toward imperial than Spanish service: from the mid-sixteenth to the mid-seventeenth centuries, thirteen members of the family served the emperor, while only two served the king of Spain.[30] One of the most notable Friulians in imperial service during the seventeenth century was Leopold I's chief minister, Johann Ferdinand Portia (1606–65), who stemmed from *condottieri* stock with alleged German roots.[31] The Friulian Colloredo family claimed a similar past and followed a similar trajectory. They alleged that their family descended from Swabian Lords of Waldsee who migrated with the Lombards.[32] Rudolfo Colloredo (1585–1657) was born in Budweis (České Budějovice) after his father, Lodovico, relocated to Central Europe and became imperial chamberlain (*Kämmerer*) to Emperor Rudolf II. Colloredo, presumably named after the emperor, who served as his godfather at the baptismal font, was a field marshal in the Long War and a coconspirator in the assassination in Wallenstein. He helped defend Prague from a Swedish onslaught at the end of the Thirty Years' War.[33]

A few generations prior to establishing their Central European line, the Colloredo became embroiled in the violent 1511 Friulian blood feud vividly depicted by Ed Muir in *Mad Blood Stirring*: a terrifying theater of ax-wielding mobs and dismembered corpses torn apart by animals. This particular round of violence in the long-standing rivalry between the local Della Torre and Savorgnan clans transformed into the biggest peasant revolt in Renaissance Italy. In the decades leading up to the 1511 violence, the Colloredo joined the Della Torre as fierce enemies of the Savorgnan. Looking back on the period, Marzio Colloredo claimed his clan had played a leading role in the feud, carefully calculating how many Savorgnan they had killed.[34]

However, the Colloredo were not just castellans at the wild edges of Italian Renaissance society. In his hagiographic 1674 narrative of the Colloredo family deeds, Galeazzo Gualdo Priorato assured the reader that "in the period of the feud they did not neglect to labor outside of the homeland as well."[35]

Priorato had already emphasized that the Colloredo family "produced in every age subjects worthy of honor and esteem in peace as well as in war, and valued not only by fellow countrymen, but also by foreigners on account of the honored employments and leading offices which they have exercised in the courts and armies of various princes."[36] He went on to list the cosmopolitan accomplishments of the Colloredo relatives who had become soldiers, courtiers, and diplomats in Venetian, Tuscan, Ferrarese, Milanese, Spanish, and Austrian service during the sixteenth century, including Rudolfo's father and two of his uncles. By the time Rudolfo and his brothers searched for a career, Priorato wrote that they "never thought of being better able to illustrate their actions with other employment than by devoting themselves all to the current service of the Most August House of Austria."[37] In his examination of the blood feud, Muir argued that Friuli was no peripheral backwater. The 1511 violence reverberated as far as the streets and canals of Venice, demanding the intervention of Venetian elites and revealing a complex weave of ties between city and countryside. The careers of Colloredo family members amplify this point. Seemingly provincial Italian nobilities were bound within webs of relationships that extended far beyond their ancestral homes.

Priorato attributed the movement of Friulian warriors into the client pools of foreign princes to Venice's increasing encroachments on Friuli's territory.[38] Rambaldo Collalto, who came from Venetian terra firma territory near Treviso and whose family claimed origins in the Margraviate of Brandenburg, found himself in a similar position. The Collalto family produced "men excellent and valorous in war" who served Venice, the pope, the French king, and the Holy Roman emperor. Rambaldo pledged allegiance to Venice but threw off Venetian ties to pursue a career under the Austrian Habsburgs.[39] In addition to his success in gaining land and other rewards in Central Europe, he registered his sons in *The Golden Book of Venetian Nobility*.[40] The Colloredo and Collalto family maneuvers between northeastern Italy and Central Europe suggest a calculated strategy for the promotion of the family line in which Italians grasped opportunities across regions.

By the end of the sixteenth century, the option of soldiering for the Habsburgs was attractive to nobles who refused to take part in the expanding government apparatus of a local ruler, or who faced some sort of legal or political obstacle in that service. Michael Mallett and J. R. Hale argued that the transformation of the regional nobility into a faithful military elite whose status and power were tied to Venice was a critical step in Venice's consolidation of power.[41] However, it is important not to overestimate this transformation, since members of these families forged transregional careers that allowed their families partially to elude the grasp of a single central power. They continued to entertain other options.

Italian noble dynasties had long exploited the ambiguities of political power in the peninsula by forging multiple ties, but Habsburg hegemony and the continuous nature of Habsburg wars beyond the peninsula dramatically expanded the geographical dimensions of these practices.

Marriage alliances between Italian dynasties and the Habsburgs facilitated the movement of men and women between the peninsula and Central Europe, contributing to the Italianization of the imperial court, where Italian was spoken as often as German.[42] Two of the Italian states identified by Hanlon as producing a high number of officers in the imperial army—Mantua and Tuscany—achieved notable marriage alliances.[43] Emperors Ferdinand II and Ferdinand III each married a Gonzaga woman (both named Eleonora) in an effort to create a stable alliance with Mantua and to protect the military corridor that ran through northern Italy. These Gonzaga empresses actively promoted Italian musicians, artists, gardeners, and doctors, as well as officers, including at least two Aulic War Council presidents: Collalto, a distant Gonzaga relative, and Annibale Gonzaga (1602–68). They were not only patrons but also "transalpine knowledge brokers" operating within dynamic, far-reaching networks.[44] In 1656, the second Empress Eleonora cofounded a twelve-member Italian academy with Archduke Leopold Wilhelm that drew together an international cadre of military-diplomatic elites whose resources, expertise, and connections helped the Habsburgs assert and defend their interests across a wide swath of Europe.[45] In the case of Tuscany, Grand Duke Cosimo II's wife was Emperor Ferdinand II's sister, Maria Maddalena of Austria. During the Thirty Years' War, Cosimo's sister, Claudia, and his daughter, Anna, both married Austrian archdukes, becoming countesses of the Tyrol.[46] Two of Cosimo's sons, Mattias and Francesco, led troops during the Thirty Years' War (Francesco fell ill and died at Regensburg in 1634). Mattias returned home to become governor of Siena and head the Tuscan militia but maintained Central European connections, employing contacts in the imperial army to offer opportunities to Tuscans abroad and to obtain specialized military services for his brother, Grand Duke Ferdinando II.[47]

The most illustrious Tuscan military career that flowered out of Medici-Habsburg ties belonged to Ottavio Piccolomini, who commanded the Spanish Army of Flanders from 1644 to 1647 and became lieutenant general of the imperial army in 1648. He oversaw the final campaign of the Thirty Years' War and represented Emperor Ferdinand III at the Peace of Nuremberg (1650) (figure 2.1).[48] Piccolomini first arrived in Central Europe in 1619, with troops financed by Grand Duke Cosimo II and a letter of recommendation from the grand duchess, Maria Maddalena, in hand.[49] Piccolomini hailed from a papal

FIGURE 2.1.   Jan Gerritsz van Bronckhorst, *Portrait of General Ottavio Piccolomini*. RMN-Grand Palais/Art Resource, New York.

family: his ancestor was Pius II. His father, Silvio, had fought in Flanders and Hungary, returning to Florence to hold the offices of grand constable of the Order of Saint Stephen, master of artillery, grand chamberlain, and captain of the grand-ducal bodyguard.[50] Ottavio Piccolomini contributed to his family's shining achievements when he attained one of the most coveted honors in imperial service: Ferdinand III named him prince of the empire in 1650. Through dynastic ties, but also due to the prominence of Tuscan figures like Piccolomini,

Florence became a stepping-stone to Habsburg service for noblemen from other parts of the peninsula.[51] For instance, Bartolomaio Strassoldo of Friuli first became a page at the Tuscan court, before obtaining a recommendation to join Piccolomini's regiment in Central Europe in 1640.[52]

While some Italian noblemen remained in Central Europe, others returned to the Italian peninsula, where they attempted to leverage experience in the imperial army for advancement. When Piero Signorini asked Mattias de' Medici to help him obtain a company to command in 1641, Mattias wrote a letter to his brother Grand Duke Ferdinando II, in which he identified Signorini as a man experienced in multiple conflicts and armies. He recounted that Signorini had "served Your Highness in the last expedition in Milan with a company" and that, before Milan, Signorini "had served many years in Germany in the office of ensign, showing himself a courageous and brave soldier on every occasion." It appears that Signorini got his first military experience in Germany, where he held a low office, standard-bearer. This early experience probably provided the grounds (and perhaps aristocratic connections) to request a higher position—captain of a company—when conflict in Milan erupted and he returned to serve the Medici. Signorini was not, however, a simple careerist traveling in pursuit of individualistic goals. In his letter to the grand duke, Mattias noted that Signorini was "loved greatly by me not only for his own merits, but also for those that Leonardo, his brother, has acquired with me in having served me currently and always with punctuality and diligence."[53] Mattias de' Medici contextualized Piero Signorini's request for a company within a longer record of services Signorini family members had supplied the Medici. The Signorini must have approached patrons through a concerted family strategy: while one member left Tuscany to gain experience and rewards in a foreign army, others continued serving closer to home.

While the prevalence of Italians at the imperial court and in the imperial army represented a continuation of long-term transregional patterns of alliance and service, the opening years of the Thirty Years' War were distinctive. By the time of the Bohemian rebellion, Italian military entrepreneurs were fervently committed to Catholic imperial rule in Central Europe and to the broader vision of militant Catholic power cultivated by Catholic Reformation propaganda and theology in the early seventeenth century. Habsburg success at White Mountain was seen as especially providential, and the decade that followed provided unusual opportunities to gain wealth, titles, and offices, encouraging a shift of focus to the Central European theater of war. However, the noblemen who arrived with visions of battlefield glory soon found themselves chasing an elusive victory.

The Papacy and Roman Noblemen

Rome greeted news of the victory at White Mountain with a wave of enthusiasm. Pope Gregory XV (r. 1621–23) and his energetic nephew, Cardinal Ludovico Ludovisi (1595–1632), were convinced that the moment for total Catholic victory—cultural, diplomatic, and military—had arrived. While his predecessor, Paul V, had sent meager subsidies, Gregory financed ten companies led by the Roman nobleman Pietro Aldobrandini by levying tithes on German and Italian clergy in the hopes that, as one cardinal wrote, "it would be seen and perceived in these victories that the armies of the Apostolic Seat yet have their part."[54] Alongside these efforts, Gregory simultaneously dispatched a new group of nuncios to courts across Europe and founded the Congregatio de Propaganda Fide (Congregation for the Propagation of the Faith), with a special focus on German issues.[55] Gregory XV's successor, the Barberini pope Urban VIII (r. 1623–44), would take a markedly different path, focusing on the protection and expansion of the Papal States, viewing Habsburg encirclement as a threat, and aligning with the French. Under Pope Innocent X (r. 1644–55), relations with the Habsburgs improved, but the papacy failed to implement its agenda at the Peace of Westphalia (1648), disapproving of the terms of peace. Gregory died just two and a half years after his election, and Aldobrandini's command of papal troops proved short-lived. Nonetheless, the militant energy from Rome in the early 1620s was a reflection both of the powerful influence of White Mountain and of this distinctive Catholic Reformation papacy's drive to assert its presence on a distant battlefield.[56]

From 1621 to 1623, a series of letters Aldobrandini sent to the papal nephew reveal what happened when papal crusading ideals were put into action. During these years, Aldobrandini moved between Prague, Vienna, Brünn (Brno), Nikolsberg (Mikulov), several garrisons in Moravia, and Brussels, while he entertained further plans to fight in Hungary and Alsace. He was responsible for financing start-up costs for his troops, as well as recruiting, mustering, and garrisoning soldiers. Direction from the papacy was vague and sometimes confused, while communications were slow. The problems that plagued Aldobrandini, including competition with other generals and a lack of needed provisions, offer a realistic look at what the generation of White Mountain faced on the ground. Montecuccoli would encounter similar issues.

Aldobrandini's military experiences in Central Europe were connected to a proud family background of providing support for the imperial army. Aldobrandini's father, Gian Francesco, had held the position of papal general during the Long War (1593–1606) under the Aldobrandini pope, Clement VIII

(r. 1592–1605). At the time, the archduke of Inner Austria was the future Emperor Ferdinand II, and the 1600 fall of Kanisza had left his territory in the path of attack.[57] In response, Ferdinand personally led troops into battle, alongside Gian Francesco. Ferdinand suffered a disastrous defeat, and Gian Francesco fell ill and died, his body sent back to Rome for burial.[58]

The Ludovisi family nourished close ties to the Aldobrandini. Decades before he became Pope Gregory XV, Alessandro Ludovisi had built his career under the Aldobrandini pope, holding various administrative and judicial positions and traveling in Clement's entourage on at least two occasions.[59] At the start of the Thirty Years' War, Aldobrandini-Ludovisi ties were strongly reshaped by Pietro Aldobrandini's uncle, Cardinal Pietro Aldobrandini (1571–1621).[60] Cardinal Aldobrandini campaigned for Ludovisi's election as pope in 1621. After Cardinal Aldobrandini's February 1621 death—the same month that Gregory XV was elected—the Aldobrandini and Ludovisi political factions merged. Gregory promoted Aldobrandini's clients as his own, including two of Pietro Aldobrandini's brothers: Cardinal Ippolito Aldobrandini, who became *camerlengo*, and Giovanni Giorgio Aldobrandini, who married Gregory's niece, Ippolita Ludovisi.[61] The papal nephew, Cardinal Ludovico Ludovisi, directed Pietro Aldobrandini's prestigious appointment as lieutenant general of papal troops.

The Moravian magnate Cardinal Franz Dietrichstein (1570–1636) was an important though distant member of the Ludovisi-Aldobrandini nexus of power. Before his appointment as papal general, Pietro Aldobrandini had volunteered for war. He obtained his first command position through Dietrichstein, who brokered a cavalry company for him in 1619. Cardinal Aldobrandini thanked Dietrichstein for helping Pietro, effusing, "everything should be attributed to (you), who has been the primary motor of his fortune."[62] Like Gregory XV and Cardinal Ludovisi, Dietrichstein had studied at the Collegium Germanicum in Rome and become a client of Clement VIII's, who elevated him to the cardinalate in 1599. Dietrichstein's wealth and power grew exponentially during the early years of the Thirty Years' War. He directed a process similar to the Prague commission overseen by Karl Liechtenstein, which resulted in the 1621 Blood Court, at which the rebels lost ownership of their properties and twenty seven were executed.[63] Native families, particularly the Liechtenstein and Dietrichstein, were the greatest beneficiaries of the confiscations, expanding their possessions and consolidating power, although loyal newcomers were also rewarded.[64] Cardinal Aldobrandini sent numerous other recommendations to Dietrichstein, including for a Roman nobleman who had given up his right of primogeniture, Torquato Conti, to become an independent adventurer.[65]

Once he became a papal general, Aldobrandini was a cog in a larger wheel of patronage that moved men between the Italian peninsula and Central Europe. Roman newssheets reported on the comings and goings of adventurers "with good bands of captains and men practiced in war," including noblemen such as Cosimo and Virginio Orsini, Pier Francesco Colonna, Paolo Sforza, and Giorgio Caetani.[66] The illustrious names of their families and the fact that war demanded enormous expenses indicate that many adventurers were not motivated by economic need.[67] Some of these noblemen served Aldobrandini as officers, including the Roman Pietro Cesarini and the Florentine Antonio Miniati.[68] In his instructions to Aldobrandini, Ludovisi acknowledged the aristocratic desire for glory that underpinned so many of these careers. He specified that Aldobrandini's mission as papal general should not only serve the emperor's needs and represent the papacy but be undertaken for Aldobrandini's personal "military glory, which one hopes for greatly and expects from your valor."[69] Other Roman noblemen in imperial service during the 1620s and 1630s, including Conti and Federico Savelli, were so intent on crafting reputations as glorious warriors that they circulated print and manuscript accounts of their deeds.[70]

In 1621, Ferdinand II eagerly accepted Roman/papal support. Although he had pushed Frederick V out of Bohemia and witnessed the dissolution of the Protestant Union, he still faced a variety of foes. Frederick V's opportunistic allies, including the voivode of Transylvania, Gábor Bethlen, and the margrave of Jägerndorf, continued to skirmish with Habsburg-allied troops in Central and Eastern Europe. Prior to White Mountain, Bethlen had attacked Royal Hungary and seized the Hungarian crown. After Frederick's 1620 loss, Bethlen and the Habsburgs started peace talks, but they dissolved because Bethlen demanded the inclusion of his Bohemian allies. Throughout the talks, he and the margrave of Jägerndorf continued to fight against the Habsburgs, aided by Moravian rebels who refused to submit, such as Count Matthis von Thurn. These opponents soon contested Habsburg authority throughout eastern Moravia. The commander of allied Catholic forces, Charles Bonaventure de Longueval, Count of Bucquoy, led twenty thousand men, and Rambaldo Collalto commanded a further five thousand against Bethlen's seventeen thousand light horse and four thousand infantrymen in the summer of 1621.[71] The troops under Aldobrandini added an additional three thousand German soldiers. Spanish auxiliaries led by Caracciolo also patrolled the region. By the time Aldobrandini started organizing his soldiers, Bucquoy was dead and was not formally replaced by Geronimo Carafa for half a year, contributing to a vacuum of authority.[72]

Although he was considered friendly to Italian noblemen, Dietrichstein was also circumspect about the arrival of foreign troops in the territories he governed.

When Emperor Ferdinand II alerted Dietrichstein to Aldobrandini's appointment and anticipated arrival in Moravia, Dietrichstein responded that he would endeavor to accommodate Aldobrandini's troops, but that Moravia was already "completely ruined, burned, and plundered."[73] Multiple companies of Spanish-backed Neapolitan and Walloon troops also traversed Moravia, demanding scarce resources from inhabitants of the devastated region. Dietrichstein aimed to strike a careful balance, conciliating Spanish allies while attempting to protect the region from what must have seemed like an unending stream of rapacious soldiers, Catholic or otherwise.[74] He needed enough men to hold the land and force the population, from whom the army extracted resources, into compliance. At the same time, he resisted inviting too many troops into Moravia: if they depleted the region, Moravia would become impossible to defend because it would be incapable of hosting any army at all.[75] Rulers and military entrepreneurs puzzled over the developing contributions system for decades, only gradually systematizing the methods by which war paid for war and reducing troop numbers.[76]

Aldobrandini soon discovered how difficult it was to lead troops in these conditions, but he nonetheless worked diligently to recruit, organize, and muster his soldiers. He submitted to regular inspections by the papal nuncio in Vienna, Carlo Carafa, and worked with the paymaster, Matteo Pini.[77] Aldobrandini shouldered financial burdens from the outset. His instructions stated that Pini would not arrive in time and so, "in order to pay out the initial money, which there befalls, Your Most Illustrious Lordship will substitute some other way of provisioning."[78] Even after he received the promised funds from Ludovisi, those funds may not have been sufficient for attracting high-quality recruits and investing in the conspicuous consumption that helped maintain aristocratic reputation.[79] Other contingencies impacted finance and the movement of money, including interruptions to the courier service and fluctuations in exchange rates.[80] In his treatise, Cinuzzi acknowledged that "many things happen in war (indeed the greater part) which come to a good end by means of money, which could not be managed otherwise."[81] For many reasons, a nobleman simply could not command a body of troops without his own methods of obtaining money, and especially credit, which was the most efficient way to gather funds at short notice.[82]

In late August 1621, Aldobrandini claimed his cavalry regiment was nearly ready for muster—a prelude to putting troops into action.[83] The infantry, which had one thousand men, was "not yet complete," and he continued to wait for weapons. Nevertheless, he was optimistic, announcing, "soldiers arrive every day." Once he received the weapons, he planned to hold a general muster (figures 2.2 and 2.3).[84] In the same letter, however, Aldobrandini remarked

FIGURE 2.2. Jacques Callot, *Enrolment of Soldiers outside a Fortified City*. The Trustees of the British Museum. To the right, a scribe and paymaster sit at a table while a soldier to the left of the table is being recruited.

FIGURE 2.3. Jacques Callot, *Review of Troops*. The Trustees of the British Museum.

that Cardinal Dietrichstein and another minister suggested he garrison his troops in Moravia rather than launch a Hungarian campaign.[85] Aldobrandini discerned a Spanish political maneuver. He reported to Ludovisi that he had asserted papal desires to his Habsburg patrons: "The intention of Our Lord and of Your Most Illustrious Lordship is that your troops would be used on occasions where they could acquire honor and reputation and not stand around idly in garrisons." Dietrichstein warned Aldobrandini that his orders would be revoked. Aldobrandini bristled, begging Ludovisi to convey papal desires directly to Ferdinand II if the emperor followed through, warning that "for the greater reputation of the Apostolic Seat, do not permit your army to remain idle." Aldobrandini's disdain for garrisoning stemmed in part from its long association with idleness and misbehavior. Leave policies were abused, soldiers might integrate with the local population by marrying or taking on a second job, while paymasters and captains siphoned off official funds for personal use.[86]

Within days, Aldobrandini received a new set of orders to muster his troops "in order to refresh [the emperor's] camp in Hungary." Soldiers continued to stream in, and, once the weapons arrived, Aldobrandini surmised that "everything will be in order."[87] He moved busily between quarters, reporting on

18 September that Carafa had inspected his cavalry and was "most satisfied."[88] However, both Aldobrandini and Carafa feared winter's rapid approach and worried about lack of provisions. Carafa, who served as Aldobrandini's advocate at the imperial court, traveled to Vienna to gain Ferdinand II's permission to garrison Aldobrandini's troops, and Aldobrandini shifted his attention to border skirmishes.[89] He still hoped to find "the opportunity to toil in the acquisition of reputation for the Apostolic Seat and for myself." He added that he also desired to flee "the difficulties with other heads [*capi*], who presently command, since I, with my reputation, am not able to obey any of those who are now in the field."[90] The imperial army was a contentious, competitive body composed of a variety of haughty nobles from different countries holding semi-autonomous commands and no formally appointed commander-in-chief.

In his letters, Aldobrandini repeatedly referred to reputation—both his own and the Holy See's. At first, he hoped to build reputation by leading papal troops on a major campaign against a heretic army, but quickly discovered that he was more likely to damage his reputation if he took his troops into battle, given the conditions on the ground. Giorgio Basta had warned that war was a "slippery profession" and the career of a soldier "fragile" because "in one moment reputation acquired over the course of many years can be lost, punishment immediately following the errors of war, without allowing for any correction as other affairs allow."[91] Honor alone was not enough in military service: officers must also strive for usefulness (*utilità*), a Baconian goal shared by a whole class of emerging experts in the early seventeenth century.[92] Aldobrandini appears to have followed that reasoning, whether he had read Basta or not. He adjusted his goals, committing troops to escort travelers through Moravia, including the papal nuncio to Poland, Cosimo de Torres, and Archduke Carl, who was visiting the duke of Saxony in Silesia.[93] Aside from a few skirmishes, Aldobrandini never achieved the campaign he and his patrons, intoxicated by White Mountain propaganda, had hoped for. By November, Aldobrandini reported that the imperial troops were incapacitated as much by the "very harsh" weather as by disagreements among the captains.[94]

In the spring of 1622, Aldobrandini perceived that better opportunities lay elsewhere. A variety of poorly unified Habsburg opponents—the Protestant Paladins—had drawn the conflict into western and northern Germany, while the fight against Bethlen resumed in the east.[95] Ferdinand II requested that the money supporting papal troops, or in the very least the army, be redirected to Alsace under Archduke Leopold. Aldobrandini told Ludovisi that he wanted to go to Alsace at the head of papal troops in order to leave Moravia where, he stated, "there is nothing more than hard work and where foreigners are not viewed well." Ludovisi eventually approved, but Aldobrandini was immobilized for months as he awaited funds to pay troops in order to disband them. Soon enough, Aldobrandini learned that he was no longer needed in Alsace.[96] Gregory XV's attention turned to the Valtelline conflict, to which he committed papal troops under his brother, Orazio Ludovisi.[97]

As the head of papal forces, Aldobrandini struggled to grasp opportunities in a timely manner. The processes of receiving papal orders and payments and organizing troops for campaigning were slow and cumbersome. By the time he was ready to engage his troops in the field, military circumstances had changed. Aldobrandini decided to disband the remaining troops and begged for leave from papal service, "so that I can send myself where I want, proffering myself on every occasion as a most devoted vassal of His Holiness and servant of Your Most Illustrious Lordship."[98] He wanted to travel to Flanders, which had resumed its position as a military hotspot with the 1621 expiration of the Twelve Years' Truce. He had not received Ludovisi's approval by October but moved forward with his plans.[99] He eventually received affirmation from Ludovisi, and by the spring of 1623—the same year that 7,500 Spanish troops under Caracciolo marched from Central Europe to Flanders to rejoin Spanish war efforts—was in Brussels.[100] Pope Gregory XV died soon after.

Inspired by a desire to show valor and win glory after White Mountain, Aldobrandini struggled with the basic task of simply maintaining his reputation while leading an army in Central Europe. Due to the slow nature of communications and the inability of his distant patrons to provide serious oversight or reliable financial backing, he operated with some degree of autonomy, and yet clearly depended on both papal and imperial authority. In the end, Aldobrandini sought to escape the office of papal general. His experience was not necessarily a failure, as he continued his military career under the papacy up to his death in 1630, but he fell short of what other members of his generation achieved in Central Europe.

Victory and Devastation: The 1620s

For other members of the generation of White Mountain, the first decade of the Thirty Years' War provided a foundation for long-term careers in imperial service and familial wealth. Between 1621 and 1656, 281 out of the 417 newly minted Bohemian noble families were German, Spanish, Italian, and Belgian.[101] Major figures such as Wallenstein, perhaps the most powerful military entrepreneur of the decade, built positions of extraordinary authority despite relatively humble noble origins.[102] Wallenstein put together an entire army for Emperor Ferdinand II to counter Bethlen's continued threat as well as the entry of the Danish king, Christian IV, into the conflict (ostensibly as a protector of imperial law, but in reality to satisfy dynastic ambitions).[103] Wallenstein promoted Italians, some of whom became his close allies: Ernesto Montecuccoli, Collalto, Galasso, and Piccolomini. While some of these noblemen switched back and forth between Catholic armies—especially the imperial, Spanish, and Catholic League armies and the armies of Italian princes—they remained faithful to the Habsburgs (and certainly avoided serving Protestant rulers).

These figures contributed to making the 1620s the most victorious decade of the war for the Habsburgs. In 1623, Pope Gregory XV helped secure the transfer of Frederick V's electoral title to Emperor Ferdinand II's ally, the duke of Bavaria, shoring up the Catholic majority among the imperial electors.[104] Jean Tserclaes, count of Tilly, and Wallenstein crushed the second Protestant alliance under Christian IV of Denmark at the end of the decade. The war may have ended with the 1629 Peace of Lübeck; however, the Habsburgs adopted a heavy-handed approach when they issued the Edict of Restitution, which proscribed Calvinism and declared any post-1552 secularization of church lands in the empire illegal, outraging their opponents and fueling further resistance. Gustavus Adolphus of Sweden saw his opportunity and invaded the empire in 1630, ostensibly on behalf of German Protestants.[105] Around this time, conflict in northern Italy erupted into the War of the Mantuan Succession (1628–31), part of a broader dynastic competition between the French Bourbons and the Spanish and Austrian Habsburgs for control of northern Italy. White Mountain may have inspired a generation of international Catholic warriors to serve in the imperial army, but it had not led to the final vanquishing of Habsburg enemies. What had started as a local dispute between the Bohemian estates and Emperor Ferdinand II morphed into a complex web of wars involving most of the ruling dynasties of Europe, as well as numerous smaller-scale princes and noble families.

Emperor Ferdinand II developed strategies to reward his allies and integrate a diverse nobility at court in Vienna. Besides the creation of titles like prince or count of the empire and the admission to military orders like the Golden Fleece, a variety of honorary, unpaid offices were distributed much more freely in Vienna than at other courts. These offices never became hereditary like they did in France. The reassignment of offices with every new ruler generated continuous competition among native and nonnative nobles.[106] Rewards thus played a key role in the emergence of a loyal aristocracy by the end of the century.[107] At the same time, Catholic devotion became a basic ingredient of success.[108] The papal nuncio, Carlo Carafa, effused that even though "few at his court . . . had been born Catholic," Ferdinand II's displays of piety (part of the myth of the *Pietas Austriaca*) inspired nobles "to abandon heresy."[109] Italians and their families had an advantage, because they had never been tainted by heresy in the first place.

Their Catholicism was unquestioned by the Habsburgs, a testament to the success of the Catholic Reformation within the Italian peninsula. As a result, their loyalty appears to have been taken for granted.

Courtly titles, honors, and offices were important, but the military entrepreneurs who succeeded in the 1620s especially benefited from Wallenstein's management of the army and increased access to credit. Captains and colonels initially advanced money to support their companies and regiments, with colonels borrowing large sums based on movable wealth (for example, silver and jewelry), property mortgages, and the anticipation of plunder and/or contributions (war taxes).[110] Salaries, which derived from contributions, ballooned from 1625 to 1635, only to decline later. In 1630, the imperial ordinance stated that a cavalry colonel received six hundred florins per month plus forage for seventeen horses, and an infantry colonel five hundred florins per month plus forage for twelve horses. In 1625, Wallenstein earned an impressive six thousand florins a month as *generalissimo*. The average foot soldier, meanwhile, took in eight florins a month, if he received anything at all. Military entrepreneurs, like court officials, collected multiple salaries for multiple roles: a general would receive a general's salary, as well as that of a colonel and captain, since he continued to fulfill those functions. If a colonel owned multiple regiments, he collected multiple colonel salaries.[111] In general, Wallenstein concentrated risk and reward in the hands of fewer, theoretically more capable and creditworthy individuals who could own multiple regiments.[112] The stakes were higher than before.

The reliance on credit during the Thirty Years' War provided for some social mobility. Even lesser nobles had a chance of financing their own regiments when an income of just five thousand florins a year from family estates was enough to receive a loan to raise a regiment. Ernst von Mansfeld started his own military career with a one-time inheritance of ten thousand florins.[113] Another change saw major merchant bankers invest in military enterprises. Hans de Witte backed Wallenstein, who had become more creditworthy than Emperor Ferdinand II. This fact resulted in enormous power, and Wallenstein took unprecedented authority over the army. By 1627, he had started authorizing new recruitment and selecting colonels without serious oversight from emperor or court. Wallenstein pursued his own strategic objectives, including obscure peace negotiations that led some to suspect treachery.[114]

The ability of colonels and generals to raise large amounts of cash at short notice depended on creditors' confidence that military entrepreneurs would repay them. The entire system rested on extortion. Wallenstein controversially altered the way contributions worked. During the 1620s, army officials started to set contributions according to army regulations without the consent of the estates. The implementation of this practice in friendly territories quickly pushed this new system to a breaking point as powerful landowning nobles and imperial rulers resisted.[115] In 1625, a quartering ordinance declared that a single regiment in Wallenstein's army must be maintained by the local populace at a rate of six thousand florins a week.[116]

Local populations bore the burdens of war finance. Prior to the Thirty Years' War, they were forced to pay a regular war tax agreed to by the estates, while they periodically dealt with marauding warriors who threatened to destroy a town or village unless a ransom was paid. The latter certainly continued during the Thirty Years' War, along with expensive "gifts" in the form of monetary compensation or goods paid to military entrepreneurs.[117] Peasants suffered the most, as we are reminded by Grimmelshausen's apt description of the military hierarchy as a tree (discussed in chapter 1), with high-ranking nobles at the very top and peasants at the bottom. In this vision of how the army worked, Grimmelshausen placed common soldiers at the tree's lowest branches, while peasants and other commoners composed the tree's roots, where they "passed their days in misery and lamentation."[118]

Some of Wallenstein's most powerful enemies were the ruling dynasties of the Holy Roman Empire whose lands and subjects suffered under Wallenstein's contributions system, including Maximilian I, the elector of Bavaria. These enemies forced Ferdinand II to remove Wallenstein from command in 1630. When Emperor Ferdinand II reinstated Wallenstein in 1631 in an emergency effort to counter the Swedish invasion, the contributions system had been revised to require imperial troops be supported on Habsburg hereditary rather than German imperial lands. When Wallenstein had lost his position in 1630—and his ability to exact contributions—de Witte knew he had made a ruinous investment and committed suicide. When de Witte initially got involved with Wallenstein, he must have incorrectly assumed that the war would end quickly in the Habsburgs' favor. De Witte's method of attaining profit was unsustainable for a longer period because the wealth required to pay back loans—goods and money—dried up as armies depleted regions.[119] The need to ravage friendly and enemy territories alike showed the obvious limitations. These activities were part of a larger frenzy of desperate and opportunistic behaviors that characterized the 1620s, including schemes to mint and debase coin to fund warfare or buy confiscated properties from 1619 to 1623, leading to hyperinflation and a breakdown in the money economy in some areas.[120]

Piccolomini built his career in these conditions. He was an ambitious warrior whose dizzying movements between Central Europe, Flanders, and northern Italy—alternating between Spanish and imperial service—reveal the choices an Italian nobleman might pursue in the 1620s. He had become close to Wallenstein by 1628, serving as the head of the *generalissimo*'s personal guard, before fighting in the War of the Mantuan Succession.[121] This conflict, triggered in 1627 when Duke Vincenzo II of Mantua died without direct heirs and a French-born relative, Duke Charles of Nevers, took the helm of government, was another turning point. When conflict broke out, Ferdinand II protected his authority in the region by committing imperial forces.[122] Piccolomini, as well as Galasso and Colloredo, served under Collalto.[123] Although, as Holy Roman emperor, Ferdinand II could have recognized Nevers's claim and resolved the Mantuan succession peacefully, one of the reasons negotiations failed was that Ferdinand had felt pressure to obtain compensation from Nevers for the Gonzaga military families allied to him. Collalto himself was a distant Gonzaga relative.[124]

During the war, military entrepreneurs, including those Gonzaga relatives who may have felt robbed of family property, ransacked the fabulous Gonzaga collections during the infamous Sack of Mantua. Total plunder extracted from the city was rumored to be worth an astounding eighteen million ducats ("twice the annual revenue of the kingdom of Naples"), and ten thousand inhabitants died.[125] The generals had first pick of the spoils. Collalto and Wallenstein (who remained in Central Europe) apparently even discussed invading the Venetian terra firma to capture lands for themselves, although the plan never came to fruition.[126] At the end of the war, Piccolomini represented Emperor Ferdinand II at the 1631 Peace of Cherasco, and his correspondence expanded, taking on the contours of a "private intelligence service."[127]

As he ascended within the imperial army, some contemporaries viewed Piccolomini with skepticism. When Collalto collected contributions for the imperial army, he sent Piccolomini to the Tuscan court to request assistance. When Piccolomini approached his "natural lord," the grand duke of Tuscany, for help in 1629, the Medici took offense.[128] The grand-ducal secretary claimed that they were prepared to welcome Piccolomini as a devoted servant and vassal, but recoiled when they realized he was actually petitioning them on behalf of another ruler.[129] However, rather than view Piccolomini as an opportunist who was disloyal to the Medici for personal gain, it is important to recognize that his maneuvers were part of a larger political environment characterized by ambiguity.[130] Piccolomini was a legitimate servant of the emperor's, and there were authentic legal grounds for Tuscany's contributions to the imperial war effort, as well as a history of Tuscan support for the imperial cause. Piccolomini has a poor historical reputation due to his role in the 1634 assassination of Wallenstein (addressed in chapter 3) and the literary image Friedrich Schiller created of him as a "traitor" and a "snake" in the 1799 trilogy *Wallensteins Ende*.[131] Rather than view Piccolomini as uniquely disloyal or depraved, however, we should evaluate his behavior alongside other challenging relationships of the period, including the rebellions of Protestant estates against Habsburg authority.

While he may not have been consistently loyal to the grand duke of Tuscany, Piccolomini displayed loyalty to the Habsburg family and the imperial Catholic rule they represented. To some degree, this loyalty emerged from the economic logic of military entrepreneurship. In order to recoup investments, military entrepreneurs relied on the Habsburg ruler to authorize contributions and the redistribution of tax revenues. For this reason, they did not operate fully autonomously, especially in the latter decades of the Thirty Years' War when contributions became more regulated.[132] The emperor also had the authority to deprive colonels of their regiments in order to reform them: a frequent practice in which troops were disbanded and/or merged with others. Even powerful and well-connected senior officers like Piccolomini endured this treatment.[133] David Parrott has argued that the army was, in fact, "an embedded instrument of imperial policy."[134] However, this instrument of imperial policy also served the interests of a network of Catholic aristocratic dynasties. Piccolomini's commitment to the Habsburg dynasty and the imperial rule they represented grew out of an understanding of the rewards his family accrued.

Many Italian noblemen in imperial service took their own initiative in joining the imperial army and used their own resources, as well as heavy-handed coercive strategies, to finance regiments. They were inspired by moments like White Mountain and long-established family patterns of service to the Habsburgs. They benefited from unrestrained, rapacious behaviors, though it would be overly simplistic to write them off as one-dimensional, evil characters sowing chaos in the decades prior to the emergence of standing armies and rational state institutions. The family business of war had its own logic. It permitted aristocratic dynasties to compete for resources on a larger geographic scale than before. At the heads of regiments, military entrepreneurs became arbiters of wealth, credit, military offices, information, and prestige within a larger web of interconnected families seeking to extend power at a time of political crisis. They were also military experts capable of adjusting their goals and strategies in response to daunting military realities.

Historians have largely overlooked the existence of a transregional military community intertwined with the confessional and cultural networks of the Italian peninsula and Central Europe. In part, this oversight stems from a neglect of the political relationship between the Italian peninsula and Habsburg Central Europe. It also reflects the fact that most works on political and military patronage networks have focused on relationships between patrons and clients within individual countries that contributed the informal power necessary to the consolidation of centralized states. Patronage networks spanning regions permeated the imperial army. Meaningful confessional, dynastic, and feudal loyalties harbored by Italian elites toward the Habsburgs, honors bestowed by the court in Vienna, and the benefits derived from the contributions system drew Italian military entrepreneurs to imperial service during the Thirty Years' War. Even their most dubious behaviors were still rather typical for early modern people. In fact, the consistent loyalty Italian noblemen developed toward the Habsburg dynasty is far more noteworthy than their moments of disloyalty to other rulers.

While Piccolomini and Collalto led imperial troops in the War of the Mantuan Succession, Montecuccoli was just starting his own career north of the Alps. Although he did not fight at White Mountain, he became a beneficiary of the relationships, knowledge, and values forged by the generation of White Mountain. His ascent to high command, however, occurred in much-changed circumstances. As the fighting continued into the 1630s, punctuated by Gustavus Adolphus of Sweden's invasion of the Holy Roman Empire and defeat of the Habsburgs at the Battle of Breitenfeld (1631) and then France's open entry into the war against the Habsburgs in 1635, fantasies of decisive victory disintegrated. Military entrepreneurs were not blind to these developments. Operating on the front lines with extraordinary responsibilities, some of them started to think differently about war and how to operate more effectively.

CHAPTER 3

The Making of an Early Modern
Military Entrepreneur

When Montecuccoli joined imperial forces in the late 1620s, he followed in the footsteps of numerous relatives, including his father, Galeotto, as well as other Italian noblemen with similar family histories. Ernesto Montecuccoli, his older male relative who was an imperial general under Wallenstein, helped Raimondo gain a string of early positions. The family business of war encompassed relatives who never went to war, but who provided political connections and helped manage family assets, some of which financed military needs. This group included Montecuccoli's mother, Anna Bigi, and two relatives, Marquis Francesco Montecuccoli and Marquis Massimiliano Montecuccoli. In 1644, Montecuccoli inherited Italian and Austrian properties from the widow of his "uncle" Girolamo Montecuccoli (Ernesto's brother), a nobleman who had established a career at the imperial court.

Montecuccoli's experiences show that the careers of military entrepreneurs were not simply the personal choices of opportunistic individuals; they were fundamentally pieces of aristocratic family strategies for gaining and maintaining power in a European landscape of interconnected conflicts. In a letter to Emperor Ferdinand III, he proudly recited the sacrifices his family had made in imperial service: "I don't speak of the Count Giovan Galeotto Montecuccoli, my father, who in his youth served and commanded three companies in the Hungarian wars, neither of Count Ernesto, my uncle, who died of three wounds as a prisoner of the Swedish in Colmar, nor of Count Girolamo his brother, who

FIGURE 3.1.   Raimondo Montecuccoli in 1646 by E. Wideman. The Trustees of the British Museum.

also died in imperial service, nor of my cousin killed, nor of my brother rendered lame in the Battle of Wittstock." Montecuccoli saw his imperial career as
the natural outgrowth of a rich family tradition of fighting—and dying—for
Habsburg causes. He claimed that the "fervor of devotion and faithfulness" he
harbored for imperial service had been "absorbed with my milk."[1] He called
upon the emperor to recognize and reward these sacrifices. At the same time,
Montecuccoli continued to serve his "natural lord," Francesco I d'Este, duke of
Modena, using the duke's influence and connections as a springboard for greater

Montecuccoli ambitions. In pursuit of their own dynastic advancement, families like the Montecuccoli sought multiple alliances.[2]

By the end of the Thirty Years' War, Montecuccoli had inherited the Austrian estate of Hohenegg, become cavalry general, earned court offices, and received some financial reimbursements. Despite this progress, ongoing challenges he faced point to the realities of life as a foreign military entrepreneur. He fell into debt, failed to earn some desired promotions, and endured hardships on campaign. Why would a foreign military entrepreneur continue to risk his life, wealth, and reputation if he was not profiting from his position? This chapter argues that, as a member of a Catholic dynasty that derived legitimacy from the fact that they were imperial vassals, Montecuccoli had religious and political reasons to conceive of his service to the Habsburgs as an act of obedience. Montecuccoli's obedience to the Habsburgs and to Catholicism provided access to a robust weave of patronage relationships extending between the Italian peninsula, Central Europe, Spain, and the Low Countries. Obedience created certain boundaries, but the opportunities available within those boundaries were rich with the promise of rewards.

During these years, Montecuccoli also contended with military theory and its relationship to experience. His generation faced problems similar to those encountered by the generation of White Mountain; however, by the 1630s and 1640s, it had become clear there was no decisive victory in sight. The acquisitive behaviors of the 1620s, in which credit financed large armies and military entrepreneurs repaid debt and sought profit through brutal methods of extortion, proved unsustainable. While contributions continued, they were more regulated. At the same time, men, horses, weapons, and foodstuffs were scarcer than ever. Montecuccoli spent most of his time and energy searching for resources to supply his regiments and traveling back and forth across large distances in response to rapidly shifting, confusing orders. In the process, he became a self-styled military expert and army reformer. While his ideas stemmed in part from book learning, they were very much a product of his experiences.

These experiences intersected with those of other Italian noblemen in Austrian Habsburg service, including the noblemen who betrayed Wallenstein in 1634 by infamously organizing their benefactor's assassination: Galasso and Piccolomini, among others. These were topsy-turvy years in which loyalties and fortunes shifted dramatically and foreigners were often viewed with mistrust. By the end of this period, Montecuccoli was torn between patrons when Francesco I d'Este went to war against Habsburg Spain in 1649. Montecuccoli remained in imperial service, rejecting Francesco's offers to join a campaign against Spain that would have made enemies of his Habsburg patrons. Despite his multiple allegiances and participation in a military environment characterized by bewildering orders, lack of provisions, poorly disciplined soldiers, and a complex interplay of dynastic interests, he remained committed to the Austrian Habsburgs.

Entering the Fray

The beginning of Montecuccoli's advancement in the imperial army coincided with one of the most notorious murders of the century. On 25 February 1634, the commander-in-chief of the imperial army, Wallenstein, was run through with a pike and killed by his own soldiers in the Bohemian border town of Eger (Cheb). The murder was organized by Wallenstein's trusted subordinates Galasso, Colloredo, Johann Aldringen, and Piccolomini and carried out by Irish and Scottish assassins, including Walter Leslie. Emperor Ferdinand II, who had become convinced that Wallenstein was secretly negotiating with the enemy, had given the conspirators the green light to arrest or kill the powerful generalissimo.[3] The assassination of Wallenstein was a coup that allowed Italian noblemen to ascend to the very top of a foreign military hierarchy. Galasso became acting commander-in-chief, followed by Piccolomini in 1648. The estates of Wallenstein and the close associates who remained loyal to him and died with him at Eger—Adam Trčka, Vilém Kinský, Christian Ilow, and Henry Neumann—were confiscated and redistributed among officers to ensure their loyalty and settle debts. This transfer of wealth amounted to over thirteen million florins. Piccolomini, Galasso, and Colloredo all received estates.[4]

Montecuccoli witnessed how the mood in the army and at court in Vienna turned against the conspirators immediately after Wallenstein's death. When Galasso stood to gain command over the army, German nobles protested. Mattias de' Medici's secretary wrote that the "German nation does not want to obey foreign captains" and that "in effect all Germans are united" in supporting an alternate candidate.[5] These German nobles felt that "Italians have too much command in this army" and that their "particular interests" threatened the emperor's service.[6] These statements indicate that German nobles perceived a faction within the imperial army working together for mutual advancement. They voiced serious concerns about Italian domination of senior positions in the army.[7] With top command positions, Piccolomini, Galasso, and Colloredo gained greater control of patronage opportunities, including the power to decide how to allocate regiments. Montecuccoli grew close to Piccolomini, and served directly under Galasso in the 1640s. Eager new Catholic recruits further elaborated this network and included the brothers of the reigning grand duke of Tuscany, Mattias and Francesco de' Medici, who received their own regiments from Piccolomini.[8] Gustavus Adolphus's shocking 1631 victory over the Habsburgs at the Battle of Breitenfeld had inspired a fresh wave of Italian noble volunteers to join the imperial army.[9] There was even discussion of forming an Italian league in alliance with the Habsburgs to fight enemies of the faith, although this never came to fruition.[10]

While some native nobles complained about Italian noblemen in the imperial army, others, including Wallenstein (who was reappointed by Ferdinand II in 1631), formed alliances with them. In 1651, Piccolomini married the daughter of Duke Julius Heinrich of Sachsen-Lauenburg, tying his fortune to a powerful German military family that had been active in the war since the Bohemian rebellion.[11] Italian military families were connected by marriage to an international cast of military elites. Another striking example is the Biglia family, who produced several imperial generals. In 1606, Maria Maddalena Biglia married Charles Bonaventure de Longueval, count of Bucquoy, who led imperial forces at the Battle of White Mountain. The Biglia were descendants of the Visconti and so created a genealogical link between the great fifteenth-century *condottieri* and seventeenth-century Habsburg military entrepreneurs.[12] Finally, the two conspirators against Wallenstein, Aldringen and Galasso, had been brothers-in-law since both married daughters of the Count d'Arco in 1630. These marriage ties mimicked the transregional marriage alliances of ruling families. Mattias and Francesco de' Medici, the sons of Grand Duke Cosimo II and Emperor Ferdinand II's sister Maria Maddalena of Austria, were the product of one such alliance.[13]

Montecuccoli would also marry into the native Central European nobility, but at the start of his career, Italian aristocratic ties were especially crucial. His two pillars of support were his own kin—especially his mother and older relatives—and his "natural" lords, the Este of Modena. Montecuccoli was not a particularly wealthy noble, but he hailed from a family of counts and marquises, some of whom controlled considerable assets in the Frignano region of the Duchy of Modena (Map 3.1). Montecuccoli became head of a branch of counts when his older brother, Fabrizio, died as a child.[14] At root, Montecuccoli's success was founded upon the capable administration of the family property by his mother, Anna Bigi, while he was still a minor, and the connections she pursued to the Este.[15] After Montecuccoli's father, Galeotto, died, Bigi relocated the family to Modena, where she appealed to the Este family for help. Cardinal Alessandro agreed to oversee the educations of both Raimondo and his brother Massimiliano, who later became a Jesuit. Montecuccoli also received holy orders and accompanied Cardinal Alessandro to Rome to attend the papal conclave that elected Urban VIII, but later obtained a dispensation

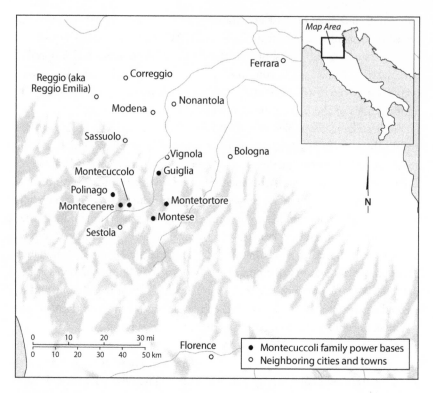

Reggio (aka Reggio Emilia) ○

○ Correggio

Modena ○

○ Nonantola

Sassuolo ○

Ferrara ○

Map Area

○ Vignola

● Guiglia

○ Bologna

Montecuccolo

Polinago ●

Montecenere ● ●

● Montetortore

N

● Montese

Sestola ○

0   10   20   30 mi

0   10   20   30   40   50 km

Florence ○

● Montecuccoli family power bases
○ Neighboring cities and towns

MAP 3.1. Montecuccoli family power bases in the Frignano region of the Modenese Apennine Mountains. Cartography by Bill Nelson.

that allowed him to exchange the tonsure for the sword. Bigi, who hailed from a Ferrarese family and left property in Ferrara to her son that he collected rent on, was a smart Italian widow dedicated to her sons' success. She expanded their Modenese patrimony, obtaining permission from Duke Cesare d'Este to follow through with her deceased husband's plan to buy back a large vegetable garden of ninety-three hectares in Modena.[16] Montecuccoli relied on his mother to send funds from home as needed to support his imperial career before her 1638 death.[17] Upon her passing, Raimondo and his brother Galeotto received equal parts of the inheritance.[18]

Montecuccoli's most important early patron in the imperial army was his relative Ernesto (of the Montese branch), who must have facilitated Montecuccoli's initial entry into the imperial army with the support of the then duke of Modena, Cesare d'Este. Collalto, who visited the Este court in 1625, took Raimondo back to the imperial army with him for his first taste of war. After a brief return to Modena, Montecuccoli formally joined the imperial army in 1627, serving in a regiment in the Low Countries under the general command of Ernesto. In 1628, he was an ensign in Johann Wangler's regiment and over the course of the next year became a captain of his own company. In 1629, he was the first imperial soldier to penetrate the town walls at the Siege of Amersfoort. Montecuccoli then traveled to Central Europe and joined Tilly's imperial forces facing off against the Swedes. He witnessed the 1631 Sack of Magdeburg, one of the most brutal events of the war, which resulted in the alleged deaths of twenty thousand inhabitants and the complete destruction of the city by fire. Several months later, Montecuccoli was captured by the Swedes at Breitenfeld and imprisoned for six months.[19] The reaction to Montecuccoli's imprisonment reveals who his protectors were. Francesco Montecuccoli, who held plenary powers over Raimondo's estate, worked with Girolamo Montecuccoli and the Modenese ambassador in Vienna, Ottavio Bolognesi, to arrange the terms of Raimondo's release and transmit funds—valued at one thousand thalers—for Montecuccoli to pay his own ransom.[20]

Cooperation between members of the Montecuccoli family had not always been a given. Montecuccolo Castle, as well as surrounding properties, had been subject to violent dispute a mere generation before Montecuccoli's lifetime. The clan had pieced together a large, coherent domain in the Frignano under Montecuccoli's ancestor, Cesare, but it had been broken apart after Cesare's 1506 death. The family divided into numerous lines, generating dissension.[21] Montecuccoli's father had fought his own uncles for the inheritance of Montecuccolo Castle until Duke Cesare d'Este took possession of the property and resolved the conflict in Galeotto's favor. In 1618, the rival Montecuccoli lords of Renno murdered Galeotto in a dispute concerning the governorship of the fortress of Brescello, leaving ten-year-old Raimondo fatherless.[22] At the time of Galeotto's death, there were eight other major family lines, including the one headed by Ernesto and Girolamo Montecuccoli, sons of the sixteenth-century diplomat Alfonso Montecuccoli.

The splintering of Montecuccoli family property and infighting were typical of many rural noble families in the Italian peninsula. A similar process contributed to a phenomenon Norbert Elias referred to as the "domestication of the nobility" in France, when members of an impoverished warrior elite turned increasingly to the courts for status and position, growing dependent on princely patronage.[23] Along these lines, Claudio Donati argued that in the Italian peninsula a "third sort of nobility"—neither urban patricians nor feudal nobles—emerged as key figures in the state-building process. Rather than oppose their local ruler, they gravitated toward his court, where their existence was punctuated by military excursions that allowed them to demonstrate virtù.[24] Military service to a prince helped many nobles consolidate family fortunes and provided these nobles with a sense of personal honor and family identity.[25]

The Montecuccoli complicate our understanding of noble military families in the age of state building by showing that families hedged their bets: not only did members pursue the patronage of local rulers, but they served other rulers, eluding the grasp of centralizing governments to some degree. War was the field that provided the most opportunities for serving foreign rulers, especially if rulers had trouble recruiting their own rebellious or otherwise resistant native nobles into the army (as Emperors Ferdinand II and III did). War was also, at root, a family business. A haughty, unruly family that may have spent the sixteenth and early seventeenth centuries feuding over a limited number of properties in the Frignano collaborated in the effort to expand dynastic holdings well beyond the Frignano.

Besides family, Montecuccoli's most ardent supporters in the first three decades of his career in imperial service were Francesco I d'Este, and the Modenese resident ambassador in Vienna, Bolognesi. Francesco, who became duke after his older brother abdicated in 1629, was the same age as Montecuccoli. He was ambitious, hoping to restore lost Este properties (especially Ferrara, forfeited to Pope Clement VIII in 1597), fully incorporate new territories (such as Correggio, awarded in 1635), and increase his status within the contentious hierarchy of princes in the Italian peninsula.[26] Although it seems strange to modern eyes that a ruler would approve of his subject fighting in a foreign army, Francesco obtained several advantages from Montecuccoli's service to Emperors Ferdinand II and III. First, most opportunities for gaining experience and knowledge of war lay beyond the Alps since the Italian peninsula was mostly pacified by the seventeenth century. As Montecuccoli claimed in 1635, "nowadays, the true military discipline blooms in Central Europe."[27] He assured Francesco that he would ultimately place the expertise he gained through serving the Habsburgs at Francesco's disposal.[28] Second, Francesco hoped to gain access to an international circulation of soldiers, horses, and weapons through Montecuccoli. If war broke out in the Italian peninsula, he expected his vassals in foreign armies to return to defend their homeland—and to bring German soldiers with them. Finally, as Montecuccoli gained the trust of his Habsburg patrons, Francesco used him in an informal diplomatic capacity alongside—and sometimes as a replacement for—Bolognesi. In 1636, Montecuccoli told Francesco, "there is no other interest in the world more primary to me than Your Most Serene Highness's service. As long as it is humanly possible, neither the length of the voyage nor the danger of the passage will ever keep me from it."[29] Montecuccoli served more than one ruler but declared supreme loyalty to Francesco I d'Este.

Francesco I d'Este's instructions were carried out in Vienna by Bolognesi, who became an ally of Montecuccoli's. If Montecuccoli was a military entrepreneur,

Bolognesi was a diplomatic entrepreneur who used his position in Vienna to represent multiple Italian families, the Este foremost. Born into an ancient family from Correggio, he started his career serving Siro da Correggio, for whom he won the title "prince of the empire" in 1616. Later, Siro was accused of debasing imperial coins and was unable to pay the exorbitant fine exacted by the Imperial Chamber. When Collalto's imperial troops entered northern Italy during the War of the Mantuan Succession, they confiscated Correggio. Bolognesi continued to represent Siro in Vienna, while coordinating with Francesco I d'Este, who eventually obtained Correggio. Bolognesi was a clever maneuverer: he deceived Siro by helping Francesco, but he simultaneously served Siro's needs by protecting Siro's territories from other possible interlopers. Even after he became Francesco's resident ambassador, he accepted diplomatic commissions from other northern Italian lords, including the Pico of Mirandola, Duke Vittorio Amedeo I of Savoy, the Republic of Genoa, the duke of Parma, and the princes of Novellara and Sabbioneta.[30]

The experiences of Bolognesi, Francesco I d'Este, and Montecuccoli grew out of the ambiguous, fractured political landscape of north-central Italy, with its numerous small lordships and history of feudal ties to the Holy Roman emperor. While the Montecuccoli had mostly accepted Este rule by the seventeenth century, family legitimacy originally stemmed from Emperor Otto IV, who enfeoffed the Montecuccoli in 1212, and Emperor Charles IV, who confirmed their rule in 1369 and allowed them to use the imperial eagle on their coat of arms. The Montecuccoli had cultivated relationships to Modena since 1173, when the *condottiere* Gherardo da Montecuccolo formed an alliance with the town—over a century before the Este gained lordship over Modena (which did not occur until 1288 under Obizzo II d'Este).[31] Guidanello da Montecuccolo (b. 1247), who headed the pro-imperial Ghibelline faction in the Frignano, violently resisted Este encroachments on Montecuccolo in the early thirteenth century, briefly turning to the commune of Bologna for assistance. The Montecuccoli operated as an independent rural power, engaged in violent struggles with local rivals such as the Guelf-allied Rastaldi family.[32] In the seventeenth century, they continued a family tradition of forming alliances beyond Modena not only to the imperial center, but also to other Italian courts and families. Some of their Modenese rivals, including members of the powerful Rangoni family, served France and Savoy.

Montecuccoli's friendship with Mattias de' Medici, who joined the imperial army as a regimental colonel in 1632 and later became general of auxiliary forces before returning to Tuscany, reflects a pattern of forming transregional aristocratic bonds. The Medici had long been patrons to the Montecuccoli. As noted in chapter 2, Montecuccoli's father, Galeotto, had commanded Tuscan troops in Hungary, while Grand Duke Cosimo II de' Medici served as Montecuccoli's older brother's godfather.[33] Montecuccoli's relative Girolamo had started his own court career as a page at the Medici court and later served Anna de' Medici when she was archduchess of the Tyrol. Girolamo's father, Alfonso, was the celebrated Tuscan diplomat who also served the grand duke as an on-call military specialist (*lancie spezzati*) alongside Piccolomini's father, Silvio. There were numerous other connections to Tuscans, including to the Piccolomini, with whom the Montecuccoli shared kin in the Bolognese Caprara family.[34] Montecuccolo was a mountain stronghold, but was not a peripheral place. The family had long exploited the possibilities of a home base located between Modena, Florence, Bologna, and Ferrara.

In this light, we can conceive of military entrepreneurs like Montecuccoli as agents of aristocratic dynasties who sought to increase wealth, credit, and political power for their families via emerging transregional opportunities. Gaining the command of a regiment in a war zone was critical to these efforts. Regimental command represented the kind of autonomy that accorded with an aristocratic family's sense of position and pride and offered rewards that were, on the one hand, material (plunder, contributions, and perhaps even confiscated properties), and, on the other hand, political (court offices and honors as a substitute for monetary reimbursement). Grand Duke Ferdinando II de' Medici expressed reservations about the expense of regiments, but Mattias and Francesco adamantly insisted that regimental command provided "reputation and utility and every advancement and that we can so much more ensure our ability to follow the profession of war."[35]

While the scions of a major ruling family expected regimental command from the outset, minor noblemen like Montecuccoli might struggle to gain ownership of the coveted regiments, even if they had start-up funds available. The fact that his uncle Ernesto held high imperial command was a windfall for Raimondo, but it was only with further powerful connections and a reputation built upon experience that he would reap the full benefits of his family position. When Montecuccoli returned to the army after his first imprisonment, Ernesto appointed him major of his infantry regiment. Soon after, he became lieutenant-colonel of Augustus von Vitzthum's regiment of cuirassiers, serving in Bavaria.[36] Despite the fact that regiments were considered property, Montecuccoli failed to inherit Ernesto's regiment after Ernesto's 1633 death. Montecuccoli continued serving in Vitzthum's regiment during a disorganized campaign intended to counter the forces of Swedish field marshal Gustav Horn. A dispute between Montecuccoli and Vitzthum nearly resulted in a duel, but Galasso ordered Vitzthum to desist.[37] After taking control of the garrison at Lindau and arresting its commander,

Franz Peter König von Mohr, Montecuccoli was placed in temporary command of the regiment, while Vitzthum took over the garrison. Montecuccoli struggled to find safe quarters for his troops, starting in Kempten then traveling to the mountains near Füssen and continuing to Passau until they finally found rest in Gmünd (after Montecuccoli made a personal trip from Passau to Vienna to appeal to Aldringen for help). All told, he must have traveled about 1,000 kilometers in the attempt to quarter troops, while the regiment traveled 511. They rested for just three weeks before marching to Regensburg (Map 3.2).[38]

Wallenstein's assassination took place during this time and was related to the problem of quartering troops. The year 1633 was difficult for the imperial army. Fighting had stalled, while political confusion and military disorganization created profound uncertainty. High-ranking officers, including Piccolomini, Galasso, and the Medici brothers, had started to blame Wallenstein for the problems the imperial army faced, including lack of appropriate winter quarters. Without a viable solution, the livelihoods of generals and subcontracting colonels were at stake. This is not the place to review the controversial and murky details of the assassination, although it is important to note that most historians do not believe that Wallenstein had malicious intentions against the empire. At root, the conspirators seem to have turned against Wallenstein because they viewed Wallenstein as an impediment to their continued advancement. In a December 1633 letter to Grand Duke Ferdinando II,

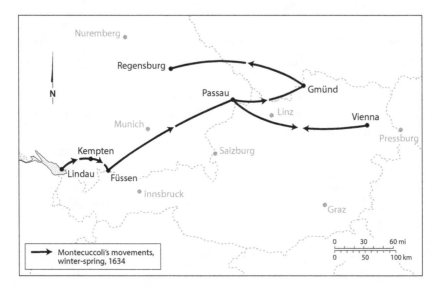

MAP 3.2.   Montecuccoli's travels in search of quarters for his troops, winter-spring 1634. Cartography by Bill Nelson.

Mattias de' Medici complained about Wallenstein, writing, "we believe that as long as this man commands the army, we cannot hope for advancement." He concluded that "all this that I write to Your Most Serene Highness is bearable for a short time, but to continue for a long time would destroy our reputation."[39] As criticism of Wallenstein reached a crescendo in both army and court in January 1634, Piccolomini informed Vienna that Wallenstein had communicated treacherous plans to him in private, and the court issued a patent to remove and arrest or kill Wallenstein.[40] Piccolomini, Galasso, Colloredo, and Aldringen chose assassination.

Approximately seven months after Wallenstein's assassination, the army under Galasso defeated the combined Swedish-German forces of the Heilbronn League at Nördlingen. At this momentous battle, the enemy forces lost around eight thousand men, and Horn was taken prisoner. This Swedish-German defeat forced the withdrawal of Swedish troops into northern Germany and laid the groundwork for the 1635 Peace of Prague, an agreement that resolved the conflict between Ferdinand II and Saxony and which other Protestant powers joined. Writing to Oxenstierna just after the battle, the Swedish general, Bernhard of Saxe-Weimar, concluded that "the great misfortune is so bad it could not be any worse."[41] Montecuccoli, who witnessed the battle, must have taken a share of the plunder, as Piccolomini ordered Vitzthum's regiment, with Montecuccoli still at its head, into the field to conduct operations after the battle had concluded.[42]

During this period, Montecuccoli, who knew Vitzthum would soon take back command, attempted but failed to gain control of his own regiment on two occasions. Both times, he traveled to Vienna and secured promises from Emperor Ferdinand II but found that the regiments in question had already been given away to others in his absence. In the first case, Emperor Ferdinand II's son, who was the king of the Romans and future Emperor Ferdinand III and had become nominal head of the army following Wallenstein's assassination, had divided Ernesto's old regiment between a cousin of Piccolomini's and another officer. This disappointment repeated after the Battle of Nördlingen: Emperor Ferdinand II agreed to bestow Aldobrandino Aldobrandini's regiment on Montecuccoli, but King Ferdinand had already awarded it to Ottaviano dell Trappola when Montecuccoli returned to the army. Close ties to patrons within the army were critical for obtaining a regiment, especially when communications between the court and army were slow.[43] During a brief period of unemployment, Montecuccoli fell back on Este patronage, seeking protection from Borso d'Este until he received a position in Annibale Gonzaga's regiment.[44]

In 1635, Montecuccoli obtained a written directive from Ferdinand II that granted him Ernesto's old regiment after he had caught the attention of Field

Marshal Melchior Hatzfeld, who alerted King Ferdinand to Montecuccoli's abilities and relayed his request for a regiment.[45] From this point forward, Montecuccoli assumed the major responsibilities of a military entrepreneur, such as recruiting men, raising credit, and subcontracting to the captains of companies. He must have excelled at his duties: he commanded four regiments at the 1636 Battle of Wittstock, where he covered the retreat of the imperial army. He arranged for his younger brother, Galeotto, to join one of his regiments, grooming his own *nipote* (nephew).[46]

With increasing responsibility came additional trouble. In 1637, Montecuccoli was arrested by order of the elector George William of Brandenburg, who alleged that Montecuccoli's troops had robbed him. While figures like George William had the loudest voices, controversies over the forced redistribution of property during the war continued more broadly. In 1635, shortly after receiving Wallenstein's estates at Náchod, Piccolomini's deputy plenipotentiary had reported exorbitant damages to the newly acquired properties and was apparently upset by Habsburg officials' overly harsh demands for a contribution for the damages. Political influence mattered greatly in these disputes, and Piccolomini eventually won concessions.[47] Following his arrest, Montecuccoli relied on friends near and far for help, including Francesco I d'Este, Ottavio Bolognesi, Matteo Galasso, Annibale Gonzaga, and Luigi Pallavicini. Hatzfeld eventually released him into the custody of Mattias de' Medici to George William's fury.[48] Montecuccoli assured Galasso that he had punished the officers responsible for the thefts (although belatedly) and traveled to Prague to explain himself in a face-to-face meeting with Emperor Ferdinand III, who had just succeeded Ferdinand II (d. 1637).[49]

Montecuccoli lost ground in the months surrounding his controversy with the elector. He also traveled home to mourn his mother's death before resuming his position in the imperial army. By the end of the 1630s, he had experienced personal setbacks and witnessed how quickly the fortunes of others also shifted. In just a matter of years, Wallenstein had been assassinated, the imperial army rejoiced at Nördlingen, the Habsburgs negotiated the Peace of Prague, and the war expanded with the formal entry of France against the Habsburgs. At the same time, Spain stopped providing support to their Austrian cousins in order to focus on the War in Flanders. Nördlingen was the last great Habsburg victory in the Empire to which Spain made considerable contributions.[50] Starting in 1638, the fighting became increasingly indecisive.

Then, in 1639, personal disaster struck: Montecuccoli was captured by the Swedes while leading troops in Bohemia and hauled away to a three-year imprisonment at the fortress in Stettin (Szczecin)—his third detainment within a ten-year period and the longest one yet.[51] Montecuccoli lost his regiment.

Forlorn, he asked his captors for access to the castle library. There he embarked upon an intellectual journey that would further alter the course of his military career.

Military Theorist and Army Reformer

When Duke Francesco I d'Este learned of Montecuccoli's capture and imprisonment in the early summer of 1639, he immediately wrote to Bolognesi of his "great displeasure." Besides the fact that Montecuccoli had "worthy qualities" and was "our vassal," Francesco pointed out that Montecuccoli's "disgrace" resulted from "most glorious actions." He hoped that Montecuccoli's release could be secured in an exchange with another prisoner and urged Bolognesi to speak to ministers and the emperor in Vienna. Other familiar faces worked to free him, including Francesco and Girolamo Montecuccoli, Mattias de' Medici, and Ottavio Piccolomini.[52] Montecuccoli languished in prison despite these efforts, because the Swedes refused to release any captives until Horn was returned.[53] Imprisonments were potentially catastrophic, because military entrepreneurs usually had to pay their own ransoms and lost regiments, access to contributions, and the means to repay creditors. They also had to pay for their own living expenses.[54] Francesco would become increasingly determined to win Montecuccoli's release as the War of Castro, a conflict that pitted an alliance of northern Italian states against Pope Urban VIII, loomed.

As he awaited the outcome of Francesco's efforts, Montecuccoli undertook a program of reading and writing. Up to this point, much of his military education had occurred on the battlefield. While in Stettin, he composed his first treatises, including *Treatise on War* (*Trattato della guerra*, 1641), a learned compilation of military wisdom organized around sets of principles, inspired by (or copied from) ancient writers such as Vegetius and Caesar, as well as moderns such as Machiavelli, Campanella, and Lipsius. Montecuccoli openly admitted that "it often pleased me to imitate Lipsius" and that he explained his own ideas "with the words of others."[55] Montecuccoli's significance lay in the way he actively combined elements of military theory and political philosophy, layering them with his own observations of the Thirty Years' War. His works represent independent thought, not simply the influence of others. Like Machiavelli and Campanella before him, Montecuccoli became an imprisoned thinker.

While he admired armchair theorists like Lipsius, Montecuccoli's experiences place him more firmly within the genre of military theory composed by officer-scholars that included Giorgio Basta, Lodovico Melzi, Henri II de

Rohan, and François de La Noue.[56] Montecuccoli adopted their conventions, criticizing the ancient and modern writers who came before him by alleging that most "have not surpassed the limits of theory," a problem he intended to remedy. He claimed, "I read attentively the principle histories of the Ancients and the better Authors who have provided precepts of war, to which I have added the examples of that which the experience of fifteen continuous years could have taught me," and he asserted that he desired to "adjust" military wisdom for modern usage. He refused to glorify his own deeds, imitating Basta and Rohan, whom he called "as modest as (they were) valorous."[57] Montecuccoli's emphasis on subordinating personal glory to objective, cool-headed reason would become a hallmark of his career. At the same time, he complained that even recent military literature was too narrow—focused on a single aspect of warfare—or too general—lacking nuanced attention to particularities.[58] By contrast, his work presented an understanding of warfare that was notably different because it was systematic, detailed, and encyclopedic.

Montecuccoli's decision to write treatises while in prison showed how critical the mastery of the art and science of war had become for officers. In the preface to *Treatise on War*, he admitted that imprisonment "awakened the mind to contemplate matters in order to prepare myself to know how to do them when the occasion of freedom permits," a statement that indicates that Montecuccoli understood the role played by letters in learning how to conduct war. Montecuccoli depicted his studies in personal terms, as a form of self-education, announcing: "If someone happens by chance to read these pages, he should know at first glance that I did not write them for him but for myself alone, and that not having had any other end than to please and delight my spirit, I directed the entire form of this work to this goal alone." And yet Montecuccoli wanted his patrons to pay attention. He insisted that his writings enabled him to "account for that which I had done when I was deprived of being able to do anything."[59] Later, when he recounted his achievements in the 1644 petition to Emperor Ferdinand III cited at the beginning of this chapter, he wrote: "And in order not to be totally useless in imperial service during the time of my captivity I observed most curiously the styles of that war, the discipline of the army, and informed myself in detail of all that I deemed to be of service to Your Majesty, offering my writings on the subject after my liberation by order of Duke Piccolomini."[60] Montecuccoli must have been distraught at his confinement in Stettin and the sudden interruption of his advancement. At the same time, he probably perceived that military treatises could be useful for self-promotion.

The science of war was vital to Montecuccoli's patrons because it was fundamentally concerned with controlling war. During the first phase of his career, Montecuccoli had witnessed disorder. He had become aware of contemporary aspirations to create order through army reforms. He was an admirer of Gustavus Adolphus, at whose death he composed an admiring ode.[61] In *Treatise on War*, Montecuccoli argued that "the science of war principally consists in only fighting when one wants to." In order to achieve this goal, it was vital "to give good order to provisions, to exercise well one's soldiers in the management of their arms, and to observe all the orders and to know well how to make one's entrenchments."[62]

Not only did the battlefield require order, so did knowledge. Montecuccoli gave his reader the impression that information about military matters was disorganized and bewildering, making it difficult to put to effective use. He isolated fundamental principles behind a vast range of military topics and then broke principles down into constituent parts, illustrating their mechanics through examples. He stressed, "it is never possible to comprehend perfectly the whole if one is ignorant of the parts that constitute it." According to his method, "the whole art of war is separated into its parts and each part into parts with the greatest brevity and with the greatest diligence that has ever been possible."[63] Montecuccoli's treatises come across as more pedagogical than earlier military writings and were intended, perhaps, to be brought on campaign for reference, in addition to being read at court. Although he wrote in solitude, Montecuccoli conceived of his work as engaging a broader audience.

Montecuccoli may have seen himself as a similar kind of figure to Galileo, who provided a model for a new career bridging the practical world of craftsmen and the theoretical universe of natural philosophers.[64] Montecuccoli explained that it was necessary "to make different experiments and to build different models so that the eye may see concretely that which the imagination formed abstractly." This was particularly true "in mechanics and in fire power, where, without practice, one can easily make errors in theory."[65] The use of firepower was especially associated with cutting-edge empirical studies, including Galileo's insights into physical motion gleaned from ballistics research. Montecuccoli emphasized his empirical orientation by claiming to write in an "unrefined" style. In typical Galilean fashion, he stated that he "paid more attention to things than to words" and hoped to distinguish his writing "for the substance of the material and not for the beauty of its ornaments."[66]

Montecuccoli must have been influenced by the first post-Galilean generation of writers and thinkers in the Italian peninsula. There, under the patronage of rulers, academies such as the Lincei, Cimento, and Investiganti made scientific experiments and observation a primary part of their activities. Piccolomini's family even boasted of direct connections to Galileo: Ottavio's brother Ascanio had been Galileo's protector after the trial, and both brothers were rumored to have been tutored by him.[67] Importantly, however, Montecuccoli's understanding of Galilean science evolved on the battlefield and in prison—not while observing scientific spectacles at court.

Treatise on War was a tour de force, announcing the arrival of a formidable military intellect. Montecuccoli's treatises were never printed during his lifetime, but circulated in manuscript form. Unusually for a writer of this period, he refrained from dedicating the work to any patron. At the same time, we know that each of his major patrons—Duke Francesco I d'Este and Emperor Ferdinand III—received a copy of *Treatise on War*. Perhaps by neglecting to dedicate his treatises to Ferdinand III or Francesco I, Montecuccoli was carefully avoiding the appearance that he served one lord over the other, leaving himself free to distribute the treatises as gifts to both. The lack of dedications in Montecuccoli's early works may reflect his awareness that he was a semiautonomous actor navigating multiple loyalties at an uncertain crossroads.

Montecuccoli was finally released in the summer of 1642. Due to the interventions of Piccolomini and Archduke Leopold Wilhelm, he received appointment to the office of sergeant general and compensation worth three thousand florins.[68] He had only briefly resumed campaigning when Francesco I d'Este demanded his swift return to Modena. "The reason for our haste," Francesco wrote in August 1642, "is the imminent revolt of all the affairs of Italy."[69] Ferdinand III agreed to a temporary leave. Bolognesi even asked him to allow Montecuccoli to keep his imperial regiment and raise additional soldiers in Central Europe to bring to Modena for use in the War of Castro. Francesco addressed Ferdinand III about the matter, arguing that "these states are Your Majesty's and to cooperate in their conservation will preserve that which is yours."[70] Ferdinand III resisted. The Thirty Years' War continued to depopulate the empire, making it harder to find soldiers, while the emperor wished to avoid antagonizing a pope already unfriendly to the Habsburgs by supplying soldiers to the forces opposing him.[71]

Having returned to Modenese service, Montecuccoli aspired to win appointment to the highest military office—field marshal, a permanent position that offered a pension.[72] Perhaps to bolster his candidacy, he composed a proposal for a Swedish-style militia for Francesco, a document that reveals the ways mobile military actors served as "conduits" of military knowledge between European regions.[73] In *Proposal*, Montecuccoli revealed an acute focus on the material resources needed for waging war: money, food, and men.[74] He focused on discipline, estimated the costs of a cavalry militia, and explained how to make a cavalry militia self-sustaining. *Proposal* followed on the heels of two shorter reports examining the Swedish army in 1642 or 1643—*Swedish*

Military Drill (*Essercizio militare svedese*, 1642) and *Report on the Manner in which the Swedes Maintain the War in Germany* (*Relazione del modo che tengono gli svedesi nella guerra della Germania*, 1642 or 1643).[75] Montecuccoli probably did not expect Francesco to implement an entirely new military system on the verge of entering a war. Rather, *Proposal* represented a long-term strategic plan that Montecuccoli might have overseen as Modenese field marshal. Francesco awarded Montecuccoli the position the following spring. For a moment, Montecuccoli may have imagined remaining permanently in Modenese service and not returning to the imperial army. In July, he achieved a notable victory at the Battle of Nonantola against numerically superior forces, an outcome that he immediately reported to his old comrade-in-arms, Mattias de' Medici, who headed allied Tuscan forces.[76]

Piccolomini also considered joining the War of Castro, but in papal service. He had been disappointed when he failed to succeed Galasso as commander-in-chief of the imperial army in 1642 and chafed against his subordinate position to Archduke Leopold Wilhelm. The Barberini family saw an opportunity to woo the disaffected general and invited Piccolomini to become supreme commander of papal forces. They lobbied hard for his service, offering cash rewards, a generous stipend, and cardinals' hats for both Piccolomini and Ascanio. Just prior to Montecuccoli's victory at Nonantola, Francesco's secretary, Fulvio Testi, reported the "most curious news" that Piccolomini had appeared in nearby Cento to pay his respects to the papal nephew, Antonio Barberini, who led the troops that were fighting against Modena and Tuscany. Piccolomini sent a messenger to Montecuccoli requesting safe passage for one of his sisters. Montecuccoli, however, suspected that Piccolomini intended to serve the pope and had sent the messenger to spy on them. The Modenese forces cautiously detained the spy.[77]

Emperor Ferdinand III dissuaded Piccolomini from joining the war against Parma, Modena, Venice, and Tuscany because he did not want to strengthen Urban VIII's hand. Instead, Ferdinand III arranged for Piccolomini to transfer to the Spanish Army of Flanders until he could be reintegrated into the imperial army.[78] However, the fact that Piccolomini nearly fought against his Medici lord and the forces led by his protégé, Montecuccoli, shows the degree to which alliances fluctuated during the era of the Thirty Years' War. Italians tended to agree about whose side they were on when fighting in Central Europe: they were uniformly Catholic, and Italian bonds of patronage were deeply embedded in a larger Spanish-Austrian system of relationships. When conflict erupted in the Italian peninsula, however, friends easily became enemies. Piccolomini's example suggests that the military careers that provided noblemen with opportunities in foreign armies had given some commanders enough autonomy to consider fighting against their natural lords. It also shows the power that Emperor Ferdinand III wielded over Piccolomini. The Medici could no longer control him, but the Habsburgs could.

Montecuccoli left Modenese service in 1643 in order to negotiate his inheritance of Austrian properties following the death of Girolamo Montecuccoli. Despite Francesco I d'Este's pleas and Montecuccoli's success as field marshal, Montecuccoli never returned to the Modenese army. Nonetheless, he maintained a relationship of service to the duke of Modena even as he assumed greater responsibilities in imperial service.

Property, Credit, and Coercion

The mid- to late 1640s were critical years in which Montecuccoli mastered his military role and became an essential servant to the Habsburgs. He inherited Hohenegg with the help of a network of supporters, started operating as a general in the imperial army, and gained his first court appointments as an imperial chamberlain and councilor of war. He cultivated closer relationships to top imperial officials, including to Ferdinand III's most trusted advisor, Maximilian von Trauttmannsdorf, and worked in coordination with the leading figures of the imperial army, especially Galasso and Archduke Leopold Wilhelm. The latter had become the nominal head of the imperial army when Ferdinand III succeeded to the imperial throne in 1637. Montecuccoli is famous for writing that there are three things needed for war: "money, money, and money."[79] His writings exhibit a refined understanding of the economic basis of warfare; he later argued for regular tax streams and centralized administration to finance warfare. However, such reforms were fantasies in 1644. In reality, Montecuccoli followed typical early modern practices, relying on family wealth and connections, as well as Francesco I d'Este and Bolognesi for support. His experiences remind us that, despite their participation in commercial activities, military entrepreneurs did not operate according to modern economic rationale. They were not focused on the goal of capital accumulation, but rather needed money as a component of pursuing the military careers that enhanced status and reputation and earned glory. In fact, many of them were profligate: for all the wealth he gained, Piccolomini died in debt.[80]

Montecuccoli was disappointed by the lack of rewards from the imperial court. He claimed impoverishment and demanded reimbursement for some of his costs. In February 1644, he won the incredible promise of thirty thousand florins from Emperor Ferdinand III, as well as the first free regiment when he returned to the battlefield, to compensate for the regiment he had lost during the War of Castro.[81] The promised compensation was delayed: two months later, Trauttmannsdorf assured him that he would receive the payment "if not all at once, then in turns," while promising start up funds for Montecuccoli's return to campaigning.[82] In August, Montecuccoli continued to ask for money, turning to another powerful minister, Wenzel Eusebius Lobkowitz, for intercession with Ferdinand III due to the fact that Montecuccoli had been forced "to send spies, messengers, and couriers, and to make other expenses."[83] By September, he had grown melodramatic, stating, "it would simply be reasonable that, after one hundred years of continuous service, which had been rendered by members of my family, there was just once a trace of imperial reward."[84]

In December, he summarized his military accomplishments, as well as his complaints, in a letter to Ferdinand III (featured in the opening paragraph of this chapter). Montecuccoli had been injured on multiple occasions, had lost his baggage four times, and had suffered imprisonment by the Swedes twice, using his own money to pay his ransom. He added that he had armed his regiment at his own cost on three occasions. Finally, when Montecuccoli left for the War of Castro (at Ferdinand III's own command, he reminded his patron), he had lost the regiment he had paid for out of his own pocket, along with his horses.[85] At an earlier stage of the war, Emperor Ferdinand II had failed to pay a debt to Wallenstein of 150,850 florins, providing the Duchy of Sagan as a gift instead.[86] Montecuccoli did not receive generous land grants from the emperor. His most important rewards were salaries and gifts in the form of money or valuable objects.[87] Titles and offices were also critical because they provided leverage to pressure court officials into siphoning money from tax revenues into his pocket, as well as the authority to forcibly extort money and goods from regions his troops passed through.

Montecuccoli inherited his property in the Habsburg hereditary lands from kin. After Girolamo Montecuccoli died, Montecuccoli returned to Vienna from the Castro War to negotiate the inheritance of Hohenegg with Girolamo's widow, Barbara Concini. After Concini died in early 1644, the property in lower Austria, valued at two hundred thousand florins, passed to Montecuccoli according to an agreement in which he would pay off the debts on the estate, as well as Concini's son by another marriage.[88] Montecuccoli triumphed over the rival heir with help from the Jesuits as well as the duke of Modena: prior to Concini's death, Francesco I d'Este appealed to the Jesuit general, Muzio Vitelleschi, for intervention with Concini's confessor to sway Concini in Montecuccoli's favor.[89] In March 1644, Montecuccoli reported to Francesco I d'Este that he had taken possession of Hohenegg, becoming a property-holding member of the Austrian aristocracy, a fact that later permitted him to argue he had been "naturalized" (*naturalizato*).[90] It took at least a year for Monte-

cuccoli to pay off the debts on the property, involving the collaboration of both
Francesco Montecuccoli and Ottavio Bolognesi. In his 1646 will, Montecuccoli named Francesco Montecuccoli's son Giambattista as his heir, suggesting
that Francesco had invested in a property his relative nearly sold off due to
the onerous debt burden.[91] Montecuccoli took occasional respite from battlefield and court at Hohenegg (he also owned a house in Vienna), where he composed his later military writings.

Montecuccoli continued to risk family wealth and personal credit in imperial service, a fact worth exploring further. The financial basis for his military
activities included revenues generated by property, loans from merchants, interest on loans he provided to other noblemen, and movable goods such as
silver plate. Montecuccoli invested in goods on his travels, sending them back
to Montecuccolo for safekeeping.[92] An agent in Modena, Pietro Ricci, who had
served Montecuccoli's father and was also a distant relative, received goods
and dispatched others—including silver—to Montecuccoli, who sent troops
to safeguard valuables en route. Ricci also managed financial transactions; another relative, Enea Caprara, assisted Montecuccoli on campaign.[93] Francesco
Montecuccoli had authority over Montecuccoli's wealth and estates and
worked with Bolognesi to transfer money and goods. When Francesco died
suddenly in 1645, Montecuccoli ordered Ricci to secure his goods and to ask
Marquis Massimiliano Montecuccoli (of the Polinago branch) to provide protection for his "jurisdictions, subjects, and properties," giving Massimiliano
full plenary power "to do as he wishes."[94] When conflict with Spain seemed
imminent in the Duchy of Modena in 1646, Montecuccoli dispatched movable goods, including silver and jewels, for safekeeping at Bolognesi's estate
in Correggio. Just before he died, Bolognesi transferred the valuables to the
monastery of San Geminiano in Modena, where Montecuccoli's sister, Anna
Beatrice, lived.[95] The Modena-based Montecuccoli family and other relatives
such as Ricci, as well as well-connected aristocratic allies like Bolognesi,
played roles in overseeing and deploying the wealth that helped finance Montecuccoli regiments in Central Europe.

Besides relying on family members, Montecuccoli also took out loans from
merchants, which he paid back from contributions as well as monetary gifts
from the emperor. In January 1645, Montecuccoli reported that he had obtained one thousand florins from the Court Chamber (or Treasury) of Styria
to pay off the loan he had taken out to secure Hohenegg.[96] He alleged that he
faced resistance to contributions from local estates. In 1646, he complained to
Lobkowitz that he was supposed to collect one thousand thalers from the
Court Chamber of Silesia to support his regiment, but the Silesians refused
to comply with Habsburg orders. As a result, Montecuccoli lamented that he

was in debt to a merchant from Breslau (Wrocław) "without knowing of any way to satisfy him since, in addition, neither my regiment nor I received a single bit of help in this past year."[97] His 1672 will mentions an outstanding debt of seven thousand florins with the Oriental Company.[98]

More significant to Montecuccoli than the mercantile credit system was the aristocratic credit system. In the family business of war, kinship networks extending across regions facilitated the borrowing and lending of money. According to the above-mentioned will, Montecuccoli owed fifty-seven thousand florins to Karl Liechtenstein and thirty-three thousand florins to Count Breuner—far greater sums than he owed any merchant. Not only did Montecuccoli take out loans from other noblemen, but he also lent money and collected interest. For instance, as he prepared to return to warfare in April 1644, Montecuccoli attempted to collect a debt of six hundred florins owed to him by a member of the Tuscan Guicciardini family. Guicciardini's uncle, Lorenzo—who had served Mattias de' Medici on campaign in Central Europe a decade earlier—repaid the loan.[99] Without the assurance provided by aristocratic connections between Florence, Modena, and Vienna, Guicciardini probably would not have secured a loan from Montecuccoli in the first place.

Finally, for Montecuccoli as for other officers in the imperial army, finance depended on extortion. It is impossible to know how much he forced out of local inhabitants in terms of both money and goods, but Montecuccoli's 1637 arrest for plundering the goods of the elector of Brandenburg shows that he was a participant in these practices. At a time when the average pay of a foot soldier was approximately 8 florins a month, Montecuccoli ordered the province of Neumark to pay 30,000 florins per month to support his regiment with an additional 1,200 florins for his personal use, 600 florins for each lieutenant-colonel, and an extra 5,000 florins for exigencies.[100] These monetary demands were vastly in excess of any compensation promised by the emperor. Montecuccoli's writings show that he understood armies only succeeded when local populations acquiesced to their presence and paid up. Without contributions, soldiers lacked provisions, leading to ill-disciplined behavior. A central feature of Montecuccoli's science of war included reforms to army financing so that soldiers received regular pay and were no longer obliged to plunder local populations.

When Montecuccoli referred to peasants in his letters, he did so as an authority figure. When he took possession of Hohenegg, he told Francesco I d'Este that "the peasants have pledged fealty to me," confirming his lordship.[101] During the War of Castro, he warned peasants not to join the opposing forces, imposing harsh punishments on anyone he believed was disloyal.[102] Although these statements signal Montecuccoli's authority, the fact that he needed to confirm peasant fealty or warn peasants against disloyalty indicates that peasants also had choices. Military entrepreneurs remained vulnerable to insubordination, and peasants were frequently violent toward soldiers. The authority that Montecuccoli demanded stemmed in large part from his ability to exert greater force, but he knew his authority also depended on convincing others of its legitimacy. For this reason, Ricci dispatched a detailed Montecuccoli family tree attesting to Montecuccoli's nobility when he claimed Hohenegg.[103] Montecuccoli was not a solitary opportunist, but a member of an aristocratic enterprise of coercion in which family members collaborated in the effort to expand their authority in new territories and political jurisdictions. Money was essential, but noble status and reputation were key to convincing numerous interested parties, from peasants to Habsburg rulers, of the legitimacy of one's expectations and demands.

Between Modena and Vienna

Montecuccoli continued to expose himself and his family to a high level of risk, including possible loss of reputation, property, and life, when he returned to the imperial army. The Thirty Years' War entered its final phase, marked by preparations for a peace congress and military strategies focused on winning advantages to bully the enemy into diplomatic concessions.[104] The French under Mazarin's direction (as of 1642) focused on a strategy of attrition in the Black Forest region and Bavaria, while the Swedish successfully prosecuted an invasion of the Habsburg hereditary lands under General Lennart Torstensson in 1642, and their Hessian allies distracted the Westphalians. The Swedish army captured important positions, including Glogau (Głogów) in Silesia and Olmütz (Olomouc) in Moravia, that would allow them to launch future attacks on the hereditary lands. Soon after, the Habsburgs lost the Second Battle of Breitenfeld. Galasso took over imperial army operations (leading to Piccolomini's disgruntled switch of service) in the hopes of mitigating further losses. At the same time, Spain no longer sent soldiers or subsidies to support Austria and received a major blow with a humiliating loss to the French at Rocroi. French propagandists hyped this victory—occurring the same month the young Louis XIV succeeded to the throne—as the signal of Spanish decline and French ascendancy.[105] Montecuccoli felt the sting of Rocroi personally: his relative, Andrea Montecuccoli of the Renno branch, was taken prisoner.

Montecuccoli experienced firsthand the fatigue of war as resources dwindled, armies shrank in size, and field operations degenerated into logistical riddles. Like Aldobrandini two decades before, Montecuccoli grew frustrated at shifting orders from Vienna and the continuous, costly demands that he transport troops across territories. During these years, he fielded numerous requests from Francesco I d'Este, working as an informal diplomat and intelligence gatherer for his natural lord. When he left Modena for Vienna in 1643, he took a cipher to communicate in secret with Francesco.[106] By 1647, the War of Castro was over, but Francesco had grown dissatisfied with the Spanish Habsburgs, whom Francesco accused of failing to provide adequate protection and rewards. He switched his alliance to France and fought against the Spanish army. Montecuccoli gingerly navigated his natural lord's rupture with the Habsburgs as he continued to advance in the imperial army.

On the battlefield, Montecuccoli learned from the disasters that befell his patrons, including Galasso's ill-fated 1644 retreat from Denmark without adequate provisions to feed his soldiers. While some decried Galasso as an "army wrecker," Montecuccoli reported on the campaign to the imperial court in January 1645 and relayed his own accounts, as well as copies of imperial orders, to Vittorio Siri, who published the works in his *Il Mercurio overo historia de' correnti tempi*. As the French propaganda blast that followed the Battle of Rocroi showed, victory came with the pen as well as with the sword. Montecuccoli relied on his own careful information gathering and writing as a means of defense against attacks on his reputation, eventually becoming a talented propagandist.

While he was pursuing inheritance negotiations for Hohenegg, Montecuccoli reported to Emperor Ferdinand III on behalf of Francesco, who continued to seek imperial support in the form of subsidies and/or soldiers.[107] In early 1644, before he returned to the battlefield, Montecuccoli was searching for an artillery general to send to Modena. He also anticipated that an upcoming reform of imperial regiments would provide officers who would "voluntarily" transfer to the wars in Italy and bring troops with them.[108] When Ferdinand III demanded that Montecuccoli return to the imperial army in April 1644, Montecuccoli kept Francesco carefully apprised, explaining that "I do not deem anything in the world equal to the honor of your grace" and conveying the news that he had informed Ferdinand III that "I was not at my liberty and that I was obliged to serve Your Highness." The emperor reassured Montecuccoli that he would write to Francesco himself about the agreement. Montecuccoli begged to be allowed to return to Modena for a few weeks, but Ferdinand III conveyed that "His Majesty's service would suffer no delay and gave me a decree in which I was ordered to be ready to depart anytime and to any place that His Majesty commands." As an incentive, Ferdinand III offered Montecuccoli the first free regiment, advancement in office, and money.[109]

In 1644, Ferdinand III expected Montecuccoli to join the imperial forces fighting the Swedes in Denmark, although his orders frequently shifted according to circumstances. In July, Galasso had reached Holstein with eighteen thousand

FIGURE 3.2. Jacques Callot, *Study of a Cavalry Skirmish*. The Trustees of the British Museum.

men after marching down the Elbe River in an attempt to confine Torstensson. Although Galasso captured Kiel and Rendsburg, the imperial army, worn down by skirmishes and pushed back as far as Bernburg, soon found itself nearly surrounded by the Swedes due to Torstensson's clever maneuvering. Galasso was forced to retreat back the same way his army had come—through a totally exhausted region—with troops that had been on half rations since August. Due to inadequate planning and the Habsburgs' dire financial position at the end of the war, imperial soldiers, far from their normal base of operations in Bohemia and suffering a shortage of transport animals, starved and deserted in high numbers.[110]

Ferdinand III was not immediately aware of the trouble Galasso's army was in. He ordered Montecuccoli to Franconia to take over command of the army led by the frequently ill Hatzfeld. In late July and early August, Montecuccoli received contradictory orders from Emperor Ferdinand III and Galasso, all of which have been printed in Siri and reveal the chaos of the moment.[111] Facing pressure from the Spanish, on 29 July Ferdinand III ordered Montecuccoli to provide five thousand men to Luigi Gonzaga for transfer to the Low Countries. Four days later, Galasso ordered Montecuccoli "not to waste another minute" and to collect all of his troops in order to advance on the Archbishopric of Bremen "as fast as possible." Galasso added that Montecuccoli should ignore any other orders apart from the emperor's. Another four days later, on 7 August, Ferdinand III confirmed his desire to send Montecuccoli's troops to the Low Countries, explaining, "it seems to us that for now the need as well as the danger is not as great in any other place than there." On 10 August and 14 August, Galasso repeated his demands that Montecuccoli march north in order to block the troops of Johann Christoph Königsmark, who was reinforcing Torstensson and threatened the empire with invasion. Ferdinand III swiftly changed his mind regarding the transfer of troops when he learned of French attacks under Louis II de Bourbon, Duke of Enghien (known as the Grand Condé), and Henri de la Tour d'Auvergne, viscount of Turenne, against Freiburg in Bavaria in early August, as well as Königsmark's approach. Finally, on 16 August, the orders started to converge in a more sensical way. Instead of transferring troops to the Low Countries, Ferdinand III told Montecuccoli to unite the troops under Hatzfeld (apparently recovered), who would lead them in support of Bavarian forces under Mercy. Montecuccoli, disappointed to lose this command position, prepared to join Galasso's forces.[112]

In the middle of receiving these confusing orders, Montecuccoli wrote a letter from Bavaria to Francesco I d'Este in which he reported that the army "had been reduced to nothing" and that he would be happy to withdraw from the region. This letter reflected complaints that were similar to a letter he wrote around the same time to Bolognesi, whose contents were examined in the opening vignette of this book and to which we return here. To Francesco and Bolognesi, Montecuccoli complained about his frequent travels, orders that continuously changed before he could accomplish anything, and the threat to his reputation that arose from leading troops in such conditions. His baggage horses were "reduced to skin and bones" and, he scoffed, more appropriate for making anatomy sketches than transporting supplies.[113] Massimiliano Montecuccoli arranged the transport of fresh horses, which were in short supply across Europe.[114] However, as Montecuccoli complained to Bolognesi, the horses were stationed in the Bohemian town Eger (Cheb) because, for some reason, his agents had not received his orders to send them to Bavaria.

No matter—due to his new orders, Montecuccoli would soon travel through Eger (Cheb) on his way to Dresden and beyond. He admitted drily that the "graces" of the imperial court "cost me greatly."[115]

Montecuccoli soon departed from Schweinfurt in Bavaria, passing through Nuremberg, Eger (Cheb), and Dresden, in order to counter Swedish forces near Bernburg and in parts of Lusatia and Saxony. His orders were malleable, as the imperial army responded to Königsmark's movements. Finally, in December, he journeyed to Linz, where he reported to the emperor, and then, early in 1645, traveled to Munich to negotiate reinforcements from the elector of Bavaria, Maximilian I. All told, he traveled approximately 1,500 kilometers in less than half a year's time. Montecuccoli was continuously reinforcing garrisons with provisions and spending his own money to earn the good will of the soldiers or to gather intelligence. He boasted that he traveled twice as fast as others (he alleged that journeys that took others fifteen–twenty days only took him eight–ten), slept half as long, and spent his free time studying the military art rather than playing games. Montecuccoli was frustrated that some of the imperial generals—Hatzfeld and Schlick—thought he was advancing too quickly for his age.[116]

In January 1645, Galasso, who had allegedly spent much of the Danish campaign drunk, was dismissed from command, while Montecuccoli, who was injured while transporting the Bavarian troops, briefly retired to Hohenegg and probably composed another treatise, *On Battle* (*Sulle battaglie*). Montecuccoli drew positive lessons from Galasso. In *On Battle*, Montecuccoli reviewed Galasso's victory at Nördlingen, which he alleged provided a textbook example of how to use the geographical features of a battle site to one's advantage.[117] In both *Military Tables* and *On the War against the Turks in Hungary*, Montecuccoli commended the deceptive strategies Galasso used against the Swedes as he retreated.[118] These two features—the strategic use of battle sites and deceptive maneuvering to escape the assault of a greater force—became hallmarks of Montecuccoli's military science, later used to great effect against the Ottoman army.

Montecuccoli continued his impressive travels in 1645, received his first court offices (imperial chamberlain and councilor of war), and continued to collect payments and gifts from patrons. He marched with troops to Bavaria, Hungary, Swabia, and Bohemia in the fight against the French, the Swedes, and allied Transylvanian forces under György Rákóczi. He made a trip to Graz to receive part of the money owed to him ("a large sum of money," he later recorded). He also traveled briefly to Modena, where Francesco presented him with "a diamond belt and a beautiful ring," before returning to Graz for the remainder of the payment Ferdinand III had promised.[119]

During this period of campaigning, Montecuccoli grew particularly close to Archduke Leopold Wilhelm. He confided to Francesco that Leopold Wilhelm "has signified to me with favors of extreme confidence that he does not want to be served in this undertaking by any other generals except for Count Puchheim and me."[120] Montecuccoli told Francesco that Leopold Wilhelm was aware of Montecuccoli's obligation to return to Modenese service "anytime that Your Highness calls me," and mentioned that the archduke would write to Francesco.[121] He continued his efforts to levy troops for Francesco, writing that, despite obstacles, "I will nevertheless continue to toil."[122]

In early January 1646, Francesco remained convinced that Montecuccoli would return to Modena, demanding that his arrival "must not be deferred much longer" and asking him to bring "one or two miners experienced in excavations."[123] A temporary lull in fighting had indeed convinced Leopold Wilhelm to grant Montecuccoli leave, but the archduke immediately revoked it when information about a new Swedish attack surfaced. When he reinstated Montecuccoli, Leopold Wilhelm offered him the promotion to cavalry general. Montecuccoli hoped Francesco would understand his desire to remain in the imperial army in such a position, writing of his "confidence" that "you will not deign to disapprove this delay on an occasion so grand."[124] This promotion opened up the possibility of greater influence over the circulation of troops, which Francesco would have appreciated.

In late 1646, Francesco once again applied pressure on Montecuccoli to return to Modena. Montecuccoli sent a relative, Alfonso Montecuccoli (of the Montecenere branch), to Vienna to ask the emperor for leave. Montecuccoli instructed him to report to Ferdinand III "the honors and benefits that the Lord Duke proposes to me" and the fact that "the fortune of these wars is very inconstant and my increasing age requires that I now establish some stable foundation." Montecuccoli sensed that the outcome of Alfonso's trip would render an important change in his life. He ordered Alfonso to begin looking for a wife for him from the Italian peninsula if the leave was accepted or from Central Europe if the leave was denied. In case his leave was denied, he also wanted his "silver, jewelry, money, and credit bonds" transported to Venice, "where I will be able to obtain them with ease."[125] Montecuccoli's leave was denied, but Leopold Wilhelm promised him the official patent for cavalry general, a position he had held only unofficially.[126] Montecuccoli seemed to be using his position between patrons to extract concessions from each of them.

Montecuccoli gained accolades during the final two years of the war, when both Galasso and Piccolomini briefly returned to lead the imperial army following Leopold Wilhelm's resignation. At Triebel in August 1647, Montecuccoli made a daring cavalry attack, and at Zusmarshausen in May 1648 he prevented catastrophe by covering the retreat of Peter Melander, who had taken over command after Galasso died in April 1647. The latter event showcased what Montecuccoli did best: resist a much larger army with limited resources (he had 800 musketeers and 2,000 cavalry, compared to the 14,500 cavalry and 7,500 infantry of the Swedish-French allied forces under Carl Gustaf Wrangel and Turenne). Perhaps thinking of Galasso, he positioned his forces carefully, so that he could use the forested terrain to his advantage. When Montecuccoli was out-flanked by the French after withstanding the enemy for an hour, Melander rushed back to help and was shot and killed in the process. Montecuccoli and many of his men made it out alive, and the bulk of Habsburg forces escaped an-nihilation. A decisive defeat would have been politically disastrous for Emperor Ferdinand III in the ongoing peace negotiations.[127]

Throughout these years of campaign action, Montecuccoli continued his efforts to send troops to Francesco I d'Este. From April to June 1647, Monte-cuccoli and Alfonso arranged to transport cavalry to Modena, but on 22 June, Montecuccoli reported that "in leaving Silesia they had been encountered by an enemy party, which took them all prisoners besides two who were killed, together with the lieutenant who conducted them." He wanted to exchange these captives for prisoners held by the imperial army, but the enemy refused, demanding a huge ransom.[128] Finally, from late August to early September, precisely when Francesco formalized his relationship to France, Raimondo sent a "qualified lieutenant" to Modena at Francesco's request.[129] As Alfonso nego-tiated Montecuccoli's leave, he simultaneously represented Francesco in Vienna in the hopes that Emperor Ferdinand III could provide the assistance Francesco needed to avoid a rupture with Spain.[130]

Francesco formally broke his alliance with Spain in August 1647, when he stipulated a formal agreement with France. At about this time, Montecuccoli reported to Ferdinand III that Francesco had accepted command of French forces in Italy, on the condition that he not fight against imperial states.[131] Any military assistance Montecuccoli procured for the duke was intended for use against the Spanish in alliance with the French. If Montecuccoli had obtained leave, he would have fought against Spanish forces. Four days prior to formal-izing the agreement with the French, Francesco sent Montecuccoli his final offer. His annoyance was evident. He told Montecuccoli, "I cannot believe any-more that the benevolence of His Majesty has so long denied the requested leave to Your Lordship, who is my subject and feudatory." If Montecuccoli wanted to return to his service, Francesco believed that he could. He warned Montecuccoli that "if Your Lordship does not come, do not think of ever hav-ing another place in my service and be certain that I will remain little satisfied with an improper and undue negative response."[132] Montecuccoli responded to Francesco's persuasions and threats by emphasizing his desire to return to Modena, but complaining that his hands were tied.[133] Francesco could have punished Montecuccoli by confiscating his estates—like Odoardo Farnese, the duke of Parma, did to his subjects who refused to join his war efforts against Spain in 1635—but Francesco refrained.[134] In November, he asked Montecuccoli to tell Ferdinand III that he had agreed to marry Vittoria Farnese, solidifying a relationship to the Duchy of Parma, which was periodically sympathetic to the French.[135] In 1648, Francesco headed a French assault on the Spanish-controlled fortress at Cremona in Milan, entering into combat against former allies.[136] Meanwhile, peace in Europe was finally struck after several trying years during which Montecuccoli documented the exhausting problems faced by the army: the overwhelming size and strength of enemy forces, the refusal of local allies to support the imperial army, and the exhaustion and poor discipline of ill-cared-for soldiers. Montecuccoli claimed to have repeatedly informed the court about these issues.[137]

Montecuccoli would have been relieved when Francesco decided to make peace with Spain; he even served as an intermediary, communicating Francesco's justifications to the emperor.[138] Montecuccoli returned to Modena in 1652 and competed in a joust, sadly killing one of his friends by accident. In the mid-1650s, Francesco realigned with the French, marrying Mazarin's niece, and fighting the Spanish again. In 1656, Montecuccoli recounted a conversation with Count Schwarzenberg about Francesco's marriage to Mazarin's niece and how such a development would, Montecuccoli wrote, create an "impediment to my fortunes since [Habsburg patrons] would no longer trust me with important offices."[139] Perhaps fortuitously for Montecuccoli, Francesco died in 1658, the same year that Leopold I (r. 1658–1705) was elected emperor.[140] Montecuccoli outlived Francesco by twenty-two years, during which time he reached the pinnacle of his career in imperial service. During the 1650s, Montecuccoli made a clear decision to abandon the duke's service in favor of the emperor's. After 1641's *On Battle*, his military treatises were all dedicated to the Habsburg monarch.

By the seventeenth century, the Spanish and Austrian Habsburg clientage network in the Italian peninsula was powerful and pervasive. As a result, Francesco's political shift toward the French reverberated uncomfortably through many Modenese kinship networks (although some dynasties such as the Rangoni served the French). Montecuccoli was an imperial general, and his cousin Andrea a Spanish governor, but Alfonso fought under Francesco when he attempted to seize Cremona from the Spanish.[141] The same circumstances would have applied to other Modenese aristocratic families who financed imperial regiments. When Francesco switched sides, he threw the international alliances of some of his aristocratic vassals into disarray. Many of these families would have recoiled at the idea of starting anew in French service.

The difficulty of establishing a reputation for faithfulness was acute in such an interconnected military and political environment characterized by weak states, informal ties, and reliance on the wealth and/or credit of many small- and medium-sized dynasties with their own particular interests. And yet faithfulness—or at least its appearance—mattered precisely because of the personal nature of power and the lack of an institutional or legal/constitutional framework for operating within. Seeing that Montecuccoli faced so many difficulties in imperial service, Francesco Montecuccoli and Bolognesi discussed Montecuccoli's permanent return to Modenese service, with Bolognesi surmising it was better for Montecuccoli "to have a mediocre but secure advantage (in Modena), than a great but uncertain hope."[142] Montecuccoli decided to remain in imperial service because, as he confided to Bolognesi, he had made "a vow of obedience."[143] Montecuccoli viewed his role in terms of vassalage rather than impersonal market forces. At the same time, he expected and negotiated for rewards. His obedience to a higher cause—the defense of the imperial Catholic world order, headed by the Habsburg dynasty—lent legitimacy to the maneuvers he undertook to satisfy his ambitions.

A year after Montecuccoli's death, the Modenese historian Pietro Gazzotti produced an account in which he reflected on Francesco's reign. In it, Gazzotti made the fascinating claim that Spanish ministers had proposed that Ferdinand III confiscate the Duchy of Modena on account of Francesco's treason. One of the candidates Gazzotti alleged they recommended to replace Francesco as duke was none other than Raimondo Montecuccoli.[144] Perhaps Gazzotti was simply airing the fantasies of a later generation. Nonetheless, this account reveals an accurate picture of a military entrepreneur whose success in imperial service implied a betrayal of his natural lord—a figure not unlike Wallenstein. One might also argue that Gazzotti imagined Montecuccoli as a seventeenth-century Francesco Sforza: a *condottiere* who nearly acquired his own state in northern Italy through military accomplishments.

Francesco I d'Este's behavior shows that military entrepreneurs who switched back and forth between alliances to different rulers were not unusually disloyal. Rulers practiced the same behaviors, traditionally depicted as legitimate in state-building literature that interprets the decisions of sovereigns in terms of reason of state. Francesco's 1647 alliance with the French was a behavior that emerged seamlessly from the Renaissance *condottiere* tradition, in which rulers and nobles alike ensured their political survival by formulating military contracts (*condotte*) and switching allegiance when better military opportunities arose.[145] In an era of faithless rulers, it was strategically wise for the Montecuccoli to distribute risk by encouraging family members to serve different rulers. This venerable military family, which had held sway in Frignano long before the Este arrived in Modena, maintained political allegiances that at times intersected with Francesco's, but also evolved in a semiautonomous way.

Understanding the Thirty Years' War entails examining layers of convoluted political relationships forged between small-scale actors—that is, between noblemen and between noblemen and minor princes—and between those actors and larger powers, as well as taking seriously the fact that every political actor—princes and minor nobles—pursued multiple allegiances as a matter of course. The Austrian Habsburg monarch—as well as the kings of Spain and France—groomed clients in northern Italy in order to protect the military corridor to Flanders and to gain access to men, money, and credit from the resource-rich peninsula. The Spanish and Austrian Habsburgs were more successful than the French at using clientage networks in the Italian peninsula.[146] Smaller-scale Italian actors, including Francesco I d'Este and the Montecuccoli family, participated in political maneuverings that reverberated as far as Central Europe, where some German nobles grew to fear the power of Italians within the imperial army following the shocking assassination of their generalissimo.

By 1648, a new question loomed for these foreign military entrepreneurs and their followers: what would happen to their careers after the war ended? What would it take to advance from the upper echelons of the imperial army to the upper echelons of court society, especially when many of the native elite were understandably hostile to newcomers? It took several years to complete the implementation of the Peace of Westphalia as the various parties to the treaty fulfilled payment obligations and/or gradually withdrew troops. By the early 1650s, it was clear to Montecuccoli that he needed a wife—preferably from a native Central European dynasty—a stable pension, and a permanent court office.

However, instead of settling down and comfortably climbing the ranks of Viennese court society, Montecuccoli found himself on the road again. This time he assumed a role closer to Bolognesi's. Appointed imperial diplomat by Ferdinand III, Montecuccoli traveled to the northern court of one of the empire's most formidable adversaries, Sweden. There he met Gustavus Adolphus's daughter, Queen Christina of Sweden, an enigmatic ruler who was on the verge of making her own stunning political and religious transformation.

CHAPTER 4

From Battlefield to Court

When Montecuccoli arrived at Queen Christina of Sweden's court in 1654, the Thirty Years' War had been officially over for less than six years. The long-desired conclusion to the war had forced a sudden change on military entrepreneurs who had spent much of their lives on campaign. Machiavelli complained that men who made war their art sought to curtail peace efforts in order to continue to enrich themselves on campaign.[1] Montecuccoli, however, did not want to keep fighting wars indefinitely: he worried about how long he could risk his life, reputation, and wealth on the exhausting campaigns of the imperial army. In 1650, Montecuccoli had an audience with Emperor Ferdinand III in which he argued that he needed "a stable footing and a secure retirement in case of accidents that could result from infirmity, lameness, old age, or some other disaster."[2] Montecuccoli faced the challenge of establishing a successful court career in which he competed for positions with the magnate class in Vienna.

For a military entrepreneur, diplomatic service often provided a bridge to the court.[3] Montecuccoli held a number of diplomatic assignments, but two stand out as particularly significant in terms of how they shaped his experience and because he kept detailed journals about what happened. They include his 1653–55 posts as imperial diplomat to Queen Christina of Sweden in Uppsala and the Spanish Netherlands and his 1666 assignment to greet Emperor Leopold I's bride, the Spanish infanta Margarita Teresa, at the Italian port of

Finale.[4] Each of these assignments played a role in his advancement, because they widened and enriched his web of patrons, opening further pathways into a lively Catholic Habsburg political universe with hubs in Vienna, Madrid, Rome, and Brussels. In between these diplomatic missions, Montecuccoli married Margarethe von Dietrichstein in 1657 and commanded imperial forces as field marshal in the Second Northern War (1655–60) and again as lieutenant general—the highest military rank possible for someone who was not a member of the Habsburg family—in the war against the Ottomans (1663–64).

Although a focus on Montecuccoli's diplomatic career temporarily shifts our gaze away from the battlefield, we must remember that these missions were nestled in-between military campaigns and that war continued to occupy his thoughts even after the Peace of Westphalia. By the end of the century, a new balance of power had emerged as the Spanish Habsburg line became extinct and England, the Dutch Republic, and Austria formed an alliance against the French. However, none of this was clear in the 1650s and 1660s. How did contemporaries, especially the cosmopolitan elites who traveled through Habsburg Europe, experience the critical decades that followed the Thirty Years' War, long before the geopolitical contours of the eighteenth century had fallen into place? What other political directions did they envisage and plan for? Although military entrepreneurs have rarely been studied outside of their military contexts, this chapter argues that they are ideal figures to analyze in order to shed light on political activity during these decades because they inhabited both battlefield and court. Montecuccoli's journals, alongside official instructions, letters, military treatises, and other documents, indicate that officers were part of a larger, mobile group of elites who exchanged scholarship and intelligence, competed over status, participated in intrigue, and volunteered for war. In particular, the journals open windows onto politics at two distinctive locales of Catholic Habsburg influence beyond the capital cities of Vienna, Madrid, or Brussels. Antwerp, where Christina lived from 1654 to 1655, and Finale, where Margarita Teresa disembarked to continue the land journey to Austria in 1666, became liminal zones in which a diverse array of cosmopolitan elites with Habsburg ties attempted to reshape status and imagine new political possibilities.

"Everything Is Overturned"

In 1650, Montecuccoli wrote a dispirited letter to Piccolomini. Piccolomini was away from Vienna, helping to negotiate the Peace of Nuremberg, which ensured the removal of Swedish troops from the Holy Roman Empire.[5] This highly placed diplomatic position revealed further remarkable possibilities for the most-elite foreign-born noblemen in imperial service. Nonetheless, the native elite closely guarded court positions, making competition in Vienna fierce. Montecuccoli perceived danger for his friend. "There is no doubt," he wrote, "that now under one pretext or another, people who naturally love themselves more than others try to gain credit for themselves and cast a shadow over Your Excellency."[6] He urged Piccolomini to return to court to combat his opponents, bemoaning the fact that "this general transformation from war to peace has altered the minds of this whole court in such a way, that one can scarcely recognize it anymore. Everything is overturned, without observing either conditions of propriety or the customary manner."[7]

Montecuccoli's statement—"everything is overturned"—is a fascinating contemporary view of how the long-desired peace was itself destabilizing. Patterns of behavior established to meet military needs changed, resulting in power shifts. No longer needed on the battlefield, military entrepreneurs had to establish positions of strength at court. War had not disappeared entirely. The conflict between Spain and France continued, involving the ongoing participation of northern Italian powers, including Modena. Emperor Ferdinand III sent twelve thousand men to assist Spain in the defense of Milan, but Montecuccoli was not involved, and Ferdinand III died shortly thereafter.[8] During the 1650s, Montecuccoli searched for ways to advance beyond the battlefield. By the end of the Thirty Years' War, he had been appointed imperial chamberlain and earned a position on the Aulic War Council, but complained that the office of chamberlain was given out to much younger noblemen, while he had been excluded from the meetings of the War Council.[9] In 1653, Piccolomini reported to Montecuccoli that Lobkowitz and other ministers were maneuvering to take over command of the army, warning that they would soon "discover their ignorance."[10]

Prior to 1657, Montecuccoli had failed to obtain another important political goal: marriage. His family members repeatedly pestered him about finding a wife, and several attempts at marriage had already fallen apart.[11] The year that he inherited Hohenegg, Montecuccoli composed a fascinating autobiographical love story that provides an intimate window into his views on love and the problems he faced in seeking a marriage partner. In "The Miserable but True Story of Morindo's Love for Arianna," a foreign soldier named Morindo courted a young lady from a high-born family named "Arianna," lady-in-waiting to "the Great Olorena." They fell in love at court in "Nivena," but their affair was doomed when Morindo departed to serve in a distant war in a country named "Atilia." The relationship crumbled while he was away because he mistakenly believed that she had become engaged to a new suitor.[12] When he learned that he had been wrong, it was too late to rekindle the courtship as Arianna truly did have a new suitor named "Linaspro."[13] While this story reproduced common literary tropes popularized by chivalric romances—especially Ariosto's *Orlando Furioso*—it also contained genuine autobiographical elements. Montecuccoli included a key at the end of the text identifying himself as Morindo, Countess Maria Anna Khevenmüller as Arianna, the Dowager Empress Eleonora as Olorena, and Spinola (a member of the famed Genoese military family) as Linaspro.[14] Montecuccoli may have wooed the young countess during a brief interlude in Vienna, after release from imprisonment in Stettin and just before leaving for Italy to serve in the War of Castro. This story captures the inherent instability of life as a military entrepreneur: for someone frequently called away to wars in distant lands, it was difficult to maintain a courtship and achieve a marriage.

Montecuccoli's troubles were partly self-inflicted: as the last chapter revealed, he could have returned permanently to Modenese service but decided to pursue other opportunities. At the time, he had told his relative Alfonso that if he stayed in Modena, he needed to pursue a marriage alliance to an Italian family. If he remained in imperial service, he wanted a German wife.[15] A marriage alliance with the right family was a critical step once he knew where he would remain. Besides continuing to serve the Austrian Habsburgs in some capacity, Montecuccoli considered at least two other options. In 1650, the Venetian and Spanish ambassadors each approached Montecuccoli about possible positions in the Venetian army and the Army of Flanders, respectively. He took these offers seriously, reporting to Piccolomini that while he wanted to await developments in Vienna, "I also would not want to lose all opportunities."[16]

Financial distress continued to plague Montecuccoli. After the war ended, the pensions of generals had been reduced by a quarter.[17] In addition to Hohenegg, Girolamo Montecuccoli had left Raimondo property in Silesia, but Raimondo had faced resistance to his ownership by local estates.[18] The matter was supposedly resolved in 1652, when Emperor Ferdinand III agreed to pay Raimondo fifty thousand florins from the revenues of the empire to replace the property.[19] Montecuccoli pursued the money, attending the Diet of Regensburg in the summer of 1653 for that purpose, but it is unclear if he ever received it.[20] The Thirty Years' War had disrupted established mechanisms for tax collection because the imperial estates had been forced to pay imperial taxes directly to local commanders, who demanded additional contributions and gifts. From 1648 to 1654, Sweden, the elector of Bavaria, and Hessen-Kassel received money raised by the imperial circles for disbanding their armies, but Ferdinand III received little.[21]

During these precarious years, Montecuccoli found ways to be useful: he traveled to the Spanish Netherlands to study and catalogue fortifications and he finished a new treatise, *Military Tables* (*Tavole militari*).[22] This was the first treatise he explicitly dedicated to Emperor Ferdinand III, echoing Machiavelli when he asserted in the dedication that war was "the only art expected of monarchs, which gives and takes away crowns and which holds religion, the fatherland, and the king himself in its charge."[23] *Military Tables* is especially fascinating because it reveals the kind of information an experienced Thirty Years' War general focused on gathering and communicating at a critical juncture when he aspired to leap into a high court position. It shared many themes with *Treatise on War*, but the information was packaged differently. *Military Tables* was more concise and systematic, resembling a manual that an officer might consult while on campaign. At the same time, *Military Tables* placed significant emphasis on building a strong foundation of mathematical knowledge prior to entering a campaign. Montecuccoli devoted the entire first section, "Precognition" (*precognizione*), to explaining the basic principles of arithmetic, geometry, and trigonometry, followed by the other two military-themed sections, "Preparation" (*preparazione*) and "Execution" (*esecuzione*). Furthermore, *Military Tables* displayed knowledge and skills that were as relevant for diplomacy as for war, including the collection, organization, and analysis of complex information. In the dedication, Montecuccoli claimed that his intent was "to reduce methodically into brief terms the vast field of the discipline" of war.[24] His later diplomatic reports followed a similar method. These were composed of a series of sequentially numbered statements with sub-points that transmuted confusing or ambiguous political realities into clear, succinct pieces of information that moved in a logical direction.[25] *Military Tables* circulated in manuscript form and spread Montecuccoli's reputation as a learned general beyond Central Europe.[26] In 1654, he contributed to the Bolognese Jesuit Mario Bettini's book on mathematics.[27]

During the period he wrote *Military Tables*, Montecuccoli studied a polymathic array of subjects. From 1645 to 1653, he composed an 850-page *zibaldone*, or commonplace book, with notes in his own hand on politics, war, medicine, alchemy, and more.[28] In the preface, he listed sixty-nine sources. He had studied two works by Lipsius (*Politicorum libri sex* and *Monita, et exempla politica*), a 1550 edition of Machiavelli's complete works (*Historia, Principe, Discorsi, Arte della Guerra*, and minor works), and a 1645 compilation of Aristotle's political thought (*Politicae Succinctae ex Aristotele potissimum erutae, libri duo, auctore m. Balthasar Cellario*). Besides *Art of War*, other books of a more directly martial theme included Rohan's *The Perfect Captain*, as well as a handful of treatises on the topics of honor, dueling, and peaceful conflict resolution, such as Marc de Vulson de La Colombière's *Theatre d'honneur et de chevalerie* and Girolamo d'Urrea's *Dialogo del vero honore militare*. Approximately one-third of the books addressed natural philosophy, especially medicine and alchemy—two topics that may have been considered practical for a general concerned with his own health and the health of his soldiers. [**See Appendix A for list of books**] As he read, Montecuccoli focused on key concepts and examples from which to derive universal principles—encyclopedic knowledge considered necessary for the practice of politics.[29]

During this formative period in Montecuccoli's education and career, enormous political and conceptual shifts were taking place as powerful, expansive territorial states emerged the victors from decades of religious and civil unrest, and new epistemological imperatives, represented by the works of Bacon, Galileo, and Descartes, among many others, gained authority. The careers of military entrepreneurs and the customs at court in Vienna appeared to be "overturned," as did traditional ways of thinking and wielding power. The war may have been over, but no one knew if peace would last, while multiple political, religious, and epistemological paths for establishing order appeared, none quite fully mapped out. A cosmopolitan culture of rationality developed as philosophers turned to reason to resolve political and theological conflicts.[30] Montecuccoli's reading list, which included Aristotelian works alongside Andreas Libavius's *Alchemia*, Giambattista della Porta's *Magiae naturalis*, and books of secrets, indicates cross-pollination between diverse veins of knowledge as contemporaries contemplated the particular problems their societies faced at mid-century.

Montecuccoli seems to have relied especially on the controversial, polymathic Dominican preacher Tommaso Campanella (1568–1639). Campanella, who had defended Galileo and argued against an Aristotelian understanding of the universe, probably influenced Montecuccoli's methodological attention to sensory experience. In Campanella's view, the ancients had committed errors of understanding that needed remedying by focus on the study of things, rather than words. Campanella was also a political thinker.[31] While *City of the Sun*, a work that describes a utopian city in harmony with nature and God, is Campanella's best-known work today, his book outlining a program for a universal Christian monarchy under the aegis of the Spanish king, *Monarchy of Spain* (*Monarchia di Spagna*), was more widely read in the seventeenth century. Campanella's ideas were explicitly apocalyptic, conveying a sense that a total change was imminent—an urgency that may have helped his works regain currency, especially at mid-century, when Europe saw a rise in millenarian beliefs. *Monarchy of Spain* was conceived under the premise that the Spanish global empire represented the final days of the Fourth Monarchy and would usher in the millennium.[32]

Montecuccoli never openly expressed millenarian ideas: when he discussed religion in his treatises, he conveyed nondogmatic, philosophical views or treated religion as a tool to inspire zeal in soldiers (the latter was a Machiavellian strategy). In Montecuccoli's view of the world, religion integrated with governance played a stabilizing rather than destabilizing role. This attitude conformed to Lipsius's own understanding of the relationship between church and state and his fusion of Stoicism and Christianity as an antidote to the inflamed religious passions that led to rebellion and war in his lifetime.[33] The political ideology of the Spanish and Austrian Habsburgs had long promoted the dynasty as the heirs to Rome, the universal rulers vested by God with the responsibility to unite the world in peace in accordance with divine plans. While this idea took on great resonance during the near-universal reign of Charles V and the growth of the Spanish Empire in the Americas, the Habsburgs and their followers continued to assert this role for Habsburg monarchs into the seventeenth century.[34] It is safe to assume that Montecuccoli perceived the Habsburgs as playing a divine role connected to the providential ordering of history in which the Last Days would eventually appear.

Montecuccoli soon found himself engaging in the post-Westphalian political moment in a new way. In the summer of 1653, he complained to his brother Massimiliano about how long it took to manage his personal affairs, explaining that he planned to ask Ferdinand III for leave in order to relocate to the Italian peninsula.[35] Just as Montecuccoli contemplated a permanent return to Italy, Ferdinand III enticed him to stay in imperial service by offering a new office—imperial diplomat—and sending him to the far northern court of the Swedish opponent against whom Montecuccoli had conducted grueling military campaigns.

Queen Christina and Her Court

When Montecuccoli arrived in Uppsala in early January 1654, Christina was on the verge of committing a spectacular act. Montecuccoli's instructions had charged him with confirming trade agreements between Sweden and Austria and exploring in secret the possibility of a marriage alliance between Christina and Emperor Ferdinand III's son, Crown Prince Ferdinand.[36] However, he soon found that Christina had other interests and plans. In June 1654, she officially abdicated the Swedish throne in favor of her cousin, Charles X. Montecuccoli was in Uppsala in the months leading up to this public act. During this period, Christina wooed him by inviting him to exclusive dances and inducting him into her mystical knightly order, the Order of the Amaranthe.[37]

In spring, Montecuccoli explained Christina's stated reasons for abdication to his correspondents and displayed open admiration for the queen. In two separate letters, he reported to Ferdinand III and Mattias de' Medici that "one may attribute [the abdication] to her transcendent spirit and to her superhuman soul, which, surpassing the sense of man and common understanding, is superior to the ordinary things of the world." Montecuccoli told Francesco I d'Este that Christina was "a miracle of Nature," and surmised about her decision to abdicate that "the great virtues shine in grand actions."[38] It appears that Christina had successfully groomed Montecuccoli—formerly a leading general of an enemy army—to serve as her own communication agent.

After abdication, Christina moved to the Habsburg-controlled Spanish Netherlands and took up residence in Antwerp. In December 1654, Christina—Gustavus Adolphus's Lutheran daughter—secretly converted to Catholicism, an event Montecuccoli witnessed, along with just five others.[39] Christina requested Montecuccoli's presence: "Having confided her thoughts in me and not wanting to reveal them to others," he wrote, "she desires that, when she writes to me, I come; and that I would be most certain of her protection and her favor on every occasion."[40] Christina became a patron to Montecuccoli, writing letters of recommendation for him, including one that she sent to Ferdinand III.[41] Christina remained in the Spanish Netherlands for a year before relocating to Rome in the autumn of 1655. Montecuccoli traveled frequently in these years, serving as an imperial diplomat at Christina's side on four missions. He visited Archduke Leopold Wilhelm in Brussels, reported to Ferdinand III in Vienna, attended the Diet of Hungary, and ultimately escorted Christina to Rome to make her grand entrance as one of the most celebrated Catholic converts of the century.

Although he appeared at times to serve Christina, Montecuccoli remained committed to his imperial patrons, Ferdinand III and Leopold Wilhelm. The Habsburgs, who were unsure how seriously to take Christina, hoped the former queen would provide Montecuccoli with intelligence on Sweden's military efforts. They also wanted her to use her perceived influence over the imperial electors in Habsburg favor. Ferdinand III's son, Ferdinand IV, had been elected king of the Romans—the successor to the emperor—but had died suddenly in July 1654. With France interfering to support a non-Habsburg candidate, the Habsburgs needed support among the imperial electors for another son, Leopold I, to succeed to the throne.[42]

Montecuccoli also sought his own benefit during these trips. When he was in Antwerp, he repeatedly visited Brussels, where Leopold Wilhelm presided as ruler of the Spanish Netherlands. Montecuccoli listened to the archduke's complaints about the "incompetence" of the officers in the Army of Flanders and other dire pronouncements.[43] Leopold Wilhelm feared that he would lose the Low Countries, along with his reputation.[44] Montecuccoli conveyed these

FIGURE 4.1. David Teniers the Younger, *Archduke Leopold Wilhelm in His Picture Gallery in Brussels*. The Erich Lessing/Art Resource, New York.

messages to Vienna, including the archduke's desire to end his governorship.[45] Leopold Wilhelm's connection to Montecuccoli involved more than shared campaign experiences: the archduke wrote Italian poetry, patronized Italian musicians, and founded an Italian literary academy in Brussels that Montecuccoli most likely attended.[46] Leopold Wilhelm held one of his audiences with Montecuccoli in his impressive picture gallery famously depicted by David Teniers the Younger.[47] [**Fig. 4.1**] In-between meetings with Leopold Wilhelm and Christina, Montecuccoli made strategic use of free time by paying and receiving visits or touring cities, fortifications, churches, and libraries. He obtained permission from Christina and Leopold Wilhelm to visit London, where he had an audience with Oliver Cromwell.[48] Montecuccoli's compulsion to write as he traveled reflected his military studiousness, as well as a probable desire for "useful cosmopolitanism": knowledge of the world developed through foreign study and ultimately employed in service to a prince.[49]

Throughout his travels, Montecuccoli interacted with a range of other elite actors. He studied court life much as he studied war, in one case diagramming where important individuals sat at the dinner table.[50] The military practice of

critically assessing one's surroundings, as well as the ability to deceive and recognize deception on the battlefield, were useful at court.[51] In Uppsala, Montecuccoli met with English, French, Spanish, and Danish diplomats, as well as
Swedish generals he had once faced off against on campaign. Christina herself was an avid reader with an interest in natural philosophy. Descartes had
stayed at her court and tutored her from October 1649 until his death from
pneumonia in February 1650.[52] To manage and further expand her manuscript
collections, Christina hired foreign scholars such as Isaac Vossius and Nicolas
Heinsius, both of whom traveled extensively for the queen, collaborating with
Lucas Holstenius in Rome and Gabriel Naudé in Paris. Naudé, who was Mazarin's librarian, fled to Christina's court during the Fronde.[53] Montecuccoli
seemed intrigued by Christina's personality and intellect, noting that "the discourses of the Queen are very quick-witted, jesting, and for the most part af-
fectionate . . . she jokes in various ways about religion."[54] Christina was an
unconventional woman and surrounded herself with a fascinating mixture of
diplomats, generals, philosophers, librarians, musicians, and artists.

The cosmopolitanism of the Spanish Netherlands involved different kinds
of interactions than Montecuccoli would have experienced in Modena, Vienna,
or Uppsala. The Spanish Netherlands were part of the Holy Roman Empire but
governed by Austrian archdukes who could receive their own diplomatic representatives from sovereign states. Montecuccoli spent time with the Spanish diplomat Antonio Pimentel and officers in the Spanish Army of Flanders, including
his cousin Andrea and members of other Italian families. Complaints about the
poor state of the army were rife: one group of officers expressed a desire to
leave the Army of Flanders and transfer to imperial service. They viewed Montecuccoli as a potential patron.[55] Due to its unique status and location at an
important crossroads (surrounded by England, France, and the Dutch Republic), the region also became a magnet for political figures seeking informal negotiations.[56] Montecuccoli met rebels such as Condé and exiles including the
former Danish governor of Norway, Hannibal Sehested. He had conversations
with a cabbalist and with an author who wrote a book on the preadamites
(men who had lived before Adam), which Montecuccoli noted was "full of the
most curious questions."[57]

As a freshly abdicated, converted queen, Christina was only the most prominent example of the "liminal personae" on display in the Spanish Netherlands: figures whom the cultural anthropologist Victor Turner might describe
as "betwixt and between the positions assigned and arrayed by law, custom,
convention, and ceremonial."[58] Although he was not as radical as Christina or
a preadamite thinker, Montecuccoli appeared to be relatively open. His studies of military science, theology, alchemy, and other topics had undoubtedly

prepared him to have conversations and develop affinities. He also observed how the intriguing figures he encountered in Antwerp were drawn into Christina's curious post-abdication designs. Christina told Montecuccoli that she intended to mediate a peace between France and Spain and, at the same time, hoped to create "the union of the Spanish, Italian, and French people under her against the Turk."[59] The pursuit of Christian peace and the slaying of non-Christians (the minions of the Antichrist) were necessary steps toward inaugurating the millennium.[60] Christina was familiar with millenarian ideas: her father had been the subject of intense millenarian speculation. Christina also owned copies of Campanella.[61]

Whether one takes Christina seriously as a millenarian political actor or not (nothing ever came of these plans), the conversations Montecuccoli witnessed in Antwerp reveal an unsettled political climate in which millenarian concepts were occasionally floated as contemporaries sought out common ground in order to imagine a new world order. After abdicating, Christina consciously chose to form a relationship to the Habsburg dynasty by moving to the Spanish Netherlands. She sought her own position in a distinctively Habsburg universe, even baselessly claiming Philip IV would place her in command of the Spanish Netherlands or Naples. She made Montecuccoli a part of these plans by choosing him to represent her wishes to the imperial court. She changed her mind frequently, however: she moved to Rome and later turned against the Habsburgs, relocating to France.

Throughout these years, war always intrigued Christina. After she had given up on the idea of mediating a peace, she warned Montecuccoli that Sweden would break its truce with Poland and start a war. She claimed if a new religious war started, she "would not be opposed to placing herself at the head of an army, to selling her property in order to raise troops, and employing her own credit in order to destroy the enemy army."[62] In this statement, Christina suggested that she would become a military entrepreneur herself, using her own wealth and credit to raise an army. She asked Montecuccoli to produce an estimate of the costs and needs for an army of six thousand infantry and two thousand cavalry and to show these plans to Leopold Wilhelm and the Spanish general Fuenseldaña.[63] This episode reminds us that courts would have been full of conversations about the possibilities of imminent warfare. Military entrepreneurs, who could quickly evaluate military plans and help put together armies at short notice, were useful figures to have around. Their skills were so relevant, in fact, that Christina even desired to emulate them herself.

Despite their skepticism about Christina, the Habsburgs—both the Spanish and the Austrian—took her seriously enough to assign diplomats to her court. In the very least, they would have seen Christina's court as a hub of information at a time when they strained to understand what was happening at various locations across Europe, aware of the military vulnerabilities created by poor communications. For her part, Christina found Montecuccoli useful as a conduit of information. She seemed to think Montecuccoli, an imperial diplomat, would represent her demands when he returned to Vienna to report to Ferdinand III, becoming her own agent while continuing in his official role as imperial diplomat. Montecuccoli continued to see Ferdinand III as his most important patron: when he completed his tasks and had no further orders, he told Christina he was leaving Antwerp to return to Vienna. Nonetheless, he appeared to satisfy most of Christina's demands and requested special favors from her. After her conversion, Montecuccoli had asked Christina if she could help him win an appointment as a cardinal, a request to which she had readily agreed. Montecuccoli received the offer of a cardinal's hat from Alexander VII but declined.[64] Montecuccoli had been a monk as a young man, just like his brother Massimiliano, but had abandoned the tonsure to become a soldier. Ironically, it was his imperial military career that provided a path to the cardinalate—a testament to the truly cosmopolitan dimensions of Habsburg Europe, where one might transform from soldier to scholar to diplomat to cardinal as one followed the circuit between battlefields and courts.

After attending the Diet of Hungary, Ferdinand dispatched Montecuccoli to join Christina on her journey to Rome. Christina sent Montecuccoli ahead of her in order to meet with Pope Alexander VII and offer her compliments to him before arriving incognito herself.[65] Urgent requests from the Viennese court, however, forced Montecuccoli to cut his trip short: Ferdinand III was preparing a military intervention in Poland to help curb Swedish aggressions.[66] Finally, in what could have been a disastrous turn of events for Montecuccoli, Ferdinand III was threatening to send troops against Montecuccoli's natural lord, Francesco I d'Este, who had allied with the French against the Spanish again.[67] Montecuccoli may have been worried about how any delay in the Italian peninsula would have been interpreted in Vienna.

Montecuccoli continued his advancement in Vienna in the late 1650s, especially after Archduke Leopold Wilhelm was recalled from the Spanish Netherlands in 1656. In 1657, Leopold Wilhelm invited Montecuccoli to join an exclusive Italian academy in Vienna whose members included Emperor Ferdinand III and the Gonzaga empress Eleonora (II). The academy was modeled on the archduke's Brussels academy.[68] After Ferdinand III died in the spring of 1657, Leopold I was finally elected emperor in 1658.[69] Leopold Wilhelm, who was Leopold I's uncle, became his nephew's most trusted advisor. Montecuccoli took command as field marshal of the auxiliary forces sent to assist Poland in the Second Northern War.[70]

Just prior to his return to battle, Montecuccoli, forty-eight years old, got married. His bride, the eighteen-year-old Margarethe von Dietrichstein, was Empress Eleonora's lady-in-waiting.[71] The alliance to the Dietrichstein family proved to be both politically important—in later years Montecuccoli was part of a powerful court faction with his brother-in-law—and provided additional financial security.[72] Margarethe's dowry was worth twenty-five thousand florins, while Emperor Ferdinand III celebrated the wedding by promising to alleviate Montecuccoli's debts.[73] Montecuccoli had continued to struggle to pay his debts, especially when Ferdinand III provided only partial reimbursements of his military costs. With Leopold Wilhelm, Eleonora Gonzaga, and the Dietrichstein family as allies, Montecuccoli could use political power to manage debt. Similarly, in Brussels, Leopold Wilhelm had helped Montecuccoli settle debts with a merchant in Passau.[74] Montecuccoli had missed the windfalls of the 1620s, but his successes at court offered important benefits.

Montecuccoli's marriage to Margarethe was a transformative event that spurred him to compose a brief autobiographical account of his life, culminating in his marriage.[75] He had studied the topic of wives and marriage in his *zibaldone*, taking notes from Cardano on how "the wife provides the foundation for the whole household, and for the nature and inclination of the children." Montecuccoli absorbed Campanella's instructions on matrimony, which Campanella claimed in his *Oeconomia* was instituted by God. Montecuccoli wrote: "To have virtuous children one must take a wife who is excellent in mind and body."[76] He may have remembered his own mother's adept management of the household after his father's death, noting in his autobiography that he had seen his mother for the last time in 1633 (she died in 1638). Montecuccoli and Margarethe had four children: three daughters and a son, Leopold Philip. Montecuccoli admired his much younger wife, depicting her in an elegy after her 1677 death as a prudent, loving mother who "understood the matters of the world with a clear light."[77] When Montecuccoli departed for the Northern War in the summer of 1657, Margarethe accompanied him. Montecuccoli's marriage into the Dietrichstein family marked his passage into a new, more entrenched phase of his imperial career.

Leopold I, aware that Montecuccoli had served both his father and grandfather faithfully and was a favorite of his uncle's, trusted Montecuccoli. In 1666—less than a decade after Montecuccoli's marriage and participation in the Northern War—Leopold presented him with another important diplomatic mission. The emperor had married the Spanish infanta, Margarita Teresa, in absentia, renewing the traditional Spanish-Austrian alliance. When Margarita Teresa traveled to join Leopold in Vienna, he asked Montecuccoli to meet his bride and her retinue at the northern Italian port of Finale in order to greet her on Leopold's behalf and to help arrange her transfer to Austrian custody. This second major diplomatic assignment of an essentially non-military nature put Montecuccoli back on familiar ground in the contentious politics of the northern Italian peninsula.

Finale

The marriage between Leopold I and Margarita Teresa occurred less than two decades after the Peace of Westphalia (1648) and just seven years after the Peace of the Pyrenees (1659), which concluded the longer war between Spain and France. In the years leading up to this marriage alliance, the uneasy climate that had characterized the period of Montecuccoli's missions to Queen Christina erupted into one of multiple large-scale conflicts. The dynasties that had emerged successfully from the Thirty Years' War initiated an interminable series of wars to defend and expand their borders. Sweden remained a threat to the Habsburgs and did indeed invade Poland as Christina predicted, triggering the Second Northern War. By the mid-1660s, new structural problems, especially Austria's ongoing vulnerabilities—to France on one frontier and the Ottoman Empire on another—had become even more evident. These problems led some, including Lobkowitz, who now served as Leopold's high steward (or chief minister) (*Obersthofmeister*), to propose a major policy realignment to appease the French. Montecuccoli opposed this policy shift, arguing that Louis XIV was untrustworthy and power hungry. During the final two decades of his life, Montecuccoli advocated military reforms to meet the demands of two-front warfare.

At the end of April 1663, in the midst of these rapidly developing tensions, the Viennese court celebrated the declaration of Leopold I's marriage to Margarita Teresa, a bride who was Leopold's cousin and niece. Philip IV's court artist, Diego Velázquez, had painted portraits of the golden-haired princess to send to Vienna so that Leopold could remain apprised of his bride's development. She is most famously depicted as the central subject of Velázquez's masterpiece, *Las Meninas*, preened upon by servants while her parents, tiny figures reflected in a mirror on the wall behind her, look on.

The festivities celebrating the union lasted for days. Montecuccoli drew a diagram of the procession he took part in, with Leopold I "at the head, along with 22 or 23 knights," snaking through the Favorita palace.[78] The 1663 celebration involved key military leaders who might otherwise be preparing Habsburg defenses: rumors circulated that the Ottomans were already approaching the frontier with an enormous army. They formally declared war on the Habsburgs in June 1663. In August 1664, Montecuccoli led the largest contingent of troops in an unexpected defeat of the Ottoman army at the Battle of St. Gotthard (Mogersdorf). For the purpose of analysis, this section focuses on the politics of the Spanish-Austrian alliance in the Italian peninsula in the 1660s, while the next chapter analyzes the Austrian confrontation with the Ottomans, including the Battle of St. Gotthard (Mogersdorf). Needless to say, contemporaries experienced these events in rapid succession.

Montecuccoli and other observers knew that profound anxiety lurked beneath the optimism of the marriage celebration between Leopold I and Margarita Teresa. In addition to the Ottoman threat, members of the Viennese court worried about the recent political maneuvers of Louis XIV. The Austrian emperor had hoped to marry Margarita Teresa's older sister, but Louis XIV secured Maria Teresa's hand in marriage as part of the Peace of the Pyrenees. Although Maria Teresa renounced her claim to the Spanish throne, the French had stipulated that this renunciation would only take effect if the Spanish paid out her full dowry, which was a financial impossibility. In this way, Louis XIV's chief negotiator, Mazarin, had carefully positioned the French king to make a claim for the inheritance of the entire global Spanish empire.[79] To make matters worse, Louis XIV and Maria Teresa had their first son in 1661. As Leopold I waited for his bride, the future of his house became increasingly dire. From 1662 to 1665, four Habsburg males on the Austrian side died. Leopold I became the head of the family after Philip IV's death and needed to produce heirs quickly to compete with Louis XIV's progeny. The young Spanish king who had succeeded Philip IV, Charles II, suffered from ill health and was not expected to live long.[80] The sooner Margarita Teresa arrived in Vienna, the better.

Mazarin's moves regarding Louis XIV's marriage to the Spanish infanta followed other concerted efforts to break up Habsburg power and divide the Spanish from the Austrians, including the exclusion of the Spanish-French conflict from the Westphalia negotiations in 1648. It foreshadowed Leopold I's secret treaties with the French regarding Austrian neutrality in the War of Devolution (1667–68), when France occupied Spanish territories in the Netherlands and Franche-Comté. The Austrian-Spanish alliance would disintegrate completely when the death of the Spanish king Charles II terminated the Spanish Habsburg line in 1700, leading to the War of the Spanish Succession (1701–14). Considering the ultimate extinction of the Spanish Habsburg dynasty, many of the political and military events of the seventeenth century have often been seen as the prelude to disaster, with Spain entering into irreversible decline. And yet the outcome of the War of the Spanish Succession was not a decisive victory for France: Austria established its hold over key parts of the former Spanish empire in Europe, including much of the Spanish Netherlands and Italian peninsula. Understanding the backdrop to this geopolitical shift requires that we take a closer look at the impressively long endurance of imperial allegiances and institutions within the Italian peninsula, as well as ongoing relationships of mutual dependence between the Habsburgs and Italian aristocratic families. The fact that the Spanish and Austrians chose northern Italy as the location for the transfer of Leopold's Spanish bride is a testament to the role this part of the world continued to play as a critical seam in the fabric of Catholic Habsburg relations.

Montecuccoli's perspective at Finale also helps to humanize an event otherwise interpreted in broad geopolitical terms as the calculated renewal of the centuries-old Spanish-Austrian alliance. By closely studying his journal, we can walk alongside him as he greeted the figures who witnessed the arrival of the bride and took part in escorting her, considering what this marriage alliance meant to them at this particular moment. Montecuccoli was in high demand everywhere he went, remarking that he received "a continuous stream of knights and gentlemen, ministers and other lords who come to see me."[81] Many of these figures appeared to belong to a northern Italian imperial network characterized by the ownership of imperial fiefs and service in the imperial army. They included the former imperial officers Fabio Visconti and Vitaliano Borromeo in Milan. In Genoa he met frequently with Giovanni Agostino Durazzo, a friend of Walter Leslie's, and with Prince and Princess Doria, who possessed an imperial fief, Louano, which Montecuccoli later visited.[82] Montecuccoli interacted with members of the Spinola family, including one "who holds imperial fiefs" and whose brother was an abbot in Vienna. Despite their imperial ties and ostensible support of the Habsburg dynasty, the relationships of Italian nobles to the Habsburgs and to one another were often contentious as they competed for status.[83] These problems were only exacerbated by Margarita Teresa's long delay in arriving due to illness and poor weather.

Among those stuck waiting was Mattias de' Medici, whose secretary, Felice Marchetti, left a detailed account of the interactions at Finale in a series of letters written to Florence (Figure 4.2). Montecuccoli's and Marchetti's accounts of Finale both focus on one particularly thorny issue that threatened to derail Margarita Teresa's transfer to Austrian custody: ceremony. Strict adherence to established ceremonies affirmed political and social hierarchies, allowing for social cohesion and the expression of relationships among nobles and rulers. In an ideal sense, the hierarchy in which nobles operated was static, attesting to divinely ordained order and the dignity of the ruler. In reality, ceremony abounded in uncertainty because power relationships continuously shifted, while no one knew which types of criteria (for example, lineage, type

FIGURE 4.2.   Studio of Justus Sustermans, *Mattias de' Medici, c. 1660.* The National Gallery of Art, Washington, DC. This portrait shows an enslaved person of African descent with a chain around his neck at Mattias's side.

of office, or seniority in office) carried the most weight.[84] These problems grew worse when groups of foreign nobles met, since they often found that they did not have an objective way to compare status.[85] The nobles who accompanied Margarita Teresa were from some of the most prestigious families in Europe. On the Spanish side, they included the Duke of Albuquerque, Francisco Fernández de la Cueva (1619–76) (viceroy of New Spain and Sicily), and the Italian cardinal Girolamo Colonna (1604–66); on the Austrian side, Cardinal

Ernst Adalbert von Harrach and Montecuccoli's brother-in-law, Ferdinand Joseph, prince of Dietrichstein. Any ceremonial problem could paralyze the political process as it not only jeopardized communication but might even prevent political actors from meeting. For instance, Montecuccoli reported that the Duke of Albuquerque refused to ride in the same carriage as Cardinal Colonna because he did not want to sit at anyone's left hand.[86]

The general ceremonial question animating Margarita Teresa's arrival was whether to follow Spanish or Austrian customs. The choice mattered because some Italian noblemen held a higher ceremonial status under the Austrian Habsburg emperor than under the Spanish king. There was no obvious solution: Margarita Teresa's status was ambiguous because, as she traveled through northern Italy, she was in transition from Spanish princess to Austrian empress. Finale was under Spanish authority, but as Margarita Teresa had already been married to Leopold I in absentia, some contemporaries considered her an empress. Margarita Teresa became another liminal figure as she moved from one dynastic hierarchy to another, altering surrounding relationships in the process. Some nobles arrived at Finale prepared to use this transitional moment in the Spanish-Austrian alliance to renegotiate their own positions vis-à-vis the Habsburgs and one another.[87] Above all, they knew that if they could persuade Margarita Teresa to use Austrian ceremonial, they could argue for an elevation of status under Spanish ceremonial based on the precedent set at Finale.

Mattias de' Medici complained vehemently of his treatment by the Spanish, who refused to use the title "highness" (altezza) with him.[88] Marchetti argued that if the new empress did not use highness, she would be in violation of precedent, since Mattias had received this treatment from three other empresses in the past.[89] The Genoese were frustrated by the same incongruity: the Marquis d'Arquati lamented that Genoa "has not asked for anything more than what she has obtained from the Emperor, that is, the title of Most Serene (Serenissima)" and blamed "the bad affection of the ruling ministers."[90] When he spoke to Spinola about the issue during a stopover in Genoa on his way to Finale, Montecuccoli learned that the Genoese had requested the title in order to mirror changes that had taken place in the ceremony Spain used with other Italian territories. However, Spinola complained that rather than reform their ceremony, the Spanish "have immediately broken (with us), not wanting to lend an ear to the treaty."[91]

When Mattias and the Genoese nobles sought help from Montecuccoli to support their claims for higher status from the Spanish, they exposed contemporary assumptions about the conferral of honorifics. Rather than view shifts in status as an exclusively top-down procedure that started with the monarch, they understood these customs as shaped both by the ways monarchs participated in them and by informal discussions among nobles at different ceremonial meeting points across Europe. Mattias and the Genoese nobles perceived that Montecuccoli was on good terms with the Spanish governor of Milan, Ponce de Leon: according to Marchetti, Montecuccoli and Ponce de Leon shared "every major confidence, often finding themselves together familiarly, and the Lord Montecuccoli dining nearly every morning with Luigi."[92] Mattias considered Montecuccoli both a client and a friend: they had maintained a regular correspondence in the decades after Mattias left the imperial army, with Montecuccoli reporting extensively on military and diplomatic events, as well as sharing personal details such as his wife's miscarriages.[93] Mattias had invested time and energy in building a reputation in Central Europe. In addition to cultivating a vast correspondence network, Mattias organized the performance of the Italian singer Atto Melani at the 1653 Diet of Regensburg with Montecuccoli's help. Melani reported back that German nobles at the diet made "lively commemorations" of Mattias "with a glass in hand."[94] Mattias's actions at Finale show that he did not merely depend upon his own illustrious family name and blood relationship to the Habsburgs. He attempted to deploy social capital accrued in the imperial army and among Central European elites in competitions for status within the Italian peninsula.

Leopold I had anticipated ceremonial difficulties and chose Montecuccoli to solve them. On the one hand, Montecuccoli had a highly visible, symbolic duty to greet the bride publicly on behalf of the emperor, a duty grounded in his military reputation as the victor at St. Gotthard (Mogersdorf). On the other hand, Leopold I appreciated Montecuccoli for far more than his alleged battlefield heroics. In his instructions, Leopold I mentioned a "special, most gracious confidence" that he held toward Montecuccoli, praising his "excellent qualities" and record of "most submissive loyalty, enthusiasm, and devotion."[95] Leopold I also noted Montecuccoli's "great dexterity, discretion, and very good conduct."[96] These were the qualities that allowed Montecuccoli to function as a "go-between" in a tense, ambiguous moment of political transition.[97]

Montecuccoli's secret instructions from Leopold I regarding ceremonial questions further reveal why these qualities mattered. Leopold I made clear that he was willing to defer to the Spanish regarding ceremonial. He asserted to Montecuccoli that "as long as Your Highness finds himself in the Spanish lands, then also the same treatment of their lands should continue." Leopold also believed that as long as Margarita Teresa belonged to a Spanish retinue, Spanish customs should prevail.[98] Nonetheless, he instructed Montecuccoli to dissemble by telling the Spaniards that he had no specific instructions. The emperor emphasized that Montecuccoli show "special confidence" toward both Ponce de Leon and the Duke of Albuquerque, and seek out their assistance on the matter.[99] Leopold I wanted Montecuccoli to ask both officials for advice about which style of dress to wear—the Spanish or the Austrian—but stated that Montecuccoli should do so "in his name and for himself alone," implying that this should appear as a personal question and not as a question from the emperor.[100]

Montecuccoli proved adept at behind-the-scenes political maneuver, relying upon a personal status that was flexible and at times nearly invisible. He often operated "incognito," relinquishing his official status as the representative of the emperor in order to avoid the strictures of ceremony. He did so when he met Ponce de Leon and was greeted at a "secret door" for precisely this purpose.[101] Following Leopold's instructions, Montecuccoli approached Ponce de Leon in Milan about the question of dress. Montecuccoli wrote that "I showed him gestures of confidence and I asked him for his advice as to how I should appear in court, whether in black or in colored dress."[102] At the same time, Leopold expected Montecuccoli to prevent conflict between the most eminent nobles involved in escorting Margarita Teresa. Most critically, the Duke of Albuquerque and Cardinal Colonna had to relinquish their official functions and the public honors associated with them so that Dietrichstein and Harrach could assume those functions and honors during the next stage of the trip.[103] Montecuccoli learned that the Duke of Albuquerque, who had been sick, planned to turn back to Spain after the transfer, but Cardinal Colonna intended to continue. Montecuccoli turned for help to a friend, Visconti, who was the head of Ponce de Leon's personal guard and who assured Montecuccoli that he would convince Colonna to leave Margarita Teresa at Trent.[104] Although less glorious than defeating the Ottomans, Montecuccoli's behind-the-scenes political work was critical for ensuring the smooth transfer of the imperial bride and for creating a veneer of cooperation among the often-incompatible elites allied to the Habsburgs.

Although Montecuccoli knew that his primary patron, Leopold I, preferred the use of Spanish ceremonial at Finale, he nonetheless took up his Tuscan friend's cause as Margarita Teresa's arrival neared. He met with Spanish officials, asserting that he had witnessed Mattias de' Medici being treated "on equal footing with the Electors of the Empire and that in the Imperial Court held prerogatives above the others."[105] Despite these efforts, the Spanish refused to budge. They feared that altering ceremonial for Mattias opened the doors to other nobles making the same claims.[106] Their fears were at least partially legitimate: the seventeenth century witnessed an inflation of noble titles. Mattias was ultimately disappointed by the treatment he received from the Spanish grandees.[107]

Montecuccoli's own opinion about Spanish titles was clear in a separate report that he wrote after the trip, titled "On the negotiations with the Republic

of Genoa regarding the ceremonies on the occasion of the passage of the imperial bride." He explained that the Spanish had claimed that ceremony must
remain "always the same" and that they would follow the example set by the
1630 arrival of Queen Maria Anna. Montecuccoli argued that the desire to keep
ceremony the same could only reasonably apply to domestic concerns and that
many modifications to ceremony had been made for "foreign royal persons."
Accordingly, the etiquette had been "modernized" in regard to Venice, Savoy,
Mantua, Modena, Parma, and Lucca. Moreover, he cited the example of the
pope, who, desiring to establish a "princely estate of the cloth," had awarded
the title of "eminence" to the cardinals, which was recognized and respected
by all. Montecuccoli referred to the "spirit of the times" as a reason for the
Spanish to adjust their ceremony with the Genoese.[108]

Montecuccoli advocated a system of titles that would work effectively across
regions, making the Spanish and Austrian Habsburg worlds more intelligible.
He conveyed a vision of nobility with truly international dimensions. Montecuccoli also spoke of the need for Madrid and Vienna to be closely connected.[109]
And yet the Spanish court appears to have been less flexible than the Austrian
court, and, as the discrepancies concerning ceremony revealed, the ideal of a
pan-Habsburg nobility was in some ways out of touch with reality. The dis-
junction between ideals and political realities was long-standing. In 1630, Olivares had insisted that "not for anything must these two houses let themselves
be divided," but in the same year the Mantuan War showed that Spanish and
Central European political priorities diverged.[110] Olivares's dictum was bla-
tantly ignored when Emperor Ferdinand III agreed to a separate peace excluding Spain at Westphalia in 1648, when Louis XIV married Maria Teresa a
decade later, and when Leopold I signed secret treaties with Louis XIV.

Nonetheless, the determination with which Genoese officials and Mattias
de' Medici pursued recognition by the Spanish court and their aspirations to
be part of a grandiose, utopian Habsburg world order indicates the lasting
power of the vision and the political benefits Habsburg honors conferred. Italian noblemen at Finale still believed that being part of the Habsburg political
universe mattered.

An international noble estate had already been forming around the emperor in
Vienna as he awarded the native and non-native noblemen who served him. The
Order of the Golden Fleece provided an ideal example of the type of award that
could be used to shape a truly pan-Habsburg nobility. In these years, Montecuccoli fought hard for admission into the order, finally receiving induction in
1668—a topic analyzed in chapter 5.[111] At the same time, Montecuccoli called
for reform in order to create a more rational hierarchy for an evolving Habsburg

world. While later nationalistic historians would view the second half of the seventeenth century as witnessing the last gasp of an antiquated Catholic dynastic order under the Habsburgs, military entrepreneurs like Montecuccoli saw things differently. Out of the destruction of the Thirty Years' War and the uncertainty that followed as peace took hold, he saw a new Habsburg Europe taking shape based upon confessional allegiance, military power, scientific knowledge, and a web of formal and informal relationships between the Habsburg dynasty and aristocratic families from the Italian peninsula to the Spanish Netherlands.

Montecuccoli became an effective diplomat because of the relative ease with which he was able to communicate with a range of political actors for whom ties to the Habsburgs—both the Spanish and Austrian—continued to shape status. His success depended not only on his military abilities, but also on his polymathic studies and mastery of the language and symbolism of the courts. Furthermore, he displayed an important willingness to sacrifice public ceremonial status in order to engage in countless invisible acts of negotiation. He traveled through the liminal zones of Habsburg influence—places such as Antwerp and Finale—and negotiated ambiguous matters that the scions of native magnate families like Dietrichstein, Harrach, or Condé may have resisted engaging in precisely because rank was not clearly defined. Military entrepreneurs at the vanguard of Counter-Reformation efforts to crush Protestant resistance in the seventeenth century are not often associated with cosmopolitanism—a concept usually identified with religious toleration, among other attributes.[112] Nonetheless, Montecuccoli's openness to relationships and ideas is a testament to a certain kind of bounded Catholic cosmopolitanism shared by an aspiring middle elite in Habsburg Europe.[113]

Finally, just because Montecuccoli was willing to sacrifice his official ceremonial status to conduct negotiations does not mean he was unconcerned about his own status and reputation. Montecuccoli continuously pushed for his own advancement even while viewing obedience as a central part of his service to the Habsburgs and critical to his reputation. His cautious behavior and willingness to subordinate personal glory to a greater good defined by the Habsburg dynasty also manifested on the battlefield. During the 1661–64 campaigns against the Ottomans, Montecuccoli produced sharp arguments about service to the Habsburgs based on his military experiences on the Hungarian frontier that later became essential components of his mature science of war.

CHAPTER 5

A Loyal Servant

During the 1660s, Montecuccoli reached the most powerful phase of his imperial military career. In the years surrounding his diplomatic mission to Finale (1666), he was appointed to the highest rank in the army, lieutenant general (1664), became president of the Aulic War Council (1668), and was inducted into the prestigious Order of the Golden Fleece (1668). He worried about the rising power of Louis XIV's France in the west but was immediately preoccupied with the renewed aggressions of the Ottoman Empire in Eastern Europe. When the Ottoman tributary György II Rákóczi, the prince of Transylvania, invaded Poland during the Second Northern War (1655–60), the Ottomans had responded by invading Transylvania, killing their upstart vassal in 1660. The Habsburgs, fearful of the Ottomans again after decades of relative peace, had attempted to help Rákóczi and his successor, János Kemény, without starting a war. Leopold I sent fifteen thousand troops to Transylvania under Montecuccoli. However, this move provoked the Ottomans, who formally declared war on the Habsburgs in the spring of 1663. Montecuccoli was involved in the defense of the hereditary lands, including when he led Habsburg troops in a surprising victory over the Ottomans at the 1664 Battle of St. Gotthard (Mogersdorf), which prevented a massive invasion. The 1661–64 campaigning on the Hungarian frontier was the next major phase of warfare after the Thirty Years' War that tested Habsburg hegemony and required the support of an international aristocracy.

During the 1660s, Montecuccoli produced formal and informal writings in which he explained events on the eastern frontier and defended his actions in the face of criticisms. These works are all critical for understanding the development of his military thought. The most comprehensive treatise produced in these years was the brief *Discourse on the War against the Turks* (*Discorso della guerra contro il Turco*, 1664), which was essentially a first draft of his magnum opus, *On the War against the Turks in Hungary* (*Della guerra col Turco in Ungheria*, 1670). *Discourse* and other, shorter writings show how a military noble whose career developed out of the Thirty Years' War applied what he understood about war to the circumstances of Eastern Europe in the 1660s. These writings are especially interesting because they were the product of an active period of warfare, completed during pauses in the fighting. While the next chapter focuses on the outcome of Montecuccoli's military science, this chapter contextualizes the development of knowledge of warfare within the turbulent politics and campaign realities of the 1660s. In these years, Montecuccoli became a propagandist in order to influence perceptions of military events among a wider court elite. His writings indicate that he fought powerful threats to his reputation that emerged in contests with native magnates as well as from the extremely challenging conditions of warfare.

Montecuccoli's main rival in the 1660s was the Croatian-Hungarian magnate Miklós Zrínyi (Nikola Zrinski), who blamed Montecuccoli for military losses leading up to St. Gotthard (Mogersdorf) (Figure 5.1). Zrínyi derisively painted Montecuccoli as a "cunctator" or "delayer" who hesitated in confronting the enemy, referring to the third-century BCE Roman general Quintus Fabius Maximus Verrucosus, who had employed a strategy of attrition against Hannibal's invading Carthaginian force. Zrínyi was a brilliant general whose family had played a leading role in frontier defense for more than a century. He circulated his own version of the events of 1661–64 but died shortly after the Battle of St. Gotthard (Mogersdorf). Zrínyi was glorified as a national hero in Croatian and Hungarian history and literature. Montecuccoli was admired in the eighteenth century, but an absence of nationalist partisans taking up his cause led to subsequent neglect of his historical significance. Although nationalistic historiography has traditionally depicted them as opposites, Zrínyi and Montecuccoli had much in common: they were both members of a cosmopolitan society of Catholic military elites locked into a relationship of mutual dependence with the Habsburg dynasty. Their rivalry shows the distinctive challenges of the Hungarian frontier, especially the mistrust between the native magnates traditionally responsible for its defense and non-Hungarian military entrepreneurs leading imperial troops.

Montecuccoli interpreted his rivalry with Zrínyi as a misunderstanding about how to wage war. In 1664, after years of difficult campaigning,

The true Portraiture of ye Noble & valient NICHOLAS Count SERINI: draw'n from the Originall sent from Hungarie to the Kings most excellent Ma:tie

Wm Faithorne sculp
Cum Privilegio Reg:

Roger L'estrange.

FIGURE 5.1. William Faithorne (after unknown artist), Miklós Zrínyi (Count Nicholas Serini), 1664. National Portrait Gallery, London/Art Resource, New York.

Montecuccoli wrote a letter to Emperor Leopold I in which he attacked un-named enemies who, he alleged, were spreading falsehoods due to "defects in information about the facts or of the Art of War" and "private passions." Mon-tecuccoli strove to create an image of himself as an officer who was expert in an objective, scientific approach to warfare. It was not necessarily an insult to be compared to Fabius Maximus: although his fighting style was unpopular, he was ultimately known as "the Shield of Rome." Montecuccoli concluded his letter to Leopold with a pearl of wisdom: "[matters] of war are of the highest impor-tance where it is not permitted to err twice and it does not help to be sorry after the fact."[1] Caution was important because a single mistake on the battlefield could prove disastrous. Rulers and statesmen had to rethink political and mili-tary values in order to survive. In letters and treatises, Montecuccoli's warning was clear: choose your servants wisely or suffer the gravest of consequences. His experiences in Hungary helped to define a vision of service based on loyalty, obedience, rationality, and the sacrifice of personal glory for a greater public good.

Eastern Front

After the Peace of Westphalia, many Europeans hoped that a unified Christian force would drive the Ottomans out of Europe once and for all. Queen Chris-tina's fantastic plot to broker peace between France and Spain and launch a new crusade fit into a broader climate of millenarian excitement shared by Catholics, Protestants, and Jews.[2] Less-radical observers had long believed that the inevitable destruction of the Ottoman Empire was part of a providential plan. Accordingly, God sent the Ottomans to attack Christians as punishment for their sins, and Christians would only prevail once they had atoned and healed internal divisions.[3] The mid-seventeenth-century reappearance of the Ottomans in military struggles in Eastern Europe and the Mediterranean lent urgency to these views and demanded immediate practical responses. The Ot-tomans had kept peace with their western neighbors for decades in order to concentrate on war against the Persian Safavids on their eastern border, but that conflict ended in 1639. By 1645, the Ottomans had started a war with Ven-ice for control of Crete, which fell in 1669. In these years, the vicissitudes of the ongoing Cretan War shaped what happened on the Hungarian frontier and vice versa.[4] The fighting in Transylvania was not peripheral, but rather closely interconnected with geopolitical developments across Europe.

The early 1660s conflicts in Eastern Europe emerged from a long history of violence on the frontier. A once-unified kingdom, Hungary had become a fragmented frontier zone between two imperial powers, the Habsburgs and the Ottomans, as a result of Suleiman the Magnificent's 1540 conquest. By the mid-sixteenth century, the former kingdom had been divided into three parts: Habsburg-dominated Royal Hungary, the Ottoman vassal-state of Transylvania, and the Ottoman-dominated region around Buda.[5] Members of the Hungarian estates desperately fortified border structures on a frontier stretching along the trans-Danubian mountains and northern section of the country. However, they could not afford large-scale fortress construction and defense without Habsburg help. Especially after the 1556 creation of the Aulic War Council, the Habsburg court drove fortifications projects, hiring Italian engineers expert in the *trace italienne* style pioneered during the Italian Wars.[6] While these efforts imported basic strategies and technologies of the military revolution into Hungary, they were not enough to prevent the Ottomans from taking individual castles when the 1594–1606 Long War broke out. The larger defense system on the frontier, however, held up, protecting the Habsburg hereditary lands and territories of the Kingdom of Hungary through the seventeenth century.[7] In general, periods of open warfare were rare: border defense usually involved the "small war" of skirmishes with daring, lightning-fast thrusts into enemy territory. The Croatian frontier overseen by the Zrínyi family became depopulated due to the violence, which included brutal, scorched-earth tactics intended to disrupt Ottoman logistical capabilities.[8]

The Habsburgs permitted ambiguous, overlapping authority in the organization of frontier defense that allowed the Aulic War Council to assert a certain amount of central control, while appeasing powerful Hungarian subjects. This approach emerged out of necessity in the effort to manage a contested region with its own local traditions of defense. In addition to maintaining the fortresses and arsenals, the council was also responsible for recruiting, arming, and provisioning border troops. Administration of finance was shared with the Aulic Treasury (*Hofkammer*) and the Hungarian Chamber (*Ungarische Kammer*).[9] Command of the frontier was divided between captains-general approved by the Aulic War Council, who were in charge of border fortresses within delineated border zones (*Grenzgebeit*), and district captains-general from among the Hungarian nobility. The latter, who included members of the Zrínyi family, oversaw smaller fortresses and feudal militia (*insurrectio* forces), including some *hajdú* troops, as well as a few hundred infantry and cavalrymen financed by the Habsburgs.[10] *Hajdú* soldiers were unique to the Hungarian theater: these infantrymen rose to prominence when they joined Istvan Bocksai's insurrection against the Habsburgs in 1604–6, forming an independent warrior class that had been promised property and legal privileges in exchange for military service. During Gábor Bethlen's rule in Transylvania, they were integrated into the nobility and became part of the feudal army. Both Rákóczi I and II exploited alliances to *hajdús* for military gain, but failed to satisfy their demands. *Hajdú* populations in both Transylvania and Upper Hungary were at times an unstable element, unjustly considered bandits by the Ottomans. They conducted border raids, along with other soldiers, including light cavalry (*hussars* or Croats who served in the imperial army) and the private forces of Hungarian nobles.[11] In 1663, Montecuccoli deemed these local traditions ineffective in the face of a large-scale Ottoman invasion.

The rare but intense periods of open warfare between the Habsburgs and Ottomans from the sixteenth century on resulted in the development of strategies aimed at fighting a numerically superior opponent. Machiavelli and later strategists associated with the military revolution had advocated caution and calculation on the battlefield in the sixteenth century. A specifically Habsburg strand of Fabian thought, undoubtedly influenced by Machiavelli, also emerged. Ogier Ghiselin de Busbecq, the imperial ambassador to Constantinople from 1556 to 1562, thought it unwise to provoke this vastly superior enemy in battle. Rather, he argued, military men and politicians "ought to take reckoning of their opportunities, their own strength, and the nature and resources of their enemy."[12] He wrote, "The Emperor Ferdinand's plan was the same as that of Fabius Maximus; after estimating his own and Soleiman's resources, he judged that the last thing which a good general ought to do was to tempt fortune and encounter the attack of so formidable an enemy in a pitched battle. He, therefore, resolved to throw all his energies into the other alternative, namely, to delay and check the tide of invasion by the construction of dykes and ramparts and every kind of fortification."[13] The imperial general and diplomat Lazarus von Schwendi presented the strategy of avoiding battle with the Ottomans in his 1571 *Discourse on War*, arguing that the Habsburg emperor should first seek peaceful terms with the Ottomans. If peace failed, generals should endeavor to interrupt supply lines and starve Ottoman troops, or else use deception rather than enter battle. At the 1567 military conference in Vienna (*Wiener Hauptgrenzberatung*), Schwendi argued for the establishment of "defense zones" carefully selected for advantageous natural features that allowed implementation of a carefully orchestrated defensive strategy.[14] Fabian strategy tends to reemerge at moments in history when armies of unequal size or power face off in the battlefield and has been connected to the evolution of guerrilla warfare.[15]

Montecuccoli's Thirty Years' War experiences confirmed the wisdom that commanders needed to choose their battles judiciously, plan carefully, and not risk disastrous outcomes.[16] In his 1641 *Treatise on War*, he reviewed the circumstances in which an army should seek battle. Examples included times when the enemy was awaiting relief that had not yet arrived, when enemy forces were cut off from each other, when one's army was strong, winter was approaching, and the surrounding countryside could not sustain many soldiers, or when the location was favorable and one's army could retreat into friendly territory if things went wrong. "In summary," he wrote, "seek battle when one has the advantage or else when it is necessitated. Advantage arises from the site, from order, from having more or better troops. Necessity arises when you see that in not fighting you would lose in every way."[17] Montecuccoli followed this section with circumstances in which one should flee battle. In his 1645 *On Battle*, similar sorts of calculations proliferate.[18] By the end of the Thirty Years' War, Montecuccoli had become a master practitioner of maneuver warfare, which permitted one to, in his words, "triumph without combat." Maneuver warfare was part of the Fabian method: it involved a series of strategic movements that deceived and disrupted the enemy, cutting troops off from one another or from their supplies.[19] Recent experience during the Second Northern War affirmed its relevance: the stalemate with Sweden had only been resolved when Montecuccoli and Frederick William, elector of Brandenburg, conducted a diversionary campaign in Swedish Pomerania to force peace talks.[20]

Generals who practiced Fabian strategies walked a fine line between taking reasonable precautions and appearing to avoid battle unnecessarily. Machiavelli famously lamented the "bloodless wars" of the mercenaries of his day, while at the same time advocating deceptive strategies explicitly designed to gain advantages over the enemy without committing to the dangers of pitched battle. This was not a contradiction in his thought, but rather reflected Machiavelli's suspicion that mercenary captains avoided battle for reasons of profit: he believed they had an interest in prolonging the activity that sustained them (warfare) and saving their investments (troops). In *Art of War*, Machiavelli's Fabrizio Colonna, the model of the virtuous commander, knew how to combine careful preparation with decisive action. After Colonna detailed the calculations required for ordering an army, his interlocutor, Luigi Alamanni, begged him to launch the attack rather than "become a Fabius Maximus, giving thought to keeping the enemy at bay and deferring battle."[21] Colonna obliged, describing a glorious imaginary battle conducted by the well-ordered army. Military treatise writers continued this discussion when they weighed the roles of prudence and valor.[22]

Zrínyi was convinced that Habsburg generals like Montecuccoli were overly cautious when confronting the Ottomans. His own confidence emerged out of a long family history of fighting the Ottomans, while he harbored a traditional Hungarian mistrust of the agents of Habsburg imperialism. One of the most memorable sixteenth-century encounters between the Ottomans and

Hungarians, the 1566 Siege of Szigetvár, played an important role in Zrínyi family lore and wider European legends. Szigetvár fell to the Ottomans but was defended valiantly by the ancestor after whom Zrínyi was named: his great grandfather, Miklós Zrínyi, the governor (ban) of Croatia, who allegedly made a heroic last stand against the Ottomans with just three hundred men (a number that echoes the legend of the ancient Greek battle of Thermopylae). The Siege of Szigetvár was memorialized in multiple books including *Historia di Zigeth, ispugnata da Suliman Re de' Turchi* (Venice, 1570), Pietro Bizarri's *Pannonicum Bellum* (Basel, 1573), and *De Sigetho Hungariae propugnacolo* (Wittenberg, 1587), as well as the Ottoman texts *The Book of Suleiman* (*Süleymanname*) and *The Ottoman Chronicle of the Szigetvár Campaign.*[23]

Nearly a century later, Zrínyi's great grandson and namesake wrote a striking elegy about the Siege of Szigetvár and his ancestor's heroic role. Miklós Zrínyi allegedly composed *The Siege of Sziget* in the army's winter quarters sometime during 1646–50, but it was not published until the nineteenth century, when it was celebrated as the first Hungarian epic poem. In depicting the siege and its outcome, Zrínyi (who admitted, "I have blended my history with legends")[24] credited his ancestor with murdering Suleiman. After exhorting his followers to give up their lives for the Hungarian cause and being struck and killed himself, Zrínyi's great grandfather was raised to heaven "on splendid wings."[25] The heroic sacrifice of the defenders of Sziget was not a defeat, but rather a signal that victory was dawning.

The vision of Hungarian independence that inspired this writing emerged from half a century of struggles and triumphs in Transylvania and the perception of a new political dawn after the Thirty Years' War. Calvinist princes including Bocskai, Bethlen, Rákóczi I, and Rákóczi II ruled Transylvania under the aegis of the Ottomans and asserted independence from the Habsburgs. Bethlen was particularly inspired in the ways he played the Habsburgs and Ottomans off one another and engaged in broader European politics: he joined the Protestant Union that supported the Bohemian rebellion against Habsburg rule during the Thirty Years' War.[26] Pope Gregory XV originally sent Aldobrandini's forces, discussed in chapter 2, to counter Bethlen's army. Montecuccoli was familiar with Bethlen's successor, Rákóczi I, who intervened in the final phase of the Thirty Years' War, laying siege to Brünn (Brno), and providing yet another front for imperial generals to defend. After the conclusion of the Thirty Years' War, Rákóczi II carried on the hope for a powerful Hungarian state but miscalculated when he invaded Poland during the Second Northern War, resulting in his 1660 assassination by the Ottomans.

During Rákóczi II's reign, in 1656, Zrínyi wrote a history of the great Hungarian Renaissance king, Mathias Corvinus (*Reflections on the Life of King*

Matthias—Mátyás király életéről való elmélkedések), which argued for the renewal of the Hungarian kingdom and included plans for a Hungarian standing army.[27] *The Siege of Sziget*, dedicated to the Hungarian nobility, explicitly called for unity. The Hungarian nobility was extremely large, with complex institutional arrangements and deep-seated animosities connected to the long history of hostilities with occupying imperial powers.[28] Many families outside of the super elite remained Protestant and deeply resented the persecution of Lutheranism or Calvinism. Some Hungarian nobles defected. In the years leading up to the Battle of St. Gotthard (Mogersdorf), this critical border region was nearly absorbed by the Ottomans.[29]

Zrínyi was frustrated by Hungarian disunity and ambivalent toward Habsburg rule. He moved back and forth between service to the emperor and defense of a borderland area often referred to as the "Zrínyi frontier" (*Zerinische Grenze*) in contemporary documents. Especially when leading skirmishes against the Ottomans as the governor of Croatia, he often operated independently with his own private forces.[30] In 1655, he attempted but failed to win election as palatine of Hungary—the highest-ranking position in the kingdom. Zrínyi was Catholic, like nearly all of the thirty–forty leading Hungarian families after 1650, many of whom instituted harsh Counter-Reformation policies on their estates.[31] He had been educated by Jesuits and traveled in Italy, developing an admiration for Homer, Virgil, Tacitus, Tasso, and Machiavelli, as well as Lipsius.[32] He wrote passionately in Hungarian and was familiar with at least four other languages. Despite the Catholicism of leading families, the Habsburgs invariably connected Hungarian separatism to Calvinism and were tormented by suspicions of disloyalty. Even the most powerful Catholic magnates were never successfully integrated into the halls of power in Vienna. In sharp contrast to the Bohemian and Austrian magnates, Hungarians were almost entirely excluded from powerful court positions.[33]

The Hungarian troubles became central issues in wider European politics, especially after the fall of the key fortress of Várad to the Ottomans in 1660. Europeans understood the importance of Transylvania, fearing how its loss would impact the Cretan War, the balance of power in Europe, and developing commercial ties in Ottoman lands.[34] With all eyes on the frontier, Leopold I begged European rulers for help, and Transylvanian politicians maneuvered for advantage. Leopold's diplomat, Ludovico Mattei, a Roman nobleman who had served in the imperial army during the Thirty Years' War and had become a councilor of war, cited the obligations of vassalage in his appeals to Italian rulers.[35] During this period, Leopold I appointed Montecuccoli military governor of Raab (Győr), the key outpost that oversaw the frontier regions. Montecuccoli was in command of the largest contingent of imperial

troops and operated alongside Zrínyi. He was also in charge of several fortifications projects.[36]

Zrínyi was active on the frontier. In 1660, he blockaded the critical border
fortress, Kanizsa, before withdrawing. In 1661, he built a bridgehead into Ottoman territory, Zrínyi-Újvár, where the Kanizsa and Mur (Mura) rivers met,
with the intention of isolating Kanizsa.[37] The Ottomans were alarmed by these
developments, which they saw as initiating a new phase of hostilities, but were
distracted by the succession of a new grand vizier, Ahmed Köprülü, after the
death of Mehmed Köprülü. A few years later, on the eve of open warfare with
the Ottomans, Zrínyi worked tirelessly. In command of thirty thousand
men, most of whom were Croatian and Hungarian troops, he destroyed the
bridge at Osijek, which the Ottomans used to cross into Hungary, and burned
the Ottoman-held town of Pécs. To many European observers—especially
Protestants—Zrínyi became a hero of providential proportions.[38] German
broadsheets publicized his glorious deeds throughout the empire, even mistakenly alleging that Zrínyi had laid siege to Szigetvár, "the ancient nest of
the Zrínyis."[39] Zrínyi's fame reached as far as England, where he was known
as "Serini." In 1664, Samuel Speed published *The Conduct and Character of Count
Nicholas Serini, Protestant Generalissimo of the Auxiliaries of Hungary*, and the
cult of Zrínyi—"Serinimania"—caught fire.[40] The fact that English contemporaries assumed Zrínyi was Protestant affirms there was broader confusion
about where his loyalties lay.

As Zrínyi conducted his daring operations, Leopold I searched for ways to
contain the Ottomans without provoking an all-out war. Montecuccoli was
the leading imperial commander forced to execute Leopold's plans in the context of deep mistrust, misinformation, fluctuating orders, and lack of provisions for the army—all while competing with Zrínyi's influence and charismatic
leadership in the army and at court.

To Transylvania and Back (1661–62)

Habsburg strategy was extremely limited at first: Montecuccoli was ordered
to attack the Ottoman strongholds at Gran (Esztergom) and Buda in order to
create a diversion. The campaign turned disastrous, however, when Montecuccoli was suddenly ordered to march with his troops into Transylvania instead. In *On the War against the Turks in Hungary*, Montecuccoli explained how,
in 1661, Habsburg plans suddenly and unexpectedly changed after the army
was already in the field. Under the influence of the prime minister, Johann Ferdinand Portia, Leopold had decided to exploit political turmoil surrounding

the death of Mehmed Köprülü to occupy Transylvania. The Ottomans reacted by granting their Transylvanian vassal, Michael Apafi, stronger governing powers, and Apafi joined Ali, the pasha of Temesvár, and Mehmed Küchük, the pasha of Várad, in besieging Habsburg positions. The full Ottoman response would come in spring 1663, when the Ottoman army, intended for service in the Cretan War, was redirected from the Dalmatian to the Austrian front.[41]

Montecuccoli had painstakingly performed all of the necessary preparations for attacks on Gran (Esztergom) and Buda: he had organized the weapons and soldiers, designated the site where the army would camp, and constructed a pontoon bridge to cross the Danube the following day. By starting with these sites, the imperial army remained close to the Danube, which was essential for supply. Everything was going according to plan, he reported, when a messenger suddenly appeared with orders from the court, demanding "the army march at once into Upper Hungary."[42] Montecuccoli was furious. Marching further east into the Hungarian wilderness presented distinct challenges. It was much more difficult to acquire sufficient provisions in a countryside that contained only 5 percent arable land, with villages spaced far apart and only nine–ten inhabitants per kilometer. The army had to clear its own path through tall grasses as there were few roads. Finally, the plain became a mosquito-ridden swamp in spring and summer, resulting in one-third or more of the army perishing from malaria.[43] In his 1670 reflection on the sudden turn of events, Montecuccoli complained that the army was not at all prepared to march into Transylvania: "No provision had been made there," he claimed, while they lacked money, time, grain, and, last but not least, the consent of the Hungarians. He noted that they had already spent months gathering enough bread in the vicinity of Komaron, transporting it along the river, supplying themselves with mills and ovens. These preparations had gone to waste.[44]

Despite his objections, Montecuccoli obeyed orders, leading approximately fifteen thousand imperial troops into Transylvania to meet an Ottoman army approximately sixty thousand strong. Montecuccoli was ordered to focus on making demonstrations, rather than engaging in direct combat, and to offer aid to the Habsburg candidate for the Transylvanian throne, Kemény, in secret. He recounted the miseries of the campaign: "The army was already affected by the problems of sickness and poverty, for even if the countryside was full of grain, they totally lacked the time, mills, and ovens for making bread on the continuous march. Nor did they have magazines for storing reserves, nor carriages for taking it with them. Thus between hunger, fever and the dysentery caused by bad water and the unwholesomeness of the air, which was burning by day and freezing by night, a great part of the army, both officers and soldiers, languished."[45] Montecuccoli drew sharp and bitter contrasts between the Habsburg and Ottoman forces. "The Turk," he insisted, had "an army three times larger than ours" that was well provided for and even received help from the inhabitants of the region. The Habsburg forces "resembled a hospital more than an army."[46] Horrified at the thought of encountering the superior army, Montecuccoli maneuvered his forces to avoid the Ottomans.[47]

Disease, injury, insufficient numbers of troops, mismanagement of military finance, lack of support among the local population, and disagreement among officials characterized the intermittent campaigning during 1661–62 and 1662–63.[48] In 1662, Kemény died in combat. Montecuccoli viewed his death as a waste, emblematic of the problems of the whole campaign. Although he admitted that Kemény was "a prince of worthy quality and long military experience," in the current expedition against the Ottomans he was "little cautious" and failed to operate according to "good rules." Montecuccoli drily surmised that Kemény, who was a Calvinist, must have behaved brashly in battle because he had already abandoned himself to his preordained fate.[49]

For the 1662 Diet of Pressburg, Portia recruited Montecuccoli to help craft imperial propaganda to influence international opinion and maintain the support of German princes. In his pamphlet, distributed at the Hungarian diet, Montecuccoli blamed Hungarian nobles for military problems, an angle that might have proven compelling to Germans but alienated Hungarian allies.[50] These efforts mirrored those of his friend, Franz Paul Lisola (1613–74), whose own dissemination of anti-French pamphlet literature served as a continuation of his diplomacy by other means.[51] In these and later pamphlets, Montecuccoli used military science as a propaganda tool. He consistently claimed that Hungarian nobles lacked the knowledge and experience to wage war properly.

In his 1662 *Response to the Slander Disseminated Here and There That the Imperial German Armies Operated Little or Not At All in the Year 1661*, Montecuccoli sarcastically referred to malicious reactions on the part of Hungarian noblemen as "Hungarian gratitude" (*gratitudine ungarica*) for the imperial army's help. He spelled out the army's achievements, which included impeding the operations of fifty thousand Ottoman troops, returning Kemény to Transylvania, stabilizing multiple areas with garrisons, and removing all armies, enemy and friendly, from Hungary. These successes occurred despite the fact that the campaign started late in the year, none of the necessary provisions had been prepared, half of the army was ill, and the Hungarians slaughtered his soldiers or else betrayed their promises of assistance.[52]

Montecuccoli devoted a section to battle itself, presumably in response to criticisms about his style of fighting. He emphasized that the warfare he practiced rejected private motives such as personal glory or honor in favor of the public good. In Montecuccoli's eyes, the desire for personal glory led to reckless behavior, which he alleged had gotten Kemény killed. "It is presumptuous," he wrote, "to form a judgment without having inspected the sites, the places, the times, the forces, and the circumstances." If a general did not restrain his appetite for personal glory, "he would run full speed into battle, without any consideration of the probability of losing or winning," concerned only for his own immortality. "But," he continued, "he who has the obligation to place the public good ahead of the private and to sacrifice himself and his soul to the obedience of orders, does not operate in this way."[53] Montecuccoli saw himself holding characteristics necessary for engaging in calculated warfare: levelheadedness, rationality, objectivity, and, perhaps most importantly, obedience. By contrast, about the Hungarians he asked, "who among these nobles (excepting very few) understands the art of war?" He claimed that of those Hungarians who had learned something about war, "many of them will not have experienced two or three campaigns—brief terms for such a long drawn out art." Transylvania, he continued, "has had such great—and indeed continuous—disturbances" that it required "the most experienced captains in the military discipline."[54] Montecuccoli's accusations seem strange, considering that Hungarian magnates had long taken responsibility for the defense of the frontier. Montecuccoli's point, however, was that formal war against the Ottomans differed substantially from conducting border raids. He believed large-scale campaigns, such as those of the Thirty Years' War and Second Northern War, provided relevant experience.

Montecuccoli composed other similar documents in these years, one of which he addressed to Leopold I.[55] In *Conjectural Judgment about the Intentions and Counsels of the Hungarians* (*Giudizio congetturale sopra le intenzioni e consigli degli ungheri*), Montecuccoli's ire toward his Hungarian rivals was clear from the opening lines. He targeted "the indiscreet zeal that the Hungarians have for maintaining their liberty," leading them to "dissolute licentiousness" and "the direct road to ruin." He continued, "the Hungarians are so jealous of maintaining their heresy, licentiousness, and wealth that they implicate themselves by continual contradictions in words, deeds, and wishes." Those contradictions included, in Montecuccoli's view, that they "desire war, but none of those things that are inseparably conjoined to war; they desire aid, but not an auxiliary army; they desire the end, but not the means." As a result, Montecuccoli argued, "a thousand rivers of inaccuracy, of pernicious designs, of terrible effects, of things diametrically opposed to one another gush forth."[56] Montecuccoli went on to complain about certain magnates who refused to cooperate with and even threatened the army. Others shared intelligence with Apafi and with "the Turk" himself.[57]

Zrínyi was outraged by the aspersions cast by Montecuccoli and other imperial officers. From the Hungarian perspective, the Habsburgs refused to provide the necessary support to free their lands from Ottoman rule, while imperial soldiers created deeper problems as they attacked locals and destroyed villages and crops. Zrínyi was furious at Montecuccoli. He addressed his own pamphlet to the "Most Excellent Leader":

> So you compelled 50,000 Turks to pull back by 50 miles? You put Prince Kemény back on the throne? You stationed new garrisons in the fortresses? You saved Transylvania? Well, well! These are great, indeed the greatest of deeds! But your glory begins and ends with these fine words. Tell me, how did Hungary benefit from your military expedition? Tell me, have you given us back Transylvania, which was in good shape when you seized it? First, restore to Transylvania Prince Kemény, who had your word and your promises of protection, and restore the happiness, peace, and plenty that you and your armies banished from the land; and then you may have your victory parade.[58]

Zrínyi was not entirely fair: Transylvania suffered violence and economic disruption long before Montecuccoli's troops arrived. He must have understood Montecuccoli's limitations, though it is possible that Hungarian nobles did not fully grasp the Habsburgs' inability to commit to a large-scale campaign, given exhaustion from the Thirty Years' War. At the same time, decades of minor fights against dispersed Ottoman troops on the frontier led to false impressions that a conquest of Ottoman territory would be easier than it was. Montecuccoli's attacks on Zrínyi for his alleged lack of experience and knowledge were also undeserved. At root, both men desired to attack Leopold's Transylvania policy, but it was not politically expedient to direct their criticisms at the emperor.[59]

Montecuccoli grounded his arguments in objective-sounding knowledge, but they were highly political, revealing the ideological contours of the emerging science of war. Zrínyi's formal treatises show that he did not approach warfare in a fundamentally different way from Montecuccoli. Zrínyi shared Montecuccoli's ideas about avoiding battle, building a standing army, conducting a great war against the Ottomans, and reforming logistics.[60] The frontier warfare that Zrínyi was familiar with was not an alien type of warfare. Montecuccoli was also a practitioner of irregular warfare and included skirmishes as part of the military art. Decades earlier, the Long War in Hungary had been a training ground for an international military elite who played an integral role in the dissemination of innovative military ideas and methods.[61]

Zrínyi and Montecuccoli also both agreed that loyalty to the common good was essential to political and military legitimacy, but they disagreed on how to define the common good. Zrínyi identified the common good with a unified

Hungarian nobility and a powerful Hungarian kingdom. Zrínyi hoped the call to defend Hungary would rally an international Christian coalition intent on defeating a common enemy, the Ottomans. Montecuccoli, by contrast, explicitly identified the common good with the Habsburg dynasty.

War against the Ottomans (1663–64)

The military situation in Hungary swiftly deteriorated when the Ottomans formally declared war on the Habsburgs in June 1663. Since April, reports had trickled in that the grand vizier was approaching with one hundred thousand men. Prior to these developments, Montecuccoli had argued strenuously to quarter troops in Hungary over the winter but had met resistance from Hungarian magnates who did not want to support the troops. Meanwhile, rather than prepare for the campaign, Portia sought peace negotiations with the Ottomans, at which Montecuccoli scoffed.[62] At the start of 1663, he commanded a mere 5,500 men and 12 cannons. In his later reflection on the war, he asked with obvious sarcasm whether one should conduct a light cavalry raid—the traditional Hungarian frontier strategy Zrínyi excelled at—in such circumstances.[63] He complained that the Hungarian *insurrectio* forces were "poorly provided for" and "inexperienced." Forced into service and fearful of the Ottomans against whom they had never fought in large-scale war, they deserted. Montecuccoli wanted to raise more Hungarian troops, but was told that border troops needed to be paid first or else they would simply abandon their posts and re-enroll as mercenaries for the pay.[64] Montecuccoli later claimed that this was about the time when he considered abandoning Habsburg service himself, but "obedience and fidelity repelled me" from such a decision.[65] He continued to conceptualize his service to the Habsburgs in terms of feudal concepts: although he was not actually a direct subject of the emperor's, he behaved as though he were.

Montecuccoli decided to leave Hungary in order to focus on defending lower Austria.[66] In response to orders from the Aulic War Council (headed by Lobkowitz) to attack the Ottoman army, he simply asked for reinforcements. Instead of laying siege to Raab (Győr), the Ottomans surprised Montecuccoli by traveling north from Buda and laying siege to one of the most important border fortresses, Neuhäusel (Érsekúvár in Hungarian, modern-day Nové Zámky). As he considered the options for relieving Neuhäusel (Érsekúvár), the imperial court ordered Montecuccoli to reinforce the castle and town of Pressburg (Pozsony in Hungarian, modern-day Bratislava)—next in the Ottomans' possible line of attack.[67] As the fortification work proceeded, Neuhäusel

(Érsekúvár) fell on 27 September, leaving the Ottomans in dangerous proximity to both Graz and Vienna and allowing them to make a raid into Moravia.[68] After the raid, the Ottomans retreated into winter quarters. They had expanded farther into Hungary than ever before.[69] Montecuccoli asked to be relieved of his command. He later grumbled that defensive actions were critically important, even if they were not as glorious as offensive campaigns.[70]

Members of the court in Vienna knew that the Ottomans would strike again in the spring of 1664. They might build on the successes of the previous year and press further into Austrian territory, possibly reaching Vienna and laying siege to the imperial city as they had in 1529 under Suleiman. In October 1663, Montecuccoli proposed a plan that started with laying siege to Gran (Esztergom). He consolidated and systematized his views, producing *Discourse* in the early spring.[71] He outlined many of the imperatives that he would explain more fully in *On the War against the Turks in Hungary*, including the need for large forces, adequate provisioning of the army, and use of the rivers that ran through Hungary to Habsburg advantage.[72] He also called for military authority to be centralized under the command of a single, supreme general. However, Montecuccoli's Danube strategy was swept aside as a result of negotiations at the 1663–64 Diet of Regensburg, where the Styrian estates and representatives of Zrínyi argued to begin the campaign to the south by laying siege to Kanizsa.[73] The diet saw an explosion of broadsheets, pamphlets, and reports attempting to sway opinion.[74] At the same time, Zrínyi undertook a daring winter campaign, advancing into Ottoman territory and capturing and burning key sites in preparation for the siege. The Habsburgs started receiving reinforcements from across Christendom.

When spring arrived, the Habsburgs were able to put an allied army of approximately 81,269 in the field.[75] Many Italian rulers had declined to provide assistance, although minor Italian feudatories contributed, and other Italian noblemen served on their own account. With the threat of Ottoman invasion looming, Pope Alexander VII provided seven hundred thousand florins and granted Leopold ecclesiastical incomes from the Austrian states, while Tuscany offered gunpowder and a plot to divert the Ottomans at sea.[76] Even Louis XIV sent troops. The forces in the field included Habsburg troops under Leopold's direct command (51,000), the imperial army (15,167 soldiers raised by the imperial circles), the French-allied Rhenish Alliance troops (13,590), separate contingents from Brandenburg, Saxony, and Bavaria (4,512 total), and an additional 15,000 men from the Hungarian feudal levies. Leopold appointed Montecuccoli to lead the largest group of Habsburg troops (29,000). The remaining Habsburg forces were divided: Louis Ratuit de Souches oversaw 8,500 in the north and Zrínyi, Strozzi, and Count Wolf Julius Hohenlohe were in charge of about 24,000 troops in the south. These generals argued about strategy; some objected that laying siege to Kanizsa diverted forces from more critical sites.[77]

The failure and abandonment of the siege of Kanisza in late May was a major turning point. Pietro Strozzi was killed. It took Montecuccoli two weeks to march south to help the imperial troops that had retreated to Zrínyi-Újvár, and what he saw when he finally arrived confirmed his suspicions. In a report, Montecuccoli blamed the siege of Kanizsa and the resulting retreat for weakening and demoralizing Habsburg forces, resulting especially in a loss of experienced soldiers. Soon after, Zrínyi-Újvár also fell.[78] Zrínyi alleged that Montecuccoli refused to fight, but Montecuccoli had in fact made serious efforts to defend Zrínyi-Újvár.[79] Montecuccoli sent a new round of letters to Vienna. In one, he reminded Walter Leslie of the "different discourses that have been composed concerning the past campaign" but asked, "How can one judge matters well without knowing the whole thread and all the circumstances?" He attached his own account, drawn from his "files" and asked Leslie to pass it along. He composed a similar note to Portia.[80]

After the fall of Kanizsa, which Leopold now blamed on the quarreling of the leading commanders, the emperor suddenly appointed Montecuccoli to supreme command. Leopold ordered Montecuccoli, who was back in Vienna, to return to the army and unite all of the troops. He wrote, "You will see the circumstances and according to your experience and valor, do that which you deem useful to the common good."[81] In his order, Leopold used the language of military treatises, which had long emphasized the careful evaluation of circumstances, the importance of experience and valor, and the goal of usefulness. His words reflected Montecuccoli's own sense of identity as an expert warrior who subordinated his own interests to a greater good upheld by the Habsburg dynasty, an identity Montecuccoli had presented in petitions to the emperor. Montecuccoli, however, was wary. On the one hand, he expressed his desire to "blindly obey" Leopold I's will and assured the emperor that "I will spare neither application nor effort, neither blood nor life in the imperial service of Your Majesty."[82] On the other hand, he lodged his dissatisfaction with how the campaigning had progressed. He also included a report on the vast discrepancies between Ottoman and imperial forces. Montecuccoli was not eager to become supreme commander if he was destined to fail, given the grim realities of the campaign. Above all, he feared loss of reputation. Leopold I immediately wrote back, reassuring Montecuccoli. He claimed, "I trust in you and therefore leave everything to your disposition." Leopold promised him "particular protection of your person" and he vowed that he would not believe anyone who wished to make "other impressions" of Montecuccoli, just as he had refused to believe the "false impressions" circulating over the course of the past year. He concluded by asking Montecuccoli to maintain "good spirits" and "be assured of my good graces."[83] Throughout his career, Montecuccoli had followed a pattern of threatening to leave imperial service permanently or at least temporarily resigning if he did not receive desired concessions from his Habsburg patron. This pattern points to a method of negotiating that ultimately belies his claims of blind obedience.

Montecuccoli accepted Leopold I's conditions and took up command, keeping the imperial court closely informed. On 8 July, he assured Leopold I that he "assiduously employ[ed]" his "studies and application" in order "not to lose even the smallest occasion for destroying the enemy . . . or in another way to promote the service of Your Majesty and public matters." He had specified, however, that his actions would be based on "good military reason and foundation." He consulted regularly with the other generals—"all (well-versed) in matters of war, most fervent with zeal, and rigorous with the enemy"—but maintained that "where the opportunity is not presented and the material is not yet sufficiently disposed, we must wait out of necessity in order not to precipitate matters."[84] Montecuccoli would later repeat these points in a December report he provided on the campaign and in his 1670 treatise.[85] Montecuccoli's messages were getting through, as other correspondence from Vienna reveals. In the weeks leading up to St. Gotthard (Mogersdorf), the papal nuncio in Vienna, Cardinal Carafa, reported on Montecuccoli's military maneuvers. Carafa explained that Montecuccoli crossed the River Mur (Mura), "flanking the enemy in order to observe his behaviors and to impede a possible invasion of Austria and Styria, hoping also to force him to turn back to the banks of the Danube where with the benefit of the natural course of the water the defense on our part will succeed more easily and more advantageously."[86] Carafa was not an eyewitness to the campaign, but his letter shows that he absorbed a picture of campaign maneuvers that reflected Montecuccoli's strategic vision, including the Danube strategy.

All eyes in Europe were focused on the eastern front. In early July, Carafa reported on Zrínyi's retreat from the battlefield to defend his own fortress, leaving Montecuccoli with only about twenty-five thousand men. In a letter to the imperial court, Zrínyi explained his frustration. He reported that Montecuccoli refused to engage the enemy, claiming to need reinforcements.[87] After a successful winter campaign, Zrínyi had watched fortified places fall, a series of failures that had started with his own botched attempt at Kanizsa. Montecuccoli's goal was to prevent an invasion of the Habsburg hereditary lands. He had too few troops to engage in a direct assault on the Ottomans. For

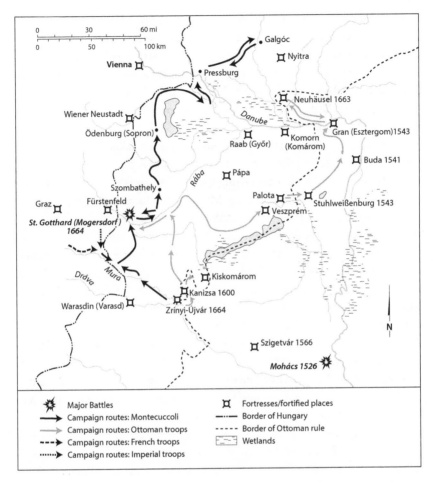

MAP 5.1. Montecuccoli's 1664 campaign on the Hungarian frontier. Cartography by Bill Nelson This map is based on data and other maps provided by György Domokos.

months, Montecuccoli's forces followed a pattern of dropping back, disappearing as the Ottomans pushed deeper into Hungarian territory (Map 5.1).

Zrínyi recognized that the Habsburgs viewed his homeland as a buffer zone to protect the dynastic and imperial heartland. If the properties of Hungarian noblemen were expendable, there was no reason to provide political support for Habsburg rule in Hungary. The Habsburgs had only been offered the crown in order to defend Hungary.[88] These were the kinds of realizations that, along with religious motives, drove some Hungarians to ally with the Ottomans. In July, Zrínyi traveled to Vienna to plead his case. Carafa assumed that Zrínyi planned to complain about Montecuccoli, "with whom he has never had a good relationship."[89] Carafa sent a copy of Zrínyi's report to Rome, and Zrínyi

circulated letters across Europe in which he attacked Montecuccoli. Within
weeks, the Viennese court received reports from the campaign that the allied
Christian and Ottoman armies had finally come face to face near the old Cister-
cian monastery of St. Gotthard (Mogersdorf), separated only by the Raab
(Rába) River. If the Ottomans succeeded in crossing the Raab (Rába), the path
to Styria, Lower Austria, and even Vienna lay open. The moment of possible
invasion had arrived.

In the days leading up to the battle, Montecuccoli had laid the groundwork
for victory by reuniting the disparate troops that composed the allied forces
at a critical moment and coordinating their movements to contain Köprülü
Fazıl Ahmed Paşa's troops along the Mur (Mura), forcing the Ottomans to
cross the Raab (Rába) at a position advantageous to the Habsburg forces and
their allies. On 31 July, the Ottomans sent part of their army across the river
via a shallow ford but found themselves grappling with a rapidly swelling river
owing to summer rains. The following afternoon, as they attempted to extend
a bridgehead, build trenches, and push into the center of the allied troops,
which formed a wide semicircle, Montecuccoli convinced the other generals
to launch a coordinated attack from the sides.[90] Years later, he recalled that
the fighting that day was "bloody, fierce, and uncertain" and that it lasted "from
9:00 in the morning until 4:00 in the afternoon."[91] The Ottoman traveler and
eyewitness to the battle Evliya Çelebi described how, after hours of enduring
"the barrage of musket and cannon fire," the Ottoman troops weakened, "but
the tricky infidels never stopped their onslaught."[92] The Ottomans attempted
to retreat across the river, leading to the drowning deaths of hundreds more.[93]
Many of the dead included the most elite Ottoman janissaries: the "sword and
shield of the Ottoman Empire," according to Montecuccoli. Their slaughter
was so great that "the histories recount few similar (slaughters)."[94]

On 3 August, Montecuccoli announced that "the blow" to the enemy "is
much greater than that which I had first judged. I believe that he will not be
able to undertake another major campaign"[95] (figure 5.2). Montecuccoli was
awed by the outcome, but also had reason to inflate his success. In reality, the
Ottoman army was not destroyed, but Köprülü made a strategic decision to
abandon the invasion and retreat. Despite a chorus of later criticism, there was
no way Montecuccoli could have launched a counteroffensive: the river had
now become disadvantageous to the allies, while they would have encountered
fresh Ottoman troops on the other side. Moreover, Montecuccoli was acutely
aware of the fact that some of the allied troops—those from France and the
Imperial Circles—would soon depart, severely reducing Christian forces.[96]

Leopold I was ecstatic at news of the victory and ordered a lavish display of
fireworks in Vienna. As a reward, he appointed Montecuccoli to the highest

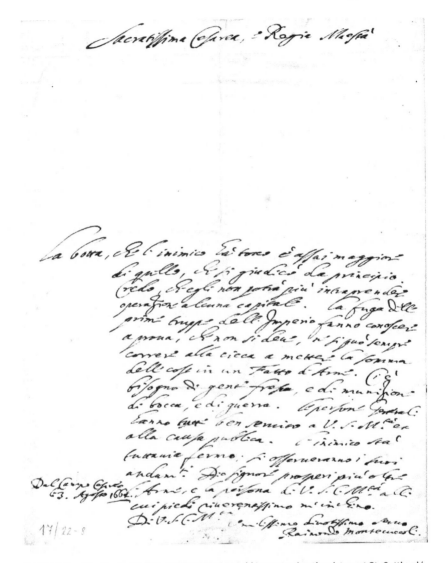

Figure 5.2. Montecuccoli's letter to Emperor Leopold I announcing the victory at St. Gotthard/ Mogersdorf. Raimondo Montecuccoli to Emperor Leopold I, from the imperial camp, 3 August 1664. Österreichische Nationalbibliothek (ÖNB), Vienna. Archival record: ÖNB, Autogr., 17/22–8.

command of the army, lieutenant general (*Generalleutnant*)—a title given out to only a handful of men during the century.[97] To the deep disappointment of their Hungarian allies, the Habsburgs quickly signed the conciliatory Peace of Vasvár, so that Leopold I could turn his attention to other problems, including Louis XIV's political machinations. Hungarian nobles responded by organizing renewed resistance to Habsburg rule that culminated in the 1674 Wesselényi

Conspiracy and a decade of heavy-handed suppression in Hungary that mirrored the Habsburg approach to Bohemia in the 1620s. Zrínyi had been so frustrated with the Habsburgs that, prior to his 1664 death, he had apparently been in secret communication with Louis XIV.[98]

Montecuccoli took pride in the award of the prestigious title of lieutenant general, previously given to Wallenstein, Galasso, and Piccolomini (and later awarded to Eugene of Savoy). He explained that lieutenant general was an "office most worthy in itself, sought after by princes and proclaimed as prestigious for being pursued as a sign of merit."[99] For a foreign military noble who claimed to have earned his position due to his knowledge and experience and who emphasized his unswerving loyalty to the Habsburgs, this was a satisfying award. He had reached the apex of the imperial army. A number of factors had made Montecuccoli fortunate at St. Gotthard (Mogersdorf), but, as Montecuccoli repeated in his writings, a good general needed to weigh these exact kinds of circumstances, understanding when and how to seize the moment. The campaign as a whole had impeded his attempts to control warfare, but the Battle of St. Gotthard (Mogersdorf) was nonetheless a vindication of his cautious yet decisive approach.

Aftermath of War

In December 1664, Montecuccoli obtained an audience with Leopold I in which he presented a new account of the campaign, prefaced by the explanatory letter referred to in the introduction of this chapter. Montecuccoli claimed that he desired to provide "direction" for the future and shed light upon "the intimate reasons for the results [of the last campaign]." He believed his account would expose: "the fallacies of those who, on account of the defect of news or of the military art, or else seduced by private passions, sought to mask the truth or to alter it, those who suppose it to be other than that which is evidently demonstrable in the original authentic consultations, in the files of the Chancellery, and in the eye-witness testimony of so many valorous, faithful officials."[100] Zrínyi had died in November during a boar hunt, but his brother, Peter, continued his efforts and met with success. An eighty-page report produced in Vienna that year detailing St. Gotthard (Mogersdorf) opened not with Montecuccoli's battlefield successes, but rather with the accomplishments of the Zrínyi brothers.[101]

In his audience with Leopold I, Montecuccoli repeated previous criticisms against his rivals, and he revealed a tendency to weaponize the evolving bureaucratic apparatus. The above passage suggests that official reports confirming his version of events had been created and archived. In a 1665 letter to the

Italian historian Galeazzo Gualdo Priorato, Montecuccoli complained that the writers of other accounts of the recent Ottoman war "don't know how to do anything else than string together the gazettes that run through common hands." In contrast to official reports and methodical treatises, he viewed information in gazettes as common and vulgar. To lend credence to such accounts was to entertain "the rumors of the town squares" without "caring or examining the truth of matters and the substance of reports." *"Misera Istoria,"* he declared, and wondered how anyone would ever be able to judge affairs of the state, the army, or the court.[102]

Priorato was in the process of writing the official history of the war in Hungary as part of a biography of Leopold I, *Historia di Leopoldo Cesare*, and absorbed Montecuccoli's views. He requested that Montecuccoli review his draft in advance, asking him to attach additional information, to cross out superfluous or false words, and to correct errors in names. Priorato also remarked on the efforts of the Zrínyi brothers to influence history "with words" rather than "deeds" and expressed surprise at their success in convincing others—even Louis, Duke d'Enghien, the Grand Condè—that they were "real masters of war."[103] Montecuccoli praised Priorato's text: "The truth diligently researched, the judgement incorrupt, expressions decorous, and all the parts which come together in a beautiful and good history." Priorato, who was hoping to advance in Vienna at the time, saw the virtue in appeasing Montecuccoli, and even emphasized their Italian background as the basis for shared views.[104] Despite these proclamations, Priorato also incorporated the writing of Miklós Zrínyi's Irish court historian, Marcus Forstall.[105]

Montecuccoli pursued other forms of recognition. In the 1664 audience, he asked for a peacetime salary of twelve thousand florins a year—he suggested the Jews of Prague pay for it—as well as induction into the highly prestigious military order, the Order of the Golden Fleece.[106] The name of the Burgundian chivalric order evoked Jason and the Argonauts, whose quest for the Golden Fleece in Colchis served as an allegory for the struggle against the Ottomans and the recapture of the Holy Sepulcher, explicit goals of the Order of the Golden Fleece. In the seventeenth century, membership in the order was the preserve of rulers—Emperor Leopold I was rarely pictured without the Golden Fleece—and powerful noblemen whose status was increasingly defined by their service and loyalty to the Spanish or Austrian Habsburg ruler.[107] For noblemen in Vienna, the order had become essential for advancement in the upper echelons of court society, although it was conferred by the Spanish king and not the emperor.

Montecuccoli claimed both Portia and Leopold I had promised to help him obtain the Golden Fleece as early as 1662—a likely enticement during the difficult campaigning in Hungary.[108] He was incensed that Zrínyi had been admitted.[109] In a letter to Lobkowitz, Montecuccoli worried that delay in obtaining the award "represents a disregard of my merits in the military field."[110] Montecuccoli had other supporters, including Leopold I; his brother-in-law, Dietrichstein; and the diplomats Lisola and Francis Eusebius Pötting (1627–78). Pötting was imperial ambassador in Madrid and a relative of Montecuccoli's by marriage: both had Dietrichstein wives. Lisola was an imperial diplomat who had negotiated with Montecuccoli in Berlin for the alliance with Brandenburg during the Second Northern War in 1658 and served in Madrid in the 1660s.[111] Lisola was part of the international web of clients drawn to imperial service for the opportunities to advance their own interests alongside a set of fervently held ideological goals. He had been born to an Italian clerk in the Franche-Comté, an imperial fief under Spanish protection until France claimed it in 1667. His anti-French orientation and relationships in Vienna made him a natural ally to Montecuccoli. Lisola and Montecuccoli agreed that if the French conquered the Spanish Netherlands and Spanish power crumbled, the emperor and his dominions would not be safe: France's ambition to expand its borders could only come at the expense of Germany.[112] Montecuccoli's induction into the Order of the Golden Fleece was complicated by the death of the king of Spain in September 1665, but Lisola continued negotiating in Madrid, arguing that Montecuccoli could offer Spain the potentially valuable "return service" of military support in Spain's ongoing struggles in Flanders.[113] Dietrichstein pressed Lobkowitz for help, and they eventually obtained a papal dispensation from Alexander VII to allow the Spanish queen to confer the order.[114] Both Montecuccoli and Dietrichstein were inducted in 1668.[115]

Leopold I's support for Montecuccoli's candidacy helps to reveal what the emperor thought of his Italian client.[116] In a letter to Pötting, Leopold I emphasized Montecuccoli's "particular experience in military matters," mentioning "first the high valor showed in the most recent expedition against the Turks as well as before and his achieved victories as well as the resulting peace for the whole of Christendom as also for the welfare of our collective House."[117] Leopold I appeared to agree with Montecuccoli's justifications for his admission: Montecuccoli merited the award based on military experience and accomplishments. In January 1666, Leopold I once again wrote letters in support of Montecuccoli to the queen of Spain and Pötting. In the letter to the queen, he repeated the recommendations he had given her late husband, citing Montecuccoli's noble lineage, service to both branches of the Habsburg family, and accomplishments in the recent Ottoman wars. Finally, he wrote of the "particular high affection" he bore for Montecuccoli and the "very great and abiding desire that he [be] dignified with the Golden Fleece and therefore his noble, proven services are rewarded with something." Leopold mentioned another justification for induction: Montecuccoli's "most loyal ability."[118] This phrase indicates that perceptions of Montecuccoli's competence were explicitly tied to his loyalty.

The victory at St. Gotthard (Mogersdorf) sealed Montecuccoli's reputation as one of the greatest generals of his age. However, as the process of his induction into the Order of the Golden Fleece reveals, his success stemmed not only from the battlefield, but also from the support of other members of a cosmopolitan Catholic aristocracy. Montecuccoli's writings—formal treatises as well as pamphlets—and network of friends and supporters bridging battlefield and court were key elements of his success.

During the early 1660s, as the Austrian Habsburgs faced the threat of a massive Ottoman invasion, Montecuccoli struggled to manage the complexities of warfare with limited resources. His ascent to the top of the military hierarchy made him an easy target for critics against whom he engaged in an unceasing battle to influence the discourse about war in Eastern Europe. Montecuccoli has gained a historical reputation as a cool-headed, systematic thinker and general, but by analyzing his writings in the context of the rivalries of the 1660s and the Hungarian frontier, we can see how his military science emerged as part of a fiery, ideological debate. The argument about the proper way to conduct war may have had origins in the late sixteenth century, but, in this instance, was profoundly shaped by the effort to navigate the complexities of the military frontier in a major new confrontation with the Ottomans. Montecuccoli was not always confident about how others perceived his reputation. He engaged in continuous acts of writing, including formal treatises, reports, letters, and countless notes, in the battle for recognition. He used the evolving idea of military science as a weapon to prove his way of waging war was correct. Loyalty was integral to his conception of how to wage war, because loyalty required the subordination of private interests to the greater good one was loyal to, supposedly resulting in clear-eyed, rational military analysis and action.[119]

Loyalty cannot be separated from ideology. Among the cosmopolitan Habsburg elite, political loyalty had become intertwined with Catholicism, especially after the Protestant rebellions that triggered the Thirty Years' War.[120] Confessional ties altered the map of Europe, permitting geographically dispersed and politically fragmented communities to nurture common interests and create powerful networks of support for struggles that had once been local.[121] The Zrínyi family were Catholic and had long defended the Hungarian border against Ottoman attacks, but Montecuccoli suspected that Zrínyi was disloyal to the Habsburgs because he put Zrínyi family interests ahead of the emperor's and argued for the union of the Hungarian nation. Furthermore, the Hungarian nobility—some of whom were indeed Protestants—occupied an ambiguous position in the larger Catholic Habsburg world. What was notably different for Montecuccoli was the way his own family's interests dovetailed with the goals of the Habsburg dynasty. By allying with the Habsburgs, multiple generations of the Montecuccoli family gained wealth and prestige.

Wars against the Ottomans had often triggered debates about the common good because Christians viewed the Ottomans as a common enemy. The 1661–64 campaigns proved no different. However, the particular variation of the discourse that emerged in these years must be set within the context of the geopolitics after the Thirty Years' War. Historians have focused on the ascent of Bourbon France in these decades. Montecuccoli was wary of the rising power of Louis XIV and viewed the French as another common enemy to rally against.[122] In his eyes, the Habsburg monarchy offered hope for unifying Catholics in the face of both Ottoman and French threats.

Fissures between Zrínyi and Montecuccoli emerged because they disagreed about what the common good was and how military force should serve broader interests.[123] Zrínyi gained an advantage in historical literature when nineteenth- and early twentieth-century Hungarian and Croatian nationalists identified him as an early hero of their causes. Montecuccoli did not fit neatly into any nationalistic literature and historians neglected his biography and treatises after the eighteenth century.[124] Nonetheless, due to his influence over eighteenth and early nineteenth-century military men, the contributions of a foreign military entrepreneur serving a fragmented, decentralized monarchy ultimately proved more influential in the long-term development of military professionalism. Montecuccoli became the model of a loyal, professional officer, emulated by multiple generations of soldiers including Eugene of Savoy, Frederick the Great, and even Napoleon. At the same time, as his disputes with Zrínyi and experiences on campaign show, war could never be an exact science like physics or mathematics because of the role of emotion, uncertainty, and unique, unpredictable events. Montecuccoli never fully achieved his science of war on the battlefield. Emerging out of contentious circumstances, it is an artifact of instability and ideological division.

CHAPTER 6

Victory at Last

Montecuccoli's experiences on the Hungarian frontier spurred him to complete his most significant and influential military treatise, *On the War against the Turks in Hungary* (*Della guerra col turco in ungheria*), in 1670. This work, sometimes referred to as the "Aphorisms," represented the culmination of decades of thinking about war and the ways scientific methods helped to understand and control war. Divided into three parts, it explained the principles of warfare, provided his definitive reflection on the controversial Hungarian campaigns, and offered a proposal for fighting a future war against the Ottomans. *On the War against the Turks in Hungary* was widely read in the eighteenth century, launching Montecuccoli into the pantheon of military thinkers.[1] Frederick the Great, Napoleon, and Clausewitz all studied this work, while Montecuccoli's successors in the army, Charles of Lorraine and Eugene of Savoy, used it as a blueprint for the 1683–99 conquest of Eastern Europe from the Ottomans.

One of the main features of *On the War against the Turks in Hungary* was Montecuccoli's focus on the development of a large standing army directly subordinate to the Austrian Habsburg ruler. Although some forms of standing armies had existed for centuries, early modern governments lacked the logistical, fiscal, administrative, and command capacities required to build and manage large, effective forces of this type, resulting in their reliance on military entrepreneurs. Prior to the Thirty Years' War, uneven experimentation with permanent forces in Habsburg Austria occurred mainly as a reaction to the Ottoman threat. Emperor Ferdinand I (r. 1556–64) was able to keep about nine thousand men on hand, while Emperor Rudolf II (r. 1576–1612) maintained regiments throughout the year for border defense during the Long War.[2] Scholars customarily view 1649 as the starting point of the Austrian Habsburg standing army, when Ferdinand III, still reeling from the effects of the Thirty Years' War, ordered nine infantry and ten cavalry regiments maintained on a permanent footing.[3] Despite these moves, troops were regularly disbanded throughout the century, including the majority of the soldiers recruited in the early 1660s to fight against the Ottomans. It was not until 1683—the period of the Siege of Vienna—that the emperor regularly maintained at least sixty thousand soldiers.[4]

The standing army was a popular idea among political theorists serving absolutist princes, though controversial to many other Europeans. Machiavelli had criticized standing armies, but, following decades of religious warfare, Lipsius and others embraced the standing army as an instrument for upholding a ruler's authority and ensuring stability. According to the military revolution thesis, Maurice of Nassau and Gustavus Adolphus adopted Lipsius's recommendations, and the standing army was eventually handed down to the modern world.[5] Other contemporaries saw standing armies as threatening to noble and ecclesiastical estates because the demands of such armies—especially regular, onerous taxation and the quartering of troops—violated rights and immunities. Many theorists and politicians emerged from the Thirty Years' War in agreement about the fact that the Holy Roman Empire required military reforms, but they disagreed on which model to follow. Whereas the emperor sought a standing army under his control funded by contributions from the estates, powerful German princes desired to maintain their own forces, which they promised to provide for collective war efforts as needed. Smaller princes who lacked the means to maintain standing armies argued for disarmament. Historians traditionally characterized different proposals about standing armies as "absolutist" or "federalist" by design, prioritizing western/central European political models and framing the eventual development of standing armies as the triumph of absolutist rulers over estates.[6] In this light, the standing army has often been interpreted as a possession of the ruler and a tool for dominating unruly elites—not only the estates but also free-wheeling military contractors who supplied force when local nobilities resisted.[7]

In reality, the development of early modern states and armies was far more complex and diverse than these traditional models allowed and involved cooperation between rulers and nobles in the effort to reach a new governing consensus. Early standing armies incorporated private mechanisms for waging war—including proprietorship of regiments—that permitted nobles to elevate their status and increase their wealth.[8] At the same time, as William Godsey has argued for Lower Austria, the estates developed into a "civilian support structure" providing critical administrative, financial, and logistical assistance for the Habsburg standing army that helped maintain public order when troops passed through various regions.[9] In this context, the development of standing armies was not a straightforward assertion of monarchical authority over noble privileges on the road to building modern, centralized nation-states, but rather a nuanced product of compromise. A remaining problem is that prevailing historiographic trends in military history continue to analyze the standing army and broader changes in power in terms of the evolution of the nation-state. If his reaction to calls for Hungarian independence were any indication, Montecuccoli would have been highly averse to the concept of the nation-state. His view of the standing army emerged out of his analysis of imperial powers, especially Rome and the Ottoman Empire.

For Montecuccoli, the maintenance of a large standing army under the direct command of the emperor was essential for fighting the Ottomans, who had the largest standing army in Europe at the time, more effectively. Every aspect of war, from battlefield tactics to provisions and logistics, transformed because of the need to keep large forces in near-continuous operation. During the first thirty years of his career, Montecuccoli had not given much thought to the Ottomans and Hungary. By the 1660s, however, his ideas about war developed in interaction with his experiences on the Hungarian frontier, where divisions and ambiguities in military authority often hampered effective action. The lessons of the Thirty Years' War remained important, but Montecuccoli's observations of the Ottoman army provided new insights and helped him reframe current military knowledge with a powerful new urgency. In *On the War against the Turks in Hungary*, Montecuccoli argued that, for the Habsburg dynasty to survive, Leopold I must emulate the military organization and culture of the Habsburgs' most formidable enemy.

Court Politics

Montecuccoli produced his magnum opus in the context of deep political rivalries at court. Although he constantly complained about impediments to his advancement (a common refrain among courtiers), he was quite powerful. In 1659, he received a position on the Privy Council (*Geheime Rat*). As early as 1661, the Venetian ambassador in Vienna reported that Montecuccoli was one of only eight men who governed the empire under Leopold—a group that included two other Italian noblemen, Johann Ferdinand Portia and Annibale

RAIMONDO
di Montecuccoli Baron di Hohenech.

FIGURE 6.1. *Portrait of Raimondo Montecuccoli.* The Trustees of the British Museum.

Gonzaga.[10] Over the course of the next thirteen years, four of the eight would die and two would be exiled, clearing the way for both Montecuccoli and Johann Adolf Schwarzenberg to become members of another select group of advisors to the emperor. After the Peace of Vasvár, Montecuccoli did not return to the battlefield for another eight years, which gave him time to secure his position at court. He sat on the Court Chamber or Treasury (*Hofkammer*) and War Council, serving as War Council president starting in 1668 and earning the noble title "High Well-Born" (*Hochwohlgeboren*) in 1669.[11] During the Wesselényi Conspiracy (1664–71), he urged Leopold to take harsh measures against the Hungarian nobility, including the reimposition of Catholicism. In 1674, he was part of a court faction that worked toward the downfall of Leopold I's chief minister, Lobkowitz, who was the leading proponent of the French policy. In 1675, the Tuscan diplomat Lorenzo Magalotti arrived in Vienna and reported that Montecuccoli held "the upper hand" when it came to political and military matters: Grand Duke Cosimo III needed to consider his influence above others.[12]

During the 1660s, Montecuccoli's major court opponent was Lobkowitz, who rose to power with the death of Portia. In 1644, as Montecuccoli struggled to establish a stable position in imperial service, he courted Lobkovitz as a patron; however, after the Thirty Years' War ended, Piccolomini warned Montecuccoli not to trust Lobkowitz.[13] Montecuccoli's relationship to Lobkowitz deteriorated when Lobkowitz's French policy became clear and when Lobkowitz served as president of the Aulic War Council.[14] Montecuccoli sent Lobkowitz updates from the battlefield and petitioned for the army's needs, often complaining about confusing orders, poor organization, and insufficient funds.[15] He started to blame Lobkowitz for military problems. By 1669, Lobkowitz had used his position of authority to create a new advisory body, the Privy Conference (*Geheime Konferenz*), from which he excluded Montecuccoli.

Montecuccoli had allies in his opposition to Lobkowitz and the French policy, including his brother-in-law, Dietrichstein, who had served as chief minister for two empresses, and Johann Maximilian Lamberg. Montecuccoli and Dietrichstein's surviving correspondence reveals their collaboration in war and politics. In 1666, Montecuccoli secured a regiment for a relative, Maximilian Dietrichstein.[16] Lamberg had Italian and Spanish connections: he had accompanied Eleonora Gonzaga from Mantua to Vienna in 1651 and became ambassador to Spain shortly thereafter. He also had family ties to Montecuccoli's in-laws, the Dietrichsteins, and eventually became father-in-law to Ferdinand Bonaventura Harrach, another ambassador to Spain, who later became a member of the Privy Conference and a friend of Montecuccoli's.[17] Finally, Johann Paul Hocher, a commoner who was a lawyer and protégé of Lobkowitz's and also served on the Privy Conference, ultimately conspired against his patron as he advanced his own career (he was ennobled in 1667).[18] Lobkowitz had other enemies, including Empress Claudia Felicitas, the daughter of Archduke Ferdinand Karl of Tyrol and Anna de' Medici. Lamberg, Dietrichstein, and Montecuccoli were members of a broad, international Habsburg network seeking to uphold the Spanish-Austrian alliance with powerful connections to one another reinforced through marriage ties, diplomatic experiences, and military patronage.[19]

In these years, Leopold I regularly sought out Montecuccoli's opinions on military and political matters, even when Montecuccoli was away from court.[20] Undoubtedly, Montecuccoli's dutiful lifelong service to Leopold's father, grandfather, and uncle, as well as Montecuccoli's record of battlefield successes, generated trust. As War Council president, Montecuccoli argued for and achieved a certain degree of standardization in terms of troop organization, weaponry, soldiers' pay, and barracks.[21] He fought against the continual efforts by some in the court—including Lobkowitz—to reduce the size of the army and repeatedly urged the emperor to develop a large standing army to oppose his enemies at a time when "all princes great and small are armed."[22] In an undated document probably written at this time called *Perpetual Militia* (*Milizia perpetua*), Montecuccoli argued for "a perpetual disposition of good, disciplined, valorous, and veteran troops," an idea he had borrowed from Lipsius, who had coined the term *"miles perpetuus."*[23] Montecuccoli justified the development of this kind of army because "the imminence of invasion by the Turk is perpetual."[24] Nonetheless, the lack of money continuously stymied reform efforts.[25]

Montecuccoli also encouraged the centralization of military authority under the Aulic War Council and greater efficiency in disbursing funds for the military. In a short tract written in 1670, *Difficulties That Occur in the Council of War* (*Difficoltà le quali occorrono nel consiglio di guerra*), he criticized the current system in which funds owed to soldiers or for fortifications projects were never paid out because the Court Chamber withheld or misused them. He argued that the Aulic War Council should be financially independent of other governing bodies. He complained of inexperienced civilians running military offices and the cumbersome chain of command that military decisions filtered through. In the past, he alleged, the president of the Aulic War Council had wielded far more influence. He wrote, "There is no state in the world that is in greater danger of war than the kingdoms of His Imperial Majesty and neither is there a place in the world where military matters are held with such little care and reflection."[26] Montecuccoli both implicitly and explicitly pointed fingers at Lobkowitz, who oversaw the various governing bodies of the court as Leopold I's chief minister. Montecuccoli even repeated a rumor that Lobkowitz had been bribed by military contractors in Silesia.[27]

When Louis XIV's aggressions toward Austria became clearer at the start of the 1670s and especially after Hungary was subdued following the magnates' conspiracy, Leopold I began to doubt the wisdom of the policy shift toward France. Despite Montecuccoli's objections on account of his age and health (he was already sixty-three years old), the emperor placed him in command of fifteen thousand troops to help the Dutch against the French in 1672.[28] In late summer, Montecuccoli set off on campaign, leading his forces through Lower Austria, where he requested and received support from the estates in the form of housing, foodstuffs, and baggage transport—a development that signaled increasing involvement of the estates in military administration.[29]

Montecuccoli, however, remained dissatisfied: Lobkowitz ordered him to avoid open warfare with the French. Similar to the early 1660s, Montecuccoli navigated an ambivalent policy with his troops, where he was not free to lead the army as he wished. By February 1673, he demanded to be removed from command and was back in court in April. As Montecuccoli struggled to explain the army's needs, he sent letters to various ministers, including both Martinitz and Dietrichstein. In particular, he instructed his messenger to meet with Dietrichstein, "in whom I have full confidence," and to beg Dietrichstein for help convincing Leopold I to adopt his strategy.[30] Montecuccoli traveled to Vienna shortly thereafter and met with Leopold I in person.

Perhaps more than anything else, the failure of the previous year's campaign convinced Leopold I to adopt Montecuccoli's plans. In the summer of 1673, Leopold I put Montecuccoli at the head of a larger army and gave him free rein to execute his military strategy. Montecuccoli's Rhine campaign against the French general Turenne pitted two of the leading generals schooled on the battlefields of the Thirty Years' War against each other, both masters of maneuver warfare. Through a series of deceptive marches and countermarches and by repeatedly cutting Turenne off from his supplies, Montecuccoli outmaneuvered his opponent, whose forces grew demoralized from months of long marches with insufficient provisions.[31] This campaign, an important setback for the French, sealed Montecuccoli's reputation as one of the greatest military commanders of the century. He campaigned against Turenne again in 1675: Turenne was killed in battle and the contest ended in a stalemate.[32]

Montecuccoli's experiences in 1673 harked back to the 1661–64 campaigns in Hungary and Transylvania. Initially appointed to lead Habsburg forces, Montecuccoli was impeded from carrying out the campaigns as he wished due to distant political decisions. Both times, Leopold I suddenly shifted strategy and appointed Montecuccoli supreme commander over Habsburg forces with the authority to conduct the campaigns as he wished. Leopold I was responding to the interests of multiple competing parties as well as to changing circumstances. Perhaps his relative flexibility was because the stakes of war were extremely high. When an initial set of plans failed, Leopold I quickly changed his mind. In each case, Montecuccoli gained a major military accomplishment and his approach to war was vindicated.

After 1672, Montecuccoli had started to appear frequently in the Privy Conference, although he was not an official member. In 1673, he composed *Poor Government of the Court Chamber—Defects of the Chamber* (*Mal governo della camera aulica—Diffetti della camera*), in which he mounted a series of blistering attacks on court officials. Montecuccoli claimed that "the bad government of the Chamber is notorious on its own account" and surmised that "from the Chamber derive the origins of the rebellion of the Hungarians, the diminished fame and authority of the Emperor, the impossibility of doing the things that are necessary for the maintenance of his dominions, and the poor, most dangerous condition to which present matters have been reduced." He railed against what he believed to be blatant corruption and mismanagement under the direction of Lobkowitz, and avoided criticizing Leopold I directly.[33] He continued other military writings, composing a final, short treatise, *On the Military Art* (*Dell'arte militare*, 1673)—a military dictionary in which he succinctly defined key concepts related to warfare in a numbered list—and producing a second version of *On Battle* (*Sulle battaglie*, 1673).[34] In 1674, Leopold I set Lobkowitz's downfall in motion, appointing a commission to investigate his activities. On 18 October, Hocher intercepted Lobkowitz on his way to court with an official decree condemning him to exile.[35] Lobkowitz's fate was ultimately tied to the success or failure of the French policy.[36]

As late as 1668, Montecuccoli downplayed his power in Vienna. In the opening lines of a document titled *On the Subject of the Imperial Disarmament* (*In suggetto del disarmamento Cesareo*), he wrote: "Short on understanding, new to office, poorly-informed about arcane matters, not rebellious by nature, I imprison my opinion in deference to others on account of my obligation and inclination. To differ from the others makes me distrust myself, but I don't have to impose complete silence upon the zeal of my most devoted service because, having no part of the discourse, I can harm nothing."[37] Montecuccoli exaggerated his lack of influence, but during the height of Lobkowitz's power in Vienna, he had indeed been excluded from certain aspects of the decision-making process. However, Montecuccoli was very much a participant in the discourse about war, not least because he continued to disseminate his views through manuscript writings. These writings culminated in Montecuccoli's magnum opus, *On the War against the Turks in Hungary*, which he presented to Emperor Leopold I in 1670. This three-part treatise ultimately outlasted all of the slanderous pamphlets and devious political maneuverings that Montecuccoli feared were tarring his reputation. It represented Montecuccoli's definitive response to his detractors and his ultimate vision of a science of war that he argued could bring order and stability to the Habsburg realms. One of the most significant features of the treatise is the centrality of Ottoman power in shaping his vision of a Habsburg standing army.

The Ottomans through Habsburg Eyes

Montecuccoli's writings on the Ottomans followed over a century of increasing military, diplomatic, and commercial interactions with the Ottoman Empire, as well as a long tradition of demonizing Muslim opponents dating back to crusade literature. Scholars puzzle over what they see as a tension between historical accounts of the rather optimistic exchanges of material goods, art, and architectural styles between East and West and the simultaneous Renaissance humanist diatribes against the Ottomans.[38] The battlefield was another site of exchange, made particularly fruitful by the soldierly imperative to learn quickly from experience and not make the same mistake twice.[39] Montecuccoli's views of the Ottoman army were not entirely accurate, since many of them were filtered through ideas about the Ottomans based on accounts of sixteenth-century conflicts. Nonetheless, his claim in *On the War against the Turks in Hungary* that his recent campaign experiences permitted him to evaluate the Ottomans with fresh eyes would have intrigued audiences who continued to fear and misapprehend this powerful neighbor.

The perception of the Ottomans as ferocious and bloodthirsty stemmed from powerful currents of thought that originally appeared in medieval crusade literature. With the expansion of the Ottoman Empire in the fifteenth century, German humanists such as Sebastian Brant further disseminated stereotypes of the Ottomans, calling for crusade.[40] Others alleged the Ottomans were not just theologically bankrupt but politically and culturally illegitimate, posing threats to Christendom on every front. Aeneas Silvius Piccolomini, later elected Pope Pius II, canonized a view of the Ottomans as the descendants of the Scythians. He deplored the fact that a people he viewed as barbarous trampled upon the most venerated of civilizations, committing atrocities. Whereas Aeneus Sylvius downplayed Ottoman military virtues, Francesco Filelfo emphasized the shame he believed Christians ought to feel: "What a disaster, what miserable fortune, that things should have sunk to so low a level that the ignoble and uncouth horde of Turks, descended from the lowliest, starving shepherds and the fugitive slaves of the Scythians, should now lord it far and wide over Christian peoples and kings, and with every day increase their power to such an extent that they now lie scarcely sixty miles from Italy!"[41] The status of other Islamic powers even rose by comparison to the Ottomans, permitting Christians to entertain alliances with Arabs and Persians.[42] In the sixteenth century, interpretations of the Ottomans as an enemy of apocalyptic proportions spread through Central Europe. Mercurino Gattinara, an Italian humanist who served Emperor Charles V as chancellor, relied on prophecies to form an eschatological vision of the clash between the Ottomans and Habsburgs, calling for crusade as well as internal reform.[43]

By the early sixteenth century, some humanists developed a more historical approach to the Ottomans that surely impacted Montecuccoli's later works.[44] In his 1504 *Commentaries*, Raffaele Maffei was critical, distinguishing between Islamic powers, considering local contexts, and refraining from the essentializing tendencies of earlier literature.[45] Perhaps the most influential views derived from Machiavelli, whose sense that empires rise and fall for secular reasons helped break down simple dichotomies between an evil, immoral East and a virtuous, Christian West. Machiavelli argued that the Ottomans were the heirs of Roman *virtù*, along with the Franks, Mamluks, Germans, and Saracens.[46] He did not emphasize Christianity as an ingredient of imperial success; if anything, Christianity had served to weaken and corrupt European states.[47] Giovanni Botero and Justus Lipsius, who were greatly indebted to Machiavelli, belonged to a group of thinkers who tried to resolve ethical objections to Machiavelli's works by attempting to integrate Christian morality into the theory and practices of realpolitik.[48] It was primarily in the writings of Lipsius that Roman military values and methods were transmitted to army reformers like Maurice of Nassau. Montecuccoli reiterated many of Lipsius's ideas, especially in the ways he comprehended the broad political context of war and the examination of its goals and motivations as essentially political in nature. Divine forces remained relevant, but mostly receded to the background as explanations for historical events.

Writings that were the product of a new phase of diplomatic relations with the Ottomans, starting in the sixteenth century after Suleiman the Magnificent's Hungarian conquest, further shaped this discourse.[49] While eschatological ideas certainly continued to inform political attitudes, some diplomatic and military reports adopted a more detached tone as diplomats attempted to stabilize relations between the two imperial powers.[50] Central Europeans developed their own discourse on the Ottomans grounded in the "inherently defensive" political culture of the Holy Roman Empire.[51] Well-known texts such as the letters by the imperial ambassador to Constantinople, Ogier Ghiselin de Busbecq, and treatises by the imperial commanders Lazarus von Schwendi and Leonhard Fronsperger argued in favor of a cautious military approach to the

Ottomans.[52] Montecuccoli absorbed the wisdom of these writers as part of his larger military and political education alongside Tacitus, Vegetius, Caesar, Machiavelli, Campanella, and Lipsius.[53]

Like Montecuccoli, these sixteenth-century writers revealed a pervasive admiration for the size, discipline, and organization of the Ottoman army. During this period, the Ottoman army evolved into a centrally funded force composed of Timariot light cavalrymen who fought in exchange for land grants (*timars*) and permanent cavalry and infantry forces paid for in cash by the government.[54] In particular, writers were fascinated by the janissaries, men from conquered Christian territories kidnapped as boys and raised for military and government positions. They became elite, highly trained infantrymen, and some served as the sultan's personal guard.[55] At the same time, Ottoman forces included a wide variety of volunteers, such as the relatives of timar-holders and janissaries, servants at garrisons or in the retinues of cavalrymen (*sipahis*) and governors (*beylerbeyis*), as well as other subjects who saw valor in war as a way to gain land grants or salaried posts.[56] Christian authors observing these Ottoman forces in the field invariably commented on their discipline and obedience in battle, as well as the cleanliness and orderliness of their camps.[57]

These writings on the Ottoman army emphasized its size and alleged ferocity, although the Ottomans' key advantage lay in organizational capacity. With a relatively well-developed state bureaucracy, Ottoman officials ably directed and supported military resources at the administrative level.[58] They regularly reallocated troops to the most vulnerable areas of the empire, making effective use of their troop numbers.[59] Finally, through decades of war against the Persian Empire on open plains, the Ottomans came as close to mastering the demanding logistics of long-distance warfare in grueling conditions as any contemporary power.[60] Ottoman planning and ambitions were limited by practical realities such as poor roads, weather, patchy resources, and the many uncertainties of war.[61] Similar to other imperial powers, resources stretched especially thin in distant regions, including the province of Buda, although the Ottomans fared better at financing border defense than the Habsburgs.[62] Overall, the Ottoman military performed best during short campaigns against the small, independent forces of Eastern European warlords.

Even as critical methods of analysis and experience with the Ottomans increased, stereotypes continued to plague the literature on the Ottomans, who provided a useful foil to Europeans urging their own societies to reform. In 1603, following an expansion of English-Ottoman trading relationships, Richard Knolles published *The Generall Historie of the Turkes*, the first comprehensive study of Ottoman history in English. Knolles acknowledged that Christian soldiers were untrained and vulgar by comparison to Ottoman soldiers, "not to speake in the meane time of the want of the auntient martiall discipline." The Ottomans, by contrast, "imitate Romans in many things" and yet remained a "barbarous empire."[63] Knolles's use of the Ottomans for criticizing Christian powers was a longstanding rhetorical tool. In 1397, Coluccio Salutati had written of Ottoman military discipline and endurance as an incitement to Christians: if barbarians practiced such virtues, surely Christians could equal or surpass them.[64] These views were paradoxical: writers asserted that the Ottomans were barbarians who practiced Rome's civilized methods better than Rome's supposedly civilized Christian heirs. Furthermore, the Ottomans were often defined as embodying both fury—an uncontrolled passion—and obedience—a quality that required passivity.[65] The idea that the Ottomans were slaves who offered the sultan blind obedience, which appears in Knolles's work as well as in Venetian ambassador accounts, grew more influential.[66]

Montecuccoli's *On the War against the Turks in Hungary* shared some of the biases of a long tradition of writing about the Ottomans, while at the same time showing a concerted effort to analyze Ottoman strengths, criticize perceived weaknesses of the Ottoman cavalry, infantry, and artillery, and provide cautious, rational responses. He took an anthropological approach, evaluating Ottoman social, cultural, and religious customs in addition to military matters.[67] Montecuccoli alleged that Habsburg officials were ignorant of the Ottomans. He wrote: "Vain error deludes those who speak of the forces of the Turk with little esteem. So many kingdoms conquered by him, never again recovered by Christians, so many fortresses taken by storm, so many pitched battles won, which convince of the foolhardiness and inadequacy of sentiments so wrong, conceits of those who, striking with the tongue instead of the sword, defeat an army with magnificent words."[68] On the one hand, statements such as these served a rhetorical purpose: if officials in Vienna were perceived as ignorant, readers might be more readily persuaded by Montecuccoli's attacks against them and his claim of unique knowledge. When he assessed the disappointing Peace of Vasvár, the contemporary traveler and diplomat Paul Rycaut accused the emperor of "backward" behavior due in part to "contempt of the *Turk*," indicating that Montecuccoli may have been imitating common literary conventions to some degree.[69]

On the other hand, Montecuccoli did indeed have relevant recent experience. In Montecuccoli's eyes, the alleged ignorance of ministers in Vienna and imperial commanders had been on full display in the most recent campaigns. The behavior of the Hungarian nobles who boldly sought reconquest of their ancestral lands and muddled orders from Vienna suggested that key parties in the last war with the Ottomans had been truly unprepared. Montecuccoli seemed to think that the problem was not just a culture of contempt for the

Ottomans, but also fear of Ottoman army size that made Christians incapable of successful battlefield action. He lamented, "Our losses have had their origin mainly in the contempt that has been made of the Turk; the dread or neglect of fighting disproportionately few against many has placed victories in the hands of barbarians."[70] While Montecuccoli continued to argue for the benefits of maneuver warfare in dealing with a more numerous enemy, he also insisted that a permanent, professional army under the authority of the emperor was central to achieving victory.

Initially Montecuccoli framed his proposal for a new war against the Ottomans with an overly simple dichotomy: "Barbarians place their advantages in their multitude and fury; but the disciplined army in order and valor."[71] Here he followed both Caesar and Machiavelli, who contrasted barbarian fury to Roman order and discipline. The founders of Greco-Roman states had given *ordine* or *ordini* to their peoples, while war itself upheld the order of state and society.[72] Valor, meanwhile, was the helpmate of rational qualities such as orderliness or prudence, providing the spiritual energy to execute well-laid plans.[73] For Montecuccoli, military order was critical for facing an opponent as frightening and overwhelming as the Ottomans. Yet the bulk of the treatise would show that Ottoman methods—especially with regard to logistics and discipline—were well-ordered and their fighting valorous. Montecuccoli's magnum opus was vulnerable to traditional prejudices against the Ottomans, but he was also clear about Ottoman strengths. He ultimately made a bold, compelling argument for the adoption of Ottoman methods in the establishment of a new military science oriented around managing the demands of a professional standing army.

Imperial Perspectives

In *On the War against the Turks in Hungary*, Montecuccoli used what he learned from the Ottomans to reframe all of the knowledge and experience he had collected about war in terms of a powerful new tool: the professional, standing army. Montecuccoli argued that in response to the "continuous, imminent danger" of the Ottomans, one must "maintain a standing body of veteran regiments of long experience."[74] However, it was not just fear of Ottoman invasion that motivated him. Montecuccoli was steeped in humanistic studies of ancient military power. Through both study and experience, he identified the Ottoman army as similar to the Roman army. Montecuccoli's text helps us to understand the perspective of a contemporary reformer who viewed Ottoman military achievements as part of the legacy of Rome.

In order to develop and maintain an effective army of permanent, disciplined forces, Montecuccoli argued that the Habsburgs needed to transform recruiting practices, institute strict programs of training and drill, reform military finance to pay soldiers regularly, overhaul the hierarchy of command and the system of promotions, and reorganize the state bureaucracy overseeing military affairs. *On the War against the Turks in Hungary* was divided into chapters that covered different aspects of the Ottoman military system and drew a map for attaining victory over it. Montecuccoli started with what he termed "preparations" (*apparecchio*), comparing the Ottomans to the Romans at the end of the section: "Long preparation produces a speedy victory," he surmised, "and it was a principle of the Romans, imitated today by the Turks, to make great but short wars. And it is a trite proverb that the wise man should not embark without biscuit."[75] His repeated, bitter criticisms of the 1661 decision to invade Transylvania without preparation indicated that he probably believed the Habsburgs violated this fundamental Roman wisdom.

Preparation for war required, above all, large numbers of regularly paid, disciplined soldiers. Montecuccoli emphasized that the "first and main advantage" of the Ottomans was the size of their army.[76] He explained that the Ottoman standing army included the impressive janissary infantrymen—"sons of European Christians"—as well as volunteers.[77] Montecuccoli recognized that this Ottoman advantage could be traced back to the establishment of their presence in Eastern Europe. He recounted the numbers of enemy soldiers Christians had faced over time, showing his command of literature on the Habsburg-Ottoman wars. Similar to other European writers on the Ottomans, he exaggerated, claiming that Suleiman the Magnificent invaded Hungary in 1526 with 300,000 men and advanced on Vienna in 1529 with 150,000.[78]

At the same time, Montecuccoli emphasized that the might of the Ottoman army depended not on sheer size, but also on the way they trained, organized, and deployed soldiers—all features of a broader culture in which war and preparation for war took precedence. He alleged that Ottoman recruits "are of the best quality" because "only the art of war is held in esteem and the sole avenue and gateway to dignity, to riches and to offices, indeed everyone who has spirit and heart employs himself in the army." He concluded that "The praise of Vegetius towards the Spartans can more rightly be given to the Turk today."[79] Ottoman military skills and sensibilities, including "the management of arms, military movements, and the habituation to orders," were all absorbed from a young age as if through their "milk."[80] Like previous writers on the Ottomans, Montecuccoli created a largely positive image of Ottoman military capabilities in order to criticize his own society.

Montecuccoli went further, integrating these ideas about a permanent, professional soldiery into a larger historical-philosophical literature that revealed the influence of Machiavelli, Campanella, and Lipsius. According to these views, history was a providential cycle in which empires rose and fell. The Ottoman Empire was currently supreme, a fact that prompted those who entertained millenarian views, including Campanella and Queen Christina of Sweden, to imagine that the conditions for apocalypse had arrived, requiring Christians to unite to defeat the Antichrist.[81] While a certain amount of apocalypticism may have influenced Montecuccoli as well, he belonged to a milder and more intentionally methodical culture of historical thinkers. He saw in the succession-of-empires theory a practical framework for understanding and responding to change rather than an impetus for enacting utopian political designs. Similar to Botero, Montecuccoli admired the Ottoman army, but he abstained from millenarian-tinged hysterics.

The Ottoman Empire was the supreme empire, Montecuccoli argued, because of their army, which was similar to the Roman army. In both cases, a large, organized army ready to fight at all times allowed these states and the commerce and arts they protected to flourish. Citing the example of Rome since the Punic Wars, he stated: "A great empire cannot maintain itself without arms." History revealed what he believed was a "universal law": "Nothing under the sun remains the same."[82] Rulers could not rest on their laurels. The continuous flux of human affairs required that they be prepared to fight at any moment. He added that many other modern nations had some kind of military force either at the ready or easily called into service, including Sweden, Holland, England, Poland, France, and the Swiss.[83]

For Montecuccoli, the Spanish Habsburgs provided the example of an empire on the wane due to a neglect of military matters. On the face of it, this complaint sounds ludicrous: Spain devoted an outsized amount of resources to waging continuous wars on multiple fronts, which some scholars have argued was the main factor in a Spanish "decline."[84] The focus of Montecuccoli's criticism, however, was on military culture. He insisted that esteem for military affairs as well as rewards and recompense for service had deteriorated in Spain.[85] The Swedes provided an alternative model. In recruitment, discipline, and effectiveness, they appeared closer to both the Ottomans and the Romans. He claimed they awarded offices based on merit, a point Montecuccoli repeatedly returned to. Ultimately, Montecuccoli preferred the Swedish system because the Swedes employed pikemen and heavy cavalry, whereas the Ottoman army fielded light troops.[86]

When he shifted his gaze back to Central Europe, Montecuccoli was critical of the tradition in which vassals fulfilling an ancient duty to defend the emperor's lands supplied military needs. This tradition was failing because the nobles lacked "talent, inclination, practice, and discipline." Whereas in the past vassals were personally obligated to fight for their lord, he alleged, many of these vassals' fiefs had been sold, given away, or taken into the possession of the church or treasury. Political and military power was far more complex than Montecuccoli's oversimplified feudal model allowed: the empire was composed of "a complex web of rights and privileges" involving not just the management of relationships between emperor and princes, but also negotiations between many different territorial rulers and their local estates.[87] Regardless of its complexity, a major problem with the system in which estates and ruler shared military authority was that for centuries it focused overwhelmingly on providing short-term defense—also the goal of the Hungarian *insurrectio* armies. Leopold I, who was forced to assert himself regularly in broader geopolitical events, needed to be capable of waging both offensive and defensive wars and wars of varying duration.[88]

Montecuccoli was troubled by what he saw as a failure on the part of hereditary nobles to serve. He complained, "In place of valorous nobles, country people currently fill in."[89] Montecuccoli recognized that poor children sent as tribute to the Ottomans could become great warriors with the right upbringing and rewards in place. After all, as Lipsius had argued, "nature brings forth some valiant men, but good order through industry makes more."[90] One assumes that under Montecuccoli's proposed military system even the most rustic recruit could become a decent soldier and perhaps even climb the ranks through merit. Despite the implications of his own vision, Montecuccoli rarely seemed to have imagined military leadership in the hands of anyone but the nobility. Yet the emperor's current set of hereditary nobles were incapable of transforming mere peasants into soldiers and leading them into war. These nobles' failure to fit the emerging mold of the dedicated professional officer, a figure Montecuccoli and other writers extolled in military treatises, was inexcusable.

Montecuccoli also opposed mercenary armies, an intriguing point of view for a military entrepreneur and yet one that makes sense in the context of the decades of difficult campaigning he endured in the imperial army. He admitted contract armies were "haphazardly put together," requiring "much money with little reward."[91] Rather than use contractors, he suggested systematizing resources by following a model that he characterized as both Swedish and Ottoman: each province should provide "a certain number of households and fields, like the *timars* for the maintenance of soldiers."[92] Recruitment had to occur continuously and could include people from different lands, including from conquered areas, provided they were Christians. Furthermore, each province could create a military academy in which "orphans, bastards, beggars, and the poor" were trained for war, "in imitation of the Janissaries of the Seraglio."[93] In another example, he called for "military seminaries" and added nobles to the list of groups to receive training.[94] To Montecuccoli, the Ottoman and the Swedish cases showed how similar kinds of military practices built powerful states. This pairing might seem unusual to modern readers used to picturing Swedish reforms in a Western European nation-state framework that starts with the Dutch and culminates in French or Prussian achievements. Montecuccoli's intriguing comparison emerged because he operated from a decidedly imperial perspective. He paired the Ottomans with the Swedes because he believed they both provided military models that met imperial (rather than anachronistic nation-state) needs.

The main reasons for opposition to the standing army were convincing: standing armies were extraordinarily costly, and they generated concerns among nobles and princes about how to maintain territorial sovereignty when the emperor's soldiers needed food and lodging on a continuous basis. For these reasons, it was expedient to disband armies in moments of peace. Montecuccoli accused his opponents of entertaining futile hopes for peace, inquiring, "Which times were ever peaceful?"[95] He reviewed more than a century's worth of continuous conflicts: from the sixteenth-century wars against the Ottomans through the Thirty Years' War, and up to the 1670 Hungarian rebellion. He lamented the fact that the imperial army was nonetheless continuously disbanded and then reconstituted, which was extremely expensive in itself.[96]

Political power lay at the heart of the argument. Montecuccoli assured nobles who feared a loss of liberty that their consent remained necessary, only that they could utter it "with a single breath" rather than grant concessions repeatedly. Standing forces would hardly be detrimental to their privileges since only a standing army could guarantee those privileges: "And tell me by grace, is there another means to maintain the state? Is there another part of Europe more subject to war than this? More immediately contiguous to the Turk? Does man remember a time when peace was ever real, neither inconstant nor doubtful?"[97] After the Thirty Years' War, many German nobles accepted that reforms were needed to prevent the profound suffering caused by the contributions system and the movements of foreign armies across German territories. Some agreed that standing armies helped maintain peace because they were seen as deterrents to war. The imperial chancellor Schönbrunn proposed an alternative at the January 1663 Reichstag when he suggested raising an army controlled from Frankfurt by a war council composed of all of the imperial estates.[98]

Even when Montecuccoli engaged explicitly in political arguments about the standing army, he invoked the Ottomans as a model of authority. He repeated the stereotypical view that the Ottoman Empire was composed of a single ruler with ultimate authority over all other subjects, who were essentially slaves.[99] Such views were drastic oversimplifications: in reality, the sultan feared rebellion and responded to the needs of the janissaries and other troops.[100] Nonetheless, while some of his contemporaries followed in the footsteps of Venetian diplomatic discourse by attacking the Ottoman Empire as an empire that lacked a powerful, propertied nobility, Montecuccoli noted the benefits of despotism.[101] Even Busbecq had reflected at length on the advantages of slavery, alleging that many ancient achievements depended on slavery and that "the Turks both publicly and privately gain much from slavery."[102]

Montecuccoli likened the authority of command in the Ottoman army to the power enjoyed by Roman dictators, another way in which the Ottomans more perfectly absorbed the lessons of Rome. Ottoman military commissions were granted "freely, absolutely, and with full authority to the Captain General" in order to "promote the service of the prince according to the usage of the Roman Republic."[103] In an emergency, which war undoubtedly was, it was more effective if a single leader, chosen for his experience, knowledge, and virtue, was granted power to execute decisions without having to negotiate or compromise. The authority of an officer over his men was not unlike the authority of a ruler over his subjects, an analogy that Lipsius had also made explicit.[104] Montecuccoli's writing was a reflection of his experiences in the Hungarian campaigns, as well as part of a broader current of thinking in which writers adopted the political and moral values of ancient Rome where authority (*auctoritas*) and discipline (*disciplina*) went hand in hand. Lipsius believed that subjects must stoically endure their political masters—even tyrants—and show constancy, rather than rebel.[105]

Montecuccoli connected military valor, a concept long cherished by the traditional nobility, to despotism. For a century or more, military theorists had helped to redefine valor, pairing it with prudence as central ingredients of successful military command. In 1604, the Sienese military theorist Imperiale Cinuzzi wrote that prudence, which depends on wisdom and control over information, "commands," while the more spiritual quality of valor "executes." Valor "consists in the ardor which proceeds partly from the spirit, partly from the body, but that from the spirit is the principle, which on account of being full of vigor and ardor and of a certain vivacity one is rendered ready to do important things and to encounter difficulties and dangers."[106] Valor made great things happen.

Montecuccoli pointed out that valor was only possible if a general had the unquestioned authority to execute plans. According to Montecuccoli, the "valor of the army" consisted partly in "the executive virtue born from the despotic, undivided command that the heads of armies have."[107] Montecuccoli remained bitter about the divided commands and acrimony produced by the 1660s Habsburg-Ottoman wars. He fumed about the use of auxiliary armies under diverse captains, which he characterized as undisciplined, untrained, and hastily thrown together. He added: "Secrets are made public. The mode is slow, speed and ease of operating are retarded and embroiled in intrigue and made difficult by consultations, deliberations, and dissensions because each has different goals, opinions, instructions, rules, and principles: whence discipline is relinquished, commands not executed, obedience disputed, operations slandered and orders confused."[108] When he arrived at the chapter titled "On Operations," which focused on the critical role played by "resolution, secrecy, and speed," he returned to the same themes.[109] "The command of the Turk," he alleged, "has resolution, secrecy, and speed because it is despotic and in the head of the army absolute and unlimited, independent." "Our style," he continued, "can be neither resolute, secret, nor unexpected." He blamed the fact that the army was composed of "German, Hungarian, French, Italian, Swedish, etc. troops," which were further divided into multifarious groups with distinct privileges, goals, and orders. These conditions produced lethargy because the process of arriving at consensus was slow and difficult while secrets continuously leaked because so many people needed to be consulted. The "remedy," he argued, was "to give absolute authority to a single head, or else give him a council of few but good, faithful, and expert men." in the manner of both the Romans and Venetians, as well as the Ottomans.[110]

Decades before, Wallenstein had assumed an unprecedented level of authority over the army and ultimately wound up assassinated. Crucially, Montecuccoli argued for an entirely different type of army composed of subjects rather than mercenaries who were highly trained, obedient, and well-paid. The ideal general to lead these troops was full of good health with a "majestic presence" and a mastery of military science acquired over the course of many years of experience. He was loyal to the emperor, subverting private passions to a common good.[111]

In the opening lines of the dedication of *On the War against the Turks in Hungary* to Emperor Leopold I, Montecuccoli made clear that he was the right man for the job. He highlighted his vast experience in the clearest terms yet: "I have lived 60 years in this world, and 43 of them in the military service of Your Imperial Majesty. Experience taught me various things in order to advance my service, and the graces that successively lifted me from the lowest level of the militia up to the supreme command of the army, with the accruing of so many other offices previously divided among many persons, now accumulated in me."[112] Since the beginning of his career, Montecuccoli had tried to distinguish himself from other competitors by pointing out his experiences of toil and sacrifice, in which he risked his life on a daily basis for the emperor. Now he attributed his rise in the Habsburg hierarchy from the "lowest level" to "supreme command" and other prestigious offices to that long experience. Montecuccoli believed that he had earned his promotions. He also revived old battles. He accused his rivals of lacking the correct knowledge about war derived from experience and principles. In part three, he argued that mastery of military science was only acquired in the field. "*Scienza*," along with "a good disposition," gave rise to "concord" and "good order," two essential ingredients of "good fortune" for a captain.[113]

As Montecuccoli was quick to point out, he had spent nearly his entire career as an active participant on campaigns experiencing firsthand the political and military transformations that he claimed demanded new conceptions of authority and obedience. Gerhard Oestreich argued that "to extol Montecuccoli is to extol Lipsius" when he explained the profound influence of Lipsius's conceptions over Montecuccoli's military science.[114] There is no doubt that Montecuccoli absorbed Lipsius. Nonetheless, his work was an original compilation of political, cultural, and military knowledge that—significantly—was tested and reflected upon as he led numerous campaigns in diverse theaters of war. His example provides a window into a curious, underexplored literary landscape where political and military theory mingled with actual battlefield experience. In particular, his circumstances resulted in distinctive views of an Ottoman power whose much-maligned despotic control was interpreted in positive terms.

After Montecuccoli's 1680 death, an international group of Habsburg officers, whose careers were defined by the harrowing Siege of Vienna (1683), implemented many of the ideas found in *On the War against the Turks in Hungary* as they conquered Eastern European territories from the Ottomans. Beyond his focus on building a large force of disciplined, regularly paid troops and a stable hierarchy of command, Montecuccoli provided a series of recommendations for combatting the Ottomans that could be put to immediate practical use. He continued to argue that the smaller Habsburg forces should avoid battle until the right set of circumstances fell into place.[115] Once they were engaged in battle, he emphasized the use of artillery as an advantage, advising Habsburg officers to combine continuous rounds of fire with cavalry charges against the Ottomans, as he had at St. Gotthard (Mogersdorf).[116] He also urged use of the Danube River, since it flowed west to east, providing transport and tactical opportunities.[117] The lessons of his doomed intervention in Transylvania had affirmed the importance of creating stable lines of communication and supply before initiating conquest. He outlined passages through geographic space, recommending which areas to secure and why, due to site location, fortifications, commercial activity, pastures, and water sources.[118]

These practical details proved useful, but Montecuccoli's broader understanding of war with the Ottomans was also critical. He pointed out that the only warfare the Habsburgs had ever experienced with the Ottomans involved conflicts in which the Ottomans carried out well-planned offensives: "The Turk does not wait for war, but brings it to the homes of others," he wrote.[119] During these campaigns, the Ottomans arrived late in the season, conquered connected spaces, and then left before winter's onset.[120] Montecuccoli argued that the Habsburgs had to make a profound shift to this pattern. Rather than react in an unplanned, haphazard way to carefully calculated Ottoman offensives—what he saw as the typical Hungarian response—he recommended that the Habsburgs themselves wage "a long and continuous war of many years," which, he asserted, was "diametrically opposed to the designs of the Turk."[121]

The series of Ottoman defeats that occurred during the Wars of the Sacred Alliance (1684–99) were mainly the result of the Habsburgs forming powerful military and diplomatic alliances and waging a long, continuous war on multiple fronts.[122] The wars that started in the sixteenth century and accelerated in the seventeenth had produced officers focused on meeting the challenges of long, continuous war. By the late seventeenth century, military servants of the Habsburgs had developed the alliances, organization, and strategies required to defeat the Ottomans. In modern military histories, the beginning of European global conquest has often been connected to the advantages Europeans gained by mastering the use of gunpowder during the military revolution. However, as Montecuccoli's experience at St. Gotthard (Mogersdorf) showed, entering into battle and using the right weapons and tactics was only part of military experience and often a small one at that. Montecuccoli spent far more time figuring out how to create the conditions—political, cultural, fiscal, and intellectual—that would give rise to a powerful army. At root, Montecuccoli admired the Ottoman army and urged the adoption of Ottoman ideas and methods by Austria. Gone was the providential narrative about the Ottomans existing as punishment for Christian sins. Montecuccoli viewed Europeans as directly responsible for past errors.

Montecuccoli's magnum opus was a call for an entirely new way of thinking about war that reflected an understanding of the military experiences of the past century, political theory, anthropological study, and new approaches to knowledge. In the eighteenth century, he was widely known as a leading European general and military theorist. He never claimed that the idea of a standing army was an original thought. His significance lies in the way he created analytical frameworks for explaining and disseminating military developments that had occurred over time in piecemeal fashion as sudden, even haphazard responses to imminent danger. His career was built upon the final flowering of the Renaissance: the lessons of Machiavelli and the Italian Wars, as well as a previous generation of humanists who not only turned to the ancients for wisdom and sought out practical applications for knowledge, but also engaged in intellectual projects to summarize and universalize knowledge. Into those rich veins, he integrated seventeenth-century political philosophy, empiricism, mathematics, and experiences from the Thirty Years' War to the later Habsburg-Ottoman conflicts. Although his career preceded the age of professions and specialization, perhaps more than anything else he helped to define the habits, practices, and mental equipment that the greatest generals would need in the age of military professionalism.

The kinds of figures who shared his understanding of the world were not necessarily rulers and ministers at the court center, but other military entrepreneurs. Sometimes considered outsiders by members of the native elite, they forged careers and knowledge upon a shifting bedrock of travel, international aristocratic and commercial networks, and military expertise. They used emerging scientific tools and collected and analyzed information to make sense of their experiences. Many of them spent their lifetimes traveling to different battlefields and courts gaining diverse knowledge in strange, unfamiliar places. By imagining war through their eyes, we can see the truly transregional dimensions of military change. At the same time, these experiences cast doubt upon the idea of the military revolution as a single, dramatic shift that set certain parts of Europe on a modernizing course. The evolution of military tactics, strategy, organization, and administration was the product of a long-term and geographically wide-ranging transmission from the Renaissance through the age of the great powers.[123]

Montecuccoli's ambitious dream of a regular standing army and efficient administration of such an army would not come to fruition in his lifetime, and subsequent generations would experience similar problems, like the disbanding of soldiers in peacetime. The Austrian Habsburg monarchy also failed to centralize military institutions on par with other powers of the late seventeenth and early eighteenth centuries because of the extremely decentralized nature of Habsburg rule. Nonetheless, army strength increased dramatically over the course of the second half of the seventeenth century, "quintupling between 1650 and 1700." As Montecuccoli had hoped, the army became all-important, especially with the onset of the "Age of Heroes" after 1683, when a new generation of commanders drove the Ottomans back from Vienna and pursued them through large parts of Eastern Europe.[124]

Over the course of many decades and at different times and in different places, political elites reimagined the ways in which power was organized and deployed. Those elites, who were far more flexible than we often give them credit for, gradually discovered and articulated new roles for themselves. The emergence, elaboration, and dissemination of military science and the development of standing armies were part of a decades-long process in which soldiers and officers moved in and out of military and court hierarchies by navigating transregional aristocratic relationships. Many elites viewed their battlefield encounters, in which large composite armies clashed, as playing instrumental roles in a grander sequence of historical events characterized by the rise and fall of empires. In this context, the interpretation of the Ottoman experience was highly instructive and had a profound impact on the development of modern military ideas and practices, even shaping the way contemporaries conceived of authority itself. Montecuccoli's thinking about war and politics represented an understanding of history as a succession of empires: after the Romans, the most powerful empire that emerged on former Roman lands and emulated Roman military power was the Ottoman Empire. The 1661–64 conflicts with the Ottomans produced a particularly influential strand of thought and action important for understanding the transmission and diffusion of military changes.

As a military reformer and officer, Montecuccoli does not fit comfortably within the narrative of state centralization, but neither does Habsburg Austria. The need to create a coherent defensive organization for the Hungarian frontier has often been seen by historians as spurring Austrian centralization, because it contributed to the emergence of the Aulic War Council in Vienna in 1556.[125] However, the Aulic War Council did not successfully centralize control over border defense until the eighteenth century, following the 1699 Treaty of Karlowitz and the creation of a brand-new system.[126] At a time when administrative efficiency was more of an aspiration than a reality, the Habsburgs permitted and even benefited from the maintenance of ambiguous, overlapping authorities.

Montecuccoli pointed out the problems in centralizing military authority under "ministers of greater authority than experience."[127] In *On the War against the Turks in Hungary*, he argued for more efficient fiscal and command structures for the military. At the same time, one could interpret his treatise as an argument for greater authority to operate as he wished in local conflicts without having to defer to a corrupt, out-of-touch court center. The cosmopolitan military nobles who cooperated with the Austrian Habsburg monarch married into distant noble families, acquired property and titles in multiple jurisdictions, and often fought in more than one army. They did not intend to contribute to a centralization of power that would reduce the scope of their own activities and resources. Montecuccoli argued that figures like him should have more power, and rulers who benefited from aristocratic mobility were not necessarily inclined to impose limits on their activities.

Epilogue
The Generation of 1683

In the final years of his life, Montecuccoli managed to avoid the battlefield but continued to serve as president of the Aulic War Council. He criticized Emperor Leopold I's advisors, quarreling with the influential Father Emmerich Sinelli, Leopold I's confessor, and the Privy Conference secretary, Christoph von Abele. Other rivals included the prince of Schwarzenberg and the Spanish ambassador of Genoese descent Marquis de los Balbases, Paolo Spinola. Spinola entangled the Tuscan diplomat Lorenzo Magalotti in his opposition to Montecuccoli, despite Magalotti's earlier positive opinion of the Modenese general.[1] When Leopold I made a military decision without consulting the Aulic War Council, Montecuccoli threatened resignation in 1679. In response, Montecuccoli's court rivals alleged that he desired to flee imperial service with ill-gotten riches.

Leopold I remained sympathetic to Montecuccoli. He explained that he could not accept Montecuccoli's departure because "my service" (*il mio servigio*) and "the public good" (*il ben publico*) depended on Montecuccoli. They lived in dangerous times and things were going badly: "I hope that you do not wish to abandon me and that you would continue in the office as you have up to now very commendably." He added that the Aulic War Council was "so well disposed" on account of Montecuccoli's "prudent direction" and assured Montecuccoli of his confidence and protection.[2] These were the words Montecuccoli needed to hear, but he also took the opportunity to mount a long-winded defense of his record, addressed to the emperor. This cycle of events was familiar: figures whom Montecuccoli did not consider to be qualified to speak on military matters had circumvented his authority, triggering an angry outburst from him. Leopold I, who appeared to view Montecuccoli as a useful and loyal servant despite rumors to the contrary, attempted to appease him, while Montecuccoli lodged a formal, written reply to the accusations.

Montecuccoli's 1680 response to his detractors is particularly interesting because he directly addressed charges of corruption and reviewed his financial record. In addition to his will, this document provides a glimpse of the sources of his wealth, especially contributions and gifts. Montecuccoli asserted that no formal complaints against him could be found in the archives of the chancelleries, and no one from the Rhine Valley, Silesia, Poland, or Hungary— major theaters in which Montecuccoli had operated—could claim to have given him money. Montecuccoli explained that when the cities of Hamburg, Lübeck, and others in northern Germany offered him three hundred thousand– four hundred thousand florins for his troops, he deposited the money with the commissioner general "without keeping even a penny for myself."[3] In 1659, the elector of Brandenburg had offered him a personal gift of thirty thousand florins, but because Montecuccoli never received imperial approval, he refused the gift "as a sign of my most humble incorruptible fidelity."[4]

Montecuccoli did admit to certain profits. He claimed that he had been regaled with "one or another trifle of horses, of chocolates, clocks, pastilles from Spain, plaster reliefs, chests, and similar little things [*e simili cosette*]," as well as a diamond-studded portrait. In his defense, he argued, "had I received some present of significance, the simple truth is that there was never any prohibition against it." All offices, whether at the imperial court or under foreign princes, had their "emoluments": "Why, then, should they be denied me?"[5] He also pointed out that he had spent large sums of money on conspicuous consumption at court, that his properties had suffered as a result of his absences, and that he had never been fully reimbursed for the 270,000 florins owed to his cousins Ernesto and Girolamo for their three regiments.[6] Montecuccoli alleged he had only received thirty thousand florins in incremental sums, in addition to one hundred thousand florins in salary. After considering his total profits in imperial service, he concluded, "I can truthfully assert that I have not increased my assets to any considerable degree."[7] This passage openly acknowledges the receipt of goods and contributions, as well as payments from the emperor. It also suggests that Montecuccoli received cash payments that he did not report. He denied that these payments violated imperial regulations, insisting they fell within the range of common and acceptable practices. Montecuccoli made an important distinction: he promoted individuals because of their merits. If they gave him gifts, they did so after their promotions as expressions of thanks. Corruption only occurred, he argued, when someone unworthy of a position provided a gift as an inducement to promotion.

Due to the obscurity of the financial record, it is difficult to know exactly how wealthy Montecuccoli was at the end of his life, but he certainly did not die impoverished. His conclusion that he did not gain anything from his career must be subjected to a healthy skepticism, especially as it was a common claim among courtiers. There were other important ways to grow wealth, including gaining tax immunities and debt relief or collecting interest on loans. For instance, in 1676, Montecuccoli became a creditor to the emperor, loaning Leopold I seventy-five thousand florins.[8] In his 1675 will, the largest part of his wealth appears to have been his estates, which he left to his only son, Leopold Philip. He provided dowries for his daughters, promised thirty thousand florins to his widow (who died before him), and left other valuable objects to friends and family, including a painting by Albrecht Dürer for Ferdinand Dietrichstein.[9]

As his 1680 defense confirms, Montecuccoli never flagged in his efforts to defend himself from attacks and to further shape his reputation as a prudent, valorous commander singularly dedicated to the Habsburg dynasty. In the opening lines, Montecuccoli pointed out that the accusations rested on the fallacy that his motivation had been "greed for money"—Machiavelli's criticism of military contractors. As this book has shown, Montecuccoli and other military entrepreneurs fought strenuously against such characterizations. Montecuccoli responded that he had served with "sincerity and integrity" and "without any other interest than that of the acquisition of His Most Merciful Imperial Graces and of honor and glory."[10] However, the fact that he remained vulnerable to charges of corruption and greed throughout his career suggests ongoing contemporary ambivalence about the ways military entrepreneurs—many of them from outside of traditional hierarchies—gained power and prestige. Not everyone bought into the image of the expert, disciplined, and virtuous warrior Montecuccoli promoted in treatises and other writings.

Nonetheless, by the end of his life, Montecuccoli had achieved great power and wealth—making him an attractive target—even if he had missed out on the windfalls of the 1620s. One of the main ingredients to his success was his enduring obedience—or at least its appearance—to a succession of three Habsburg emperors. Obedience forced him to make sacrifices, but these sacrifices were short-term. His experiences in imperial service from the 1630s through the 1670s are a testament to the incremental nature of rewards available to talented and well-connected military entrepreneurs capable of adapting to changes in warfare and committed to long-term Habsburg service.[11] His career trajectory diverged from that of Wallenstein, who rose quickly to a stratospheric height before crashing down again. Other Italian noblemen in imperial service had displayed a similar kind of obedience to the Habsburgs. It originally emerged from feudal bonds, confessional commitments, and family ties—all of which meant that they maintained multiple loyalties—but it evolved into a particular devotion to the person of the Habsburg emperor because of the nature of the rewards.

At the same time, Montecuccoli did not always behave like a perfectly loyal, obedient vassal. When it suited him, he changed shape, becoming a client who entertained multiple patronage opportunities. In fact, one might argue that he actively exploited the inherent ambiguity of his status as either a subject or a client (or both at the same time)—another indication that political position was malleable in the seventeenth century. Montecuccoli never openly defied the emperor or fought against imperial or Spanish forces, but he actively negotiated with Habsburg patrons, threatened to leave imperial service on multiple occasions, and criticized imperial policy (directing criticisms at court ministers rather than the emperor). He played his cards well. The fact that Leopold I recommended the title prince of the empire for Montecuccoli in 1675, with the support of the electors of Mainz, Brandenburg, Saxony, and the Palatinate, is a reflection of support and admiration for Montecuccoli among some of the most powerful figures in the empire.[12] In 1678, Montecuccoli was asked to become the protector of the Akademie der Naturforscher, or Sacri Romani Imperii Academia Caesaro-Leopoldina Naturae Curiosorum, later known as the German National Academy of Sciences Leopoldina—a request that reflected an understanding of Montecuccoli's reputation both as a respected scholar and as an important patron in Vienna.[13] Eight months after composing his 1680 defense, Montecuccoli died in Linz at age seventy-two. His body was transported back to Vienna and laid to rest in the Jesuit church.[14]

After his death, Montecuccoli's reputation was initially a product of how contemporaries read accounts of the 1663–64 war against the Ottomans, above all his own. Portions of his writings, especially those covering the Habsburg-Ottoman wars, were published and entered into circulation across the continent for the first time around the turn of the century. The first publication occurred in a 1692 Italian-language work dedicated to Vittorio Amedeo II, duke of Savoy, who oversaw an expansion of the Savoyard army starting in 1690.[15] A Spanish translation was published the following year. While these publications featured only a draft of Montecuccoli's magnum opus (referred to as *Sistema dell'arte bellica*), a more complete, though problematic, Italian-language edition of his works was published soon after, in 1704, by Heinrich von Huyssen, the tutor of Russian tsar Peter the Great's son, Alexei Petrovich. Publications in other languages along with subsequent editions of those publications followed: in Latin in 1716, in French in 1712, 1734, 1735, 1760, 1769, 1770, 1777, and 1785–87, and in German in 1736. [See Appendix B]

In 1775, at the height of Montecuccoli's posthumous international fame, the Modenese count Agostino Paradisi composed an elegy to him for the annual opening of the University of Modena, which he sent to Frederick the Great. In an attached letter, Paradisi proclaimed Montecuccoli to be "the greatest captain in modern Italy, who could not be equaled by Turenne, and surpassed only by Frederick the Great."[16] The fact that the most iconic military men of the eighteenth century were compared to Montecuccoli and aspired to equal or surpass his achievements attests to his eighteenth-century status. This attention continued through the beginning of the nineteenth century, when Ugo Foscolo and Giuseppe Grassi published further Italian-language editions of Montecuccoli's works.[17] However, sometime after Napoleon's death, Montecuccoli started to disappear from view, becoming an obscure figure by the second half of the nineteenth century—when the foundations of the historical discipline were laid. From 1899 to 1901, Alois Veltzé revived international interest in Montecuccoli with his four-volume German translation of a wide variety of Montecuccoli's writings, including military treatises and correspondence. However, the absence of an obvious national historiography to affiliate Montecuccoli with impeded his full reintegration into the canon of military thinkers.

Montecuccoli's works, as well as the example he had set in his lifetime, nonetheless had a major impact on the generation of officers who succeeded him in the imperial army, the "generation of 1683."[18] These men witnessed the Ottoman Siege of Vienna or were inspired by the dramatic relief of the siege to participate in the subsequent conquest of Eastern Europe. They were consumed with a zeal for Habsburg service that mirrored what the generation of White Mountain had felt. Antonio Carafa (1642–92) was present at the relief of the Siege of Vienna after having started his career as part of Montecuccoli's forces. He was a Neapolitan nobleman who fled his native land after committing a murder in the early 1660s. First, he stopped in Malta to join a relative in the Knights of St. John and battle Muslim enemies in the Mediterranean, distinguishing himself at the siege of Djidjelli. Shortly thereafter, probably excited by news of Montecuccoli's recent victory against the Ottomans, he traveled to Vienna where his relative, Carlo Carafa, served as papal nuncio. Carlo Carafa introduced him to figures who became powerful allies, including Empress Dowager Eleonora Gonzaga, and Antonio joined Habsburg forces in 1665. During the 1683 Siege of Vienna, Charles of Lorraine sent Carafa to beg the king of Poland, Jan Sobieski, for immediate intervention. Once Sobieski's army entered Silesia, Carafa returned to the Polish king's side in order to guide his army to Vienna. On 12 September, the combined Christian forces swarmed down from the surrounding hills and vanquished the Ottomans. Carafa eventually earned admission into the Order of the Golden Fleece and served as the general commissary of the imperial army and the imperial plenipotentiary to the Italian princes in 1691.[19] His hardline views of Hungarians were similar to Montecuccoli's. In 1687, he presided over the Massacre at Eperjes (Prešov) in Hungary at which twenty-four Protestants who had supported the Hungarian leader Imre Thököly were executed[20]

According to his biographer and fellow Neapolitan, Giambattista Vico (1668–1744), Carafa had been close enough to Montecuccoli to be consulted by him on difficult military matters. Vico's account of Carafa's life, *De rebus gestis Antonj Caraphaei* (1716), is essentially a portrait of a new kind of loyal military officer. Vico characterized Carafa as courageous, austere, and methodical, a commander who cared more about service to the emperor than personal glory, planned carefully for battle, and studied warfare. Vico, who is more widely known for writing an anti-Cartesian treatise, *The New Science*, had been commissioned by Carafa's heir to write the biography. He must have read recently published portions of Montecuccoli's treatises or manuscript copies, considering how closely his depiction of Carafa conforms to Montecuccoli's self-image. Vico concluded that Carafa had also been underestimated by those who were ignorant of military science.[21]

Two slightly later figures, Eugene of Savoy (1663–1736) and Luigi Ferdinando Marsigli (1658–1730), show how the patterns of expertise and professionalism embodied by Montecuccoli developed into the eighteenth century. Eugene of Savoy eventually occupied a role similar to Montecuccoli's, but Eugene became the iconic figure of Austria's rise and the prototype of the dedicated, disciplined, professional military officer. He had been a subject of Louis XIV, although his father descended from the dukes of Savoy and his mother was Olympia Mancini, one of Mazarin's nieces. By the time Eugene was ready to begin a military career, the French court had turned against his mother. She fled into exile, and Eugene lost important social and political allies. Rejected by Louis XIV, Eugene turned to connections in the Italian peninsula in order to establish a career in Central Europe under Leopold. Due to marriage ties between the House of Savoy and German princes, Eugene had German relatives who helped him, including the elector of Bavaria, Maximillian Emmanuel, and Louis of Baden, whose uncle was the president of the Aulic War Council. Eugene's financial stability during the early part of his career came from Vittorio Amedeo II, the reigning duke of Savoy, who granted him the revenues of two Piedmontese abbeys (and to whom the earliest known publication of Montecuccoli's treatises had been dedicated).[22]

The parallels between Eugene and Montecuccoli are noteworthy. Eugene also served three successive Habsburg emperors and initiated army reforms. He was the first president of the Aulic War Council since Montecuccoli who was also an active commander.[23] Eugene read Montecuccoli's works and, similar to Carafa, appears to have imitated Montecuccoli's model or was at least perceived as doing so. Eugene carefully guarded his reputation as a military expert. According to his twentieth-century biographer, he studied intensively, exposed himself to physical discomfort, pursued rigid discipline, sought to maintain self-control at all times, and was deeply loyal and obedient to the emperor. Eugene excelled when faced with circumstances of "almost inevitable defeat" and was less effective when he operated at an advantage.[24] Under Eugene's leadership, Habsburg forces routed the Ottoman army at the Battle of Zenta in 1697, effectively ending the war. Eugene took over supreme command of the imperial forces in 1708 during the War of the Spanish Succession, working in coordination with the duke of Marlborough to inflict multiple defeats on the French army. He secured Habsburg influence over the Italian peninsula and the Netherlands before returning to the eastern frontier to crush a resurgent Ottoman power. Eugene's career witnessed the resolution of the conflicts on two fronts—against France and the Ottomans—that Montecuccoli had struggled to grasp. Finally, Eugene responded to Habsburg military weaknesses and to personal criticisms in a way that was remarkably similar to Montecuccoli. Eugene believed that the ministers who attacked him were men "who like to puff themselves up with brave words, but who have not the smallest understanding or experience of war." He complained that he received "neither money nor supplies" and threatened resignation.[25] In 1705, Eugene apparently refused to lead the army in its poor state, citing the potential ruin to his honor and reputation.[26] Through the Aulic War Council, Eugene attempted to implement reforms to improve the quality of commanders, forbid the sale of commissions in regiments, and instill strict, uniform discipline across the army.[27]

Eugene's contemporaries viewed him as a dedicated professional officer. They commended him for his courage, loyalty, seriousness of purpose, caution, objectivity, and incorruptible nature. The French marshal Villars, who had served both alongside and against Eugene and was a friend off the battlefield, commented that Eugene "is thought a brave man, having as much good sense as spirit, enjoying studying and being set on becoming the good officer he is certainly capable of becoming; he is full of ambition, zealous about anything which has to do with glory but even more to be commended by his sincere and true devotion to duty." In 1692, the English minister Paget characterized Eugene as "a very worthy person, and greatly esteemed for a prudent goodly commander." When Rüdiger Starhemberg, the president of the Aulic War Council at the time, recommended placing Eugene in command of the imperial forces in 1697, he wrote, "[He knew] no one with more understanding, experience, application and zeal for Your Majesty's Imperial service, or with a more generous and disinterested temper, and possessing the esteem of his soldiers to a greater extent than the prince." The duke of Marlborough commented on Eugene's "merit."[28] Their language reflects a long-standing discourse about war initially developed by military entrepreneurs over a century before.

Marsigli, a contemporary of Eugene's, provides a different sort of coda to the history of Italian noblemen in imperial service, one that points to certain limitations to these careers. Originally from Bologna, Marsigli would one day claim that his original interest in mathematics was inspired by his desire to become a soldier—similar to Descartes.[29] As a member of the second post-Galilean generation, he employed mathematics and new techniques and instruments in the investigation of physical properties. He was voracious in his studies. Marsigli eventually produced major treatises on the oceans (1725) and the Danube (1726) and is considered to be a father of the earth sciences. He exemplified the fruitful interchange between war and science at the turn of the eighteenth century, though ultimately failed at a Habsburg career when he was dishonorably discharged in 1704.

Before seeking a position in the imperial army, Marsigli recognized the benefits of close study of both Hungary and the Ottoman Empire. He traveled in the Ottoman Empire and studied Hungarian history and the roots of Hungarian rebellion.[30] He received an introduction to Leopold I and pledged his service to the emperor prior to the Siege of Vienna but was captured by the Ottomans when the siege transpired. After a brief stint grinding and roasting coffee for the encamped forces, Marsigli was taken as a slave to Bosnia. He was eventually ransomed and returned to soldiering for the Habsburgs. Marsigli formed friendships with Carafa and another prominent Italian general, Enea Caprara, who had been a protégé of Montecuccoli's and Piccolomini's nephew. Marsigli spent two decades in Habsburg service and ultimately used his cartographic skills to help demarcate the new border separating the Ottoman and Habsburg empires in 1699.[31]

Similar to Montecuccoli, Marsigli used writings, sketches, and maps in order to demonstrate his expertise and recommend himself to patrons. He excelled at the genre of scientific military writing. For instance, the completion of a survey of fortifications would earn him a letter of recommendation. Marsigli studied his environment and sought ways to be useful even—and perhaps especially—during breaks or lulls in military activity. In the preface to one of his works, he claimed that he would serve the emperor with his pen during a halt in military activity and describe the furthest regions of Hungary.[32] On his way to Vienna in 1682, Marsigli had taken a route that allowed him to inspect the military border with France. He had pointedly stopped in Regensburg, "where I lingered three days in order to inform myself of the order and manner with which the ministers of the empire convene here." At his first meeting with Leopold, he gave the emperor a report and a sketch based on what he had seen in the borderlands, "the first thing of mine that he saw."[33] Later, he offered suggestions on how to rebuild trade between the Habsburg and Ottoman empires and even proposed a medical frontier during periods of plague in the east.[34] His claim to be an authority on the Ottomans was eventually backed up by a treatise, *Stato militare dell'imperio Ottomanno*.[35] He was offered but declined employment under other patrons, including Queen Christina of Sweden, who apparently hoped to involve him in plans for a naval attack on the Ottomans.[36]

Marsigli was less dedicated to military endeavors than Eugene or Montecuccoli: at one point, Marsigli left his regiment in someone else's charge so that he could travel for his studies. He was alleged to have committed gross mistakes, and lost positions as a result. Caprara grew to resent Marsigli after Marsigli supplied him with erroneous information during a campaign.[37] In 1703, Marsigli was partly responsible for the surrender of the Fortress of Breisach to the French. Marsigli had been second-in-command to Count d'Arco and both men felt justified in defying official orders to continue fighting when they perceived how dire their circumstances were. Eugene, who had just taken over the presidency of the Aulic War Council with an agenda to enforce stricter discipline throughout the army, was appalled. Arco was executed the following year, and Marsigli had his sword broken over him to symbolize his dishonor.[38] Their actions at Breisach contradicted basic values of obedience and loyalty. Marsigli returned to the Italian peninsula, where he later commanded papal forces against the Habsburgs, but mostly focused on scientific studies.

Despite the troubled nature of his military career, Marsigli's experiences in Central and Eastern Europe provided the foundation for his scholarship. By the end of the seventeenth century, however, the many-sided, entrepreneurial figures for whom warfare was a gateway to multifaceted knowledge about the world were disappearing. Montecuccoli and Marsigli were creatures of the late Renaissance and its encyclopedic tendencies, approaching a new age of specialization. Through decades of success on campaign, Montecuccoli became a military expert for whom science and scholarship were useful in terms of how they served the needs of armies and rulers. Marsigli's penetrating scientific studies on diverse topics related to the eastern frontier were not enough to turn him into a successful officer, particularly in the face of reputation-ruining events like his disobedience and capitulation at Breisach. However, he was admitted to the Royal Society in 1691 and founded the Institute of Sciences and Arts in Bologna in 1715. He was committed to scholarship for its own sake, as was Descartes, who had also abandoned the military career that provided him with his first immersion in engineering and mathematics.[39] Although historians do not necessarily group these figures together, Marsigli, Eugene, Descartes, Carafa, and Montecuccoli can all be understood as members of an early modern cohort of learned aristocratic warriors who traveled widely for war and, in the process, grappled with key problems—political, military, and/or epistemological—of their generations.

Long after Montecuccoli's lifetime, nobles continued to rely on their own wealth and credit to finance troops, which some of them, such as Montecuccoli's successor, Charles of Lorraine, even leased out to other rulers.[40] It was not until the reforms of Charles VI (r. 1711–40) that officers were explicitly banned from extorting payments from the populace.[41] Even during Maria Theresa's reign (r. 1740–80), magnate families such as the Esterházys and Pálffys continued to use their own wealth and credit to raise regiments, while Prince Liechtenstein spent ten million florins of his own wealth on work connected to military reforms.[42] Eighteenth-century rulers who ceased to rely on military entrepreneurs and started maintaining standing forces still participated in military entrepreneurship by contracting out their armies to other rulers as a way to pay for them.[43] Meanwhile, individual nobles and merchants became contractors charged with supplying specific items such as uniforms and weapons. In France, a country that boasted one of the most centralized military systems in Europe, the state did not take on the responsibility of providing arms to its own soldiers until 1727.[44] After achieving her goal of doubling tax revenues, Maria Theresa was the first Habsburg ruler to finance a standing army of over one hundred thousand men in 1754, but she failed to pay for numerous other needs, such as provisioning magazines or building new fortresses.[45] In Habsburg Austria, the last privileges of regimental ownership were not eradicated until 1868, when the colonel of a regiment completed his full transformation into "a mere military functionary."[46]

Habsburg forces remained markedly international in composition, partly due to the Habsburg monarchy's wide geographical reach. According to István Deák, up until the fall of the Austro-Hungarian Empire, the Austrian army cultivated a multinational officer corps that owed personal fealty to the emperor and were committed to the supranational ideology that supported Habsburg power.[47] The origins of the special relationship between Habsburg monarchs and the army have been traced back to Maria Theresa—the "mother" of the troops who offered noble status to all officers after thirty years of service—as well as to the earlier period of conquest on the eastern frontier, when the army grew in size to confront the Ottomans.[48] The Thirty Years' War also represented an important phase of development, because Emperor Ferdinand II lacked military support from his rebellious estates and relied on a new kind of army: the privately raised forces of military entrepreneurs, figures who expressed personal devotion to the emperor. Wallenstein was the most famous example of this type, but he became far too powerful, was not perceived as sufficiently loyal, and was held in suspicion until he was assassinated. Montecuccoli's experiences from the 1630s on are more instructive. They provide useful details on the evolution of a military entrepreneur-officer into a devoted Habsburg servant, while showing how loyalties, as well as the traditions of service that produced them, were a product of wider political, cultural, and military patterns dating back to the Renaissance and Reformation.

While Italian military entrepreneurs are fascinating in themselves, what is most significant is the ways their experiences and ideas reflect the politics and culture of seventeenth-century Habsburg Europe. Close study of their careers reveals politically fractured territories, composed of diverse, interconnected communities where multiple loyalties were common. In this context, we can reevaluate the nature of Habsburg power, which attracted so many noblemen willing to commit their wealth, credit, safety, and reputations to the Habsburg cause. In the case of Italian noblemen in imperial service, connections to the dynasty were often an outgrowth of Spanish Habsburg dominance in the peninsula; at the same time, Italian nobles cultivated their own distinctive imperial traditions and increasingly looked toward Central Europe for military opportunities from the Thirty Years' War forward. By the end of the century, the pan-Christian allusions of Habsburg rule continued to attract recruits from across Europe—especially to defend against the Ottomans—but Austrian Habsburg ambitions had grown much more assertive, while the Spanish Habsburgs ceased to exist. Austria contended with France and the Ottomans, despite a continued lack of effective centralized government or the kind of standing, professional military forces associated with modern state power. Military entrepreneurs played a major role in the birth pangs of a new Habsburg Europe oriented around the Austrian branch of the family, even as Montecuccoli complained loudly of his poor treatment and longed for a future in which careers like his own were no longer needed.

APPENDIX A

Montecuccoli's List of Books

Manoscritti che trattano di diverse materie (KA: NL Montecuccoli, B/492: 194; in Veltzé, *Ausgewaehlte Schriften*, 1:115–18)
Autori e loro abbreviature (abbreviations omitted)

1. Le Conseiller d'Estat in 16 imprimé à Paris 1641.
2. Fr. Baconi de Verulamio sermones fideles sive Interiora Rerum in 16. Lugd. Batav. 1641.
3. Justi Lipsii. Politicorum libri sex. Lugd. Batav. in 32. 1634.
4. J. Lipsii Monita, et Exempla Politica, in 32. Amsterdam. 1630.
5. Le Prince de Balzac in 8, à Paris 1642.
6. Politicae Succinctae ex Aristotele potissimum erutae, libri duo, auctore M. Balthasar Cellario. Jenae in 16. 1645.
7. Arn. Clapmarius de Arcanis rerum p. in 16. Amsterodami 1641. Item Christophorus Besoldus.
8. Aulicus inculpatus in 32. Amsterodami 1644.
9. Cyriaci Lentuli Augustus in 16. Amsterodami 1645.
10. Le Parfait Ambassadeur, à Paris 1642.
11. Frederici de Marsolaer legatus. Amsterodami 1644 in 16.
12. Las Obras, y Relaciones de Ant. Perez. 1644 in 8.
13. Tutte le opere di Nicolò Macchiavelli; Historia, Principe, Discorsi, Arte della guerra, operette. 1550 in 4o.

14. Le Ministre d'estat de Silhon. Paris 1643 in 16.

15. Le Politique très-Chrestien sur les actions du Cardinal de Richelieu. Paris 1647 in 16.

16. Cardani Arcana Politica. Lugduni Batavorum 1635 in 32.

17. Campanella, Monarchia Hispanica 1640 in 16.

18. Les oeuvres de Balzac, à Paris par Leonard Fuchet. 1628 in 8.

19. Aphorismi Politici, et Militaris Danaei, Lugduni Batavorum ex officina Jacobi Marci. Ao. 1639 in 16o.

20. Le Parfait Capitaine de Rohan. Paris 1642.

21. Argenis Barclai (Barclay). Frankfurt 1630 in 4.

22. Thomae Campanellae Metaphysica

23. Eiusdem libri septem de Medicinalibus

24. Campanellae Grammatica

    25. Logicorum libri tres

    26. Rhetoricorum liber unus

    27. Poeticorum liber unus

    28. Historiographia

    29. Astrologicorum libri 7

    30. Physiologia

    31. Moralia

    32. Politica

    33. Oeconomica

    34. Apologia pro Galileo

    35. Prodromus philosophiae instaurandae

    36. Atheismus triumphatus

    37. de Gentilismo non retinendo

    38. de Praedestinatione, Electione, Reprobatione Tractatus

39. Valerianus Magnus

40. Baconus Verulamius

41. Joannes (Rud.) Glauberus de furnis novis Philosophicis

42. Joannis (Rud.) Glauberi opus minerale

43. Théâtre d'honneur et de chevalerie de la Colombière (Vulson sieur)

44. Neue vollkommentlich Kumeterbuch durch Jacobum Theodorum Tabernaemontanum. Gedruckt zu Frankfurt 1625 in 2o.

45. Johannis Schröderi M.D. Pharmacopoeia Medico-Chymica. Ulmae 1649 in 4o.

46. Oeconomia ruralis, et domestica, hiebevor von M. Joanne Colero beschreiben, jetzo aber auff ein Neues vermehret und verbessert. Gedruckt zu Mayntz 1645 in 2o.

47. Medulla destillatoria, et Medica durch Conradum Khunrath Lipsen-
    sem. Hamburg 1638 in 4o.
48. Myrothecium, Chirurgia, Palladium: Spagyrica Joannis Fabri Mon-
    speliensis Argentorati. 1632 in 8.
49. Joannis Baptistae Portae Neapolitani Magiae Naturalis libri viginti
    Hanoviae 1644 in 8.
50. Ortus Medicinae; opuscula Medica de lithiasi, Febribus, Humoribus,
    Peste. Authore Joanne Baptista von Helmont. Amsterodami 1648 in 4.
51. Alchymia Andreae Libavii recognita, emendata, et aucta. Francofurti
    duobus tomis comprehensa 1606, 1613 in 2.

    Sunt varia opuscula. Alchymia, Commentariorum Alchymiae pars I.
    pars 2. Syntagma Arcanorum Chymicorum. Tractatus Chymicus.
    Defensio Syntagmatis Chymici. Examen Philosophiae novae. Analysis
    Confessionis fratrum de rosea Cruce.

52. Tyrocinium Chymicum Joannis Beguini. Vittenbergae anno 1640 in 8.
53. Zachariae Brendelii Chimia. Jenae 1641 in 8.
54. Secreti del Reverendo Donno Alessio Piemontese. In Pesaro 1558 in 8.
55. Joannis Hartmanni Praxis Chymiatrica. Genevae 1647 in 8.
56. Marci Cornacedini Methodus in pulverem purgantem; in 8. Genevae
    1647
57. Oswaldi Crollii Basilica Chymica. Tractatus de signaturis internis
    rerum. Francofurti in 4.
58. Cl.V. Lazari Riverii Praxis Medicae Tomus Primus. Lugduni 1649 in 4.
59. Manuscritti
60. Zacutus Lusitanus: de medicorum principum historia; Coloniae
    1629 n 8.
De praxi medica admiranda. Amsterdam 1639.
61. I secreti della Signora Isabella Cortese. In Venetia 1603 in 8.
62. Raimondo Lullo de' Secreti di Natura libri due. Alberto Magno delle
    cose minerali, e metalliche libri cinque. Il tutto traddotto da M.
    Pietro Lauro. In Venezia 1557 in 8.
63. Secreti diversi, e miracolosi raccolti dal Falloppia, et approvati da altri
    medici di gran fama. In Venezia 1565 in 8.
64. Dialogo del Vero Honore Militare di D. Girolamo d'Urrea
65. Il Duello del Fausto da Longiano
66. Il Duello dell'Alciato
67. Il duello del Mutio Justinopolitano
68. Trattato di Gio Battista Olevano
69. Bernhardus Varenius

APPENDIX B

Earliest Publications of Montecuccoli's Works

In Veltzé, *Ausgewaehlte Schriften*, 1: XI–XIII

L'attione bellica del conte Montecuccoli. Edited by G. B. Zappata. Turin, 1692. Italian.

Arte universal de la guerra del principe Raymondo Montecuccoli etc. Edited by B. D. Chafrion. Milan, 1693. Spanish.

Memorie del general principe di Montecuccoli. Edited by Heinrich von Huyssen. 2 vols. Cologne, 1704. Italian.

Memorie del general principe di Montecuccoli. Edited by Filoni. Cologne and Ferrara, n.d. Italian.

Mémoires de Montecuccoli, etc. Paris, 1712. French. Further editions: Amsterdam, 1734; Strassburg, 1735; Paris, 1760.

Commentarium generales artis bellicae aphorismos continens a. R. principe Montecuccoli. Edited by P. M. Bonbardi. Vienna, 1716. Latin.

Besondere und geheime Kriegsnachrichten des Fürsten Raimund Montecuccoli. Leipzig, 1736. German.

Commentaires sur les mémoires de Montecuccoli vom Grafen L. Turpin de Crissée. 3 vols. Paris, 1769. French. 2nd ed.: 3 vols. Amsterdam, 1770.

Commentaires sur les commentaires du comte Turpin de Crissée von Warnery. Wrocław, 1777. 2nd ed.: Hannover, 1785–87.

Opere di Raimondo Montecuccoli. Illustrated by Ugo Foscolo. Edited by L. Mussi. 2 vols. Milan, 1807. Italian.

Opere di Raimondo Montecuccoli. Edited by G. Grassi. 2 vols. Turin, 1821. Italian.

NOTES

The following abbreviations are used in the notes:

ADG	Ambasciatori della Germania
AFA	Alte Feldakten
AG	Archivio Gonzaga
ASF	Archivio di Stato di Firenze, Florence, Italy
ASM	Archivio di Stato di Mantova, Mantua, Italy
ASMo	Archivio di Stato di Modena, Modena, Italy
ASSi	Archivio di Stato di Siena, Italy
ASV	Archivio Segreto Vaticano, Vatican City, Rome, Italy
Autogr.	Autographen-Sammlung
Barb. lat.	Barberini Latino
BAV	Biblioteca Apostolica Vaticana, Vatican City, Rome, Italy
BE	Biblioteca Estense, Modena, Italy
BN	Biblioteca Nazionale, Rome, Italy
BUB	Biblioteca Universitaria di Bologna, Bologna, Italy
DBI	*Dizionario biografico degli Italiani*
Doc. Boh.	*Documenta Bohemica bellum tricennale illustrantia*
FHKA	Finanz- und Hofkammerarchiv
FM	Fondo Marsili
HHStA	Haus-, Hof- und Staatsarchiv, Vienna, Austria
HKP	Hofkammerprotokollen
MDP	Mediceo del Principato
MZA	Moravský zemský archiv v Brně, Brno, Czech Republic
NAP	Národní archiv v Praze, Prague, Czech Republic
NL: Montecuccoli	Nachlaβ Raimund Montecuccoli
OMeA SR	Obersthofmeisteramt—Sonderreihe
ÖNB	Österreichische Nationalbibliothek, Vienna, Austria
ÖSTA-KA	Österreichisches Staatsarchiv-Kriegsarchiv, Vienna, Austria
RAC	Rodinný archiv Collaltů
RAD	Rodinný archiv Ditrichstejnů

RAL   Rodinný archiv Lobkovic
RAP   Rodinný archiv Piccolomini
SOAL   Státní oblastní archiv v Litoměřicích, Litoměřice-
                Žitenice, Czech Republic
SOAZ   Státní oblastní archiv v Zámrsku, Zámrsk, Czech Republic

Introduction

1. In fact, just a week earlier, Ferdinand III, who had mistakenly believed conflicts in Central Europe were under control, had ordered Montecuccoli to transfer his troops to the command of the Spanish Army of Flanders for service in the Low Countries. As he received these orders from Ferdinand, Montecuccoli also received letters from the lieutenant general campaigning in Denmark—Matteo Galasso—urgently demanding he march toward Denmark. This episode is analyzed in chapter 3.

2. Raimondo Montecuccoli to Ottavio Bolognesi, 13 August 1644, in *Opere di Raimondo Montecuccoli*, ed. Ugo Foscolo (Milan: Luigi Mussi, 1808), 2:252–53.

3. Montecuccoli to Bolognesi, 13 August 1644, in Foscolo, *Opere*, 2:252–53. A letter to Ferdinand III's advisor, Maximilian, Count von Trauttmansdorff, is also revealing. See Raimondo Montecuccoli to Count von Trauttmansdorf, 22 April 1644, Foscolo, *Opere*, 2:249–52.

4. Michael Roberts, "The 'Military Revolution', 1560–1660," in *The Military Revolution Debate: Readings on the Military Transformation of Early Modern Europe*, ed. Clifford J. Rogers (Boulder, CO: Westview Press, 1995), 13–35; Geoffrey Parker, *The Military Revolution: Military Innovation and the Rise of the West, 1500–1800*, 2nd ed. (New York: Cambridge University Press, 1996); and Jeremy Black, *A Military Revolution? Military Change and European Society 1550–1800* (Atlantic Highlands, NJ: Humanities Press, 1991).

5. Fritz Redlich, "Military Entrepreneurship and the Credit System in the 16th and 17th Centuries," *Kyklos*, 10 (1957): 186–93. See also David Parrott, *The Business of War: Military Enterprise and Military Revolution in Early Modern Europe* (Cambridge: Cambridge University Press, 2012), 79–80.

6. Some historians use the term "military entrepreneur" and others use "military enterpriser." The classic study is Fritz Redlich, *The German Military Enterpriser and His Work Force: A Study in European Economic and Social History*, 2 vols. (Wiesbaden: F. Steiner, 1964). Also essential: Parrot, *Business of War*. M. S. Anderson characterizes the period from 1618 to 1660 as "the age of the entrepreneur." M. S. Anderson, *War and Society in Europe of the Old Regime, 1618–1789* (Stroud: Sutton, 1998), 33–76.

7. Redlich, *German Military Enterpriser*, 1:156; Golo Mann, *Wallenstein, His Life Narrated* (New York: Holt, Rinehart and Winston, 1976).

8. Georg Schreiber, *Raimondo Montecuccoli: Feldherr, Schriftsteller und Kavalier: Ein Lebensbild aus dem Barock* (Graz: Styria, 2000); Thomas Barker, *The Military Intellectual and Battle: Raimondo Montecuccoli and the Thirty Years' War* (Albany: State University of New York Press, 1975). See also Fabio Martelli's recent body of work on Montecuccoli, especially: Raffaella Gherardi and Fabio Martelli, *La pace degli eserciti e dell'economia: Montecuccoli e Marsili alla Corte di Vienna* (Bologna: Il Mulino, 2009).

9. Piero Pieri, *Guerra e politica negli scrittori italiani* (Milan: Riccardo Ricciardi Editore, 1954), 72–135; Azar Gat, *The Origins of Military Thought from the Enlightenment to Clause-*

witz (Oxford: Clarendon Press, 1989), 13–24. Modern publications of Montecuccoli's collected works are available in Italian and German: Raimondo Montecuccoli, *Le opere di Raimondo Montecuccoli*, 3 vols., 2nd ed., ed. Raimondo Luraghi and Andrea Testa (Rome: Stato maggiore dell'esercito, Ufficio storico, 2000); Alois Veltzé, ed. and trans., *Ausgewaehlte Schriften des Raimund Fürsten Montecuccoli, General-lieutenant und Feldmarschall*, 4 vols. (Vienna: W. Braumüller, 1899–1901). The only treatise published in English is *On Battle* (1645), which can be found in Barker, *Military Intellectual*, 73–173.

10. Gregory Hanlon, *The Twilight of a Military Tradition: Italian Aristocrats and European Conflicts, 1560–1800* (London: UCL Press, 1998).

11. Harms Kaufmann, *Raimondo Graf Montecuccoli 1609–1680: Kaiserlicher Feldmarschall, Militärtheoretiker und Staatsmann* (Vienna: Kaufmann, 1974), 10.

12. Schiller's masterpiece was debuted in 1798–99 and first published in 1800. For an examination of the influence of Schiller's iconic work, see Steffan Davies, *The Wallenstein Figure in German Literature and Historiography, 1790–1920* (Leeds: Maney Publishing, 2010).

13. Redlich, *German Military Enterpriser*, vol. 1, esp. 1:296–305.

14. Hanlon, *Twilight*, 94–100.

15. Hanlon, *Twilight*, 202–19.

16. Charles Ingrao, *The Habsburg Monarchy, 1618–1815* (Cambridge: Cambridge University Press, 1994), 121.

17. Montecuccoli, *Le opere*, 1:253.

18. For details about the family, see Tommaso Sandonnini, *Il Generale Raimondo Montecuccoli e la sua famiglia, note storico-biografico* (Modena: G. Ferraguti, 1913).

19. The Austrian Habsburgs ruled the hereditary lands directly. After 1627, the Bohemian crownlands (Bohemia, Silesia, and Moravia) also became hereditary. Lusatia was part of the Bohemian crownlands until its territories were absorbed by Saxony after 1635. The Austrian Habsburgs' position as elected kings of Hungary prompted their claims of rightful rule in Croatia and Transylvania.

20. Daniel Nexon, *The Struggle for Power in Early Modern Europe* (Princeton, NJ: Princeton University Press, 2009).

21. Angelantonio Spagnoletti, *Stato, aristocrazie e ordine di Malta nell'Italia moderna* (Rome: École française de Rome; Bari: Universita degli studi, 1988), 49.

22. J. R. Hale, "Armies, Navies and the Art of War," in *The New Cambridge Modern History*, vol. 3, *The Counter-Reformation and Price Revolution, 1559–1610*, ed. R. B. Wernham (Cambridge: Cambridge University Press, 1968), 540–69.

23. On the fusion of experience, technical know-how, and theory in the making of the Scientific Revolution see, for instance, Pamela O. Long, *Artisan/Practitioners and the Rise of the New Sciences 1400–1600* (Corvallis: Oregon State University Press, 2011). For the relationship to authority, see Peter Dear, "Mysteries of State, Mysteries of Nature: Authority, Knowledge and Expertise in the Seventeenth Century," in *State of Knowledge: The Co-Production of Science and Social Order*, ed. Sheila Jasanoff (New York: Routledge, 2004), 206–24; Eric Ash, *Power, Knowledge, and Expertise in Elizabethan England* (Baltimore, MD: Johns Hopkins University Press, 2004).

24. Two excellent examples of this approach are Harold J. Cook, *The Young Descartes: Nobility, Rumor, and War* (Chicago: University of Chicago Press, 2018), and Michael Wintroub, *The Voyage of Thought: Navigating Knowledge across the Sixteenth-Century World* (Cambridge: Cambridge University Press, 2017).

25. René Descartes, *Discourse on Method and Related Writings* (New York: Penguin, 2000), 10.

26. Cook, *Young Descartes*, and Daniel Riches, "Military Affairs as a Force for Integration across Early Modern Frontiers" (paper presented at the Society for Military History, Ogden, UT, 19 April 2008). I would like to thank Daniel Riches for sharing this unpublished conference paper with me. On political and cultural agents, see Hans Cools, Marika Keblusek, and Badeloch Noldus, eds., *Your Humble Servant: Agents in Early Modern Europe* (Hilversum: Uitgeverij Verloren, 2006).

27. Steven Gunn, David Grummitt, and Hans Cools assert that the problems in understanding the relationship between war and state building could be remedied by greater examination of the interaction between war and other dynamic features of early modern life. See Steven Gunn, David Grummitt, and Hans Cools, "War and the State in Early Modern Europe: Widening the Debate," *War in History* 15, no. 4 (2008): 371–88.

28. Jacob Burckhardt, *The Civilization of the Renaissance in Italy* (London: Penguin Books, 1990).

29. Montecuccoli to Bolognesi, 13 August 1644, in Foscolo, *Opere*, 2:253.

30. David Parrott, "The Military Enterpriser in the Thirty Years' War," in *War, Entrepreneurs, and the State in Europe and the Mediterranean, 1300–1800*, ed. Jeff Fynn-Paul (Leiden: Brill, 2014), 63–86, esp. 84.

31. For the early eighteenth century, see Guy Rowlands, *Dangerous and Dishonest Men: The International Bankers of Louis XIV's France* (New York: Palgrave Macmillan, 2015), 21. On the "aristocratic credit system," see Redlich, *German Military Enterpriser*, 5:1, 5:31.

32. For instance, see chapter 3.

33. Nuanced views of the relationship between war and state building that prioritize understanding war in terms of how it relates to the development of the nation-state include John Brewer, *The Sinews of Power: War, Money, and the English State, 1688–1783* (Cambridge, MA: Harvard University Press, 1990); Philippe Contamine, ed., *War and Competition between States* (New York: Oxford University Press, 2000); and Jan Glete, *War and the State in Early Modern Europe: Spain, the Dutch Republic and Sweden as Fiscal-Military States, 1500–1660* (London: Routledge, 2002).

34. William Beik, *Absolutism and Society in Seventeenth-Century France: State Power and Provincial Aristocracy in Languedoc* (Cambridge: Cambridge University Press, 1985); Sharon Kettering, *Patronage in Sixteenth- and Seventeenth-Century France* (Aldershot: Ashgate, 2002); and Antoni Mączak, ed., *Klientelsysteme im Europa der frühen Neuzeit* (Munich: Oldenbourg, 1988).

35. Peter H. Wilson, *Europe's Tragedy: A History of the Thirty Years' War* (London: Allen Lane, 2009), 623–24; Parrott, *Business of War*, 156–95.

36. R. J. W. Evans, *The Making of the Habsburg Monarchy, 1550–1700: An Interpretation* (Oxford: Clarendon Press, 1979); R. J. W. Evans and T. V. Thomas (eds.), *Crown, Church, and Estates: Central European Politics in the Sixteenth and Seventeenth Centuries* (London: Macmillan, 1991). For a summary of historiography on Habsburg absolutism, see Petr Mat'a and Thomas Winkelbauer, "Introduction," in *Die Habsburgermonarchie, 1620 bis 1740: Leistungen und Grenzen des Absolutismusparadigmas*, ed. Petr Mat'a and Thomas Winkelbauer (Stuttgart: Franz Steiner Verlag, 2006), 7–42.

37. These diaries have been published in their original Italian: Montecuccoli, *Le opere*, 3:279–397 and 3:398–431.

38. Roberts, "Military Revolution."

39. Geoffrey Parker, "The 'Military Revolution, 1560–1660'—A Myth?," in *The Military Revolution Debate: Readings on the Military Transformation of Early Modern Europe*, ed. Clifford J. Rogers (Boulder, CO: Westview Press, 1995), 37–54.

40. Pamela H. Smith, *The Business of Alchemy: Science and Culture in the Holy Roman Empire* (Princeton, NJ: Princeton University Press, 1994); Mario Biagioli, *Galileo, Courtier: The Practice of Science in the Culture of Absolutism* (Chicago: University of Chicago Press, 1994); Bruce T. Moran, ed., *Patronage and Institutions: Science, Technology, and Medicine at the European Court, 1500–1750* (Rochester, NY: Boydell Press, 1991); Paula Findlen, *Possessing Nature: Museums, Collecting, and Scientific Culture in Early Modern Italy* (Berkeley: University of California Press, 1994).

41. Jan Glete views rulers, ministers, and military leaders in the new fiscal-military state as entrepreneurs. See Jan Glete, "Warfare, Entrepreneurship, and the Fiscal-Military State," in *European Warfare, 1350–1750*, ed. Frank Tallett and D.J.B. Trim (Cambridge: Cambridge University Press, 2010), 300–321; Redlich, *German Military Enterpriser*, 5:1–2; and Anderson, *War and Society*, 33–76.

42. Michael Mallett, *Mercenaries and Their Masters: Warfare in Renaissance Italy* (Totowa, NJ: Rowman and Littlefield, 1974).

43. Österreichisches Staatsarchiv, Kriegsarchiv (ÖStA KA), Nachlaß (NL), Vienna: Montecuccoli, B/492: 51, *Private Notizen*, 15 April 1672. The ring was valued at 270 florins.

44. Veltzé provides a description of archival manuscript sources pertaining to Montecuccoli. See Veltzé, *Ausgewaehlte Schriften*, 1:xli–cxxxi.

45. John Lynn, *Giant of the Grand Siècle: The French Army, 1610–1715* (Cambridge: Cambridge University Press, 1997), 6. Studies of similar groups include Friedrich Edelmayer, *Söldner und Pensionäre: Das Netzwerk Philipps II. im Heiligen Römischen Reich* (Vienna: Verlag für Geschichte und Politik, 2002); David Worthington, *Scots in Habsburg Service, 1618–1648* (Leiden: Brill, 2004); and Eduardo de Mesa, *The Irish in the Spanish Armies in the Seventeenth Century* (Rochester, NY: Boydell and Brewer, 2014).

1. The Order of War

1. Montecuccoli, *Le opere*, 1:141.

2. Quoted in Gunther E. Rothenberg, "Maurice of Nassau, Gustavus Adolphus, Raimondo Montecuccoli, and the 'Military Revolution' of the Seventeenth Century," in *Makers of Modern Strategy from Machiavelli to the Nuclear Age*, ed. Peter Paret (Princeton, NJ: Princeton University Press, 1986), 61.

3. Niccolò Machiavelli, *Art of War*, ed. and trans. Christopher Lynch (Chicago: University of Chicago Press, 2003), 4.

4. Hale, "Armies, Navies and the Art of War," 177.

5. Noblemen in armies were military entrepreneurs, save for low-ranking officers who had not invested personal wealth in a body of troops and for independent adventurers who financed their own retinues but were not under contract to a prince. Many noblemen claimed to have started out as foot soldiers, but they usually did so in a relative's regiment and were quickly promoted to formal office if they remained in the army.

6. Mallett, *Mercenaries and Their Masters*, 6–24; William Caferro, *John Hawkwood: An English Mercenary in Fourteenth-Century Italy* (Baltimore, MD: Johns Hopkins University Press, 2006), 62–94, esp. 63, 69–71.

7. William McNeill, *The Pursuit of Power: Technology, Armed Force, and Society since A.D. 1000* (Chicago: University of Chicago Press, 1982), 69–79; quote on 69.

8. William Caferro, *Mercenary Companies and the Decline of Siena* (Baltimore, MD: Johns Hopkins University Press, 1998).

9. Caferro, *John Hawkwood.*

10. Mallett, *Mercenaries and Their Masters*, 49–50, 104, 221–28.

11. Mallett, *Mercenaries and Their Masters*, 188–92; Michael Mallett and Christine Shaw, *The Italian Wars, 1494–1559: War, State and Society in Early Modern Europe* (Harlow: Pearson, 2012).

12. J. R. Hale, *War and Society in Renaissance Europe, 1450–1620* (Baltimore, MD: Johns Hopkins University Press, 1985), 127–29.

13. Reinhard Baumann, *Landsknechte: Ihre Geschichte und Kultur vom späten Mittelalter bis zum Dreißigjährigen Krieg* (Munich: C. H. Beck, 1994); Peter Burschel, *Söldner im Nordwestdeutschland des 16. und 17. Jahrhunderts* (Göttingen: Vandenhoeck & Ruprecht, 1994).

14. Machiavelli, *Art of War*, 13.

15. Machiavelli, *Art of War*, 19.

16. Baldesar Castiglione, *The Book of the Courtier*, trans. George Bull (New York: Penguin, 1976), 40–42.

17. For this discussion, see Castiglione, *Book of the Courtier*, 88–94.

18. Castiglione, *Book of the Courtier*, 284.

19. Castiglione, *Book of the Courtier*, 287.

20. On the reception of *The Book of the Courtier* into the seventeenth century, see Peter Burke, *The Fortunes of the Courtier: The European Reception of Castiglione's Cortegiano* (Hoboken, NJ: Wiley, 2014). Burke argues that Castiglione's ideas went out of fashion around 1650, when an even more cynical view of princely power emerged.

21. Jan Papy, "Justus Lipsius and Neo-Stoicism," in *The Routledge Companion to Sixteenth Century Philosophy*, ed. Henrik Lagerlund and Benjamin Hill (New York: Routledge, 2017), 203. Robert Bireley labeled Lipsius an "anti-Machiavellian" for the way he attempted to resolve ethical objections to Machiavelli's works by integrating Christian morality with his ideas. See Robert Bireley, *The Counter-Reformation Prince: Anti-Machiavellianism or Catholic Statecraft in Early Modern Europe* (Chapel Hill: University of North Carolina Press, 1990), 72–100.

22. Quoted in Bireley, *Counter-Reformation Prince*, 75.

23. Montecuccoli, *Le opere*, 1:128. On the trend toward Ramist logic, see Walter J. Ong, *Ramus, Method, and the Decay of Dialogue: From the Art of Discourse to the Art of Reason* (Cambridge, MA: Harvard University Press, 1983).

24. For the influence of imperial humanism, see Thomas Dandelet, *The Renaissance of Empire in Early Modern Europe* (New York: Cambridge University Press, 2014).

25. Fernando Gonzalez de Leon, "'Doctors of Military Discipline': Technical Expertise and the Paradigm of the Spanish Soldier in the Early Modern Period," *Sixteenth Century Journal* 27, no. 1 (Spring 1996): 61–85.

26. Steven A. Walton, "State Building through Building for the State: Domestic and Foreign Expertise in Tudor Fortifications," in "Expertise and the Early Modern State," ed. Eric Ash, special issue, *Osiris* 25 (2010): 68.

27. Dear, "Mysteries of State," 206–24.

28. Roberts, "Military Revolution, 1560–1660."

29. Parker, "'Military Revolution, 1560–1660'—A Myth?," 20–21, 38.

30. Standing armies and military administrations developed in one generation might shrink or vanish in the next. See Parker, "'Military Revolution, 1560–1660'—A Myth?," 40.

31. On the continued importance of manuscript sources and the many intersections between print and manuscript cultures, see David McKitterick, *Print, Manuscript and the Search for Order, 1450–1830* (Cambridge: Cambridge University Press, 2003).

32. Miguel Martinez, *Front Lines: Soldiers' Writing in the Early Modern Hispanic World* (Philadelphia: University of Pennsylvania Press, 2016); Paul Scannell, *Conflict and Soldiers' Literature in Early Modern Europe: The Reality of War* (London: Bloomsbury Academic, 2015); Yuval Harari, *Renaissance Military Memoirs: War, History and Identity, 1450–1600* (Woodbridge: Boydell Press, 2004); and Adam McKeown, *English Mercuries: Soldier Poets in the Age of Shakespeare* (Nashville, TN: Vanderbilt University Press, 2009).

33. Gonzalez de Leon, "'Doctors of Military Discipline.'"

34. Parker, "'Military Revolution, 1560–1660'—A Myth?," 40.

35. Gonzalez de Leon, "'Doctors of Military Discipline,'" 85.

36. David R. Lawrence, *The Complete Soldier: Military Books and Military Culture in Early Stuart England, 1603–1645* (Leiden: Brill, 2009).

37. Parker, "'Military Revolution, 1560–1660'—A Myth?"; Mallett and Shaw, *Italian Wars*, 177–97.

38. The Army of Flanders was the largest army in Europe after the Ottoman army. Geoffrey Parker, *The Army of Flanders and the Spanish Road, 1567–1659: The Logistics of Spanish Victory and Defeat in the Low Countries' Wars* (Cambridge: Cambridge University Press, 1972).

39. Walton, "State Building," 76–78.

40. Montecuccoli mentioned all of these writers as influences on his own writing in the preface to his first treatise, *Trattato della guerra* (1641). See Montecuccoli, *Le opere*, 1:131.

41. Imperiale Cinuzzi, *La vera militar disciplina antica e moderna* (Siena: S. Marchetti, 1604), 1:1. On this family, see Antonio Sestigiani, *Compendio istorico di sanesi nobili, brevi cenni su famiglie nobili di Siena, notizie di personaggi illustri o riguardevoli, provenienza geografica, eseguito da A. Sestigiani nel 1696*, vol. 1, lett. A–0, Archivio di Stato di Siena (ASSi), ms. A 11, f. 197v.

42. Anna E. C. Simoni, "Soldiers' Tales: Observations on Italian Military Books Published at Antwerp in the Early Seventeenth Century," in *The Italian Book, 1465–1800: Studies Presented to Dennis E. Rhodes on His 70th Birthday*, ed. Denis V. Reidy (London: British Library, 1993), 267.

43. Simoni, "Soldiers' Tales," 267.

44. Brancaccio served in Flanders from 1602 to 1609 and again in the 1620s and 1630s. Lelio Brancaccio, *I carichi militari* (Antwerp: Ioachimo Trognesio, 1610). See the dedication.

45. Giorgio Basta, *Il governo della cavalleria leggiera* (Venice: Bernardo Gionti, Battista Ciotti, 1612). See the prefatory note, "A' Cortesi Lettori," p. 2.

46. Cinuzzi, *La vera militar disciplina*, 1:2.

47. Henri Rohan, *Le parfait capitaine: Autrement l'abregé des guerres des commentaires de Cesar: Augmenté d'vn traicté de l'interest des princes & estats de la Chrestienté* (Paris: s.n., 1639); quoted in Jonathan Dewald, *Aristocratic Experience and the Origins of Modern Culture: France, 1570–1715* (Berkeley: University of California Press, 1993), 55–56.

48. Edgar Zilsel, *The Social Origins of Modern Science* (Dordrecht: Kluwer Academic Publishers, 2000); Long, *Artisan/Practitioners*.

49. Erik A. Lund, *War for the Every Day: Generals, Knowledge, and Warfare in Early Modern Europe, 1680–1740* (Westport, CT: Greenwood Press, 1999), 5; Lesley B. Cormack, "Mathematics and Empire: The Military Impulse and the Scientific Revolution," in *The Heirs of Archimedes: Science and the Art of War through the Age of Enlightenment*, ed. Brett D. Steele and Tamera Dorland (Cambridge, MA: MIT Press, 2005).

50. Henry Guerlac, "Vauban: The Impact of a Science of War," in *Makers of Modern Strategy from Machiavelli to the Nuclear Age*, ed. Peter Paret (Princeton, NJ: Princeton University Press, 1986), 68–69.

51. Matteo Valleriani, *Galileo Engineer* (Dordrecht: Springer, 2010).

52. Cinuzzi, *La vera militar disciplina*, 1:6.

53. Michael Roberts, *Gustavus Adolphus and the Rise of Sweden* (London: English Universities Press, 1973), 103–4, 107–12.

54. Giorgio Basta, *Il Mastro di campo generale* (Venice: G.B.Ciotti,, 1606), 1.

55. Cinuzzi, *La vera militar disciplina*, 1:21.

56. Cinuzzi, *La vera militar disciplina*, 1:18.

57. Lawrence, *Complete Soldier*, 59–60.

58. Parker, "'Military Revolution, 1560–1660'—A Myth?," 40–42. The English reception of continental ideas has been examined in Lawrence, *Complete Soldier*, 36–45.

59. Cinuzzi, *La vera militar disciplina*, 1:27.

60. Cinuzzi, *La vera militar disciplina*, 1:6–7.

61. Brancaccio, *I carichi*, 41–42.

62. Brancaccio, *I carichi*, 46.

63. Basta, *Il Mastro*, 1.

64. Gonzalez de Leon, "'Doctors of Military Discipline'"; Parrott, *Business of War*, 154–73.

65. Cinuzzi, *La vera militar disciplina*, 1:6.

66. Simoni, "Soldiers' Tales," 269.

67. Johann Grimmelshausen, *The Adventures of Simplicius Simplicissimus*, ed. and trans. Mike Mitchell (Sawtry: Dedalus, 1999), 53–54.

68. Noble status of one sort or another was perhaps the most commonly shared characteristic of military entrepreneurs. See Parrott, "Military Enterpriser," 65–66.

69. Wintroub, *Voyage*, 67–68.

70. J. R. Hale, "Printing and the Military Culture of Renaissance Venice," *Medievalia et Humanistica* 8 (1977): 21–62; Anthony Grafton and Lisa Jardine, "'Studied for Action': How Gabriel Harvey Read His Livy," *Past and Present* 129 (1990): 30–78.

71. Mario Biagioli, "The Social Status of Italian Mathematicians, 1450–1600," *History of Science* 27 (1989): 41–95.

72. Ash, *Power, Knowledge, and Expertise*.

73. Valleriani, *Galileo Engineer*, 196–97.

74. For the Spanish case, see González de Leon, "'Doctors of Military Discipline,'" 61–85.

75. J. R. Hale, "The Military Education of the Officer Class in Early Modern Europe," in *Cultural Aspects of the Italian Renaissance: Essays in Honour of Paul Oskar Kristeller*, ed. C. H. Clough (Manchester: Manchester University Press, 1976), 440–61.

76. Parker, "'Military Revolution, 1560–1660'—A Myth?," 41.

77. Simoni, "Soldiers' Tales," 277.

78. Lawrence, *Complete Soldier*, 57.

79. Simoni, "Soldiers' Tales," 257.

80. Gonzalez de Leon, "'Doctors of Military Discipline,'" 81.

81. Gonzalez de Leon, "'Doctors of Military Discipline,'" 80.

2. The Generation of White Mountain

1. Johann Philipp Abelinus and Matthaeus Merian, "The Battle of White Mountain (November 8, 1620)," excerpt from *Theatrum Europaeum* in *The Thirty Years' War, A Documentary History*, ed. and trans. Tryntje Helfferich (Indianapolis, IN: Hackett Publishing Company, 2009), 50–51.

2. Brennan C. Pursell, *The Winter King: Frederick V of the Palatinate and the Coming of the Thirty Years' War* (Aldershot: Ashgate, 2003).

3. Christoph Kampmann, *Europa und das Reich im Dreissigjährigen Krieg: Geschichte eines europäischen Konflikts* (Stuttgart: Kohlhammer Verlag, 2013), 36–38, and Geoffrey Parker, ed., *The Thirty Years' War*, 2nd rev. ed. (London: Routledge, 1997), 43–63.

4. Wilson, *Europe's Tragedy*, 294–99. From 1618 to 1620, Pope Paul V sent 304,000 thalers to Emperor Ferdinand II and 204,000 thalers to the Catholic League. See Giampiero Brunelli, *Soldati del papa: Politica militare e nobiltà nello Stato della Chiesa, 1560–1644* (Rome: Carocci, 2003), 190.

5. The same pope named a new basilica in Rome Santa Maria della Vittoria, rededicating the church to the Virgin Mary in thanks for the victory.

6. István Deák, *Beyond Nationalism: A Social and Political History of the Habsburg Officer Corps, 1848–1918* (New York: Oxford University Press, 1990).

7. Tomáš Bílek, *Dějiny konfiskací v Čechách po r. 1618*, 2 vols. (Prague: V kommissi u F. Řivnáce, 1882); Karl Richter, "Die böhmischen Länder von 1471–1740," in *Handbuch der Geschichte der böhmischen Länder*, vol. 2, ed. Karl Bosl (Stuttgart: A. Hiersemann, 1974), 284, 290; Tomáš Knoz, "Die Konfiskationen nach 1620 in (erb)länderübergreifender Perspektive: Thesen zu wesentlichen Wirkungen, Aspekten und Prinzipien des Konfiskationsprozesses," in *Die Habsburgermonarchie, 1620 bis 1740: Leistungen und Grenzen des Absolutismusparadigmas*, ed. Petr Mat'a and Thomas Winkelbauer (Stuttgart: Franz Steiner Verlag, 2006), 99–130.

8. Josef V. Polišenský, *The Thirty Years' War*, trans. Robert Evans (Berkeley: University of California Press, 1971), 198.

9. Aurelio Musi, "L'Italia nel sistema imperiale spagnolo," in *Nel sistema imperiale: L'Italia Spagnola*, ed. Aurelio Musi (Naples: Edizioni Scientifiche Italiane, 1994), 51–66.

10. Compared to eleven out of the fifty-five newer families. See Gregory Hanlon, "The Decline of a Military Aristocracy: Siena 1560–1740," *Past and Present* 155, no. 1 (1997): 69–73.

11. Benedetto Croce, "I Caracciolo d'Avellino," in *Uomini e cose della vecchia Italia*, 3rd. ed. (Bari: G. Laterza, 1956), 151; Hanlon, *Twilight*, 73–74. For a list of captains, see Vittorio Mariani and Varo Varanini, *Condottieri italiani in Germania [. . .] con 38 Carte, 26 Facsimili, 75 Ritratti* (Milan: Garzanti, 1941), 121–22. This fascist-era dictionary was a piece of propaganda and contains numerous errors but nonetheless drew attention to the sheer numbers of Italian noblemen in Habsburg armies. See Hanlon, *Twilight*, 5–7.

12. Parker, *Army of Flanders*, 27–29, 31–32.

13. Angelantonio Spagnoletti, *Principi italiani e Spagna nell'eta barocca* (Milan: B. Mondadori, 1996), 32. See also two collections of essays: Thomas James Dandelet and John A. Marino, eds., *Spain in Italy: Politics, Society, and Religion 1500–1700* (Leiden: Brill, 2007); and Enrique García Hernán and Davide Maffei, eds., *Guerra y sociedad en la Monarquía Hispánica: Politica, estrategia y cultura en la Europa moderna (1500–1700)*, 2 vols. (Madrid: Ediciones del Laberinto, 2006).

14. Gregory Hanlon, *The Hero of Italy: Odoardo Farnese, Duke of Parma, His Soldiers, and His Subjects in the Thirty Years' War* (Oxford: Oxford University Press, 2014), 12.

15. Angelantonio Spagnoletti, "L'Aristocrazia napoletana nelle guerre del primo seicento: tra pratica delle armi e integrazione dinastica," in *I Farnese: Corti, guerra e nobilità in antico regime: Atti del convegno di studi Piacenza, 24–26 novembre 1994*, ed. Antonella Bilotto, Pietro Del Negro, and Cesare Mozzarelli (Rome: Bulzoni editore, 1997), 445–68.

16. Gianvittorio Signorotto, "Guerre spagnoli, ufficiali lombardi," in Bilotto, Del Negro, and Mozzarelli, *I Farnese*, 367–96.

17. José Martínez Millán, "Alessandro Farnese, la corte di Madrid e la monarchia cattolica," in Bilotto, Del Negro, and Mozzarelli, *I Farnese*. For Naples, see Giuseppe Galasso, *Alla periferia dell'impero: Il Regno di Napoli nel periodo spagnolo (secoli XVI–XVII)* (Turin: Einaudi, 1994); and Tommaso Astarita, *The Continuity of Feudal Power: The Caracciolo di Brienza in Spanish Naples* (Cambridge: Cambridge University Press, 2004).

18. After the Battle of White Mountain, Emperor Ferdinand II commissioned Caracciolo to travel to Madrid in order to thank the Spanish king for his help. Raffaele M. Filamondo, *Il genio bellicoso di Napoli, memorie istoriche d'alcuni capitani celebri napolitani: C'han militato per la Fede, per lo Re, per la Patria nel secolo trascorso raccolte* (Naples: D. A. Parrino, 1714), 607–19; E. William Monter, "Caracciolo, Tommaso," in *Dizionario biografico degli Italiani* [hereafter *DBI*], ed. Alberto Mario Ghisalberti (Rome: Istituto dell'Enciclopedia Italiana, 1976), 19:459–62. Andrea Cantelmo and Caracciolo's commander, Carlo Spinello, were Neapolitan commanders with similar trajectories.

19. Thomas Barker, *Army, Aristocracy, Monarchy: Essays on War, Society and Government in Austria, 1618–1780* (Boulder, CO: Social Science Monographs, 1982), 70.

20. Robert Rebitsch, *Matthias Gallas (1588–1647): Generalleutnant des Kaisers zur Zeit des Dreissigjährigen Krieges: Eine militärische Biographie* (Münster: Aschendorff, 2006), 30–33. On the political status of the Prince-Bishopric of Trento during the Thirty Years' War, see Claudio Donati, *Ai confini d'Italia: Saggi di storia trentina in età moderna*, (Bologna: Mulino, 2008), 43–66.

21. Cesare Campori, *Raimondo Montecuccoli: la sua famiglia e i suoi tempi* (Florence: G. Barbèra, 1876), 6–7, 12.

22. Campori, *Raimondo Montecuccoli*, 83.

23. Wilson, *Europe's Tragedy*, 83.

24. Salvatore Pugliese, *Le prime strette dell'austria in italia* (Milan: Treves, 1932), 34. See also Karl Otmar von Aretin, *Das alte Reich, 1648–1806* (Stuttgart: Klett Cotta, 1993), 1:112–15 and 201–208; L. Auer, "Zur Rolle Italiens in der österreichischen Politik um das spanischen Erbe," *Mitteilungen des österreichischen Staatsarchivs* 31 (1978): 52–72; Cinzia Cremonini, "I feudi imperiali italiani tra Sacro Romano Impero e monarchia cattolica (seconda metà XVI–inizio XVII secolo)," in *L'impero e l'Italia nella prima età moderna*, ed. Matthias Schnettger and Marcello Verga (Bologna: Il Mulino, 2006), 41–65.

25. Some Italian nobles probably had legitimate Germanic ancestors, though even Scottish soldiers like Walter Leslie made similar allegations, suggesting these claims were part of a discourse foreign nobles adopted when searching for ways to justify advancement in imperial service. See Worthington, *Scots in Habsburg Service*, 205, 208.

26. Pugliese, *Le prime strette*, 7–8, 12.

27. Robert Von Friedeburg, "'Lands' and 'Fatherlands': Changes in the Plurality of Allegiances in the Sixteenth-Century Holy Roman Empire," in *Networks, Regions and Nations: Shaping Identities in the Low Countries, 1300–1650*, ed. Judith Pollmann and Robert Stein (Leiden: Brill, 2010), 266–67.

28. Pugliese, *Le prime strette*, 13–14, 115, 119–20.

29. Hanlon, *Twilight*, 243.

30. Corrado Argegni, *Condottieri, capitani, tribuni* (Milan: E. B. B. I., Instituto editoriale italiano B. C. Tosi, 1936–37), 3:286–89.

31. Galeazzo Gualdo Priorato, *Vite et azzioni di personaggi militari, e politici* (Vienna: M. Thurnmayer, 1674), 437–59. See also Jean Bérenger, *Finances et Absolutisme autrichien dans la seconde moitié du XVIIème siècle* (Lille: Atelier Reproduction des Theses Universite Lille III, 1975), 1:39–46.

32. Priorato, *Vite et azzioni*, 187–98.

33. Robert Rebitsch, Jenny Öhman, and Jan Kilián, *1648: Kriegführung und Friedensverhandlungen. Prag und das Ende des Dreißigjährigen Krieges* (Innsbruck: Innsbruck University Press, 2018), 179–243.

34. Ed Muir, *Mad Blood Stirring: Vendetta in Renaissance Italy* (Baltimore, MD: Johns Hopkins University Press, 1998), 47, 180.

35. Priorato, *Vite et azzioni*, 191.

36. Priorato, *Vite et azzioni*, 188.

37. Priorato, *Vite et azzioni*, 193.

38. Priorato, *Vite et azzioni*, 190.

39. Priorato, *Vite et azzioni*, 179–82. On the Italian Collalto family, see Pier Angelo Passolunghi, *I Collalto: Linee, documenti, genealogie per una storia del casato* (Villorba: B&M edizioni, 1987); Collalto, Rambaldo, in Ghisalberti, *DBI*, 5:26, 5:783. On the Central European Collalto line, see Zdeněk Kazlepka, *Ostrov italského vkusu: Umelecký mecenát Antonia Rambalda, hrabete z Collalto a San Salvatore, mezi Itálií, Vídní a Moravou v první polovine 18. století* (Brno: Barrister & Principal: Moravská galerie, 2011).

40. Collalto's patent for admission into the Moravian Land Diet can be found in Moravský zemský archiv (MZA), Rodinný Archiv Collaltů (RAC), značka 169G, k. č. 5,

inv. č. 133, 1–13. Ferdinand II wrote to Cardinal Dietrichstein about his decision to admit Collalto, in *Doc. Boh.*, no. 707. Collalto's sons' admission to *The Golden Book of Venetian Nobility* can be found in: MZA, RAC, značka 169G, inv. č. 2455.

41. Michael Mallett and J. R Hale, *The Military Organization of a Renaissance State: Venice, c. 1400 to 1617* (Cambridge: Cambridge University Press, 1984).

42. Alessandro Catalano, "L'italiano lingua di cultura dell'Europa centrale nell'età moderna / Italština v novodobých dějinách středoevropských kultur," in *Humanitas latina in Bohemis*, ed. G. Cadorini and J. Špička (Kolín: Albis, Treviso: G. Cadorini, 2007), 117–68. According to Antonio Carafa's 1628 papal nuncio report, Emperor Ferdinand II "[spoke] continuously in Italian or German." Antonio Carafa, *Relazione di Germania*, 1628, Archivio Segreto Vaticano (ASV), Segretario di Stato di Germania (Segr. Stato, Germania), 26-A, f. 64v.

43. Hanlon's study of fascist-era dictionaries showed sixty-four officers from Florence, twenty-seven from Siena, and twenty-seven from Mantua were active in Austrian Habsburg service in the period 1560–1710. Hanlon, *Twilight*, 243.

44. Matthias Schnettger, "Kaiserinnen und Kardinäle: Wissensbroker(innen) zwischen dem Kaiserhof und Italien im 17. Jahrhundert," in *Transferprozesse zwischen dem Alten Reich und Italien im 17. Jahrhundert*, ed. Sabina Brevaglieri and Matthias Schnettger (Bielefeld: Transcript Verlag, 2018), 129. The correspondence of the first empress Eleonora contains evidence of her patronage requests. See Archivio di stato di Mantova (ASM), Archivio Gonzaga (AG), Lettere imperiali (E.II.2), b. 434–35 and Haus-, Hof- und Staatsarchiv (HHStA), Familienkorrespondenz, 31. On the two empresses, see Giambattista Intra, "Le due Eleonore Gonzaga Imperatrice," in *Atti e memorie della R. Accademia Virgiliana di Mantova, Biennio 1891–1892* (Mantua: s.n., 1893).

45. Herbert Seifert, "Akademien am Wiener Kaiserhof der Barockzeit," in *Akademie und Musik-Erscheinungsweisen und Wirkungen des Akademiegedankens in Kultur- und Musikgeschichte: Institutionem, Veranstaltungen, Schriften: Festschrift für Werner Braun zum 65. Geburtstag*, ed. Wolf Frobenius, Nicole Schwindt-Gross, and Thomas Sick (Saarbrücken: SDV, 1993), 215–17. Notes from meetings of the academy can be found in Österreichische Nationalbibliothek (ÖNB), Handschriften-Sammlung, Signatur 10108.

46. Anna married Claudia's son in 1646. Gaetano Pieraccini, *La stirpe de' Medici di Cafaggiolo: Saggio di ricerche sulla transmissione ereditaria dei caratteri biologici* (Florence: Vallechi, 1924–25), 2:545–52.

47. Carla Sodini, *L'ercole tirreno: Guerra e dinastia medicea nella prima metà del '600* (Florence: Olschki, 2001), 129–236.

48. On this phase of his career, see Rebitsch, Öhman, and Kilián, *1648*, 89–160.

49. On the grand duke's early contributions to the war, see Sodini, *L'ercole tirreno*, 64–67.

50. Barker, *Army, Aristocracy, Monarchy*, 69–71. Imperiale Cinuzzi mentioned Silvio Piccolomini in his 1612 treatise. See chapter 1.

51. Examples of letters of recommendation from the grand dukes to Piccolomini can be found in Státní oblastní archiv v Zámrsku (SOAZ), Rodinný archiv Piccolomini (RAP), inv. č. 11029–67. The duke of Parma had a similar reputation that attracted recruits during the War in Flanders. Wilson, *Europe's Tragedy*, 133.

52. Argegni, *Condottieri, capitani, tribuni*, 3:286.

53. Mattias de' Medici to Grand Duke Ferdinando II, Siena, 30 September 1641, Archivio di stato di Firenze (ASF), Mediceo del Principato (MDP) 5396, f. 247r.

54. Cardinal B. Cesi to Cardinal L. Ludovisi, 24 May 1621; quoted in Brunelli, *Soldati del papa*, 190. For Aldobrandini's instructions, see *Instruttione a VS Illma Sigre D. Pietro Aldobrandini Tnte Gnale di N Sre per la levata da farsi in Germania di un Reggimento di fanti catholici che S. Sta. da per aiuto alla Maestà dell'Imperatore Ferdinando*, Rome, 1 June 1621, Archivio Segreto Vaticano (ASV), Miscellanea Armadio II (Misc., Arm. II), vol. 177, f. 86r.

55. Mario Rosa, "The 'World's Theatre': The Court of Rome and Politics in the First Half of the Seventeenth Century," in *Court and Politics in Papal Rome, 1492–1700*, ed. Gianvittorio Signorotto and Maria Antonietta Visceglia (Cambridge: Cambridge University Press, 2002), 80–81; Guido Braun, "Akteure, Medien und Institutionen in den Prozessen von Wissensproduktion über das Reich an der römischen Kurie in den 1620er Jahren. Nuntius Carlo Carafa und die Propaganda Fide-Kongregation," in Brevaglieri and Schnettger, *Transferprozesse zwischen dem Alten Reich*, 218–19.

56. As a "stage" for demonstrating military valor, Central Europe occupied a role similar to Flanders at the turn of the century. Brunelli, *Soldati del papa*, 202. On the relationship between pope and emperor, see Alexander Koller, *Imperator und Pontifex. Forschungen zum Verhältnis von Kaiserhof und römischer Kurie im Zeitalter der Konfessionalisierung (1555–1648)* (Münster: Aschendorff, 2012).

57. Robert Bireley, *Ferdinand II, Counter-Reformation Emperor, 1578–1637* (New York: Cambridge University Press, 2014), 62–63.

58. Hanlon, *Twilight*, 84–85; Giampiero Brunelli, *La santa impresa: Le crociate del papa in Ungheria: 1595–1601* (Rome: Salerno Editrice, 2018). Montecuccoli's father, Galeotto, had also been present at this battle.

59. Klaus Jaitner, ed., *Die Hauptinstruktionen Gregors XV: Für die Nuntien und Gesandten an den europäischen Fürstenhöfen, 1621–1623* (Tübingen: M. Niemeyer, 1997), 1:75–76.

60. Maria Antonietta Visceglia, "Fazioni e lotta politica nel Sacro Romano Collegio nella prima metà del Seicento," in *La corte di Roma tra Cinque e Seicento: "Teatro" della politica europea*, ed. Gianvittorio Signorotto and Maria Antonietta Visceglia (Rome: Bulzoni, 1998), 78.

61. Renato Lefevre, "Il patrimonio romano degli Aldobrandini nel Seicento," in *Archivio della Società romana di Storia patria*, 82 (1959): 18; Jaitner, *Hauptinstruktionen*, 1:106–12. For the Aldobrandini family tree, see Christoph Weber, *Genealogien zur Papstgeschichte* (Stuttgart: Hiersemann, 1999), 1: 30.

62. Cardinal Aldobrandini to Cardinal Dietrichstein, Rome, 7 September 1619, MZA, Rodinný Archiv Ditrichstejnů (RAD), Franz Dietrichstein correspondence, k. č. 427. For letters concerning Aldobrandini and another Italian soldier, see HHStA, Rom Hofkorrespondenz, 8, 10.

63. Josef Válka, *Dějiny Moravy díl 2: Morava Reformace Renesance a Baroka: Vlastivěda moravská země a lid nová řada svazek 6* (Brno: Muzejní a vlastivědná společnost, 1995), 98–114, esp. 101 and 106; Tomáš Parma, *František kardinál Dietrichstein a jeho vztahy k římské kurii: Prostředky a metody politické komunikace ve službách moravské církve* (Brno: Matice Moravská, 2011).

64. For a careful analysis of changes in Bohemia and Moravia, see Alessandro Catalano, *La Boemia e la riconquista delle coscienze: Ernst Adalbert von Harrach e la controriforma in europa centrale (1620–1667)* (Rome: Edizioni di storia e letteratura, 2005), 52–58; as well

as Vaclav Bůzek and Petr Mat'a, "Wandlungen des Adels in Böhmen und Mähren im Zeitalter des 'Absolutismus' (1620–1740)," in Ronald G. Asch, *Der europäische Adel in der Frühen Neuzeit: Eine Einführung* (Köln: Böhlau, 2008), 303–7. Thomas Winkelbauer's erudite study of Liechtenstein is also revealing. See Thomas Winkelbauer, *Fürst und Fürstendiener: Gundaker von Liechtenstein, ein österreichischer Aristokrat des konfessionellen Zeitalters* (Vienna: Oldenbourg, 1999), 24–46.

65. Conti joined Bucquoy's army, became close to Wallenstein, and participated in the suppression of Bohemian rebels during the 1620s, earning the nickname "the Devil." Stefano Andretta, "Conti, Torquato," in Ghisalberti, *DBI*, 5:28, 5:481.

66. Roman newssheet of 13 April 1619; quoted in Brunelli, *Soldati del papa*, 200. See also "Istruzioni al cavalier Virginio Orsini quando andò in Germania," in Sodini, *L'ercole tirreno*, 262.

67. Brunelli, *Soldati del papa*, 200.

68. Aldobrandini originally intended to put Conti in charge of a regiment, but Conti had been captured. Conti and Miniati are mentioned in Pietro Aldobrandini to Cardinal Ludovico Ludovisi, Vienna, 18 September 1621, Biblioteca Vaticana (BV), Barberini latino (Barb. lat.), f. 7r. Cesarini is mentioned in Pietro Aldobrandini to Cardinal Ludovico Ludovisi, Iglau (Jihlava), 4 November 1621, BV, Barb. lat., 7058, f. 14v. On Miniati, see Eugenio Gamurrini, *Istoria geneaologica delle famiglie nobili Toscane, et Umbre* (Florence: Nella stamperia di Francesco Onofri, 1668), 1:138–40.

69. *Instruttione*, ASV, Misc., Arm. II, vol. 177, f. 88r.

70. *Viaggi dell' ecc.mo Signore D. Torquato Conti e le cose accadutegli successivamente dall'anno 1614 sino al 1631*, Biblioteca Vittorio Emanuele, MSS. Ges., n. 314, ff. 223–36; Cecilia Mazzetti di Pietralata, "Federico Savelli, tugendhafter Adliger, Militär und Diplomat," in Brevaglieri and Schnettger, *Transferprozesse zwischen dem Alten Reich*, 161–205. On the Savelli, see Irene Fosi, "La famiglia Savelli e la rappresentanza imperiale a Roma nella prima metà del Seicento," in *Kaiserhof—Papsthof (16.–18. Jahrhundert)*, ed. Richard Bösel, Grete Klingenstein, and Alexander Koller (Vienna: Verlag der österreichischen akademie der wissenshaften, 2006), 67–76.

71. Wilson, *Europe's Tragedy*, 323–25.

72. Bucquoy's absence was felt until 1625, when a figure with comparable prominence, Wallenstein, finally filled the leadership vacuum. After Bucquoy's death, Maximillian Liechtenstein assumed command of imperial troops, with Spanish forces remaining under Caracciolo. Wilson, *Europe's Tragedy*, 324.

73. Ferdinand II to Cardinal Dietrichstein, Vienna, 28 June 1621, in *Documenta Bohemica*, vol. 3, no. 85; Cardinal Dietrichstein to Ferdinand II, Brünn, 4 July 1621, in *Documenta Bohemica*, vol. 3, no. 102.

74. Josef Polišenský and Frederick Snider, *War and Society in Europe, 1618–1648* (Cambridge: Cambridge University Press, 1978), 81–84, 87–88. For Dietrichstein's correspondence with these figures, see *Documenta Bohemica*, vol. 3, passim.

75. For this problem, see Tryntje Helferrich, "A Levy in Liège for Mazarin's Army: Practical and Strategic Difficulties in Raising and Supporting Troops in the Thirty Years' War," in *JEMH* 11, no. 6 (2007): 475–500.

76. John Lynn, "How War Fed War: The Tax of Violence and Contributions during the Grand Siècle," in *Journal of Modern History* 65, no. 2 (June 1993): 286–310. On the decreasing size of armies, see Parrott, *Business of War*, 124–25.

77. Avvisi di Roma, 5 June 5 1621, in BV, *Urb. lat.* 1089, f. 410r. See also *Instruttione*, ASV, Misc., Arm. II, vol. 177, f. 87r. Pini was nominated *collaterale generale* in 1607. See Brunelli, *Soldati del papa*, 232n144. Dieter Albrecht, "Zur Finanzierung des Dreißigjährigen Krieges. Die Subsidien der Kurie für Kaiser und Liga 1618–1635," *Zeitschrift für bayerische Landesgeschichte* 19 (1956): 541.

78. *Instruttione*, ASV, Misc., Arm. II, vol. 177, f. 87v.

79. Lynn, *Giant of the Grand Siècle*, 234–41.

80. Pietro Aldobrandini to Cardinal Ludovico Ludovisi, Trigla, 26 August 1621, BV, Barb. lat., 7058, f. 2r; Pietro Aldobrandini to Cardinal Ludovico Ludovisi, Vienna, 19 March 1622, BV, Barb. lat., 7058, f. 21r,

81. Cinuzzi, *La vera militar disciplina*, 2:5. Military treatises spilled more ink on the topic of valor, but finance was a more critical issue facing armies and their leaders. See Lynn, *Giant of the Grand Siècle*, 221–47.

82. Lynn, *Giant of the Grand Siècle*, 30.

83. Pietro Aldobrandini to Cardinal Ludovico Ludovisi, Iglau (Jihlava), 26 August 1621, BV, Barb. lat., 7058, f. 2r. J. R. Hale refers to the muster as a "positive initiation rite" among sixteenth-century Landsknechts. See Hale, *War and Society*, 150–51.

84. Pietro Aldobrandini to Cardinal Ludovico Ludovisi, Iglau (Jihlava), 26 August 1621, BV, Barb. lat., 7058, f. 2r.

85. Pietro Aldobrandini to Cardinal Ludovico Ludovisi, Iglau (Jihlava), 26 August 1621, BV, Barb. lat., 7058, f. 2v. Days earlier, Ferdinand II mentioned the plan in a letter to Wallenstein. See Ferdinand II to Albrecht Wallenstein, Vienna, 22 August 1621, in *Documenta Bohemica*, vol. 3, no. 196.

86. Hale, *War and Society*, 133.

87. Pietro Aldobrandini to Cardinal Ludovico Ludovisi, Iglau (Jihlava), 1 September 1621, BV, Barb. lat., 7058, f. 4r.

88. Pietro Aldobrandini to Cardinal Ludovico Ludovisi, Vienna, 18 September 1621, BV, Barb. lat., 7058, f. 6r.

89. Pietro Aldobrandini to Cardinal Ludovico Ludovisi, Vienna, 18 September 1621, BV, Barb. lat., 7058, f. 6r. See also Cardinal Dietrichstein to Ferdinand II, Brünn (Brno), 17 September 1621, in *Documenta Bohemica*, vol. 3, no. 221. On the papal nuncio's role, see Braun, "Akteure, Medien und Institutionen," 207–40, as well as Rotraut Becker, "Aus dem Alltag des Nuntius Malatesta Baglioni. Nichtdiplomatische Aufgaben der Wiener Nuntiatur um 1635," in *Quellen und Forschungen aus italienischen Archiven und Bibliotheken* 65 (1985): 328–40.

90. Pietro Aldobrandini to Ludovico Ludovisi, Vienna, 18 September 1621, BV, Barb. lat., 7058, f. 6rv.

91. Basta, *Il governo*, 9.

92. Basta, *Il governo*, 28. See also Katherine Neal, "The Rhetoric of Utility: Avoiding Occult Associations for Mathematics through Profitability and Pleasure," *History of Science* 37 (1999): 151–78.

93. Aldobrandini to Ludovisi, Trigla, 13 October 1621, BV, Barb. lat., 7058, f. 11r.

94. Pietro Aldobrandini to Ludovico Ludovisi, Iglau (Jihlava), 4 November 1621, BV, Barb. lat., 7058, f. 14rv.

95. Wilson, *Europe's Tragedy*, 325–31.

96. Pietro Aldobrandini to Ludovico Ludovisi, Vienna, 27 August 1622, BV, Barb. lat., 7058, ff. 35rv. Ludovico Ludovisi, Rome, 17 September, 1622, BV, Barb. lat., 7058, f. 36r.

97. Brunelli, *Soldati del papa*, 190.

98. Pietro Aldobrandini to Ludovico Ludovisi, Vienna, 9 September 1622, BV, Barb. lat., 7058, f. 38r.

99. Pietro Aldobrandini to Ludovico Ludovisi, Vienna, 26 October 1622, BV, Barb. lat., 7058, f. 39r. This is the last letter until he wrote from Brussels in April 1623.

100. BV, Barb. lat., 7058, f. 41r.

101. Wilson, *Europe's Tragedy*, 351–54.

102. Though Wallenstein was born a minor nobleman, his newfound wealth came from marriage to a rich widow and from his purchases of confiscated properties using debased currency he had minted himself.

103. On the mechanics of Wallenstein's rise, see Geoff Mortimer, *Wallenstein: The Enigma of the Thirty Years' War* (Basingstroke: Palgrave Macmillan, 2010).

104. Dieter Albrecht, "Der Heilige Stuhl und die Kurübertragung von 1623," in *Quellen und Forschungen aus italienischen Archiven und Bibliotheken* 34 (1954): 236–49. For disagreements on the Catholic side, see Alessandro Catalano, "La politica della curia romana in Boemia," in Bösel, Klingenstein, and Koller, *Kaiserhof—Papsthof*, 105–21.

105. Richard Bonney, *The Thirty Years' War 1618–1648* (Oxford: Osprey, 2002), 39–42.

106. By contrast, French-born courtiers dominated positions at the French court by the early seventeenth century. Honorary offices started to expand under Ferdinand II, who became emperor at the start of the Thirty Years' War. Jeroen Duindam, *Vienna and Versailles: The Courts of Europe's Dynastic Rivals, 1550–1780* (Cambridge: Cambridge University Press, 2003), 71–72, 123–24; see 59–60 for the dominance of French-born courtiers in France.

107. James Van Horn Melton, "The Nobility in the Bohemian and Austrian Lands, 1620–1780," in *The European Nobilities in the Seventeenth and Eighteenth Centuries*, vol. 2, *Northern and Central Europe*, ed. H. M. Scott (New York: Longman, 1995), 110–43.

108. Karin J. MacHardy, *War, Religion and Court Patronage in Habsburg Austria: The Social and Cultural Dimensions of Political Interaction, 1521–1622* (New York: Palgrave Macmillan, 2003).

109. Carlo Carafa, *Relazione di Germania* (1628), ASV, Segr. Stato Germania 26-A, ASV, ff. 58v and 59v; Guido Braun, "Kaiserhof, Kaiser und Reich in der 'Relazione' des Nuntius Carlo Carafa (1628)," in Bösel, Klingenstein, and Koller, *Kaiserhof—Papsthof*, 77–104. See also Anna Coreth, *Pietas Austriaca* (West Lafayette, IN: Purdue University Press, 2004).

110. Redlich, "Military Entrepreneurship and the Credit System," 187.

111. For comparison, in 1620 the salary of a high-ranking court official and powerful native noble, Gundaker von Liechtenstein, totaled five hundred florins a month, plus an additional three hundred once he became president of the Hofkammer. Redlich, *German Military Enterpriser*, 1:308–15.

112. Parrott, *Business of War*, 116–20.

113. Parrott, "Military Enterpriser," 66; Walter Krüssmann, *Ernst von Mansfeld (1580–1626): Grafensohn, Söldnerführer, Kriegsunternehmer gegen Habsburg im Dreißigjährigen Krieg* (Berlin: Duncker & Humblot, 2010), 30–51.

114. Redlich, *German Military Enterpriser*, 1:230–31. See also Wilson, *Europe's Tragedy*, 395–99.

115. Fritz Redlich, "Contributions in the Thirty Years' War," *Economic History Review* 12, no. 2 (1959): 247–49.

116. Under these conditions, a military entrepreneur with just ten thousand florins for an initial investment was capable of recovering his investment and profiting handsomely. Parrott, *Business of War*, 118.

117. Redlich, *German Military Enterpriser*, 1:331–43.

118. Grimmelshausen, *Adventures of Simplicius*, 53–54.

119. At one point, 98 percent of the money de Witte had borrowed to finance Wallenstein's army was set against anticipated contributions. Anton Ernstberger, *Hans de Witte, Finanzman Wallensteins* (Wiesbaden: Steiner, 1954), 196.

120. Charles P. Kindelberger, "The Economic Crisis of 1619 to 1623," *Journal of Economic History* 51 (1991): 149–75; and Kampmann, *Europa und das Reich*, 45–46. Contemporary broadsheets reveal what ordinary people experienced. See Martha White Paas, *The Kipper und Wipper Inflation, 1619–23: An Economic History with Contemporary German Broadsheets*, broadsheet descriptions by John Roger Paas, trans. George C. Schoolfield (New Haven, CT: Yale University Press, 2012).

121. The regiment Alt-Piccolomini was created that year. Trčka facilitated the introduction to Wallenstein. For these events, see Barker, *Army, Aristocracy, Monarchy*, 72–77. Multiple Piccolomini family members died in imperial service, including Ottavio's brother, his nephew, and his illegitimate son, showing the remarkable extent of this particular family's sacrifice for the Habsburg cause. Barker, *Army, Aristocracy, Monarchy*, 97–98.

122. As Holy Roman emperor, Ferdinand II had the right to confirm or deny Nevers's rule, and his wife, the Gonzaga empress Eleonora, hoped to entice Nevers into the imperial camp. However, Olivares, fearful of a potential French ally in Mantua, allowed Spanish-allied troops to invade the Mantuan dependency, Monferrato, and lay siege to Casale. This military move put an end to negotiations and set off a chain of events that drew aggressive reactions from both the French and Nevers. Wilson, *Europe's Tragedy*, 438–40, 443–46; J. H. Elliott, "Spain and the War," in *The Thirty Years' War*, ed. Geoffrey Parker, 2nd rev. ed. (London: Routledge, 1997), 95–98; and David Parrott, "A *Prince Souverain* and the French Crown: Charles de Nevers 1580–1637," in *Royal and Republican Sovereignty in Early Modern Europe: Essays in Memory of Ragnhild Hatton*, ed. Robert Oresko, G. C. Gibbs, and H. M. Scott (Cambridge: Cambridge University Press, 1997), 149–87.

123. Pietro Aldobrandini was in charge of the papal garrison at Ferrara.

124. Letters and other documents from Emperor Ferdinand II to Collalto regarding the Mantuan War can be found in MZA, RAC, z. G169, including "Letters from Ferdinand II to Rambaldo Collalto concerning the campaign to Italy" (1629), k. 1708; and "Two handwritten letters from Ferdinand II to Rambaldo Collalto giving him authority for negotiating matters of war and peace" (1630), k. 1712. On Piccolomini's role as an envoy, see the entire letter "Instruktion an Oberst Piccolomini," reprinted in *Documenta Bohemica*, vol. 4, no. 914.

125. Wilson, *Europe's Tragedy*, 444; Giambattista Intra, *Il sacco di Mantova* (Milan: Tip. della Perseveranza, 1872).

126. See Moriz Ritter, "Wallensteins Eroberungspläne gegen Venedig 1629," *Historische Zeitschrift* 93 (1904).

127. Barker, *Army, Aristocracy, Monarchy*, 77–81, quote on 77.

128. Pugliese, *Le prime strette*, 123.

129. Andrea Cioli to Marchese Coloredo, no date, *Negotio del fondo di Collalto Generale dell' Armi di Cesare in Italia l'anno 1629. Lettere peri Negotio del . . . Conte di Collalto . . . dell'Armi Cesarea in Italia 1629 et 30*, ASF, MDP, 4480.

130. Salvatore Pugliese argued that the whole incident epitomized the "ambiguous custom" that the imperial court used more generally toward Tuscany. See Pugliese, *Le prime strette*, 123–27, quote on 124.

131. Friedrich Schiller, *The Robbers/Wallenstein*, trans. F. J. Lamport (New York: Penguin Books, 1979), 385, 429, 472.

132. Parrott, "Military Enterpriser," 78.

133. Redlich, *German Military Enterpriser*, 1:171–72; Otto Elster, *Die Piccolomini—Regimenter während des 30jähr. Krieges: bes. das Kürassier—Regiment Alt—Piccolomin* (Vienna: Seidel & Sohn, 1903), 83–84.

134. Parrott, "Military Enterpriser," 78.

3. The Making of an Early Modern Military Entrepreneur

1. Raimondo Montecuccoli to Emperor Ferdinand III, 14 December 1644, in Foscolo, *Opere*, 2:258–59. See also a copy of his petition to Emperor Ferdinand III a few months later: 11 April 1644, Archivio di stato di Modena (ASMO), Ambasciatori della Germania (ADG), 96B. On the service of Montecuccoli's family see Campori, *Raimondo Montecuccoli*, 21–22.

2. For a similar example, see Cecilia Mazzetti di Pietralata, "Federico Savelli, tugendhafter Adliger, Militär und Diplomat," in Brevaglieri and Schettger, *Transferprozesse*, 161–205.

3. Wilson, *Europe's Tragedy*, 535–42; Robert Rebitsch, *Wallenstein: Biografie eines Machtmenschen* (Vienna: Böhlau, 2010); Mortimer, *Wallenstein*.

4. *Doc. Boh.*, vol. 1, 154; Bílek, *Dějiny konfiskací v Čechách po r. 1618*, 2:680, 2:775. The Spanish king granted Piccolomini the Duchy of Amalfi in the Kingdom of Naples after Piccolomini transferred to the Spanish Army of Flanders in 1635. Hanlon, *Twilight*, 257.

5. Lorenzo Guicciardini to Andrea Cioli, Naitott, 30 March 1634, ASF, MDP, 4472, 101–2.

6. Lorenzo Guicciardini to Andrea Cioli, Naistott, 14 April 1634, ASF, MDP, 4472, ff. 114–15. In 1642, Piccolomini faced accusations that he had acted arrogantly around Germans. Ottavio Piccolomini to de Magni, Prague, 29 December 1642, in *Doc. Boh.*, vol. 6, no. 1376.

7. Hanlon, *Twilight*, 98. The terms "Italian," "Spanish," or "foreign" seem to have been imprecise labels for cohesive groups of patrons and clients who advanced from outside of the traditional noble hierarchy of the Habsburg hereditary lands. Many of these outsiders were Italian and Spanish, but some were Scottish, Irish, Walloon, and even Czech or German.

8. For the appointment of the Medici brothers as colonels, see Decree of Alberto, Duke of Michelburg, ASF, MDP 4471, f. 2r.

9. Imperial diplomats had scoured Catholic Europe for support, begging allies in the Italian peninsula to provide money "for the needs of the Emperor, and all of Germany, devastated by the King of Sweden." *Alcuni fogli*, ASF, MDP 6379, f. 238. See also f. 239.

10. Pugliese, *Le prime strette*, 128–29.

11. Alena Pazderová, "Francesco Ottavio Piccolomini in Archival Documents," in *Siena in Prague: History, Art, Society*, ed. Alena Pazderová and Lucia Bonelli Conenna (Prague: National Gallery, 2000), 28.

12. Redlich, *German Military Enterpriser*, 1:303.

13. See chapter 2.

14. A century after Montecuccoli's death, the commune of Montecuccolo, over which he held lordship, registered 316 inhabitants. Lodovico Ricci, *Corografia dei territorj di Modena, Reggio e degli altri stati già appartenenti alla Casa d'Este* (Modena: Per gli Eredi di Bartolomaio Soliani, 1806), 167.

15. Bigi was a cultivated noblewoman from Ferrara, the granddaughter of Este secretary and historian Giambattista Pigna. Barker, *Military Intellectual*, 8.

16. Campori, *Raimondo Montecuccoli*, 9, 14–21.

17. For an example, see Campori, *Raimondo Montecuccoli*, 14. On Montecuccoli's early life and education see Barker, *Military Intellectual*, 8–9.

18. Sandonnini, *Il generale*, 2:77.

19. Barker, *Military Intellectual*, 9–16.

20. Campori, *Raimondo Montecuccoli*, 59–61.

21. *Atti e memorie della R. Deputazione di Storia Patria per le Provincie Modenesi* (Modena: Deputazioni, 1870), 5:13–28. For details on the early history of the family, their possessions, and their participation in martial pursuits, see Girolamo Tiraboschi, *Memorie storiche modenesi col codice diplomatico*, vol. 3 (Modena: Società Tipografica, 1794).

22. Campori, *Raimondo Montecuccoli*, 8, 12–13.

23. Norbert Elias, *The Civilizing Process: [Sociogenetic and Psychogenetic Investigations]*, trans. Edmund Jephcott (New York: Urizen Books, 1978).

24. Claudio Donati, "The Profession of Arms and the Nobility in Spanish Italy: Some Considerations," in *Spain in Italy: Politics, Society, and Religion 1500–1700*, ed. Thomas Dandelet and John A. Marino (Leiden: Brill, 2007), 303. See also Claudio Donati, "Il 'militare' nella storia dell'Italia moderna, dal Rinascimento all'età napoleonica," in *Eserciti e carriere militari nell'Italian moderna*, ed. C. Donati (Milan: Edizioni Unicopli 1998), 7–39.

25. Cesare Mozzarelli, *Antico regime e modernità* (Rome: Bulzoni, 2008); Gregory Hanlon, "In Praise of Refeudalization: Princes and Feudatories in North-Central Italy from the Sixteenth to the Eighteenth Century," in *Sociability and Its Discontents: Civil Society, Social Capital and their Alternatives in Late Medieval and Early Modern Europe*, ed. Nicholas Eckstein and Nicholas Terpstra (Turnhout: Brepols, 2009), 213–25.

26. Riccardo Rimondi, *Estensi: Storia e leggende, personaggi e luoghi di una dinastia millenaria* (Ferrara: Cirelli & Zanirato, 2004), 213–26; Luciano Chiappini, *Gli Estensi: mille anni di storia* (Ferrara: Corbo, 2001), 459–82.

27. Raimondo Montecuccoli to Francesco I d'Este, Hagenau, 13 December 1635, ASMO, ADG, 96B.

28. Ernesto Montecuccoli expressed similar sentiments. Campori, *Raimondo Montecuccoli*, 23.

29. Raimondo Montecuccoli to Francesco I d'Este, near Aschersleben, 26 April 1636, ASMO, ADG, 96B.

30. Tiziano Ascari, "Bolognesi, Ottavio," in *DBI*, vol. 11; Fernando Manzotti, "Le fine del Principato di Correggio nelle relazioni italo-imperiali del periodo italiano della guerra dei trent'anni," in *Atti e mem. della deputazione di storia patria per le Antiche province Modenesi*, ser. 8, 6 (1954): 43–59.

31. Girolamo Tiraboschi, *Dizionario topografico-storico degli stati Estensi* (Modena: Tipografia Camerale, 1825), 2:90, 2:92, 2:95.

32. Tiraboschi, *Memorie storiche*, vol. 3, passim. On Guidinello and the Guelf-Ghibelline rivalry in Frignano, see 131–49.

33. Campori, *Raimondo Montecuccoli*, 10.

34. The *lancie spezzati* dined with the grand duke and received pensions. Hanlon, *Twilight*, 63, 207.

35. Mattias and Francesco de' Medici to Grand Duke Ferdinando II de' Medici, Vaisenfelz, 13 November 1632, ASF, MDP, 4471, f. 190r.

36. Barker, *Military Intellectual*, 16–18.

37. Barker, *Military Intellectual*, 16–19. Veltzé, *Ausgewaehlte Schriften*, 4:22; Vitzthum to Galasso, Lindau, 6 December 1633, ÖStA KA, Alte Feldakten (AFA), 1634/12/221/2.

38. Raimondo Montecuccoli, *Ristretto della mia annuaria in Allemagna 1632–1644*, in ÖStA KA, NL: Montecuccoli, B/492: 27; see also Veltzé, *Ausgewaehlte Schriften*, 4:22.

39. Mattias de' Medici to the grand duke of Tuscany, Pilsen, 24 December 1633, ASF, MDP, 4471, ff. 662r–63v.

40. The content of his accusation is in Heinrich Srbik, *Wallensteins Ende: Ursachen, Verlauf und Folgen der Katastrophe* (Salzburg: O. Müller, 1952), 106–7.

41. Wilson, *Europe's Tragedy*, 549.

42. The order is dated 21 September 1634, ÖSTA KA, AFA, 1634/71/9.

43. For a similar point, see Michael Kaiser, "Jan von Werth zwischen Wittelsbach und Habsburg. Kriegsunternehmertum und Patronage im Dreißigjährigen Krieg," *Zeitschrift für bayerische Landesgeschichte* 75 (2012): 137.

44. Barker, *Military Intellectual*, 22–25.

45. Barker, *Military Intellectual*, 27. The directive is located in ÖSTA KA, AFA 1635/7/11, and has been reprinted in Barker, *Military Intellectual*, 28–29.

46. Galeotto was injured in battle and became disabled. He was murdered by a servant in 1642.

47. The deputy plenipotentiary, Paolo Orsini, reported 159,000 guilders in damages at Náchod. Alena Pazderová, "Francesco Ottavio Piccolomini," 27–28.

48. Montecuccoli discusses the incident in *Ristretto* in KA, NL: Montecuccoli, B/492: 27. See also Veltzé, *Ausgewaehlte Schriften*, 4:25–26.

49. He claimed that one of the officers had deserted after murdering a common soldier. Montecuccoli to Galasso, Dessau, 15 February 1638, ÖSTA KA, AFA, 1638/2/16. Events from this period of Montecuccoli's life are detailed in his autobiographical writings, including: *Ristretto della mia annuaria in Allemagna 1632–1644*, in KA: NL Montecuccoli, B/492: 27; *Autobiografische Notizen R. Montecuccolis zu seinem Leben von 1627 bis 1657*, in KA: NL Montecuccoli, B/492: 40; and *Ristretto delle occasioni principali della guerra, nelle quali si è trovato il conte Raimondo Montecuccoli e delle cariche, ch'egli ha essercitato fin al anno*

1664, in KA: NL Montecuccoli, B/492: 70. Veltzé has printed and translated these writings into German. On the Brandenburg issue, see Veltzé, *Ausgewaehlte Schriften*, 4:136–37.

50. Ronald G. Asch, *The Thirty Years' War: The Holy Roman Empire and Europe, 1618–48* (New York: St. Martin's Press, 1997), 126–31, 150.

51. Barker, *Military Intellectual*, 38–40.

52. Dispatches from Modena to Ottavio Bolognesi, 20 June 1639, ASMO, ADG, 94. Montecuccoli thanked Francesco for his help. See Raimondo Montecuccoli to Francesco I d'Este, Stettin, 8 March 1640, ASMO, ADG, 87. See also Girolamo Graf Montecuccoli to Ottavio Bolognesi, Innsbruck, 14 June 1639, and Francesco Montecuccoli to Ottavio Bolognesi, Modena, 29 July 1639, ÖNB, *Autographen-Sammlung* (Autogr.), 27/66-1; Campori, *Raimondo Montecuccoli*, 118–20.

53. Pieri, *Guerra e politica*, 93. Jean de Werth, at the time a general in Bavarian service, suffered a long imprisonment from 1638 to 1642 for the same reason. Kaiser, "Jan von Werth," 135–66.

54. Parrott, "Military Enterpriser," 74–75; Kaiser, "Jan von Werth," 142–44.

55. Montecuccoli, *Le opere*, 1:128.

56. See chapter 1.

57. Montecuccoli, *Le opere*, 1:127–29.

58. Montecuccoli, *Le opere*, 1:127–29.

59. Montecuccoli, *Le opere*, 1:127.

60. Petition to Emperor Ferdinand III, 11 April 1644, ASMO, ADG, 96b.

61. "Alla memoria di Gustavo Adolfo Re de' Sveci, Vandali e Goti," in Campori, *Raimondo Montecuccoli*, 546–49.

62. Montecuccoli, *Le opere*, 1:235.

63. Montecuccoli, *Le opere*, 1:128.

64. Biagioli, "Social Status"; Valleriani, *Galileo Engineer*.

65. Montecuccoli, *Le opere*, 1:130.

66. Montecuccoli, *Le opere*, 1:130.

67. Barker alleges that Ottavio's brother Enea helped facilitate Galileo's position as Tuscan court mathematician. See Barker, *Army, Aristocracy, Monarchy*, 70–72.

68. Campori, *Raimondo Montecuccoli*, 134.

69. Francesco I d'Este to Ottavio Bolognesi, Modena, 28 August 1642, in Fulvio Testi, *Lettere* (Bari: Laterza, 1967), vol. 3, no. 1568.

70. Francesco I d'Este to Ferdinand III, Modena, 28 August 1642, in Testi, *Lettere*, vol. 3, no. 1569.

71. Davide Maffi, *Il baluardo della corona: Guerra, esercito, finanze e società nella Lombardia seicentesca (1630–1660)* (Florence: Le Monnier, 2007), 103–4. Despite these concerns, Francesco obtained 1,100 Swedish prisoners from the imperial army, as well as 300 Swiss mercenaries. The Montecuccoli family supplied 250 of their own subjects. Campori, *Raimondo Montecuccoli*, 138–39, 146, 160–61.

72. His competition was the Modenese infantry general and Este relative Camillo Bevilacqua. "Compendio di una scrittura di Raimondo Montecuccoli esistente nell'archivio di stato a Modena intitolata: Pretensioni del conte Raimondo Montecuccoli sopra la proposizione di farlo mastro di campo generale di S.A.S," in Campori, *Raimondo Montecuccoli*, 550–52. See also 140–41.

73. Caferro, *John Hawkwood*, 334.

74. Montecuccoli, *Le opere*, 3:78.

75. Montecuccoli, *Le opere*, 3:71–77.

76. Raimondo Montecuccoli to Mattias de' Medici, from the camp at Modena, 22 July 1643, quoted in Campori, *Raimondo Montecuccoli*, 168.

77. Fulvio Testi to Cardinal Rinaldo d'Este, from the camp in Secco, 13 June 1643, quoted in Testi, *Lettere*, vol. 3, no. 1659.

78. Campori, *Raimondo Montecuccoli*, 133–34. On the papacy's martial pursuits and relationships at this time, see Brunelli, *Soldati del papa*, 241–72.

79. Montecuccoli, *Le opere*, 2:301.

80. Redlich, *German Military Enterpriser*, 1:400. See also, for instance, Stephanie Haberer, *Ott Heinrich Fugger (1592–1644): Biographische Analyse typologischer Handlungsfelder in der Epoche des Dreißigjährigen Krieges* (Augsburg: Wissner, 2004).

81. Raimondo Montecuccoli to Pietro Ricci, Vienna, 6 February 1644, in *Lettere inedite di Raimondo Montecuccoli al dottori Pietro e Carlo Ricci*, ed. Canonico B. Ricci (Modena: Tipi del Commercio, 1907), 23.

82. Raimondo Montecuccoli to Francesco I d'Este, Vienna, 16 April 1644, ASMO, ADG 96b. Montecuccoli believed he would receive the full payment from the Court Chamber of Styria. Raimondo Montecuccoli to Mattias de' Medici, Vienna, 14 May 1644, ASF, MDP 5434, ff. 306–7.

83. Raimondo Montecuccoli to Wenzel Eusebius Lobkowitz, Lobring/Cobring(?), 1 August 1644, Státní oblastní archiv Litoměřice-Žitenice (SOAL), "Von der kaiserlichen armee," c. 157, p. 5. The Lobkovitz collection has moved to Nelahozeves Castle since I consulted it.

84. Campori, *Raimondo Montecuccoli*, 204.

85. Raimondo Montecuccoli to Emperor Ferdinand III, 14 December 1644, in Foscolo, *Opere*, 2:258.

86. Richard Bassett, *For God and Kaiser: The Imperial Austrian Army, 1619–1918* (New Haven, CT: Yale University Press, 2015), 28.

87. See the epilogue for a summary of gifts and payments Montecuccoli received over the course of his lifetime.

88. Raimondo Montecuccoli to Pietro Ricci, Vienna, 6 February 1644, in Ricci, *Lettere*, 23.

89. Francesco I d'Este to Muzio Vitelleschi, Modena, 16 December 1643, Testi, *Lettere*, vol. 3, no. 1737; Campori, *Raimondo Montecuccoli*, 190–91. He needed to prove his nobility by producing a family tree. Raimondo Montecuccoli to Pietro Ricci, Vienna, 9 April 1644, in Ricci, *Lettere*, 24.

90. Raimondo Montecuccoli to Ottavio Piccolomini, copy of his audience with the emperor, Vienna, 9 March 1650, SOAZ, RAP, inv. č. 12416, p. 290. The family established a fidei commissum to ensure continuity of ownership.

91. "Atti d'ultima volontà di Raimondo Montecuccoli: Testamento do Raimondo Montecuccoli," in Sandonnini, *Il generale*, 63.

92. Raimondo Montecuccoli to Pietro Ricci, Venice, 10 December 1643, in Ricci, *Lettere*, 22.

93. Ricci, *Lettere*, 2.

94. Raimondo Montecuccoli to Pietro Ricci, Glattau in Bohemia, 22 June 1645, in Ricci, *Lettere*, 29–30.

95. Campori, *Raimondo Montecuccoli*, 233.

96. Raimondo Montecuccoli to Pietro Ricci, Vienna, 25 January 1645, in Ricci, *Lettere*, 28.

97. Raimondo Montecuccoli to Wenzel Eusebius Lobkowitz, Prague, 7 October 1646, SOAL, c. 157, f. 17v. The whole letter is ff. 25r–27v. Montecuccoli hoped Lobkowitz would help him since "Your Excellency has always honored me with your protection and grace" (25r). Two years earlier, Montecuccoli made a similar complaint. See Raimondo Montecuccoli to Wenzel Eusebius Lobkowitz, 12 August 1644, SOAL, c. 157, 9.

98. Veltzé, *Ausgewaehlte Schriften*, 4:172.

99. Raimondo Montecuccoli to Pietro Ricci, Vienna, 23 April 1644, and Raimondo Montecuccoli to Pietro Ricci, Dresden, 2 October 1644, in Ricci, *Lettere*, 24–25, 27.

100. Bassett, *For God and Kaiser*, 26; John Mitchell, *Life of Wallenstein, Duke of Friedland* (London: James Fraser, 1837), 108.

101. Raimondo Montecuccoli to Francesco I d'Este, Vienna, 12 March 1644, ASMO, ADG 96b.

102. Campori, *Raimondo Montecuccoli*, 160–61.

103. Raimondo Montecuccoli to Pietro Ricci, Vienna, 9 April 1644, in Ricci, *Lettere*, 24.

104. On this phase, see Kampmann, *Europa und das Reich*, 128–79.

105. Wilson, *Europe's Tragedy*, 635–39, 661–62, 667–69.

106. Campori, *Raimondo Montecuccoli*, 208.

107. See the letter and enclosed petition in Raimondo Montecuccoli to Francesco I d'Este, Vienna, 26 December 1643, ASMO, ADG, 96B.

108. Raimondo Montecuccoli to Francesco I d'Este, Vienna, 2 January 1644, ASMO, ADG, 96b; and Campori, *Raimondo Montecuccoli*, 192–93.

109. Raimondo Montecuccoli to Francesco I d'Este, Vienna, 23 April 1644, ASMO, ADG, 96B.

110. Wilson, *Europe's Tragedy*, 689–90, and Kampmann, *Europa und das Reich*, 147.

111. The letters can be found in Vittorio Siri, *Il Mercurio overo historia de' correnti tempi (1635–1655) di Vittorio Siri* (Casale: Per Giorno del Monte, 1655), 4:173–76.

112. The letters are: Lettera del Tenente Generale Galasso al Tenente Maresciallo Conte Montecuccoli, Dal campo appresso Oldesto, 3 August 1644; Lettera del Galasso al Conte Montecuccoli, Dal campo Imperiale a Bornholm, 10 August 1644; Lettera del Galasso al Conte Montecuccoli, Dal Campo Imperiale a Kiel, 14 August 1644; Lettera del Galasso al Conte Montecuccoli, Dal campo Imperiale a Mellen, 24 August 1644; Ordini dell'Imperadore al Conte Montecuccoli, di Ebersdorf, 29 July 1644; Lettera dell'Imperadore al Conte Montecuccoli, Vienna, 7 August 1644; Lettera dell'Imperadore al Conte Montecuccoli, Vienna, 16 August 1644; Lettera dell'Imperadore al Conte Montecuccoli, Erbersdorf, 3 September 1644, in Siri, *Il Mercurio*, 4:173–76. Quotes are on 4:173 and 4:175.

113. Raimondo Montecuccoli to Ottavio Bolognesi, 13 August 1644, in Foscolo, *Opere*, 2:252–53.

114. Montecuccoli reported to Ricci from Dresden in October that he had received horses "safe and sound" from Massimiliano Montecuccoli. Raimondo Montecuccoli to Pietro Ricci, Dresden, 2 October 1644, in Ricci, *Lettere*, 26.

115. Raimondo Montecuccoli to Ottavio Bolognesi, 13 August 1644, in Foscolo, *Opere*, 2:252–53.

116. Campori, *Raimondo Montecuccoli*, 218–19.

117. Montecuccoli, *Le opere*, 2:17–18.

118. Montecuccoli, *Le opere*, 2:153, 2:321.

119. Veltzé, *Ausgewaehlte Schriften*, 4:140–41. He stopped at Linz, where he reportedly lost the ring the duke of Modena had given him.

120. Raimondo Montecuccoli to Francesco I d'Este, Vienna, 22 July 1645, ASMO, ADG, 96B.

121. Raimondo Montecuccoli to Francesco I d'Este, from the imperial camp at Teben in Hungary, 5 August 1645, ASMO, ADG, 96B.

122. Raimondo Montecuccoli to Francesco I d'Este, from the camp at Teben, 27 August 1645, ASMO, ADG, 96B.

123. Minuti Ducale, Modena, 5 January 1646, ASMO, ADG, 96B; Raimondo Montecuccoli to Francesco I d'Este, Modena, no date, 1646, ASMO, ADG, 96B.

124. Raimondo Montecuccoli to Francesco I d'Este, Budweis, [25 December] 1645, ASMO, ADG, 96B; Budweis, 10 January 1646, ASMO, ADG, 96B.

125. Montecuccoli copied the instructions in a letter to Francesco. Raimondo Montecuccoli to Francesco I d'Este, Freiberg, 24 December 1646, ASMO, ADG, 96B.

126. Raimondo Montecuccoli to Francesco I d'Este, Freiberg, 24 December 1646, ASMO, ADG, 96B; Campori, *Raimondo Montecuccoli*, 250–51.

127. Wilson, *Europe's Tragedy*, 740–43. Nonetheless, Bérenger argues that Montecuccoli underestimated how bad the defeat was in terms of the larger campaign strategy. See Jean Bérenger, *Turenne* (Paris: Fayard, 1987), 258–60, esp. 260. For detailed coverage of these campaigns, see Rebitsch, Öhman, and Kilián, *1648*.

128. Raimondo Montecuccoli to Francesco I d'Este, Breßlau, 29 April 1647, ASMO, ADG, 96B; Baden, 22 June 1647, ASMO, ADG, 96B.

129. Raimondo Montecuccoli to Francesco I d'Este, the imperial camp, 20 August 1647, ASMO, ADG, 96B; Pilsen, 5 September 1647, ASMO, ADG, 96B.

130. Campori, *Raimondo Montecuccoli*, 256–57.

131. Campori, *Raimondo Montecuccoli*, 263.

132. *Minuti Ducale*, Modena, 23 August 1647, ASMO, ADG, 96B.

133. Raimondo Montecuccoli to Francesco I d'Este, Pilsen, 5 September 1647, ASMO, ADG, 96B.

134. Hanlon, *Hero of Italy*, 52.

135. Francesco I d'Este to Raimondo Montecuccoli, Modena, 3 November 1647, ASMO, ADG, 96B.

136. Luigi Simeoni, *Francesco I d'Este e la politica italiana del Mazarino* (Bologna: N. Zanichelli, 1921), 73–135.

137. Raimondo Montecuccoli to Wenzel Eusebius Lobkowitz, Prague, 7 October 1646, SOAL, c. 157, ff. 25r–27v.

138. Campori, *Raimondo Montecuccoli*, 279–80.

139. Montecuccoli, *Le opere*, 3:355.

140. Ferdinand III considered a military intervention against Francesco but died in 1657. After his death, the Viennese court was preoccupied by Leopold I's election as emperor and Austria's involvement in the Second Northern War. In 1658, Montecuc-

coli was appointed field marshal of the imperial auxiliary forces in that war, a position for which Leopold Wilhelm probably recommended him after Hatzfeld's death.

141. Campori, *Raimondo Montecuccoli*, 264.

142. Quoted in Campori, *Raimondo Montecuccoli*, 200.

143. Montecuccoli to Bolognesi, 13 August 1644, in Foscolo, *Opere*, 2:253.

144. Campori, *Raimondo Montecuccoli*, 324.

145. Mallett and Shaw, *Italian Wars*, 1–5.

146. David Parrott, "Italian Soldiers in French Service, 1500–1700. The Collapse of a Military Tradition," in *Italiani al servizio straniero in età moderna*, ed. Paola Bianchi, Davide Maffei, and Enrico Stumpo (Milan: FrancoAngeli, 2008), 38–39.

4. From Battlefield to Court

1. Machiavelli, *Art of War*, 13.

2. Montecuccoli to Piccolomini, copy of his audience with the emperor, Vienna, 9 March 1650, SOAZ, RAP, inv. č. 12416, 292.

3. Petr Maťa, *Svět české aristokracie (1500–1700)* (Prague: Nakl. Lidové noviny, 2004), 465–77.

4. The journals have been published in their original Italian in Montecuccoli, *Le opere*, 3:279–397 and 3:398–431.

5. Otto Elster, *Piccolomini-studien* (Leipzig: G. Müller-Mann, 1911), 119–34.

6. Montecuccoli to Piccolomini, Vienna, 13 August 1650, SOAZ, RAP, inv. č. 12464, 485.

7. Montecuccoli to Piccolomini, Vienna, 13 August 1650, SOAZ, RAP, inv. č. 12464, 486. Piccolomini was already at the end of his career and would die at his country estate six years later.

8. Pugliese, *Le prime strette*, 145–48.

9. Montecuccoli to Piccolomini, copy of his audience with the emperor, Vienna, 9 March 1650, SOAZ, RAP, inv. č. 12416. Montecuccoli was one of seventy-six imperial chamberlains appointed between 1623 and 1649. Many of the others were native nobles, but the list included members of the Piccolomini, Collalto, Strassoldo, and Gonzaga families, along with a handful of other foreigners. See Haus-, Hof- und Staatsarchiv (HHStA), Obersthofmeisteramt—Sonderreihe (OMeA SR) 184, ff. 1–2. On these offices and the *cursus honorum* at the Austrian Habsburg court, see Duindam, *Vienna and Versailles*, 90–128.

10. Piccolomini to Montecuccoli, Regensburg, 27 January 1653, ÖStA KA, NL: Montecuccoli, B/492: 254a. In later decades, Montecuccoli openly struggled with Lobkowitz. See chapter 6.

11. For instance, Montecuccoli, *Le opere*, 3:313–14. On marriage as a basic requirement for a successful court career in Vienna, see Maťa, *Svět*, 429.

12. Raimondo Montecuccoli, *Historia miserabile, mà vera de gli amori di Morindo per Arianna*, ÖNB, Autogr., 17/22-2, 1–2.

13. Montecuccoli, *Historia miserabile*, ÖNB, Autogr., 17/22-2, 2.

14. Nivena was Vienna and Atilia was Italy.

15. See chapter 3.

16. Raimondo Montecuccoli to Ottavio Piccolomini, Vienna, 6 February 1650, SOAZ, RAP, inv. č. 12412, 273–74, quote on 274.

17. Raimondo Montecuccoli to Ottavio Piccolomini, copy of his audience with the emperor, Vienna, 9 March 1650, SOAZ, RAP, inv. č. 12416, 289.

18. The property had originally been acquired by Ernesto, who left his properties to his brother Girolamo.

19. Raimondo Montecuccoli to Massimiliano Montecuccoli, Prague, 27 November 1652, in Veltzé, *Ausgewaehlte Schriften*, 4:254; and Regensburg, 9 June 1653, in Veltzé, *Ausgewaehlte Schriften*, 4:256.

20. The demands for compensation of German military entrepreneurs in the Swedish army were impossible for the empire to satisfy, but impacted negotiations at Osnabrück. See Parrott, "Military Enterpriser," 81.

21. Peter Wilson, *The Heart of Europe: A History of the Holy Roman Empire* (Cambridge, MA: Belknap Press of Harvard University Press, 2016), 451–52.

22. John Mears, *Count Raimondo Montecuccoli: Practical Soldier and Military Theoretician* (PhD diss., University of Chicago, 1964), 97–98. See also Veltzé, *Ausgewaehlte Schriften*, 4:248.

23. Montecuccoli, *Le opere*, 2:127. These treatises have been published in Montecuccoli, *Le opere*, vols. 1 and 2.

24. Montecuccoli, *Le opere*, 2:127.

25. Montecuccoli, *Le opere*, 3:386–97.

26. On the circulation of his works, see Kurt Peball, "Raimund Fürst Montecuccoli 1609–1680. Gedanken zum Leben und Werk eines großen österreichischen Feldherrn," *Österreichische Militärische Zeitschrift* 2 (1964): 303.

27. Montecuccoli's letter to Bettini was printed in Mario Bettini, *Recreationum mathematicarum apiaria novissima duodecim* [. . .] (Bononiae: Sumptibus J. B. Ferronii, 1659), 10. See also Denise Aricò, "Una corrispondenza fra il gesuita bolognese Mario Bettini e Raimondo Montecuccoli," *Filologia e critica* (May–August 2006): 288–312.

28. ÖStA KA, NL: Montecuccoli, B/492: 194.

29. For a similar case, see Erik Thomson, "Axel Oxenstierna and Books," *Sixteenth Century Journal* 38 (2007): 705–29.

30. Stephen Toulmin, *Cosmopolis: The Hidden Agenda of Modernity* (Chicago: University of Chicago Press, 1992), 70–71.

31. He had been arrested twice: first by the Inquisition for heresy in 1594 and then for his role in connection to a conspiracy to overthrow Spanish rule in Naples in 1599. For the latter offense, he spent twenty-seven years in prison and was later forced into exile in France, where he died. John Headley, *Tommaso Campanella and the Transformation of the World* (Princeton, NJ: Princeton University Press, 1997). See also Germana Ernst, *Tommaso Campanella: The Book and the Body of Nature* (Dordrecht: Springer, 2010).

32. According to the Book of Daniel, the Fourth Monarchy would precede the establishment of the Kingdom of God on earth. In early modern interpretations, the Fourth Monarchy was often identified as the Roman Empire/Holy Roman Empire. Campanella saw all of the realms over which the Habsburgs maintained influence—the Spanish and Austrian lands, as well as the Holy Roman Empire—as part of a single empire. Not everyone agreed with these views of the Habsburg realms nor thought that the Holy Roman Empire was a direct continuation of the Roman Empire. See W. Stanford Reid, "The Four Monarchies of Daniel in Reformation Historiography," *Historical Reflections/Réflexions Historiques* 8, no. 1 (Spring 1981): 115–23. A published ver-

sion of Campanella's work is available: Tommaso Campanella, *Monarchie d'Espagne: texte inédit*, ed. Germana Ernst (Paris: Presses universitaires de France, 1997).

33. Lipsius was a Catholic convert.

34. Marie Tanner discusses the origins and evolution of the mythic image of the emperor, culminating in the reign of Philip II. See Marie Tanner, *The Last Descendant of Aeneas: The Hapsburgs and the Mythic Image of the Emperor* (New Haven, CT: Yale University Press, 1993), esp. 119–30. On the universal mission of the Austrian Habsburgs, see Evans, *Making*. For the Spanish Habsburgs, see also Anthony Pagden, *Lords of All the World: Ideologies of Empire in Spain, Britain and France c. 1500–c. 1800* (New Haven, CT: Yale University Press, 1995).

35. Raimondo Montecuccoli to Massimiliano Montecuccoli, Munich, 19 August 1653, in Veltzé, *Ausgewaehlte Schriften*, 4:257.

36. Campori, *Raimondo Montecuccoli*, 293.

37. Montecuccoli, *Le opere*, 3:292. Christina inducted other foreign diplomats into the order as well, including the two Spanish ambassadors Antonio Pimentel and Bernardino de Rebolledo.

38. Montecuccoli to Emperor Ferdinand III, Uppsala, 27 February 1654, ÖNB, Autogr., 17/22–5; Montecuccoli to Mattias de' Medici, Uppsala, 27 February 1654, ASF, MDP, f. 5452, fol. 718r; Montecuccoli to Francesco I d'Este, Regensburg, 4 May 1654, ASMO, ADG, b. 96b. A diamond-studded miniature portrait of the queen was listed among Montecuccoli's most precious possessions in 1675. See ÖStA KA, NL: Montecuccoli, B/492: 24, 22.

39. Besides the Dominican priest who performed the ceremony, the other witnesses were all Spanish diplomatic and military officials, including Pimentel and the Spanish minister and general, Fuenseldaña. Montecuccoli, *Le opere*, 3:339.

40. Montecuccoli, *Le opere*, 3:348.

41. Montecuccoli, *Le opere*, 3:326.

42. Christina was not optimistic about such a possibility. Montecuccoli, *Le opere*, 3:325. However, she traveled to Cologne to discuss the matter with the archbishops of Trier and Mainz. Susanna Åkerman, *Queen Christina of Sweden and Her Circle: The Transformation of a Seventeenth-Century Philosophical Libertine* (Leiden: E. J. Brill, 1991), 217–18.

43. Montecuccoli, *Le opere*, 3:311. Since 1649, Leopold Wilhelm had been trying to convince Philip IV to give Montecuccoli a permanent position in the Army of Flanders. Renate Schreiber, *"Ein Galeria nach meinem Humor": Erzherzog Leopold Wilhelm* (Vienna: Kunsthistorisches Museum-Museumsverband, 2004), 74.

44. Montecuccoli, *Le opere*, 3:373.

45. Montecuccoli, *Le opere*, 3:390–91, 3:395–96.

46. Renate Schreiber, "Mit Degen und Feder—Erzherzog Leopold Wilhelm als Verfasser italienischer Gedichte," in *Fürst und Fürstin als Künstler*, ed. Annette Cremer, Mathias Müller, and Klaus Pietschmann (Munich: DKV, 2018), 6–7, 11, 13; Seifert, "Akademien am Wiener Kaiserhof der Barockzeit," 215–17. Schreiber has published some of Leopold Wilhelm's poetry in Schreiber, *Ein Galeria*, 131–43.

47. Montecuccoli, *Le opere*, 3:311.

48. Montecuccoli, *Le opere*, 3:322.

49. Daniel Riches, *Protestant Cosmopolitanism and Diplomatic Culture: Brandenburg-Swedish Relations in the Seventeenth Century* (Leiden: Brill, 2013), 164.

50. Montecuccoli, *Le opere*, 3:299.

51. On military deception and political maneuvering, see Caferro, *John Hawkwood*, 18–19.

52. Paul Douglas Lockhart, *Sweden in the Seventeenth Century* (Basingstoke: Palgrave Macmillan, 2004), 71.

53. Eva Nilsson Nylander, *The Mild Boredom of Order: A Study in the History of the Manuscript Collection of Queen Christina of Sweden* (Lund: Lund University, 2011), 51–54; Thomson, "Axel Oxenstierna," 708–9.

54. Montecuccoli, *Le opere*, 3:291–92. Montecuccoli to Piccolomini, Uppsala, 10 February 1654, SOAZ, RAP, inv. č. 12528, 763. Regarding Queen Christina's religious doubts and skepticism, see Åkerman, *Queen Christina*, 14–43.

55. Montecuccoli, *Le opere*, 3:375. On Andrea Montecuccoli, see Campori, *Raimondo Montecuccoli*, 279.

56. Toby Osborne, *Dynasty and Diplomacy in the Court of Savoy: Political Culture and the Thirty Years' War* (Cambridge: Cambridge University Press, 2002), 196–201; Geoffrey Parker, "The Decision-Making Process in the Government of the Catholic Netherlands under 'the Archdukes,' 1596–1621," in *Spain and the Netherlands, 1559–1659: Ten Studies*, ed. Geoffrey Parker (Short Hills, NJ: Enslow Publishers, 1979), 164–76.

57. Montecuccoli, *Le opere*, 3:343.

58. Victor W. Turner, *The Ritual Process: Structure and Anti-Structure* (Chicago: University of Chicago Press, 1969), 95. Turner bases his ideas on Van Gennep's work. See Arnold Van Gennep, *The Rites of Passage* (Chicago: University of Chicago Press, 1960).

59. Montecuccoli, *Le opere*, 3:328.

60. Norman Cohn, *The Pursuit of the Millennium: Revolutionary Millenarians and Mystical Anarchists of the Middle Ages* (New York: Oxford University Press, 1981).

61. Nylander, *Mild Boredom*, 113.

62. Montecuccoli, *Le opere*, 3:370.

63. Montecuccoli obeyed, but neither the archduke nor Fuenseldaña thought Christina's ideas were viable. Montecuccoli, *Le opere*, 3:378–80.

64. Montecuccoli, *Le opere*, 3:343, 3:371. Henry Schwarz, *The Imperial Privy Council in the Seventeenth Century* (Westport, CT: Greenwood Press, 1972), 310.

65. Galeazzo Gualdo Priorato and Girolamo Graziani, *Historia della Sacra Real Maestà di Christina Alessandra Regina di Suetia, &c.* (Modena: Appresso Bartolomeo Soliani, 1656), 220. On Montecuccoli's role in Rome, see also Campori, *Raimondo Montecuccoli*, 314–15, 318.

66. Campori, *Raimondo Montecuccoli*, 320.

67. Simeoni, *Francesco I d'Este*, 179–98.

68. The Vienna academy included another Italian nobleman who had participated in the Brussels academy and followed Leopold Wilhelm to Vienna. Montecuccoli, *Le opere*, 3:373–74; Schreiber, "Mit Degen," 11–14; Seifert, "Akademien am Wiener Kaiserhof," 215–17. Notes from two of the meetings of this academy can be found in ÖNB, Handschriften-Sammlung, Signatur 10108. See also Schreiber, *Ein galeria*, 139–41.

69. On Leopold Wilhelm's influence at court, see Schreiber, *Ein Galeria*, 160–62.

70. Campori, *Raimondo Montecuccoli*, 322–60. For reports on this conflict, see Adalbert Franz Fuchs, *Briefe and den Feldmarschall Raimund Grafen Montecuccoli: Beiträge zur Geschichte des nordischen Krieges in den Jahren 1659–1660* (Vienna: C. W. Stern, 1910).

71. See the correspondence regarding the marriage: Empress Eleonora to Dietrichstein, Vienna, 3 March 1657, MZA, RAD, 1247; Montecuccoli to Dietrichstein, Vienna, 3 March 1657, MZA, RAD 1247; and Montecuccoli to Dietrichstein, Vienna, 17 March 1657, MZA, RAD 1247.

72. Schwartz, *Imperial Privy Council*, 185. On the Dietrichstein family see Evans, *Making*, 172, 203–4, 209.

73. "Concept zu seinem Testamente (1672)," in Veltzé, *Ausgewaehlte Schriften*, 4:172; Raimondo Montecuccoli to Massimiliano Montecuccoli, Vienna, 10 March 1657, in Veltzé, *Ausgewaehlte Schriften*, 4:273.

74. Montecuccoli, *Le opere*, 3:342, 3:346, 3:348, 3:356.

75. *Autobiographische Notizen Raimunds Montecuccoli zu seinem leben von 1627 bis 1657*, ÖStA KA, NL: Montecuccoli, B/492: 40.

76. ÖStA KA, NL: Montecuccoli, B/492: 194.

77. *Private Notizen*, ÖStA KA, NL: Montecuccoli, B/492: 51.

78. *Raimund Montecuccolis Entwurf eines Zeremoniells am kaiserlichen Hofe in Wien für den 27. April 1663*, ÖStA KA, NL: Montecuccoli, B/492: 81. On the celebrations of this union in Madrid, see *Verdadera relación de las fiestas y recibimiento que en Barcelona se hizo á la Majestad Cesárea de la Serma. Sra. D.a Margarita de Austria, emperatriz de Alemania, y juntamente de su embarcaciór, Y acompañamiento* (Madrid, 1666).

79. John P. Spielman, *Leopold I of Austria* (New Brunswick, NJ: Rutgers University Press, 1977), 45; Jiří Mikulec, *Leopold I: Život a Vláda Barokního Habsburka* (Prague: Paseka, 1997).

80. Spielman, *Leopold I*, 53.

81. Montecuccoli, *Le opere*, 3:404.

82. Montecuccoli, *Le opere*, 3:413. For Agostino Durazzo, see Montecuccoli, *Le opere*, 3:407–10; for the Spinola and Doria families, see Montecuccoli, *Le opere*, 3:408.

83. For instance, after a perceived insult from the Maltese, Genoa sent five additional armed galleys to roam the waters at Finale. Felice Marchetti, "Lettere con la Segria di Stato. Negoziati del S. Segrio di Stato Marchetti essendo co' l Sermi Principe Mattia nel viaggio al Finale per ricevir l'infanta di Spagna sposa dell'imper Leopoldo l'anno 1666," ASF, MDP, 6381, f. 558.

84. On these issues, see the essays in Ralph Kauz, Giorgio Rota, and Jan Paul Niederkorn, *Diplomatisches Zeremoniell in Europa und im Mittleren Osten in der Frühen Neuzeit* (Vienna: Verlag der Österreichischen Akademie der Wissenschaften, 2009). The acting out of ceremony itself could produce uncertainty since the environment was often ambivalent. For example, the left hand might appear to confer higher status than the right, or the front and back of a procession could be argued to be of equal importance. See Duindam, *Vienna and Versailles*, 181–88.

85. Although long-term interactions between courts had resulted in the standardization of some behavior, many aspects of ceremony were court specific. William J. Roosen, "Early Modern Diplomatic Ceremonial: A Systems Approach," *Journal of Modern History* 52 (September 1980): 452–76.

86. Montecuccoli, *Le opere*, 3:407–8.

87. On brides as classic liminal figures, see Van Gennep, *Rites of Passage*, 116.

88. Marchetti, "Lettere," ASF, MDP, 6381, f. 427.

89. Marchetti, "Lettere," ASF, MDP, 6381, f. 413.

90. Marchetti, "Lettere," ASF, MDP, 6381, f. 409.

91. Montecuccoli, *Le opere*, 3:407.

92. Marchetti, "Lettere," ASF, MDP, 6381, f. 450.

93. Montecuccoli considered it was his "duty" or "debt" to write to Mattias after Mattias helped secure his release from prison. Montecuccoli to Mattias de' Medici, Vienna, 14 May 1644, ASF, MDP 5434, ff. 306–7. For the report on Margarethe von Dietrichstein's miscarriage, see Montecuccoli to Mattias de' Medici, Vienna, 23 May 1666, ASF, MDP 5414, f. 946.

94. Atto Melani to Mattias de' Medici, ASF, MDP, 5455, f. 227. See also Raimondo Montecuccoli to Mattias de' Medici, Regensburg, 14 July 1653, ASF, MDP, 5415, f. 525.

95. "Instruction fuer den Grafen Montecuccoli zur Reise nach Finale," in Veltzé, *Ausgewaehlte Schriften*, 3:319.

96. "Instruction," in Veltzé, *Ausgewaehlte Schriften*, 3:324.

97. Van Gennep, *Rites of Passage*, 122.

98. "Instruction," in Veltzé, *Ausgewaehlte Schriften*, 3:324.

99. "Instruction," in Veltzé, *Ausgewaehlte Schriften*, 3:320–21.

100. Veltzé, *Ausgewaehlte Schriften*, 3:322.

101. Veltzé, *Ausgewaehlte Schriften*, 3:280.

102. Veltzé, *Ausgewaehlte Schriften*, 3:401.

103. Albuquerque and Colonna would only be able to participate as private persons, thus sacrificing public honors associated with the official ceremony. Finale, 28 July 1666, Memoriale (Recapitulation meines Auftrages.), in Veltzé, *Ausgewaehlte Schriften*, 4:292.

104. Montecuccoli, *Le opere*, 3:403. In his instructions, the emperor had explicitly stated that he did not want Cardinal Colonna or the duke of Albuquerque to continue with Margarita Teresa to Vienna. See "Instruction," in Veltzé, *Ausgewaehlte Schriften*, 3:323.

105. Montecuccoli, *Le opere*, 3:417–18.

106. Montecuccoli, *Le opere*, 3:418.

107. Marchetti, "Lettere," ASF, MDP, 6381, f. 587. For Montecuccoli's exchange with the duke, during which the duke opted to use the Spanish style, see Montecuccoli, *Le opere*, 3:426–27. According to the duke, the grandees of Spain reserved "Highness" for sovereign princes. Montecuccoli, *Le opere*, 3:428–30.

108. "Ueber die Verhandlungen mit der Republik Genua, bezueglich des Ceremoniells gelegentlich der Durchreise der kaiserlichen Braut," in Veltzé, *Ausgewaehlte Schriften*, 3:328.

109. Montecuccoli, *Le opere*, 3:429.

110. Olivares is quoted in John Elliott, *The Count-Duke of Olivares: The Statesman in an Age of Decline* (New Haven, CT: Yale University Press, 1986), 369.

111. See chapter 5.

112. Margaret C. Jacob, *Strangers Nowhere in the World: The Rise of Cosmopolitanism in Early Modern Europe* (Philadelphia: University of Pennsylvania Press, 2006), 1–12.

113. For a similar phenomenon, see Riches, *Protestant Cosmopolitanism*.

5. A Loyal Servant

1. Montecuccoli to Leopold I, Vienna, 15 December 1664, ÖStA KA, AFA, 1664-13-29.

2. See chapter 4.

3. Norbert Haag, "'Erbfeind der Christenheit': Türkenpredigten im 16. und 17. Jahrhundert," in *Repräsentationen der islamischen Welt im Europa der Frühen Neuzeit*, ed. Gabriele Haug-Moritz (Münster: Aschendorff, 2010), 127–49; Margaret Meserve, *Empires of Islam in Renaissance Historical Thought* (Cambridge, MA: Harvard University Press, 2008).

4. Montecuccoli collected information on the war in Crete. ÖStA KA, NL: Raimund Montecuccoli, B/492: 254b.

5. Paul Lendvai, *The Hungarians. A Thousand Years of Victory in Defeat*, trans. Ann Major (Princeton, NJ: Princeton University Press, 2003), 94–95; Pál Fodor, "Ottoman Policy towards Hungary, 1520–1541," *Acta Orientalia Academiae Scientiarum Hungaricae* 45, no. 2–3 (1991): 271–345.

6. Gábor Ágostan, "Habsburgs and Ottomans: Defense, Military Change and Shifts in Power," *Turkish Studies Association Bulletin* 22, no. 1 (Spring 1998): 131–32; Gunther Rothenberg, *The Austrian Military Border in Croatia, 1522–1747* (Urbana: University of Illinois Press, 1960); Winfried Schulze, *Landesdefension und Staatsbildung: Studien zum Kriegswesen des innerösterreichischen Territorialstaates (1564–1619)* (Vienna: Böhlau, 1973); Kurt Vessely, "The Development of the Hungarian Military Frontier until the Middle of the Eighteenth Century," *Austrian History Yearbook* 9–10 (1973–74): 55–110.

7. Ágostan, "Habsburgs and Ottomans," 133; Bérenger, *Finances et Absolutisme autrichien*, 2:338–39.

8. Jean Nouzille, *Histoire de frontières: L'Autriche et l'Empire ottomon* (Paris: Berg International Editeurs, 1991), 64.

9. Ágostan, "Habsburgs and Ottomans," 133–34.

10. At times, single individuals held both offices, although Hungarians were only permitted to serve as border-fortress captains-general in areas deemed less critical to the defense of the Austrian lands. See Géza Pálffy, "The Hungarian-Habsburg Border Defence Systems," in *Ottomans, Hungarians, and Habsburgs in Central Europe: The Military Confines in the Era of Ottoman Conquest*, ed. Géza Dávid and Pál Fodor (Leiden: Brill, 2000), 43–44, 59.

11. Nouzille, *Histoire*, 89; Bérenger, *Finances et Absolutisme autrichien*, 2:335–52.

12. Ogier Ghiselin de Busbecq, *The Turkish Letters of Ogier Ghiselin de Busbecq, Imperial Ambassador at Constantinople, 1554–1562: Translated from the Latin of the Elzevir Edition of 1663*, trans. Edward Seymour Forster (Baton Rouge: Louisiana State University Press, 2005), 238.

13. Busbecq, *Turkish Letters*, 240.

14. Pálffy, "Hungarian-Habsburg Border Defence Systems," 50–51; Beatrice Heuser, *Strategy before Clausewitz: Linking Warfare and Statecraft, 1400–1830* (Abingdon: Routledge, 2018).

15. Later practitioners included George Washington, "the American Fabius."

16. Gat, *Origins of Military Thought*, 22.

17. Montecuccoli, *Le opere*, 1:251. The whole section is 1:249–54.

18. Montecuccoli, *Le opere*, 2:15.

19. Jurgen Brauer and Hubert van Toyll, *Castles, Battles, and Bombs: How Economics Explains Military History* (Chicago: University of Chicago Press, 2008), 136–37; Parrott, *Business of War*, 77.

20. Mears, *Count Raimondo Montecuccoli*, 106; Robert I. Frost, *The Northern Wars: War, State and Society in Northeastern Europe, 1558–1721* (Harlow: Longman, 2000).

21. Machiavelli, *Art of War*, 3:78, 3:70.

22. See chapter 2.

23. George Gömöri, "Introduction," in Miklós Zrínyi, *The Siege of Sziget*, trans. László Kőrössy (Washington, DC: Catholic University of America Press, 2011); Nouzille, *Histoire*, 71.

24. Zrínyi, *Siege*, 3.

25. Zrínyi, *Siege*, 250–51. Quote on 251. For an overview of Zrínyi's poetry and the Italian influences on his writing, see Bene Sándor, "A költő Zrínyi Miklós / Miklós Zrínyi, the Poet," in *Zrínyi-Album / Zrínyi Album*, ed. Sándor Bene et al. (Budapest: Zrínyi Kiadó, 2016), 174–250.

26. Ágnes R. Várkonyi, "Gábor Bethlen and His European Presence," *Hungarian Historical Review* 2, no. 4 (2013): 695–732.

27. Leslie S. Domonkos, "The Battle of Mohács as a Cultural Watershed," in *From Hunyadi to Rákóczi War and Society in Late Medieval and Early Modern Hungary*, ed. János M. Bak and Béla K. Király (New York: Brooklyn College Press, 1982), 210.

28. Paula Sutter Fichtner, *The Habsburg Monarchy, 1490–1848* (Basingstoke: Palgrave Macmillan, 2003), 48.

29. Georg B. Michels, "'They Have Become Turks (Seindt Türkhen Worden)': Anti-Habsburg Resistance and Turkification in Seventeenth-Century Hungary," in *The Humanities in a World Upside Down*, ed. Ignacio López-Calvo (Newcastle-upon-Tyne: Cambridge Scholars, 2017), 12–35.

30. József Kelenik, "A keresztény világ bajnoka / The Champion of the Christian World," in Bene et al., *Zrínyi-Album / Zrínyi Album*, 117, 119–27. Zrínyi rescued Emperor Ferdinand III at Eger when the Swedish forces of Carl Gustaf Wrangel launched a surprise attack.

31. Evans, *Making*, 240, 247.

32. Zrínyi owned copies of the works of Lipsius, whose *Constantia* and *Politica* were published in Hungarian in 1641, and quoted Lipsius in his own writings. See Gerhard Oestreich, *Neostoicism and the Early Modern State*, ed. Gerhard Oestreich, Brigitta Oestreich and H. G Koenigsberger, trans. David McLintock (Cambridge: Cambridge University Press, 1982), 101–2. On the influence of Lipsius in Hungary, see Tibor Klaniczay, "Probleme der ungarischen Spätrenaissance (Stoizismus und Manierismus)," in *Renaissance und Humanismus in Mittel- und Osteuropa: Eine Sammlung von Materialien*, ed. J. Irmscher (Berlin: Akademie-Verl., 1962), 2:61–94.

33. Their separateness was affirmed by their continued use of the Hungarian language and dress while at court in Vienna. Evans, *Making*, 257–61.

34. Ágnes R. Várkonyi, "The Preservation of Statehood," in *History of Transylvania*, vol. 2, *From 1606 to 1830*, ed. Béla Köpeczi et al. (Boulder, CO: Social Science Monographs, 2002), 233–35.

35. Pugliese, *Le prime strette*, 150; Giampiero Brunelli, "Mattei, Ludovico, detto Luigi," in *DBI*.

36. Raffaella Gherardi, "An der Grenze zwischen der Habsburgermonarchie und dem Osmanischen Reich: Raimondo Montecuccoli und das italienische Militär in Wien," in *Die Schlacht von Mogersdorf / St. Gotthard und der Friede von Eisenburg / Vasvar*

1664: Rahmenbedingungen, Akteure, Auswirkungen und Rezeption eines europäischen Ereignisses, ed. Karin Sperl, Martin Scheutz, and Arno Strohmeyer (Eisenstadt: Amt der Burgenländischen Landesregierung, Hauptreferat Landesarchiv und Landesbibliothek, 2016), 171–93.

37. György Domokos, *Kő és tűz, Erődépítészet- és tüzérségtörténeti tanulmányok* [Stone and Fire: Studies about the History of Fortification and Artillery] (Budapest: Nemzeti Kulturális Alap, 2021), 585.

38. Kelenik, "A keresztény világ bajnoka," 149. Jan Amos Comenius wrote about his mystical significance. Nóra G. Etényi, "Zrínyi Miklós a Német-római Birodalom nyilvánosságában/Miklós Zrínyi through the Public Eye in the Holy Roman Empire," in Bene et al., *Zrínyi-Album/Zrínyi Album*, 293–95.

39. Etényi, "Zrínyi Miklós," 309–11.

40. Gömöri, "Introduction," xiii–xiv.

41. Montecuccoli, *Le opere*, 2:394. See also Géza Perjés, "The Zrínyi-Montecuccoli Controversy," in *From Hunyadi to Rákóczi: War and Society in Late Medieval and Early Modern Hungary: War and Society in Eastern and Central Europe*, ed. János M. Bak and Béla K. Kiraly (New York: Brooklyn College Press, 1982), 3:342–43; Rothenberg, *Austrian Military Border*, 81.

42. Montecuccoli, *Le opere*, 2:394.

43. Peter Broucek, "Logistische Fragen der Türkenkriege des 16. und 17. Jahrhunderts," *Vorträge zur Militärgeschichte* 7 (1986): 35–60.

44. Montecuccoli, *Le opere*, 2:395.

45. Montecuccoli, *Le opere*, 2:397–98.

46. Montecuccoli, *Le opere*, 2:399–400.

47. Details of this campaign can be found in Galeazzo Gualdo Priorato, *Historia di Leopoldo Cesare, continente le cose piu memorabili successe in Europa, dal 1656. sino al 1670* [. . .], vol. 2 (Vienna: Gio. Battista Hacque, 1670).

48. Thomas Barker, *Double Eagle and Crescent: Vienna's Second Turkish Siege and Its Historical Setting* (Albany: State University of New York Press, 1967), 24; Charles Ingrao, *The Habsburg Monarchy, 1618–1815* (Cambridge: Cambridge University Press, 1994), 65–66.

49. Montecuccoli, *Le opere*, 2:405.

50. Várkonyi, "Preservation," 247–48.

51. Markus Baumanns, *Das publizistische Werk des kaiserlichen Diplomaten Franz Paul Freiherr von Lisola (1613–1674): Ein Beitrag zum Verhältnis von absolutistischem Staat, Öffentlichkeit und Mächtepolitik in der frühen Neuzeit* (Berlin: Dunker & Humblot, 1994).

52. Raimondo Montecuccoli, *Risposta alle calunnie che qua e là si vanno disseminando che l'armi alemanne cesaree abbiano poco o nulla operato l'anno 1661*, in Montecuccoli, *Le opere*, 3:147–48.

53. Montecuccoli, *Le opere*, 3:150.

54. Montecuccoli, *Le opere*, 3:148.

55. The documents are: *Conjectural Judgment about the Intentions and Counsels of the Hungarians (Giudizio congetturale sopra le intenzioni e consigli degli ungheri), Most Humble Opinion Regarding the Preservation of Hungary and Transylvania (Umilissimo parere intorno alla conservazione dell'Ungheria, e della Transilvania)*, and *Combination of War against the Turk in Transylvania and Hungary (Combinazione della guerra contr'al Turco in Transilvania,*

ed Ungheria). Umilissimo parere was addressed to Leopold. These documents have been printed in Montecuccoli, *Le opere*, vol. 3.

56. Montecuccoli, *Le opere*, 3:126.

57. Montecuccoli, *Le opere*, 3:126–27.

58. Quoted in Várkonyi, "Preservation," 248.

59. Kelenik, "A keresztény világ bajnoka," 131; Perjés, "Zrínyi-Montecuccoli Controversy," 341–42.

60. Kelenik, "A keresztény világ bajnoka," 167–71; Bene, "A költő Zrínyi Miklós," 250–60, 265–71.

61. On the significance of the Hungarian-Ottoman wars as a key though overlooked site of the military revolution, see József Kelenik, "The Military Revolution in Hungary," in Dávid and Fodor, *Ottomans, Hungarians, and Habsburgs*, 117–59.

62. Bérenger, *Finances et Absolutisme autrichien*, 1:42; Montecuccoli, *Le opere*, 2:405–10.

63. The 5,535 men included 365 "Croats." Montecuccoli, *Le opere*, 2:410–11.

64. Montecuccoli, *Le opere*, 2:412–13. Montecuccoli remained negative about the prospects of Hungarian feudal levies. See 2:414.

65. Montecuccoli, *Le opere*, 2:411.

66. Rothenberg, *Austrian Military Border*, 81; Veltzé, *Ausgewaehlte Schriften*, 2:391–92.

67. Montecuccoli commissioned Colonel Joseph Priami. See György Domokos, "From Imprisoned Embezzler to Commander: The Appointment of Joseph Priami to Commander of Bratislava, 1663," *Vojenská História* [Journal of Military History, Slovakia] 21, no. 4 (2019): 7.

of Bratislava, 1663."

68. Nouzille, *Histoire*, 73; Caroline Finkel, *Osman's Dream: The Story of the Ottoman Empire 1300–1923* (New York: Basic Books, 2005), 266–67.

69. Klára Hegyi, "The Ottoman Network of Fortresses in Hungary," in Dávid and Fodor, *Ottomans, Hungarians, and Habsburgs*, 170.

70. Montecuccoli, *Le opere*, 2:422.

71. This manuscript was dated 1 March 1664.

72. On the size of Habsburg forces, see Montecuccoli, *Le opere*, 2:220–21.

73. The lands of the Styrian estates would be better defended if Zrínyí took Kanisza, lost during the Long Turkish War. Lobkowitz, however, had agreed with Montecuccoli's proposal. Kelenik, "A keresztény világ bajnoka," 134–44; 153–55.

74. Etényi, "Zrínyi Miklós," 315–21.

75. Figures presented are effective strength. The paper strength of total forces was 97,713. For a summary of all figures, see Peter H. Wilson, *German Armies: War and German Politics, 1648–1806* (London: UCL Press, 1998), 42.

76. Pugliese, *Le prime strette*, 152–55.

77. Kelenik, "A keresztény világ bajnoka," 134–44; 153–55.

78. *Relazione della campagna dell'Armata Cesarea nell'Anno MDCLXIV*, ÖStA KA, AFA, 1664/13/29, ff. 4rv; Montecuccoli, *Le opere*, 2:430.

79. Montecuccoli only retreated when it was clear his smaller forces could no longer sustain the Ottoman assault. Nonetheless, his strenuous defense of the fortress allowed the main body of allied Christian troops time to prepare the defense of Muraköz, Lower Austria, and the region around the Raab (Rába) River. See Kelenik, "A keresztény világ bajnoka," 159–65; Domokos, *Kő és tűz*, 598–605.

80. Montecuccoli to Leslie, Vienna, 2 June 1664, ÖStA KA, AFA, 1661–1664/10; Montecuccoli to Portia, Vienna, 25 May 1664, ÖStA KA, AFA, 1661–1664/9. Montecuccoli's "files" included stacks of careful observations that he made throughout the time he spent on the battlefield. Such files include, for instance, a series of "questions" (*quistioni*) that he posed on 10 July about the "main operation" (*operazione capitale*): ÖStA KA, AFA, 1661–1664/92.

81. Order from Leopold to Montecuccoli, appointing him supreme commander on 4 June 1664, from Linz. The Italian is: "Voi vedrete le congiunture, e secondo la Vostra esperienza, & il Vostro valore farete quelle, che stimarete utile al bene commune." Priorato, *Historia*, V. 2, 1670. Appendix.

82. Montecuccoli to Leopold, Vienna, 6 June 1664, in Priorato, *Historia*, 2:1670, Appendix.

83. Leopold to Montecuccoli, Linz, 9 June 1664, in Priorato, *Historia*, 2:1670, Appendix.

84. ÖStA KA, AFA, 1661–1664/91.

85. The report is *Relazione*, ÖStA KA, AFA, 1664/13/29.

86. Carafa to secretary of state, Vienna, 19 July 1664, Archivio Segreto Vaticano (ASV), Segr. Stato Germania, ff. 38rv.

87. Carlo Carafa to secretary of state, 5 July 1664, ASV, Segr. Stato Germania 177, f. 6r.

88. Fichtner, *Habsburg Monarchy*, 48.

89. Carafa to secretary of state, 12 July 1664, ASV, Segr. Stato Germania 177, f. 19v.

90. Fabio Martelli, "The Battle of Mogersdorf, Saint Gotthard in the Eyes of Montecuccoli: A Victory and the Consequences," in Sperl, Scheutz, and Strohmeyer, *Die Schlacht von Mogersdorf*, 195–99.

91. Montecuccoli, *Le opere*, 2:446.

92. Evliya Çelebi, *An Ottoman Traveller: Selections from the Book of Travels of Evliya Çelebi*, trans. Robert Dankoff and Sooyong Kim (London: Eland Publishing, 2010), 227.

93. In addition to Martelli's work, analysis of this battle can be found in: Ferenc Tóth and Jean Bérenger, *Saint-Gotthard 1664: Une bataille européenne* (Panazol: Lavauzelle, 2007); Leopold Toifl, "Die Schlacht von Mogersdorf, St. Gotthard am 1. August 1664," in Sperl, Scheutz, and Strohmeyer, *Die Schlacht von Mogersdorf*, 151–69. The classic work is Wilhelm Nottebohm, *Montecuccoli und die Legende von St. Gotthard (1664)* (Berlin: R. Gaertners Verlagsbuchhandlung, H. Heyfelder, 1887); there is also a detailed account in Georg Wagner, "Die Schlacht von St. Gotthard-Mogersdorf und das Oberkommando Raimund Montecuccolis," in *Atti del convegno di studi su Raimondo Montecuccoli nel terzo centenario della battaglia sulla Raab* (Modena: Accademia Nazionale di Scienze, Lettere, e Arti, 1964), 155–234.

94. Montecuccoli, *Le opere*, 2:446.

95. Montecuccoli to Emperor Leopold I, the imperial camp, 3 August 1664, ÖNB, Autogr., 17/22–8.

96. Martelli, "Battle of Mogersdorf," 199–200.

97. Italian rulers chimed in with praise for Montecuccoli, including Grand Duke Ferdinando II de Medici. Ferdinand II Medici to Raimondo Montecuccoli, Florence, 30 August 1664, ÖNB, Autogr., 17/13-2.

98. Lendvai, *Hungarians*, 131–32.

99. Montecuccoli, *Le opere*, 2:450. On Montecuccoli asking to be made prince of the empire in 1665, see Veltzé, *Ausgewaehlte Schriften*, 4:316, 4:319, 4:339–40.

100. Montecuccoli to Leopold, Vienna, 15 December 1664, ÖStA KA, AFA, 1664/XIII.

101. Etényi, "Zrínyi Miklós," 325.

102. Montecuccoli to Priorato, Guarino, 18 March 1666, ÖStA KA, NL: Montecuccoli, B/492: 166–92.

103. Montecuccoli to Priorato, Vicenza, 23 October 1665, ÖStA KA, NL: Montecuccoli, B/492: 166–92.

104. He declared that "to write the history of the Roman Emperor, it seems appropriate to me to write about it to an Italian," adding, "Italians are more curious than other nations about History." Montecuccoli to Priorato, Guarino, 18 March 1666, ÖStA KA, NL: Montecuccoli, B/492: 166–192.

105. Etényi, "Zrínyi Miklós," 337. See Priorato, *Historia*.

106. *Notizen über Audienzen am 13.12.1664 und am 15.12.1664*, Vienna, 13 December 1664, ÖStA KA, NL: Montecuccoli, B/492: 186.

107. Tanner, *Last Descendant*, 146–61.

108. *Notizen über Audienzen am 13.12.1664 und am 15.12.1664*, Vienna, 13 December 1664, ÖStA KA, NL: Montecuccoli, B/492: 186.

109. An den Fürsten Lobkowitz (Mündlich.), Vienna, 13 December 1664, in Veltzé, *Ausgewaehlte Schriften*, 4:312.

110. Montecuccoli an den Fürsten Lobkowitz, Raab, 28 November 1665, in Veltzé, *Ausgewaehlte Schriften*, 4:322; Graf Dietrichstein an Montecuccoli, Vienna, 17 December 1665, in Veltzé, *Ausgewaehlte Schriften*, 4:323–24.

111. For his reports, see A. F. Pribram, ed., "Die Berichte des kaiserlichen Gesandten Franz von Lisola aus den Jahren 1655–1660," *Archiv für oesterreichische Geschichte* 70 (1887).

112. Mears, *Count Raimondo Montecuccoli*, 104; Schwarz, *Imperial Privy Council*, 160.

113. Baron Lisola an Montecuccoli, Madrid, 18 October 1665, in Veltzé, *Ausgewaehlte Schriften*, 4:320.

114. Graf Dietrichstein an Montecuccoli, Vienna, 17 December 1665, in Veltzé, *Ausgewaehlte Schriften*, 4:323–24.

115. Montecuccoli an Count Pötting, Vienna, 4 July 1668, in Veltzé, *Ausgewaehlte Schriften*, 4:329–30.

116. "Antwort des Kaisers," in Veltzé, *Ausgewaehlte Schriften*, 4:313.

117. Kaiser Leopold an den Grafen Pötting, Vienna, 15 January 1665, in Veltzé, *Ausgewaehlte Schriften*, 4:314.

118. Kaiser Leopold an die Königin von Spanien, Vienna, 14 January 1666, in Veltzé, *Ausgewaehlte Schriften*, 4:327.

119. Lipsius discussed the importance of defending the common good. Oestreich, *Neostoicism*, 41.

120. Lipsius emphasized religious unity among a ruler's subjects as key to stability. See Bireley, *Counter-Reformation Prince*, 88–91.

121. Nexon, *Struggle*.

122. He noted, "France is a house with few friends, for the most part only enemies, which envies the House of Austria . . . the French spirit is notably unstable, their faith

slippery, and their king is proud and magnanimous, ever fortunate in undertakings in which he has not encountered any obstacle." Montecuccoli, *Le opere*, 3:211.

123. Michael Behmen, "Der gerechte und der notwendige Krieg: 'Necessitas' und 'utilitas reipublicae' in der Kriegstheorie des 16. und 17. Jahrhunderts," in *Staatsverfassung und Heeresverfassung in der europäischen Geschichte der frühen Neuzeit*, ed. Barbara Stollberg-Rilinger and Johannes Kunisch (Berlin: Duncker und Humbolt, 1986), 42–106.

124. For Zrínyi, the Hungarian nation was composed of propertied noblemen and excluded the vast majority of Hungarians. It has been easier for modern audiences to sympathize with Zrínyi's commitment to national liberty, especially when those audiences confuse Zrínyi's nationalism with the modern version.

6. Victory at Last

1. Rothenberg, "Maurice of Nassau," 32–63; and Gat, *Origins of Military Thought*, 13–24.

2. Eugen Heischmann, *Die Anfänge des stehenden Heeres in Österreich* (Vienna: Österr. Bundesverl., 1925), 222–23; Major Alphons Freiherrn von Wrede, *Geschichte der k. und k. Wehrmacht* (Vienna: Siedel, 1898), 1:30; Hermann Meynert, *Geschichte der k. k. österreichischen Armee, ihrer Heranbildung und Organisation, so wie ihrer Schicksale, Thaten und Feldzüge, von der Frühesten bis auf die jetzige Zeit* (Vienna: C. Gerold und Sohn, 1854), 3:77.

3. Wrede, *Geschichte*, 1:13. On the scholarly debate about this start date, see Rothenberg, "Maurice of Nassau," 1; Walter Hummelberger, "Der Dreissigjährige Krieg und die Entstehung des Kaiserlichen Heeres," in *Unser Heer: 300 Jahre Österreichisches Soldatentum in Krieg und Frieden* (Vienna: Fürlinger, 1963), 3. On the general development, see Gerhard Papke, "Von der Miliz zum Stehenden Heer: Wehrwesen im Absolutismus," in *Handbuch der Deutschen Militärgeschichte 1648–1939* (Munich: Bernard & Graefe, 1979): 1:1–311. Several regiments first organized during the Thirty Years' War—including regiments owned by both Wallenstein and Piccolomini—were in continuous operation until 1918. See Wrede, *Geschichte*, vol. 3. Phillip Hoyos, "Die kaiserliche Armee 1648–1650," in *Der Dreißigjährige Krieg: Schriften des Heeresgeschichtlichen Museums in Wien*, ed. Hugo Schneider (Vienna: Österreichischer Bundesverlag für Unterricht, 1976), 169–232.

4. John Mears, "Count Raimondo Montecuccoli: Servant of a Dynasty," *Historian* 32, no. 3 (May 1970): 399; Bérenger, *Finances et absolutisme autrichien*, 2:370–80.

5. On the differences between Machiavelli and Lipsius, see Oestreich, *Neostoicism and the Early Modern State*, 72–73. Although his analysis of Lipsius remains useful, Oestreich's work must be treated with caution due to its associations with National Socialism. See Peter N. Miller, "Nazis and Neostoics: Otto Brunner and Gerhard Oestreich before and after the Second World War," *Past and Present* 176 (August 2002): 144–86.

6. Wilson, *German Armies*, 22–23, 26–34.

7. Hans Meier-Welcker, *Deutsches Heereswesen in Wandel der Zeit ein Überblick über d. Entwicklung vom Aufkommen d. stehenden Heere bis zur Wehrfrage d. Gegenwart* (Frankfurt: Bernhard & Graefe, Verl. f. Wehrwesen, 1956), 9; Hans Meier-Welcker, *Handbuch zur deutschen Militärgeschichte, 1648–1939*, vol. 1, *Von der Miliz zum stehenden Heer* (Munchen: Bernhard & Graefe, 1979).

8. David Parrott, "From Military Enterprise to Standing Armies: War, State, and Society in Western Europe, 1600–1700," in *European Warfare, 1350–1750*, ed. Frank Tallett and D. J. B Trim (Cambridge: Cambridge University Press, 2010), 74–95; Guy Rowlands, *The Dynastic State and the Army under Louis XIV: Royal Service and Private Interest, 1661–1701* (Cambridge: Cambridge University Press, 2002). See also David Parrott, *Richelieu's Army: War, Government, and Society in France, 1624–1642* (Cambridge, New York: Cambridge University Press, 2006); Sara E. Chapman, *Private Ambition and Political Alliances: The Phélypeaux de Pontchartrain Family and Louis XIV's Government, 1650–1715* (Rochester, NY: University of Rochester Press, 2004).

9. William Godsey, *The Sinews of Habsburg Power: Lower Austria as A Fiscal-Military State, 1650–1820* (Oxford: Oxford University Press, 2018), 152.

10. Besides Montecuccoli, the group included Johann Ferdinand Portia, Johann Weikhard Auersperg, Annibale Gonzaga, Ernst Oettingen, Johann Adolf Schwarzenberg, Johann Franz Trautson, and Lobkowitz. See Schwarz, *Imperial Privy Council*, 152.

11. This title permitted a noble to hold landed property *in allodium* (rather than as a fief) and to pass on a family coat of arms. HHStA, Reichsregister, Leopold I, Bd. 16, 1663–1674, ff. 1–2, 1–634.

12. Campori, *Raimondo Montecuccoli*, 513.

13. In July 1644, Montecuccoli thanked Lobkowitz for his "favors," promising to "embrace" service to Lobkowitz "with great ambition." Raimondo Montecuccoli to Wenzel Eusebius Lobkowitz, Wittenberg, 12 July 1644, SOAL, c. 157, f. 1r. See chapters 3 and 4.

14. On the French policy, see chapter 4.

15. For an example, see Raimondo Montecuccoli to Wenzel Eusebius Lobkowitz, undated (probably 1658), SOAL, Žitenice, c. 157, f. 115r.

16. Montecuccoli to Dietrichstein, Vienna, 17 October 1666, MZA, RAD, 88, f. 132. For other instances, see Montecuccoli to Dietrichstein, Vienna, 22 November 1666, MZA, RAD, 88, f. 116; Montecuccoli to Dietrichstein, Giavrino, 9 April 1668, MZA, RAD, 88, f. 161.

17. Lamberg succeeded Lobkowitz as Obersthofmeister in 1675. See Schwarz, *Imperial Privy Council*, 274–76, 150, 167. On the complex networks surrounding the Gonzaga empresses and Cardinal Harrach, see Schnettger, "Kaiserinnen und Kardinäle," 127–60.

18. Evans, *Making*, 294. Hocher conducted the trials of the Hungarian magnates in 1671. See Schwarz, *Imperial Privy Council*, 247–49; Bérenger, *Finances et Absolutisme autrichien*, 1:62–65.

19. Dietrichstein would occupy Lobkowitz's old position as Leopold's chief minister in 1683.

20. Julius Grossman, "Die Geschäftsordnung in Sachen der äusseren Politik am Wiener Hofe zu Kaiser Leopolds und Lobkowitz Zeiten," *Forschungen zur deutschen Geschichte* 12 (1871–72): 457–74.

21. Mears, *Count Raimondo Montecuccoli*, 126–27, 129–30.

22. Montecuccoli, *Le opere*, 3:213.

23. Bireley, *Counter-Reformation Prince*, 93.

24. Montecuccoli, *Le opere*, 3:231.

25. On the difficulties in implementing reform on the Hungarian frontier, see Istvan Czignany, *Reform vagy kudarc? Kísérletek a magyarországi katonaság beillesztésére a Habsburg Birodalom haderejébe 1600–1700* (Budapest: Balassi Kiadó, 2004).

26. Montecuccoli, *Le opere*, 3:217.

27. Veltzé, *Ausgewaehlte Schriften*, 3:396, 3:401.

28. Mears, *Count Raimondo Montecuccoli*, 144–47.

29. Godsey, *Sinews*, 151.

30. *Instruzione al Capitano Leopoldo*, Nuremberg, 5 March 1673, ÖStA KA, NL: Montecuccoli, B/492: 245. See also Ferdinand Dietrichstein to Raimondo Montecuccoli, Vienna, 17 March 1673, ÖStA KA, NL: Montecuccoli, B/492: 245.

31. Bérenger, *Turenne*, 399–400; Rothenberg, "Maurice of Nassau," 58.

32. On both campaigns, see Bérenger, *Turenne*, 392–400, 411–13; Barker, *Military Intellectual*, 46.

33. Montecuccoli, *Le opere*, 3:225. See also Montecuccoli, *Notes Concerning the Aulic Chamber (Notizie sopra la camera aulica)*, in *Le opere*, 3:229–30.

34. Montecuccoli, *Le opere*, 2:553–79, 2:583–617.

35. Schwarz, *Imperial Privy Council*, 186–87. On the succession of new "confidants" after 1674 see Evans, *Making*, 144–45.

36. On Lobkowitz, see Bérenger, *Finances et Absolutisme autrichien*, 1:57–61.

37. Montecuccoli, *Le opere*, 3:210.

38. Francesca Trivellato, "Renaissance Italy and the Muslim Mediterranean in Recent Historical Work," *Journal of Modern History* 82 (March 2010): 127–55. For recent volumes examining cultural transfers, see Marlene Kurz et al., eds., *Das Osmanische Reich und die Habsburgermonarchie: Akten des internationalen Kongresses zum 150-jährigen Bestehen des Instituts für Österreichische Geschichtsforschung, Wien, 22.–25. September 2004* (Vienna: R. Oldenbourg, 2005); Almut Höfert and Armando Salvatore, *Between Europe and Islam: Shaping Modernity in a Transcultural Space* (Brussels: P. I. E. Peter Lang, 2005).

39. See Montecuccoli's wisdom on this topic in chapter 5.

40. Antje Niederberger, "Das Bild der Türken im deutschen Humanismus am Beispiel der Werke Sebastian Brants (1456–1521)," in Kurz et al., *Das Osmanische Reich*, 181–204.

41. Meserve, *Empires of Islam*, 81.

42. Meserve, *Empires of Islam*, 3–5.

43. Franz Bosbach, "*Imperium Turcorum* oder *Christianorum Monarchia*—Die Osmanen in der heilsgeschichtlichen Deutung Mercurino Gattinaras," in Kurz et al., *Das Osmanische Reich*, 167–80. See also Franz Fuchs, ed., *Osmanische Expansion und europäischer Humanismus* (Wiesbaden: Harrassowitz, 2005); Bodo Guthmüller and Wilhelm Kühlmann, *Europa und die Türken in der Renaissance* (Berlin: De Gruyter, 2000).

44. One of the first histories to provide a relatively neutral, accurate assessment of the Ottoman military was Marcantonio Sabellico's universal history, *Enneads* (1504). Other "relatively detached" histories followed from Johannes Adelphus (1513), GianMaria Angiolello (after 1514), Giovanni Battista Cipelli (known as Egnatius, 1516), and Andrea Cambini (1528). See Meserve, *Empires of Islam*, 240–41.

45. Meserve, *Empires of Islam*, 242–44.

46. John M. Najemy, "Machiavelli between East and West," in *From Florence to the Mediterranean and Beyond: Essays in Honour of Anthony Molho*, ed. Diogo Ramada Curto et al. (Florence: Olschki, 2009), 133–34.

47. Najemy, "Machiavelli," 140–41.

48. Bireley, *Counter-Reformation Prince*, 72–100.

49. On the integration of the Ottomans into the European diplomatic system, see Arno Strohmeyer, "Das Osmanische Reich—ein Teil des europäischen Staatensystems der Frühen Neuzeit?," in Kurz et al., *Das Osmanische Reich*, 149–65.

50. Ralf C. Müller, "Der umworbene 'Erbfeind': Habsburgische Diplomatie an der Hohen Pforte vom Regierungsantritt Maximilians I. bis zum 'Langen Türkenkrieg'—ein Entwurf," in Kurz et al., *Das Osmanische Reich*, 251–80. By contrast, sermons continued to play to stereotypes. See Haag, "'Erbfeind,'" 127–49.

51. Wilson, *German Armies*, 1.

52. See chapter 5.

53. He cites his sources in the appendix to *On the War against the Turk in Hungary*. See Montecuccoli, *Le opere*, 2:536–50.

54. Rhoads Murphey, *Ottoman Warfare* (London: UCL Press, 1999), 35–36.

55. As time passed, fiscal limitations forced the sultan to rely increasingly upon temporary contract soldiers or "overnight soldiers" similar to European rulers. Murphey, *Ottoman Warfare*, 46. Approximately fifty thousand of the seventy-five thousand were Timariots, and twenty thousand were members of the Sultan's standing forces. Murphey, *Ottoman Warfare*, 49.

56. Pál Fodor, "Volunteers in the Ottoman Army," in *Ottomans, Hungarians, and Habsburgs in Central Europe: The Military Confines in the Era of Ottoman Conquest* (Leiden: Brill, 2000), 229–63. Fodor estimates at least 20 percent of Ottoman armies were composed of volunteers in the sixteenth century.

57. Stephen Turnbull, *The Ottoman Empire, 1526–1699* (New York: Routledge, 2003), 19–21. Busbecq spent three months observing an Ottoman military camp. He commented extensively on the Ottoman army. See also Busbecq, *Turkish Letters*, 110–14, 149–59.

58. Murphey, *Ottoman Warfare*, 49.

59. Murphey, *Ottoman Warfare*, 56.

60. For instance, they established a system of grain-storage depots throughout their territory. Murphey, *Ottoman Warfare*, 70. Busbecq attributed their provisioning abilities to their experiences fighting Persia in semiarid steppe terrain. Busbecq, *Turkish Letters*, 110.

61. Murphey, *Ottoman Warfare*.

62. Gábor Ágostan, "The Costs of the Ottoman Fortress-System in Hungary," in Dávid and Fodorm, *Ottomans, Hungarians, and Habsburgs*, 195–228; Caroline Finkel, "The Cost of Ottoman Warfare and Defence," *Byzantinische Forschungen* 16 (1990): 91–103.

63. To Knolles, the Ottomans were barbaric because of other practices, such as fratricide in the royal family. Richard Knolles, *The Generall Historie of the Turkes: From the First Beginning of That Nation to the Rising of the Othoman Familie* [. . .] (London: A. Islip, 1603), 3.

64. Meserve, *Empires of Islam*, 75.

65. Machiavelli thought easterners, "orientali," possessed obedience. Najemy, "Machiavelli," 135.

66. Knolles, *Generall Historie*, 3. See also Lucette Valensi, *The Birth of the Despot: Venice and the Sublime Porte* (Ithaca, NY: Cornell University Press, 2009).

67. Martelli, "Battle of Mogersdorf," 203.

68. Montecuccoli, *Le opere*, 2:388.

69. Paul Rycaut, dedicatory epistle, in *The History of the Present State of the Ottoman Empire* (London: John Starkey and Henry Brome, 1670).

70. Montecuccoli, *Le opere*, 2:492.

71. For both Caesar and Machiavelli, the barbarians were the western tribes that opposed Roman expansion.

72. See chapter 1.

73. Montecuccoli, *Le opere*, 2:463. The contrast between "fury" and "valor" is telling. "Fury" suggested passion and savagery.

74. Montecuccoli, *Le opere*, 2:467–68.

75. Montecuccoli, *Le opere*, 2:465.

76. Montecuccoli, *Le opere*, 2:489.

77. Montecuccoli, *Le opere*, 2:466.

78. Montecuccoli, *Le opere*, 2:489–90. The historic size of the Ottoman army is difficult to determine. See Fodor, "Volunteers in the Ottoman Army," 230–34. According to Rhoades Murphey, the Ottomans were never capable of deploying more than seventy-five thousand men at any given moment, although this number does not include auxiliary contingents. Murphey, *Ottoman Warfare*, 46, 49. Even at its lowest estimates, the Ottoman army was far larger than any army of its Christian rivals.

79. Montecuccoli, *Le opere*, 2:466.

80. Montecuccoli, *Le opere*, 2:486.

81. See chapter 4.

82. Montecuccoli, *Le opere*, 2:468–69.

83. Montecuccoli, *Le opere*, 2:471.

84. John Elliott, *The Revolt of the Catalans: A Study in the Decline of Spain, 1598–1640* (Cambridge: Cambridge University Press, 1963). The idea that Spain declined during the seventeenth century is contested. See, for instance, Christopher Storrs, *The Resilience of the Spanish Monarchy, 1665–1700* (Oxford: Oxford University Press, 2006).

85. Montecuccoli, *Le opere*, 2:470.

86. Martelli, "Battle of Mogersdorf," 204.

87. Wilson, *German Armies*, 10–11.

88. On the way these needs initiated a shift toward absolutism, see Oestreich, *Neostoicism*, 234.

89. Montecuccoli, *Le opere*, 2:470.

90. Justus Lipsius, *Six Bookes of Politickes or Civil Doctrine*, trans. William Jones (London: Richard Field, 1594), book. 5, p. 13. Cited in Gunther E. Rothenberg, "Maurice of Nassau, Gustavus Adolphus, Raimondo Montecuccoli, and the 'Military Revolution' of the Seventeenth Century," in *Makers of Modern Strategy from Machiavelli to the Nuclear Age*, ed. Peter Paret, Gordon A. Craig, and Felix Gilbert (Princeton, NJ: Princeton University Press), 41.

91. Montecuccoli, *Le opere*, 2:470–71.

92. Montecuccoli, *Le opere*, 2:469.

93. Montecuccoli, *Le opere*, 2:474.

94. Montecuccoli, *Le opere*, 2:487.

95. Montecuccoli, *Le opere*, 2:471, 2:409.

96. Montecuccoli, *Le opere*, 2:471.

97. Montecuccoli, *Le opere*, 2:473.

98. Wilson, *German Armies*, 40.

99. Montecuccoli, *Le opere*, 2:481.

100. Finkel, *Osman's Dream*, 153–54.

101. A contemporary of Montecuccoli's, the traveler and diplomat Paul Rycaut also argued that the Ottoman Empire was an empire of slaves. In his *Present State of the Ottoman Empire*, Rycaut alleged that the Ottoman Empire was a tyranny since it lacked a powerful, propertied nobility, providing European states with an example of poor government. See Linda T. Darling, "Ottoman Politics through British Eyes: Paul Rycaut's 'Present State of the Ottoman Empire,'" *Journal of World History* 5, no. 1 (Spring 1994): 71–97. Montesquieu would develop these ideas further in his theory of oriental despotism.

102. Busbecq, *Turkish Letters*, 101. After discoursing on slavery's benefits, Busbecq concluded the passage by writing off these statements as "not meant very seriously." Busbecq, *Turkish Letters*, 102.

103. Montecuccoli, *Le opere*, 2:481.

104. Bireley, *Counter-Reformation Prince*, 94.

105. Oestreich, *Neostoicism*, 6, 55, 268. See also Martelli, "Battle of Mogersdorf," 203.

106. Imperiale Cinuzzi, *La vera militar disciplina*, 2:37.

107. Montecuccoli, *Le opere*, 2:480–81.

108. Montecuccoli, *Le opere*, 2:494.

109. Montecuccoli, *Le opere*, 2:521.

110. Montecuccoli, *Le opere*, 2:522.

111. Montecuccoli, *Le opere*, 2:482. See chapter 5.

112. Montecuccoli, *Le opere*, 2:253.

113. Montecuccoli, *Le opere*, 2:485. On generals see 2:482.

114. Oestreich, *Neostoicism*, 81.

115. Montecuccoli, *Le opere*, 2:531–33.

116. Montecuccoli, *Le opere*, 2:496–97, 2:534.

117. Montecuccoli, *Le opere*, 2:512.

118. Montecuccoli, *Le opere*, 2:514–15.

119. Montecuccoli, *Le opere*, 2:512.

120. Montecuccoli, *Le opere*, 2:510–11.

121. Montecuccoli, *Le opere*, 2:508.

122. Murphey, *Ottoman Warfare*, 9–11.

123. On the evolutionary nature of military change, see Clifford J. Rogers, "The Military Revolutions of the Hundred Years War," in *The Military Revolution Debate: Readings on the Military Transformation of Early Modern Europe*, ed. Clifford J. Rogers (Boulder, CO: Westview Press, 1995), 76–77.

124. Michael Hochedlinger, *Austria's Wars of Emergence: War, State and Society in the Habsburg Monarchy, 1683–1797* (London: Longman, 2003), 102–4, 111; quote on 103. Bérenger, *Finances et Absolutisme autrichien*, 2:332–92.

125. The classic interpretation is Thomas Fellner and Heinrich Kretschmayr, *Die österreichische Zentralverwaltung. I. Abt. Von Maximilian I. bis zur Vereinigung der öster-*

reichischen und böhmischen Hofkanzlei (1749), vol. 1, *Geschichtliche Übersicht* (Vienna: Veröffentlichungen der Kommission für neuere Geschichte Österreichs, 1907), 234–41.

126. Pálffy, "Hungarian-Habsburg Border Defence Systems," 62–63. Lazarus von Schwendi advocated local centralization in 1567. Pálffy, "Hungarian-Habsburg Border Defence Systems," 47.

127. Montecuccoli, *Opere,* 2:396.

Epilogue: The Generation of 1683

1. Campori, *Raimondo Montecuccoli,* 513–21.

2. Leopold to Montecuccoli, Prague, 21 February 1680, in Sandonnini, *Il Generale,* 2:57.

3. *Dimostrazione di non aver punto avvantaggiato le facoltà patrimoliali e d'aver servito senza interesse,* Prague, 23 February 1680, in Sandonnini, *Il generale,* part 2, 53–54.

4. *Dimostrazione,* in Sandonnini, *Il generale,* 2:54.

5. *Dimostrazione,* in Sandonnini, *Il generale,* 2:54–55.

6. Some in Vienna contended that Ernesto had received two hundred thousand florins from Wallenstein—nearly, but not entirely, enough to fund his regiments. Campori, *Raimondo Montecuccoli,* 80–81.

7. *Dimostrazione,* in Sandonnini, *Il generale,*2:55.

8. Finanz- und Hofkammerarchiv (FHKA), Hofkammerprotokollen (HKP), 1 July 1676, Bd. 923, f. 301.

9. *Copia del testamento, tranquillita e riposo dell'anima del Signor Conte di Montecuccoli,* 30 October 1680, in Sandonnini, *Il generale,*2:64–69. Bérenger stated that Montecuccoli's total wealth reached three million florins, but I have not been able to determine this figure based on the 1680 will. Without taking the value of properties into consideration, Montecuccoli's will discussed the distribution of fifty thousand florins. Hohenegg, his main property, was valued at two hundred thousand florins in 1644. See chapter 3.

10. *Dimostrazione,* in Sandonnini, *Il generale,* 2:55.

11. Parrott, "Military Enterpriser," 63–86.

12. There is no record of the formal bestowal of this title, but Montecuccoli's son, Leopold Philip, was made a prince of the empire after Raimondo's death. *Copia di viglietto dell'imperatore al Montecuccoli con cui gli promette la dignità di Principe dell'Impero,* in Sandonnini, *Il generale,* 2:56.

13. On the Akademie der Naturforscher, see Schwarz, *Imperial Privy Council,* 310–11.

14. Veltzé, *Ausgewaehlte Schriften,* 4:358.

15. Geoffrey Symcox, *Victor Amadeus II: Absolutism in the Savoyard State, 1675–1730* (Berkeley: University of California Press, 1983).

16. Agostino Paradisi, *Elogio del Principe Raimondo Montecuccoli* (Parma: Bodoni, 1796), 3–4, 11–12; letter to Frederick at end of text.

17. Peball, "Raimund Fürst Montecuccoli," 303. There is no English-language publication of *On the War against the Turk.* A bibliography of publications can be found in Veltzé, *Ausgewaehlte Schriften,* 1:xli–xc.

18. The phrase "generation of 1683" comes from Lund, *War for the Every Day,* 21–63. Lund is referring to the generation of generals who served the emperor from 1686 to 1723.

19. See Giambattista Vico's portrait of Carafa: Giambattista Vico, *De rebus gestis Antonj Caraphaei* (Naples: Excudebat Felix Musca, 1716). Prešov is located in modern-day Slovakia. On Carafa's life, see "Carafa, Antonio," in *DBI*, 19:485–94; Filamondo, *Il genio bellicoso*, 54–73; Hanlon, *Twilight*, 212–15.

20. Jean Bérenger, *A History of the Habsburg Empire* (New York: Longman, 1994), 333.

21. Vico, *De rebus gestis*.

22. Derek McKay, *Prince Eugene of Savoy* (London: Thames and Hudson, 1977), 11–12.

23. Hochedlinger, *Austria's Wars*, 95, 113, 120, 140–41, 164–65, 178, 182–83, 185–86, 195. The most comprehensive, detailed biography of Eugene is Max Braubach, *Prinz Eugen von Savoyen: eine Biographie*, 5 vols. (Munich: R. Oldenbourg, 1963).

24. McKay, *Prince Eugene*, 230; on his battle strategy, see 84.

25. He wrote these lines to the Jesuit Father Bischoff in spring 1702. Quoted in McKay, *Prince Eugene*, 63.

26. Braubach, *Prinz Eugen*, 2:97–98.

27. McKay, *Prince Eugene*, 71.

28. McKay, *Prince Eugene*, 28, 35, 42, 87; other revealing statements by contemporaries can be found at 156–57.

29. John Stoye, *Marsigli's Europe, 1680–1730: The Life and Times of Luigi Ferdinando Marsigli, Soldier and Virtuoso* (New Haven, CT: Yale University Press, 1994), 28.

30. For documents he produced related to these themes, see Biblioteca Universitaria di Bologna, Fondo Marsili, ms. 28, 57, and 70.

31. Luigi Ferdinando Marsili, *Autobiografia de Luigi Ferdinando Marsili: Messa in luce nel II centenario dalla morte di lui dal Comitato marsiliano*, ed. Emilio Lovarini (Bologna: N. Zanichelli, 1930). Raffaella Gherardi has produced numerous studies of Marsigli. See Raffaella Gherardi, *La politica, la scienza, le armi: Luigi Ferdinando Marsili e la costruzione della frontiera dell'impero e dell'europa* (Bologna: CLEUB, 2010); Raffaella Gherardi, *Potere e costituzione a Vienna fra sei e settecento: Il "buon ordine" di Luigi Ferdinando Marsili* (Bologna: Il Mulino, 1980); Gherardi and Martelli, *La pace degli eserciti e dell'economia*. Two volumes of Marsigli's observations on the Croatian and Transylvanian border have been published: Luigi Ferdinando Marsili, *Relazioni dei confini della Croazia e della Transilvania a Sua Maesta Cesarea*, ed. Raffaella Gherardi, 2 vols. (Modena: Mucchi Editore, 1986). John Stoye's excellent biography remains critical. See Stoye, *Marsigli's Europe*.

32. Marsili, *Autobiografia*, 161.

33. Marsili, *Autobiografia*, 36, 38.

34. Stoye, *Marsigli's Europe*, 195–97, 199–200.

35. Luigi Ferdinando Marsili, *Stato militare dell'imperio ottomanno: L'état militaire de l'empire ottoman* (Graz: Akadem. Druck- u. Verlagsanst., 1972). Marsigli's activities are an example of what Eric Ash has termed "action at a distance," in which experts provided vital information that helped a court or commercial center expand control over its peripheries. See Eric Ash, "Introduction: Expertise and the Early Modern State," in *Expertise: Practical Knowledge and the Early Modern State*, ed. Eric Ash, Osiris, vol. 25 (Chicago: University of Chicago Press, 2010), 16–18.

36. Stoye, *Marsigli's Europe*, 56.

37. Stoye, *Marsigli's Europe*, 132–33; for another incident in which he was suspended, see 143–44.

38. Stoye, *Marsigli's Europe*, 216–52.

39. Stoye, *Marsigli's Europe*, 12, 111.

40. Redlich, *German Military Enterpriser*, 2:6–7.

41. Redlich, *German Military Enterpriser*, 2:19–21, 2:57–58, 2:46–47. Redlich discusses eighteenth-century parallels to seventeenth-century contracting practices and values throughout vol. 2.

42. Christopher Duffy, *The Army of Maria Theresa: The Armed Forces of Imperial Austria, 1740–1780* (New York: Hippocrene Books, 1977), 24.

43. Redlich, *German Military Enterpriser*, 2:94–95.

44. Redlich, *German Military Enterpriser*, 2:21–22. On later versions of these careers, see essays in Jeff Fynn-Paul, ed., *War, Entrepreneurs, and the State in Europe and the Mediterranean, 1300–1800* (Leiden: Brill, 2014).

45. Duffy, *Army of Maria Theresa*, 123–24.

46. Deák, *Beyond Nationalism*, 17.

47. Deák, *Beyond Nationalism*, esp. 3–24.

48. Duffy, *Army of Maria Theresa*; Deák, *Beyond Nationalism*; Hochedlinger, *Austria's Wars*.

Sources

Archives

Austria

Finanz- und Hofkammerarchiv, Vienna, Austria
  Hofkammerprotokollen
Haus-, Hof- und Staatsarchiv, Vienna, Austria
  Familienkorrespondenz
  Obersthofmeisteramt—Sonderreihe
  Reichsregister Leopold I
  Rom Hofkorrespondenz
Österreichische Nationalbibliothek, Vienna, Austria
  Autographen-Sammlung
  Handschriften-Sammlung
Österreichisches Staatsarchiv/Kriegsarchiv, Vienna, Austria
  Alte Feldakten
  Nachlaß Raimund Montecuccoli

Czech Republic

Moravský zemský archiv v Brně, Brno, Czech Republic
  Rodinný archiv Collaltů
  Rodinný archiv Ditrichstejnů
Národní archiv v Praze, Prague, Czech Republic
  Sbírka opisů cizí archivy, Vatikán Řím Itálie
Státní oblastní archiv v Litoměřicích, Litoměřice-Žitenice, Czech Republic
  Rodinný archiv Lobkovic
Státní oblastní archiv v Zámrsku, Zámrsk, Czech Republic
  Rodinný archiv Piccolomini

Italy

Archivio di Stato di Firenze, Florence, Italy
  Mediceo del Principato
Archivio di Stato di Mantova, Mantua, Italy
  Archivio Gonzaga
Archivio di Stato di Modena, Modena, Italy
  Ambasciatori della Germania

Archivio per materie, Capitani
Archivio per materie, Letterati
Archivio di Stato di Siena, Italy
  Manoscritti
Archivio Segreto Vaticano, Vatican City, Rome, Italy
  Miscellanea Armadio II
  Segr. Stato Germania
  Segr. Stato Principi
  Segr. Stato Soldati
Biblioteca Apostolica Vaticana, Vatican City, Rome, Italy
  Barberini Latino
Biblioteca Estense, Modena, Italy
  Autografoteca Campori
Biblioteca Nazionale, Rome, Italy
  MSS. Gesuitici
Biblioteca Universitaria di Bologna, Bologna, Italy
  Fondo Marsili

Printed Primary Sources

Abelinus, Johann Philipp, and Matthaeus Merian. "The Battle of White Mountain
    (November 8, 1620)." Excerpt from *Theatrum Europaeum* in *The Thirty Years'
    War, A Documentary History*, edited and translated by Tryntje Helfferich,
    49–55. Indianapolis, IN: Hackett Publishing Company, 2009.
Basta, Giorgio. *Il governo della cavalleria leggiera*. Venice: Bernardo Gionti, Battista
    Ciotti, 1612.
——. *Il mastro di campo generale di Giorgio Basta conte d'Hvst*. Venice: G. B. Ciotti,
    1606.
Bettini, Mario. *Recreationum mathematicarum apiaria novissima duodecim* [. . .].
    Bononiae: Sumptibus J. B. Ferronii, 1659.
Brancaccio, Lelio. *I carichi militari*. Antwerp: Ioachimo Trognesio, 1610.
Busbecq, Ogier Ghiselin de. *The Turkish Letters of Ogier Ghiselin de Busbecq, Imperial
    Ambassador at Constantinople, 1554–1562: Translated from the Latin of the Elzevir
    Edition of 1663*. Translated by Edward Seymour Forster. Baton Rouge:
    Louisiana State University Press, 2005.
Campanella, Tommaso. *Monarchie d'Espagne: Texte inédit*. Edited by Germana Ernst.
    Paris: Presses universitaires de France, 1997.
Castiglione, Baldassarre. *The Book of the Courtier*. Translated by George Bull. New
    York: Penguin, 1976.
——. *Il libro del cortegiano*. Milan: Garzanti, 1981.
Çelebi, Evliya. *An Ottoman Traveller: Selections from the Book of Travels of Evliya Çelebi*.
    Translated by Robert Dankoff and Sooyong Kim. London: Eland Publishing,
    2010.
Cinuzzi, Imperiale. *La vera militar disciplina antica e moderna*. 2 vols. Siena: S.
    Marchetti, 1604.
Descartes, René. *Discourse on Method and Related Writings*. New York: Penguin, 2000.

Filamondo, Raffaele M. *Il genio bellicoso di Napoli, memorie istoriche d'alcuni capitani celebri napolitani: C'han militato per la Fede, per lo Re, per la Patria nel secolo trascorso raccolte.* Naples: D. A. Parrino, 1714.

Foscolo, Ugo, ed. *Opere di Raimondo Montecuccoli.* 2 vols. Milan: Luigi Mussi, 1808.

Fuchs, Adalbert Franz, ed. *Briefe an den Feldmarschall Raimund Grafen Montecuccoli: Beitraege zur Geschichte des nordischen Krieges in den Jahren 1659–1660.* Vienna: C. W. Stern, 1910.

Gamurrini, Eugenio. *Istoria geneaologica delle famiglie nobili Toscane, et Umbre.* Vol. 1. Florence: Nella stamperia di Francesco Onofri, 1668.

Gimorri, Adriano, ed. *I viaggi. Opera inedita pubblicata a cura di Adriano Gimorri e preceduta da una notizia sulla vita e sulle opere dell'autore.* Modena: Società Tipografica Modenese, Antica Tipografia Soliani, 1924.

Grimmelshausen, Johann. *The Adventures of Simplicius Simplicissimus.* Edited and translated by Mike Mitchell. Sawtry: Dedalus, 1999.

Harrach, Ernst Adalbert. *Die Diarien und Tagzettel des Kardinals Ernst Adalbert Von Harrach (1598–1667).* Edited by Katrin Keller and Alessandro Catalano. 7 vols. Vienna: Böhlau, 2010.

Jaitner, Klaus, ed. *Die Hauptinstruktionen Gregors XV: Für die Nuntien und Gesandten an den europäischen Fürstenhöfen, 1621–1623.* Vol. 2. Tübingen: M. Niemeyer, 1997.

Knolles, Richard. *The Generall Historie of the Turkes from the First Beginning of That Nation to the Rising of the Othoman Familie: With All the Notable Expeditions of the Christian Princes against Them [. . .].* London: Adam Islip, 1603.

La Noue, François de. *Discours politiques et militaires.* Edited by F. E. Sutcliffe. Geneva: Droz librairie, 1967.

Lipsius, Justus. *Six Bookes of Politickes or Civil Doctrine.* Translated by William Jones. London: Richard Field, 1594.

Machiavelli, Niccolò. *Art of War.* Edited and translated by Christopher Lynch. Chicago: University of Chicago Press, 2003.

Marsili, Luigi Ferdinando. *Autobiografia de Luigi Ferdinando Marsili: Messa in luce nel II centenario dalla morte di lui dal Comitato marsiliano.* Edited by Emilio Lovarini. Bologna: N. Zanichelli, 1930.

———. *Relazioni dei Confini della Croazia e della Transilvania a Sua Maesta Cesarea.* 2 vols. Edited by Raffaella Gherardi. Modena: Mucchi Editore, 1986.

———. *Stato militare dell'imperio ottomanno: l'état militaire de l'empire ottoman.* Graz: Akadem. Druck- u.Verlagsanst, 1972.

Melzi, Ludovico. *Regole militari del cavalier Melzo sopra il governo e servitio della cavalleria.* Anversa: Appresso Gioachimo Trognæsio (IS), 1611.

Montecuccoli, Raimondo. *Le opere di Raimondo Montecuccoli.* Edited by Raimondo Luraghi and Andrea Testa. 3 vols. 2nd ed. Rome: Stato maggiore dell'esercito, Ufficio storico, 2000.

Paradisi, Agostino. *Elogio del Principe Raimondo Montecuccoli.* Parma: Bodoni, 1796.

Pribram, A. F., ed. "Die Berichte des kaiserlichen Gesandten Franz von Lisola aus den Jahren 1655–1660." *Archiv für Oesterreichische Geschichte* 70 (1887).

Priorato, Galeazzo Gualdo. *Historia di Leopoldo Cesare, continente le cose piu memorabili successe in Europa, dal 1656. sino al 1670 [. . .].* Vienna: Gio. Battista Hacque, 1670.

——. *Vite et azzioni di personaggi militari e politici*. Vienna: Appresso Michele Thurn-mayer, 1674.

Priorato, Galeazzo Gualdo, and Girolamo Graziani. *Historia della Sacra Real Maestà di Christina Alessandra Regina di Suetia, &c*. Modena: Appresso Bartolomeo Soliani, 1656.

Ricci, Canonico B., ed. *Lettere inedite di Raimondo Montecuccoli al dottori Pietro e Carlo Ricci*. Modena: Tipi del Commercio, 1907.

Rohan, Henri. *Le parfait capitaine: Autrement l'abregé des guerres des commentaires de Cesar: Augmenté d'vn traicté de l'interest des princes & estats de la Chrestienté*. Paris: s.n., 1639.

Rycaut, Paul. *The History of the Present State of the Ottoman Empire*. London: John Starkey and Henry Brome, 1670.

Schiller, Friedrich. *The Robbers/Wallenstein*. Translated by F. J. Lamport. New York: Penguin Books, 1979.

Siri, Vittorio. *Il Mercurio overo historia de' correnti tempi (1635–1655) di Vittorio Siri*. Vol. 4. Casale: Per Giorno del Monte, 1655.

Testi, Fulvio. *Lettere*. Vol. 3. Bari: Laterza, 1967.

Veltzé, Alois, ed. and trans. *Ausgewaehlte Schriften des Raimund Fürsten Montecuccoli, General-Lieutenant und Feldmarschall*. 4 vols. Vienna: W. Braumüller, 1899–1901.

Verdadera relación de las fiestas y recibimiento que en Barcelona se hizo á la Majestad Cesárea de la Serma. Sra. D.a Margarita de Austria, emperatriz de Alemania, y juntamente de su embarcaciór, Y acompañamiento. Madrid 1666.

Vico, Giambattista. *De rebus gestis Antonj Caraphaei*. Naples: Excudebat Felix Musca, 1716.

Zrínyi, Miklós. *Arznei gegen das türkische Gift*. Excerpt in *Ungarns Geschichte und Kultur in Dokumenten*, edited and translated by Julius von Farkas, 60–70. Wiesbaden: Otto Harrassowitz, 1966.

——. *The Siege of Sziget*. Translated by László Kőrössy. Washington, DC: Catholic University of America Press, 2011.

Secondary Sources

Ágostan, Gábor. "The Costs of the Ottoman Fortress-System in Hungary." In *Ottomans, Hungarians, and Habsburgs in Central Europe: The Military Confines in the Era of Ottoman Conquest*, edited by Géza Dávid and Pál Fodor, 195–228. Leiden: Brill, 2000.

——. "Empires and Warfare in East Central Europe, 1550–1750: The Ottoman-Habsburg Rivalry and Military Transformation." In *European Warfare, 1350–1750*, edited by Frank Tallett and D. J. B Trim, 110–34. Cambridge: Cambridge University Press, 2010.

——. "Habsburgs and Ottomans: Defense, Military Change and Shifts in Power." *Turkish Studies Association Bulletin* 22, no. 1 (Spring 1998): 126–41.

Åkerman, Susanna. *Queen Christina of Sweden and Her Circle: The Transformation of a Seventeenth-Century Philosophical Libertine*. Leiden: E. J. Brill, 1991.

Albrecht, Dieter. "Der Heilige Stuhl und die Kurübertragung von 1623." *Quellen und Forschungen aus italienischen Archiven und Bibliotheken* 34 (1954): 236–49.

——. "Zur Finanzierung des Dreißigjährigen Krieges. Die Subsidien der Kurie für Kaiser und Liga 1618–1635." *Zeitschrift für bayerische Landesgeschichte* 19 (1956): 534–67.

Álvarez-Ossorio Alvariño, Antonio. "The State of Milan and the Spanish Monarchy." In *Spain in Italy: Politics, Society, and Religion 1500–1700*, edited by Thomas James Dandelet and John A. Marino, 99–132. Leiden: Brill, 2007.

Anderson, M. S. *War and Society in Europe of the Old Regime, 1618–1789*. Stroud: Sutton, 1998.

Aretin, Karl Otmar von. *Das alte Reich, 1648–1806*. Vol. 1. Stuttgart: Klett Cotta, 1993.

Argegni, Corrado. *Condottieri, capitani, tribune*. Vol. 3. Milan: E. B. B. I., Instituto editoriale italiano B. C. Tosi, 1936–37.

Aricò, Denise. "Una corrispondenza fra il gesuita bolognese Mario Bettini e Raimondo Montecuccoli." *Filologia e critica* (May–August 2006): 288–312.

Asch, Ronald. *The Thirty Years' War: The Holy Roman Empire and Europe, 1618–48*. New York: St. Martin's Press, 1997.

Ash, Eric. "Introduction: Expertise and the Early Modern State." In *Expertise: Practical Knowledge and the Early Modern State*, edited by Eric Ash, 1–24. Osiris, vol. 25. Chicago: University of Chicago Press, 2010.

——. *Power, Knowledge, and Expertise in Elizabethan England*. Baltimore, MD: Johns Hopkins University Press, 2004.

Astarita, Tommaso. *The Continuity of Feudal Power: The Caracciolo di Brienza in Spanish Naples*. Cambridge: Cambridge University Press, 2004.

Atti e memorie della R. Deputazione di Storia Patria per le Provincie Modenesi. Vol. 5. Modena: Deputazioni, 1870.

Auer, L. "Zur Rolle Italiens in der österreichischen Politik um das spanischen Erbe." *Mitteilungen des österreichischen Staatsarchivs* 31 (1978): 52–72.

Barker, Thomas. *Army, Aristocracy, Monarchy: Essays on War, Society, and Government in Austria, 1618–1780*. Boulder, CO: Social Science Monographs, 1982.

——. *Double Eagle and Crescent: Vienna's Second Turkish Siege and Its Historical Setting*. Albany: State University of New York Press, 1967.

——. *The Military Intellectual and Battle: Raimondo Montecuccoli and the Thirty Years' War*. Albany: State University of New York Press, 1975.

Bassett, Richard. *For God and Kaiser: The Imperial Austrian Army, 1619–1918*. New Haven, CT: Yale University Press, 2015.

Baumann, Reinhard. *Landsknechte: Ihre Geschichte und Kultur vom späten Mittelalter bis zum Dreißigjährigen Krieg*. Munich: C. H. Beck, 1994.

Baumanns, Markus. *Das publizistiche Werk des kaiserlichen Diplomaten Franz Paul Freiherr von Lisola (1613–1674): Ein Beitrag zum Verhältnis von absolutistischem Staat, Öffentlichkeit und Mächtepolitik in der frühen Neuzeit*. Berlin: Dunker & Humblot, 1994.

Becker, Rotraut. "Aus dem Alltag des Nuntius Malatesta Baglioni. Nichtdiploma-tische Aufgaben der Wiener Nuntiatur um 1635." *Quellen und Forschungen aus italienischen Archiven und Bibliotheken* 65 (1985): 328–40.

Behmen, M. "Der gerechte und der notwendige Krieg: 'Necessitas' und 'utilitas reipublicae' in der Kriegstheorie des 16. und 17. Jahrhunderts." In *Staatsverfassung und Heeresverfassung in der europäischen Geschichte der frühen Neuzeit*, edited by Barbara Stollberg-Rilinger and J. Kunisch, 42–106. Berlin: Duncker & Humbolt, 1986.

Beik, William. *Absolutism and Society in Seventeenth-Century France: State Power and Provincial Aristocracy in Languedoc.* Cambridge: Cambridge University Press, 1985.

Bene, Sándor. "A költő Zrínyi Miklós/Miklós Zrínyi, the Poet." In *Zrínyi-Album/Zrínyi Album*, edited by Sándor Bene et al., 174–250. Budapest: Zrínyi Kiadó, 2016.

Bérenger, Jean. *Finances et Absolutisme autrichien dans la seconde moitié du XVIIème siècle.* 2 vols. Lille: Atelier Reproduction des Theses Universite Lille III, 1975.

——. *A History of the Habsburg Empire.* New York: Longman, 1994.

——. *Turenne.* Paris: Fayard, 1987.

Biagioli, Mario. *Galileo, Courtier: The Practice of Science in the Culture of Absolutism.* Chicago: University of Chicago Press, 1994.

——. "The Social Status of Italian Mathematicians, 1450–1600." *History of Science* 27 (1989): 41–95.

Bianchi, P., D. Maffi, and E. Stumpo, eds. *Italiani al servizio straniero in età moderna.* Milan: Angeli, 2008.

Bílek, Tomáš. *Dějiny konfiskací v Čechách po r. 1618.* 2 vols. Prague: V kommissi u F. Řivnáce, 1882.

Bilotto, Antonella, Pietro Del Negro, and Cesare Mozzarelli. *I Farnese: Corti, guerra e nobilità in antico regime: Atti del convegno di studi Piacenza, 24–26 novembre 1994.* Rome: Bulzoni editore, 1997.

Bireley, Robert. *The Counter-Reformation Prince: Anti-Machiavellianism or Catholic Statecraft in Early Modern Europe.* Chapel Hill: University of North Carolina Press, 1990.

——. *Ferdinand II, Counter-Reformation Emperor, 1578–1637.* New York: Cambridge University Press, 2014.

Black, Jeremy. *A Military Revolution? Military Change and European Society 1550–1800.* Atlantic Highlands, NJ: Humanities Press, 1991.

Bonney, Richard. *The Thirty Years' War 1618–1648.* Oxford: Osprey, 2002.

Bosbach, Franz. "*Imperium Turcorum* oder *Christianorum Monarchia*—Die Osmanen in der heilsgeschichtlichen Deutung Mercurino Gattinaras." In *Das Osmanische Reich und die Habsburgermonarchie: Akten des internationalen Kongresses zum 150-jährigen Bestehen des Instituts für Österreichische Geschichtsforschung, Wien, 22.–25. September 2004*, edited by Marlene Kurz, Martin Scheutz, Karl Vocelka, and Thomas Winkelbauer, 167–80. Vienna: R. Oldenbourg, 2005.

Braubach, Max. *Prinz Eugen von Savoyen: Eine Biographie.* 5 vols. Munich: R. Oldenbourg, 1963.

Brauer, Jurgen, and Hubert van Toyll. *Castles, Battles, and Bombs: How Economics Explains Military History.* Chicago: University of Chicago Press, 2008.

Braun, Guido. "Kaiserhof, Kaiser und Reich in der Relazione des Nuntius Carlo Caraffa (1628)." In *Kaiserhof—Papsthof (16.–18. Jahrhundert)*, edited by Richard Bösel, Grete Klingenstein, and Alexander Koller, 77–104. Vienna: Verlag der österreichischen akademie der wissenshaften, 2006.

Brevaglieri, Sabina, and Matthias Schnettger, eds. *Transferprozesse zwischen dem Alten Reich und Italien im 17. Jahrhundert. Wissenskonfigurationen, Akteure, Netzwerke.* Bielefeld: Transcript Verlag, 2018.

Brewer, John. *The Sinews of Power: War, Money, and the English State, 1688–1783.* Cambridge, MA: Harvard University Press, 1990.

Broucek, Peter. "Logistische Fragen der Türkenkriege des 16. und 17. Jahrhunderts." *Vorträge zur Militärgeschichte* 7 (1986): 35–60.

Brunelli, Giampiero. *La santa impresa: Le crociate del papa in Ungheria: 1595–1601.* Rome: Salerno Editrice, 2018.

———. "'Prima maestro, che scolare': Nobiltà romana e carriere militari nel Cinque e Seicento." In *La nobiltà romana in età moderna: Profili istituzionali e pratiche sociali*, edited by Maria Antonietta Visceglia, 89–132. Rome: Carocci 2001.

———. "'Soldati della scuola vecchia di Fiandra': Nobiltà ed esercizio delle armi nello stato della chiesa fra cinque e seicento." In *I Farnese: Corti, guerra e nobiltà in antico regime: Atti del convegno di studi Piacenza, 24–26 novembre 1994*, edited by Antonella Bilotto, Pietro Del Negro, and Cesare Mozzarelli, 421–44. Rome: Bulzoni editore, 1997.

———. *Soldati del papa: Politica militare e nobiltà nello Stato della Chiesa: 1560–1644.* Rome: Carocci, 2003.

Burckhardt, Jacob. *The Civilization of the Renaissance in Italy.* London: Penguin Books, 1990.

Burke, Peter. *The Fortunes of the Courtier: The European Reception of Castiglione's Cortegiano.* Hoboken, NJ: Wiley, 2014.

Burschel, Peter. *Söldner im Nordwestdeutschland des 16. und 17. Jahrhunderts.* Göttingen: Vandenhoeck & Ruprecht, 1994.

Bůzek, Vaclav, and Petr Mat'a. "Wandlungen des Adels in Böhmen und Mähren im Zeitalter des "Absolutismus" (1620–1740)." In *Der europäische Adel in der Frühen Neuzeit: Eine Einführung*, edited by Ronald G. Asch, 287–321 Cologne: Böhlau, 2008.

Caferro, William. *John Hawkwood: An English Mercenary in Fourteenth-Century Italy.* Baltimore, MD: Johns Hopkins University Press, 2006.

———. *Mercenary Companies and the Decline of Siena.* Baltimore, MD: Johns Hopkins University Press, 1998.

———. "Warfare and Economy in Renaissance Italy 1350–1450." *Journal of Interdisciplinary History* 39 (2008): 167–209.

Campori, Cesare. *Raimondo Montecuccoli: La sua famiglia e i suoi tempi.* Florence: G. Barbèra, 1876.

Catalano, Alessandro. *La Boemia e la riconquista delle coscienze: Ernst Adalbert von Harrach e la controriforma in europa centrale (1620–1667).* Rome: Edizioni di storia e letteratura, 2005.

———. "La politica della curia romana in Boemia." In *Kaiserhof—Papsthof (16.–18. Jahrhundert)*, edited by Richard Bösel, Grete Klingenstein, and Alexander Koller, 105–21. Vienna: Verlag der österreichischen akademie der wissenshaften, 2006.

———. "L'Educazione del principe: Ferdinand August Leopold von Lobkowitz e il suo primo viaggio in Italia." *Porta Bohemica* 2 (2003): 104–27.

———. "L'italiano lingua di cultura dell'Europa centrale nell'età moderna /Italština v novodobých dějinách středoevropských kultur." In *Humanitas latina in*

Bohemis, edited by G. Cadorini and J. Špička, 117–68. Kolín: Albis; Treviso: G. Cadorini, 2007.

Chapman, Sara E. *Private Ambition and Political Alliances: The Phélypeaux de Pontchartrain Family and Louis XIV's Government, 1650–1715*. Rochester, NY: University of Rochester Press, 2004.

Chiappini, Luciano. *Gli estensi: mille anni di storia*. Ferrara: Corbo, 2001.

Cohn, Norman. *The Pursuit of the Millennium: Revolutionary Millennarians and Mystical Anarchists of the Middle Ages*. New York: Oxford University Press, 1981.

Contamine, Philippe, ed. *War and Competition between States*. New York: Oxford University Press, 2000.

Cook, Harold J. *The Young Descartes: Nobility, Rumor, and War*. Chicago: University of Chicago Press, 2018.

Cools, Hans, Marika Keblusek, and Badeloch Noldus, eds. *Your Humble Servant: Agents in Early Modern Europe*. Hilversum: Uitgeverij Verloren, 2006.

Coreth, Anna. *Pietas Austriaca*. West Lafayette, IN: Purdue University Press, 2004.

Cormack, Lesley B. "Mathematics and Empire: The Military Impulse and the Scientific Revolution." In *The Heirs of Archimedes: Science and the Art of War through the Age of Enlightenment*, edited by Brett D. Steele and Tamera Dorland, 181–203. Cambridge, MA: MIT Press, 2005.

Cremonini, Cinzia. "I feudi imperiali italiani tra Sacro Romano Impero e monarchia cattolica (seconda metà XVI–inizio XVII secolo)." In *L'impero e l'Italia nella prima età moderna*, edited by Matthias Schnettger and Marcello Verga, 41–65. Bologna: Il Mulino, 2006.

Croce, Benedetto. "I Caracciolo d'Avellino." In *Uomini e cose della vecchia Italia*. 3rd. ed. Bari: G. Laterza, 1956.

Czignany, Istvan. *Reform vagy kudarc? Kísérletek a magyarországi katonaság beillesztésére a Habsburg Birodalom haderejébe 1600–1700*. Budapest: Balassi Kiadó, 2004.

Dandelet, Thomas James. *The Renaissance of Empire in Early Modern Europe*. New York: Cambridge University Press, 2014.

Dandelet, Thomas James, and John A Marino, eds. *Spain in Italy: Politics, Society, and Religion 1500–1700*. Leiden: Brill, 2007.

Darling, Linda T. "Ottoman Politics through British Eyes: Paul Rycaut's 'Present State of the Ottoman Empire.'" *Journal of World History* 5, no. 1 (Spring 1994): 71–97.

Davies, Steffan. *The Wallenstein Figure in German Literature and Historiography, 1790–1920*. Leeds: Maney Publishing, 2010.

Deák, István. *Beyond Nationalism: A Social and Political History of the Habsburg Officer Corps, 1848–1918*. New York: Oxford University Press, 1990.

Dear, Peter. "Mysteries of State, Mysteries of Nature: Authority, Knowledge and Expertise in the Seventeenth Century." In *State of Knowledge: The Co-Production of Science and Social Order*, edited by Sheila Jasanoff, 206–24. New York: Routledge, 2004.

Dewald, Jonathan. *Aristocratic Experience and the Origins of Modern Culture: France, 1570–1715*. Berkeley: University of California Press, 1993.

Domokos, György. "From Imprisoned Embezzler to Commander: The Appointment of Joseph Priami to Commander of Bratislava, 1663." *Vojenská História* [Journal of Military History, Slovakia] 21, no. 4 (2019): 7–28.

——. *Kő és tűz, Erődépítészet- és tüzérségtörténeti tanulmányok* [Stone and Fire: Studies about the History of Fortification and Artillery]. Budapest: Nemzeti Kulturális Alap, 2021.

Domonkos, Leslie S. "The Battle of Mohács as a Cultural Watershed." In *From Hunyadi to Rákóczi: War and Society in Late Medieval and Early Modern Hungary*, edited by János M. Bak and Béla K. Király, 203–24. New York: Brooklyn College Press, 1982.

Donagan, B. "The Web of Honour: Soldiers, Christians, and Gentlemen in the English Civil War." *Historical Journal* 44 (2001): 365–89.

Donati, Claudio. *Ai confini d'Italia: saggi di storia trentina in età moderna*. Bologna: Mulino, 2008.

——. "Il 'militare' nella storia dell'Italia moderna, dal Rinascimento all'età napoleonica." In *Eserciti e carriere militari nell'Italian moderna*, edited by C. Donati, 7–39. Milan: Edizioni Unicopli, 1998.

——. "The Profession of Arms and the Nobility in Spanish Italy: Some Considerations." In *Spain in Italy: Politics, Society, and Religion 1500–1700*, edited by Thomas Dandelet and John A. Marino, 299–324. Leiden: Brill, 2007.

Duffy, Christopher. *The Army of Maria Theresa: The Armed Forces of Imperial Austria, 1740–1780*. New York: Hippocrene Books, 1977.

Duindam, Jeroen. *Vienna and Versailles: The Courts of Europe's Dynastic Rivals, 1550–1780*. Cambridge: Cambridge University Press, 2003.

Edelmayer, Friedrich. *Söldner und Pensionäre: Das Netzwerk Philipps II. im Heiligen Römischen Reich*. Vienna: Verlag für Geschichte und Politik, 2002.

Elias, Norbert. *The Civilizing Process: [Sociogenetic and Psychogenetic Investigations]*. Translated by Edmund Jephcott. New York: Urizen Books, 1978.

Elliott, John. *The Count-Duke of Olivares: The Statesman in an Age of Decline*. New Haven, CT: Yale University Press, 1986.

——. *The Revolt of the Catalans: A Study in the Decline of Spain, 1598–1640*. Cambridge: Cambridge University Press, 1963.

——. "Spain and the War." In *The Thirty Years' War*, edited by Geoffrey Parker, 103–109. 2nd rev. ed. London: Routledge, 1997.

Elster, Otto. *Die Piccolomini—Regimenter während des 30jähr. Krieges: bes. das Kürassier—Regiment Alt—Piccolomin*. Vienna: Seidel & Sohn, 1903.

——. *Piccolomini-Studien*. Leipzig: G. Müller-Mann, 1911.

Ernst, Germana. *Tommaso Campanella: The Book and the Body of Nature*. Dordrecht: Springer, 2010.

Ernstberger, Anton. *Hans de Witte, Finanzman Wallensteins*. Wiesbaden: Steiner, 1954.

Etényi, Nóra G. "Zrínyi Miklós a Német-római Birodalom nyilvánosságában / Miklós Zrínyi through the Public Eye in the Holy Roman Empire." In *Zrínyi-Album / Zrínyi Album*, edited by Sándor Bene, 282–337 et al. Budapest: Zrínyi Kiadó, 2016.

Evans, R. J. W. *The Making of the Habsburg Monarchy, 1550–1700: An Interpretation*. Oxford: Clarendon Press, 1979.

Evans, R. J. W., and T. V. Thomas, eds. *Crown, Church, and Estates: Central European Politics in the Sixteenth and Seventeenth Centuries*. London: Macmillan, 1991.

Fellner, Thomas, and Heinrich Kretschmayr. *Die österreichische Zentralverwaltung. I. Abt. Von Maximilian I. bis zur Vereinigung der österreichischen und böhmischen*

Hofkanzlei (1749). Vol. 1, *Geschichtliche Übersicht*. Vienna: Veröffentlichungen der Kommission für neuere Geschichte Österreichs, 1907.

Fichtner, Paula Sutter. *The Habsburg Monarchy, 1490–1848*. Basingstoke: Palgrave Macmillan, 2003.

Findlen, Paula. *Possessing Nature: Museums, Collecting, and Scientific Culture in Early Modern Italy*. Berkeley: University of California Press, 1994.

Finkel, Caroline. "The Cost of Ottoman Warfare and Defence." *Byzantinische Forschungen* 16 (1990): 91–103.

——. *Osman's Dream: The Story of the Ottoman Empire 1300–1923*. New York: Basic Books, 2005.

Fodor, Pál. "Ottoman Policy towards Hungary, 1520–1541." *Acta Orientalia Academiae Scientiarum Hungaricae* 45, no. 2–3 (1991): 271–345.

——. "Volunteers in the Ottoman Army." In *Ottomans, Hungarians, and Habsburgs in Central Europe: The Military Confines in the Era of Ottoman Conquest*, edited by Géza Dávid and Pál Fodor, 230–34. Leiden: Brill, 2000.

Fosi, Irene. "La famiglia Savelli e la rappresentanza imperiale a Roma nella prima metà del Seicento." In *Kaiserhof—Papsthof (16.–18. Jahrhundert)*, edited by Richard Bösel, Grete Klingenstein, and Alexander Koller, 67–76. Vienna: Verlag der österreichischen akademie der wissenshaften, 2006.

France, John, ed. *Mercenaries and Paid Men: The Mercenary Identity in the Middle Ages: Proceedings of a Conference Held At University of Wales, Swansea, 7th–9th July 2005*. Leiden: Brill, 2008.

Frigo, Daniela, ed. *Politics and Diplomacy in Early Modern Italy: The Structure of Diplomatic Practice, 1450–1800*. Cambridge: Cambridge University Press, 2000.

Frost, Robert I. *The Northern Wars: War, State and Society in Northeastern Europe, 1558–1721*. Harlow, Longman, 2000.

Fuchs, Franz, ed. *Osmanische Expansion und europäischer Humanismus*. Wiesbaden: Harrassowitz, 2005.

Fynn-Paul, Jeff, ed. *War, Entrepreneurs, and the State in Europe and the Mediterranean, 1300–1800*. Leiden: Brill, 2014.

Galasso, Giuseppe. *Alla periferia dell'impero: Il Regno di Napoli nel periodo spagnolo (secoli XVI–XVII)*. Turin: Einaudi, 1994.

Gat, Azar. *The Origins of Military Thought from the Enlightenment to Clausewitz*. Oxford: Clarendon Press, 1989.

Gherardi, Raffaella. "An der Grenze zwischen der Habsburgermonarchie und dem Osmanischen Reich: Raimondo Montecuccoli und das italienische Militär in Wien." In *Die Schlacht von Mogersdorf/St. Gotthard und der Friede von Eisenburg/ Vasvar 1664: Rahmenbedingungen, Akteure, Auswirkungen und Rezeption eines europäischen Ereignisses*, edited by Karin Sperl, Martin Scheutz, and Arno Strohmeyer, 171–93. Eisenstadt: Amt der Burgenländischen Landesregierung, Hauptreferat Landesarchiv und Landesbibliothek, 2016.

——. *La politica, la scienza, le armi: Luigi Ferdinando Marsili e la costruzione della frontiera dell'impero e dell'europa*. Bologna: CLEUB, 2010.

——. *Potere e costituzione a Vienna fra sei e settecento: Il "buon ordine" di Luigi Ferdinando Marsili*. Bologna: Il Mulino, 1980.

Gherardi, Raffaella, and Fabio Martelli. *La pace degli eserciti e dell'economia: Montecuccoli e Marsili alla corte di Vienna.* Bologna: Società editrice il Mulino, 2009.

Glete, Jan. *War and the State in Early Modern Europe: Spain, the Dutch Republic and Sweden as Fiscal-Military States, 1500–1660.* London: Routledge, 2002.

——. "Warfare, Entrepreneurship, and the Fiscal-Military State." In *European Warfare, 1350–1750,* edited by Frank Tallett and D. J. B. Trim, 300–321. Cambridge: Cambridge University Press, 2010.

Godsey, William. *The Sinews of Habsburg Power: Lower Austria as A Fiscal-Military State, 1650–1820.* Oxford: Oxford University Press, 2018.

Gömöri, George. "Introduction." In Miklós Zrínyi, *The Siege of Sziget,* translated by László Kőrössy, xi–xxiv. Washington, DC: Catholic University of America Press, 2011.

Gonzalez de Leon, Fernando. "'Doctors of Military Discipline': Technical Expertise and the Paradigm of the Spanish Soldier in the Early Modern Period." *Sixteenth Century Journal* 27, no. 1 (Spring 1996): 61–85.

Grafton, Anthony, and Lisa Jardine. "'Studied for Action': How Gabriel Harvey Read His Livy." *Past and Present* 129 (1990): 30–78.

Grossman, Julius. "Die Geschäftsordnung in Sachen der äusseren Politik am Wiener Hofe zu Kaiser Leopolds und Lobkowitz Zeiten." *Forschungen zur deutschen Geschichte* 12 (1871–72): 457–74.

Guerlac, Henry. "Vauban: The Impact of a Science of War." In *Makers of Modern Strategy from Machiavelli to the Nuclear Age,* edited by Peter Paret, 64–90. Princeton, NJ: Princeton University Press, 1986.

Gunn, Steven. "War and the Emergence of the State: Western Europe, 1350–1600." In *European Warfare, 1350–1750,* edited by Frank Tallett and D. J. B. Trim, 105–21. New York: Cambridge University Press, 2010.

Gunn, Steven, David Grummitt, and Hans Cools. "War and the State in Early Modern Europe: Widening the Debate." *War in History* 15, no. 4 (2008): 371–88.

Guthmüller, Bodo, and Wilhelm Kühlmann. *Europa und die Türken in der Renaissance.* Berlin, Boston: De Gruyter, 2000.

Guthrie, William. *From White Mountain to Nordlingen, 1618–1635.* Westport: Greenwood Press, 2002.

——. *The Later Thirty Years' War: From the Battle of Wittstock to the Treaty of Westphalia.* Westport: Greenwood Press, 2003.

Haag, Norbert. "'Erbfeind der Christenheit': Türkenpredigten im 16. und 17. Jahrhundert." In *Repräsentationen der islamischen Welt im Europa der Frühen Neuzeit,* edited by Gabriele Haug-Moritz, 127–49. Münster: Aschendorff, 2010.

Haberer, Stephanie. *Ott Heinrich Fugger (1592–1644): Biographische Analyse typologischer Handlungsfelder in der Epoche des Dreißigjährigen Krieges.* Augsburg: Wissner, 2004.

Hale, J. R. "Armies, Navies and the Art of War." In *The New Cambridge Modern History.* Vol. 3, *The Counter-Reformation and Price Revolution, 1559–1610,* edited by R. B. Wernham, 540–69. Cambridge: Cambridge University Press, 1968.

——. "The Military Education of the Officer Class in Early Modern Europe." In *Cultural Aspects of the Italian Renaissance: Essays in Honour of Paul Oskar*

Kristeller, edited by C. H. Clough, 440–61. Manchester: Manchester University Press, 1976.

——. "Printing and the Military Culture of Renaissance Venice." *Medievalia et Humanistica* 8 (1977): 21–62.

——. *War and Society in Renaissance Europe, 1450–1620*. Baltimore, MD: Johns Hopkins University Press, 1985.

Hanlon, Gregory. "The Decline of a Military Aristocracy: Siena 1560–1740." *Past and Present* 155, no. 1 (1997): 69–73.

——. *The Hero of Italy: Odoardo Farnese, Duke of Parma, His Soldiers, and His Subjects in the Thirty Years' War*. Oxford: Oxford University Press, 2014.

——. "In Praise of Refeudalization: Princes and Feudatories in North-Central Italy from the Sixteenth to the Eighteenth Century." In *Sociability and Its Discontents: Civil Society, Social Capital and Their Alternatives in Late Medieval and Early Modern Europe*, edited by Nicholas Eckstein and Nicholas Terpstra, 213–25. Oxford: Oxford University Press, 2009.

——. *Italy 1636: Cemetery of Armies*. Oxford: Oxford University Press, 2016.

——. *The Twilight of a Military Tradition: Italian Aristocrats and European Conflicts, 1560–1800*. London: UCL Press, 1998.

Harari, Yuval. *Renaissance Military Memoirs: War, History and Identity, 1450–1600*. Woodbridge: Boydell Press, 2004.

Headley, John. *Tommaso Campanella and the Transformation of the World*. Princeton, NJ: Princeton University Press, 1997.

Hegyi, Klára. "The Ottoman Network of Fortresses in Hungary." In *Ottomans, Hungarians, and Habsburgs in Central Europe: The Military Confines in the Era of Ottoman Conquest*, edited by Géza Dávid and Pál Fodor, 163–93. Leiden: Brill, 2000.

Heischmann, Eugen. *Die Anfänge des stehenden Heeres in Österreich*. Vienna: Österr. Bundesverl., 1925.

Helferrich, Tryntje. "A Levy in Liège for Mazarin's Army: Practical and Strategic Difficulties in Raising and Supporting Troops in the Thirty Years' War." *JEMH* 11, no. 6 (2007): 475–500.

Hernán, Enrique García, and Davide Maffei, eds. *Guerra y sociedad en la Monarquía Hispánica: Politica, estrategia y cultura en la Europa moderna (1500–1700)*. 2 vols. Madrid: Ediciones del Laberinto, 2006.

Heuser, Beatrice. *Strategy before Clausewitz: Linking Warfare and Statecraft, 1400–1830*. Abingdon: Routledge, 2018.

Hochedlinger, Michael. *Austria's Wars of Emergence: War, State and Society in the Habsburg Monarchy, 1683–1797*. London: Longman, 2003.

Höfert, Almut, and Armando Salvatore. *Between Europe and Islam: Shaping Modernity in a Transcultural Space*. Brussels: P. I. E. Peter Lang, 2005.

Hoyos, Phillip. "Die kaiserliche Armee 1648–1650." In *Der Dreißigjährige Krieg: Schriften des Heeresgeschichtlichen Museums in Wien*, edited by Hugo Schneider, 169–232. Vienna: Österreichischer Bundesverlag für Unterricht, 1976.

Hummelberger, Walter. "Der Dreissigjährige Krieg und die Entstehung des Kaiserlichen Heeres." In *Unser Heer: 300 Jahre Österreichisches Soldatentum in Krieg und Frieden*, 1–48. Vienna: Fürlinger, 1963.

Ingrao, Charles. *The Habsburg Monarchy, 1618–1815.* Cambridge: Cambridge University Press, 1994.

Intra, Giambattista. *Il sacco di Mantova.* Milan: Tip. della Perseveranza, 1872.

——. "Le due Eleonore Gonzaga Imperatrice." In *Atti e Memorie della R. Accademia Virgiliana di Mantova, Biennio 1891–1892.* Mantua: s.n., 1893.

Jacob, Margaret C. *Strangers Nowhere in the World: The Rise of Cosmopolitanism in Early Modern Europe.* Philadelphia: University of Pennsylvania Press, 2006.

Kaiser, Michael. "Jan von Werth zwischen Wittelsbach und Habsburg. Kriegsunternehmertum und Patronage im Dreißigjährigen Krieg." *Zeitschrift für bayerische Landesgeschichte* 75 (2012): 135–66.

Kampmann, Christoph. *Europa und das Reich im Dreißigjährige Krieg. Geschichte eines europäische Konflikts.* Stuttgart: Kohlhammer Verlag, 2013.

Kaufmann, Harms. *Raimondo Graf Montecuccoli 1609–1680: Kaiserlicher Feldmarschall, Militärtheoretiker und Staatsmann.* Wien: Kaufmann, 1974.

Kauz, Ralph, Giorgio Rota, and Jan Paul Niederkorn, eds. *Diplomatisches Zeremoniell in Europa und im Mittleren Osten in der Frühen Neuzeit.* Vienna: Verlag der Österreichischen Akademie der Wissenschaften, 2009.

Kazlepka, Zdeněk. *Ostrov italského vkusu: Umelecký mecenát Antonia Rambalda, hrabete z Collalto a San Salvatore, mezi Itálií, Vídní a Moravou v první polovine 18. stoleti.* Brno: Barrister & Principal: Moravská galerie, 2011.

Kelenik, József. "A keresztény világ bajnoka / The Champion of the Christian World." In *Zrínyi-Album / Zrínyi Album,* edited by Sándor Bene et al., 108–73. Budapest: Zrínyi Kiadó, 2016.

——. "The Military Revolution in Hungary." In *Ottomans, Hungarians, and Habsburgs in Central Europe: The Military Confines in the Era of Ottoman Conquest,* edited by Géza Dávid and Pál Fodor, 117–59. Leiden: Brill, 2000.

Kettering, Sharon. *Patronage in Sixteenth- and Seventeenth-Century France.* Aldershot: Ashgate, 2002.

Kindelberger, Charles P. "The Economic Crisis of 1619 to 1623." *Journal of Economic History* 51 (1991): 149–75.

Klaniczay, Tibor. "Probleme der ungarischen Spätrenaissance (Stoizismus und Manierismus)." In *Renaissance und Humanismus in Mittel- und Osteuropa: Eine Sammlung von Materialien.* Vol. 2, edited by Johannes Irmscher, 61–94. Berlin: Akademie-Verl., 1962.

Knoz, Tomáš. "Die Konfiskationen nach 1620 in (erb)länderübergreifender Perspektive: Thesen zu wesentlichen Wirkungen, Aspekten und Prinzipien des Konfiskationsprozesses." In *Die Habsburgermonarchie, 1620 bis 1740: Leistungen und Grenzen des Absolutismusparadigmas,* edited by Petr Mat'a and Thomas Winkelbauer, 99–130. Stuttgart: Franz Steiner Verlag, 2006.

Koenigsberger, H. G. *The Habsburgs and Europe, 1516–1660.* Ithaca, NY: Cornell University Press, 1971.

Koller, Alexander. *Imperator und Pontifex: Forschungen zum Verhältnis von Kaiserhof und römischer Kurie im Zeitalter der Konfessionalisierung (1555–1648).* Münster: Aschendorff, 2012.

Kortepeter, Carl Max. *Ottoman Imperialism during the Reformation: Europe and the Caucasus.* New York: New York University Press, 1972.

Kottmann, Karl A, ed. *Millenarianism and Messianism in Early Modern European Culture*. Vol. 2, *Catholic Millenarianism: From Savonarola to the Abbé Grégoire*. Dordrecht: Kluwer Academic Publishers, 2001.

Kroener, Berhard R. "'The Soldiers Are Very Poor, Bare, Naked, and Exhausted': The Living Conditions and Organizational Structure of Military Society during the Thirty Years' War." In *1648: War and Peace in Europe: Politics, Religion, Law, and Society*, edited by Klaus Bussmann and Heinz Schilling, 285–91. Münster-Osnabrück: Westfalisches Landsmuseum für Kunst und Kulturgeschichte, 1998.

Krüssmann, Walter. *Ernst von Mansfeld (1580–1626): Grafensohn, Söldnerführer, Kriegsunternehmer gegen Habsburg im Dreißigjährigen Krieg*. Berlin: Duncker & Humblot, 2010.

Kurz, Marlene, Martin Scheutz, Karl Vocelka, and Thomas Winkelbauer, eds. *Das Osmanische Reich und die Habsburgermonarchie: Akten des internationalen Kongresses zum 150-jährigen Bestehen des Instituts für Österreichische Geschichtsforschung, Wien, 22.–25. September 2004*. Vienna: R. Oldenbourg, 2005.

Lawrence, David R. *The Complete Soldier: Military Books and Military Culture in Early Stuart England, 1603–1645*. Leiden: Brill, 2009.

Lefevre, Renato. "Il patrimonio romano degli Aldobrandini nel Seicento." *Archivio della Società romana di Storia patria* 82 (1959): 1–24.

Lendvai, Paul. *The Hungarians: A Thousand Years of Victory in Defeat*. Translated by Ann Major. Princeton, NJ: Princeton University Press, 2003.

Liliencron, Rochus, ed. *Allgemeine Deutsche Biographie* [. . .]: *Auf Veranlassung* [. . .]. Leipzig: Duncker & Humblot, 1875.

Lindström, Peter, and Svante Norrhem. *Flattering Alliances: Scandinavia, Diplomacy, and the Austrian-French Balance of Power, 1648–1740*. Translated by Charlotte Merton. Lund: Nordic Academic Press, 2013.

Lockhart, Paul Douglas. *Sweden in the Seventeenth Century*. Basingstoke: Palgrave Macmillan, 2004.

Long, Pamela O. *Artisan/Practitioners and the Rise of the New Sciences 1400–1600*. Corvallis: Oregon State University Press, 2011.

Lund, Erik A. *War for the Every Day: Generals, Knowledge, and Warfare in Early Modern Europe, 1680–1740*. Westport, CT: Greenwood Press, 1999.

Lynn, John. *Giant of the Grand Siècle: The French Army, 1610–1715*. Cambridge: Cambridge University Press, 1997.

——. "How War Fed War: The Tax of Violence and Contributions during the Grand Siècle." *Journal of Modern History* 65, no. 2 (June 1993): 286–310.

——. *The Wars of Louis XIV 1667–1714*. London: Routledge, 2014.

MacHardy, Karin J. *War, Religion and Court Patronage in Habsburg Austria: The Social and Cultural Dimensions of Political Interaction, 1521–1622*. New York: Palgrave Macmillan, 2003.

Maczak, Antoni, ed. *Klientelsysteme im Europa der frühen Neuzeit*. Munich: Oldenbourg, 1988.

Maffi, Davide. *Il baluardo della corona: Guerra, esercito, finanze e società nella Lombardia seicentesca (1630–1660)*. Florence: Le Monnier Università, 2007.

Mallett, Michael. *Mercenaries and Their Masters: Warfare in Renaissance Italy*. Totowa, NJ: Rowman and Littlefield, 1974.

Mallett, Michael, and J. R. Hale. *The Military Organization of a Renaissance State: Venice, c. 1400 to 1617*. Cambridge: Cambridge University Press, 1984.

Mallett, Michael, and Christine Shaw. *The Italian Wars, 1494–1559: War, State and Society in Early Modern Europe*. Harlow: Pearson, 2012.

Mann, Golo. *Wallenstein, His Life Narrated*. New York: Holt, Rinehart and Winston, 1976.

Manzotti, Fernando. "Le fine del Principato di Correggio nelle relazioni italo-imperiali del periodo italiano della guerra dei trent'anni." In *Atti e mem. della deputazione di storia patria per le Antiche province Modenesi* 8, no. 6 (1954): 43–59.

Mariani, Vittorio, and Varo Varanini. *Condottieri italiani in Germania* [. . .] *con 38 Carte, 26 Facsimili, 75 Ritratti*. Milan: Garzanti, 1941.

Martelli, Fabio. "The Battle of Mogersdorf, Saint Gotthard in the Eyes of Montecuccoli: A Victory and the Consequences." In *Die Schlacht von Mogersdorf/ St. Gotthard und der Friede von Eisenburg/Vasvar 1664: Rahmenbedingungen, Akteure, Auswirkungen und Rezeption eines europäischen Ereignisses*, edited by Karin Sperl, Martin Scheutz, and Arno Strohmeyer, 195–205. Eisenstadt: Amt der Burgenländischen Landesregierung, Hauptreferat Landesarchiv und Landesbibliothek, 2016.

Martinez, Miguel. *Front Lines: Soldiers' Writing in the Early Modern Hispanic World*. Philadelphia: University of Pennsylvania Press, 2016.

Mat'a, Petr. *Svět české aristokracie (1500–1700)*. Prague: Nakl. Lidové noviny, 2004.

Mat'a, Petr, and Thomas Winkelbauer. *Die Habsurgermonarchie 1620 bis 1740: Leistungen und Grenzen des Absolutismusparadigmas*. Stuttgart: Steiner, 2006.

——. "Introduction." In *Die Habsburgermonarchie, 1620 bis 1740: Leistungen und Grenzen des Absolutismusparadigmas*, edited by Petr Mat'a and Thomas Winkelbauer, 7–42. Stuttgart: Franz Steiner Verlag, 2006.

McKay, Derek. *Prince Eugene of Savoy*. London: Thames and Hudson, 1977.

McKeown, Adam. *English Mercuries: Soldier Poets in the Age of Shakespeare*. Nashville, TN: Vanderbilt University Press, 2009.

McKitterick, David. *Print, Manuscript and the Search for Order, 1450–1830*. Cambridge: Cambridge University Press, 2003.

McNeill, William. *The Pursuit of Power: Technology, Armed Force, and Society since A.D. 1000*. Chicago: University of Chicago Press, 1982.

Mears, John. *Count Raimondo Montecuccoli: Practical Soldier and Military Theoretician*. PhD diss., University of Chicago, 1964.

——. "Count Raimondo Montecuccoli: Servant of a Dynasty." *Historian* 32, no. 3 (May 1970): 392–409.

——. "The Thirty Years' War, the 'General Crisis,' and the Origins of a Standing Professional Army in the Habsburg Monarchy." *Central European History* 21, no. 2. (June 1988): 122–41.

Meier-Welcker, Hans. *Deutsches Heereswesen in Wandel der Zeit ein Überblick über d. Entwicklung vom Aufkommen d. stehenden Heere bis zur Wehrfrage d. Gegenwart*. Frankfurt: Bernhard & Graefe, Verl. f. Wehrwesen, 1956.

——. *Handbuch zur deutschen Militärgeschichte, 1648–1939*. Vol. 1, *Von der Miliz zum stehenden Heer*. Munchen: Bernhard & Graefe, 1979.

Mesa, Eduardo de. *The Irish in the Spanish Armies in the Seventeenth Century*. Rochester, NY: Boydell and Brewer, 2014.

Meserve, Margaret. *Empires of Islam in Renaissance Historical Thought*. Cambridge, MA: Harvard University Press, 2008.

Meynert, Hermann. *Geschichte der k. k. österreichischen Armee, ihrer Heranbildung und Organisation, so wie ihrer Schicksale, Thaten und Feldzüge, von der Frühesten bis auf die jetzige Zeit*. 4 vols. Vienna: C. Gerold und Sohn, 1854.

Michels, Georg B. "'They Have Become Turks (Seindt Türkhen Worden)': Anti-Habsburg Resistance and Turkification in Seventeenth-Century Hungary." In *Humanities in a World Upside Down*, edited by Ignacio López-Calvo, 12–35. Newcastle-upon-Tyne: Cambridge Scholars: 2017.

——. "When Will the Turks Attack? Habsburg Espionage and Actionable Intelligence in the Age of Grand Vezir Ahmed Köprülü (1661–1676)." In *Seeing Muscovy Anew: Politics, Institutions, Culture: Essays in Honor of Nancy Shields Kollmann*, edited by Daniel Bruce Rowland et al., 303–22. Bloomington: Slavica, 2017.

Mikulec, Jiří. *Leopold I: Život a vláda barokního Habsburka*. Prague: Paseka, 1997.

Millán, José Martínez. "Alessandro Farnese, la corte di Madrid e la monarchia cattolica." In *I Farnese: Corti, guerra e nobilità in antico regime: Atti del convegno di studi Piacenza, 24–26 novembre 1994*, edited by Antonella Bilotto, Pietro Del Negro, and Cesare Mozzarelli, 93–116. Rome: Bulzoni editore, 1997.

Miller, Peter N. "Nazis and Neostoics: Otto Brunner and Gerhard Oestreich before and after the Second World War." *Past and Present* 176 (August 2002): 144–86.

Mitchell, John. *Life of Wallenstein, Duke of Friedland*. London: James Fraser, 1837.

Moran, Bruce T. "German Prince-Practitioners: Aspects in the Development of Courtly Science, Technology, and Procedures in the Renaissance." *Technology and Culture* 22, no. 2. (April 1981): 253–73.

——, ed. *Patronage and Institutions: Science, Technology, and Medicine at the European Court, 1500–1750*. Rochester, NY: Boydell Press, 1991.

Mortimer, Geoff. *Wallenstein: The Enigma of the Thirty Years' War*. Basingstoke: Palgrave Macmillan, 2010.

——. "War by Contract, Credit and Contribution: The Thirty Years' War." In *Early Modern Military History*, edited by Geoff Mortimer, 101–17. Basingstroke: Palgrave Macmillan, 2004.

Mozzarelli, Cesare. *Antico regime e modernità*. Rome: Bulzoni, 2008.

Muir, Ed. *Mad Blood Stirring: Vendetta in Renaissance Italy*. Baltimore, MD: Johns Hopkins University Press, 1998.

Müller, Klaus. *Das kaiserliche Gesandtschaftswesen im Jahrhundert nach dem Westfälischen Frieden: (1648–1740)*. Bonn: Röhrscheid, 1976.

Müller, Ralf C. "Der umworbene 'Erbfeind': Habsburgische Diplomatie an der Hohen Pforte vom Regierungsantritt Maximilians I. bis zum 'Langen Türkenkrieg'—ein Entwurf." In *Das Osmanische Reich und die Habsburgermonarchie: Akten des internationalen Kongresses zum 150-jährigen Bestehen des Instituts für Österreichische Geschichtsforschung, Wien, 22.–25. September 2004*, edited by Marlene Kurz, Martin Scheutz, Karl Vocelka, and Thomas Winkelbauer, 251–80. Vienna: R. Oldenbourg, 2005.

Münkler, Herfried. *Der Dreißigjährige Krieg: Europäische Katastrophe, deutsches Trauma 1618–1648*. Berlin: Rowolt, 2017.

Murphey, Rhoads. *Ottoman Warfare*. London: UCL Press, 1999.

Musi, Aurelio. "L'Italia nel sistema imperiale spagnolo." In *Nel sistema imperiale: L'Italia Spagnola*, edited by Aurelio Musi, 51–66. Naples: Edizioni Scientifiche Italiane, 1994.

Najemy, John M. "Machiavelli between East and West." In *From Florence to the Mediterranean and Beyond: Essays in Honour of Anthony Molho*, edited by Diogo Ramada Curto, Eric R. Dursteler, Julius Kirshner, and Francesca Trivellato, 127–45. Florence: Olschki, 2009.

Neal, Katherine. "The Rhetoric of Utility: Avoiding Occult Associations for Mathematics through Profitability and Pleasure." *History of Science* 37 (1999): 151–78.

Negri, Paolo. "Disegni di Cristina Alessandra di Svezia per un'impresa contro il regno di Napoli." *Archivio della Reale Società Romana di storia patria* 32 (1909): 107–72.

Nexon, Daniel. *The Struggle for Power in Early Modern Europe*. Princeton, NJ: Princeton University Press, 2009.

Niederberger, Antje. "Das Bild der Türken im deutschen Humanismus am Beispiel der Werke Sebastian Brants (1456–1521)." In *Das Osmanische Reich und die Habsburgermonarchie: Akten des internationalen Kongresses zum 150-jährigen Bestehen des Instituts für Österreichische Geschichtsforschung, Wien, 22.–25. September 2004*, edited by Marlene Kurz, Martin Scheutz, Karl Vocelka, and Thomas Winkelbauer, 181–204. Vienna: R. Oldenbourg, 2005.

Nottebohm, Wilhelm. *Montecuccoli und die Legende von St. Gotthard (1664)*. Berlin: R. Gaertners Verlagsbuchhandlung, H. Heyfelder, 1887.

Nouzille, Jean. *Histoire de frontières: L'Autriche et l'Empire ottoman*. Paris: Berg International Editeurs, 1991.

Nylander, Eva Nilsson. *The Mild Boredom of Order: A Study in the History of the Manuscript Collection of Queen Christina of Sweden*. Lund: Lund University, 2011.

Oestreich, Gerhard. *Neostoicism and the Early Modern State*. Edited by Gerhard Oestreich, Brigitta Oestreich, and H. G Koenigsberger. Translated by David McLintock. Cambridge: Cambridge University Press, 1982.

Ong, Walter J. *Ramus, Method, and the Decay of Dialogue: From the Art of Discourse to the Art of Reason*. Cambridge, MA: Harvard University Press, 1983.

Oresko, Robert, and David Parrott. "Reichsitalien and the Thirty Years' War." In *1648: War and Peace in Europe*, vol. 1, edited by Klaus Bussmann and Heinz Schilling, 141–60. Munich: Bruckmann, 1998.

Osborne, Toby. *Dynasty and Diplomacy in the Court of Savoy: Political Culture and the Thirty Years' War*. Cambridge: Cambridge University Press, 2002.

Paas, Martha White. *The Kipper und Wipper Inflation, 1619–23: An Economic History with Contemporary German Broadsheets*. Translated by George C. Schoolfield. New Haven, CT: Yale University Press, 2012.

Pagden, Anthony. *Lords of All the World: Ideologies of Empire in Spain, Britain and France c. 1500–c. 1800*. New Haven, CT: Yale University Press, 1995.

Pálffy, Géza. "The Hungarian-Habsburg Border Defence Systems." In *Ottomans, Hungarians, and Habsburgs in Central Europe: The Military Confines in the Era of Ottoman Conquest*, edited by Géza Dávid and Pál Fodor, 3–33. Leiden: Brill, 2000.

Papke, Gerhard. "Von der Miliz zum Stehenden Heer: Wehrwesen im Absolutis-mus." In *Handbuch der Deutschen Militärgeschichte 1648–1939*, vol. 1, 1–311. Munich: Bernard & Graefe, 1979.

Papy, Jan. "Justus Lipsius and Neo-Stoicism." In *The Routledge Companion to Sixteenth Century Philosophy*, edited by Henrik Lagerlund and Benjamin Hill, 203–21. New York: Routledge, 2017.

Parker, Geoffrey. *The Army of Flanders and the Spanish Road, 1567–1659: The Logistics of Spanish Victory and Defeat in the Low Countries' Wars*. Cambridge: Cambridge University Press, 1972.

——. "The Decision-Making Process in the Government of the Catholic Nether-lands under 'the Archdukes,' 1596–1621." In *Spain and the Netherlands, 1559–1659: Ten Studies*, edited by Geoffrey Parker, 164–76. Short Hills, NJ: Enslow Publishers, 1979.

——. *The Dutch Revolt*. Ithaca, NY: Cornell University Press, 1977.

——. "The 'Military Revolution, 1560–1660'—A Myth?" In *The Military Revolution Debate: Readings on the Military Transformation of Early Modern Europe*, edited by Clifford J. Rogers, 37–54. Boulder, CO: Westview Press, 1995.

——. *The Military Revolution: Military Innovation and the Rise of the West, 1500–1800*. 2nd ed. New York: Cambridge University Press, 1996.

——, ed. *The Thirty Years' War*. 2nd rev. ed. London: Routledge, 1997.

Parma, Tomáš. *František kardinál Dietrichstein a jeho vztahy k římské kurii: Prostředky a metody politické komunikace ve službách moravské církve*. Brno: Matice Moravská, 2011.

Parrott, David. *The Business of War: Military Enterprise and Military Revolution in Early Modern Europe*. Cambridge: Cambridge University Press, 2012.

——. "From Military Enterprise to Standing Armies: War, State, and Society in Western Europe, 1600–1700." In *European Warfare, 1350–1750*, edited by Frank Tallett and D. J. B. Trim, 74–95. Cambridge: Cambridge University Press, 2010.

——. "Italian Soldiers in French Service, 1500–1700: The Collapse of a Military Tradition." In *Italiani al servizio straniero in età moderna*, edited by Paola Bianchi, Davide Maffei, and Enrico Stumpo, 15–40. Milan: FrancoAngeli, 2008.

——. "The Military Enterpriser in the Thirty Years' War." In *War, Entrepreneurs, and the State in Europe and the Mediterranean, 1300–1800*, edited by Jeff Fynn-Paul, 63–86. Leiden: Brill, 2014.

——. "*A Prince Souverain* and the French Crown: Charles de Nevers 1580–1637." In *Royal and Republican Sovereignty in Early Modern Europe: Essays in Memory of Ragnhild Hatton*, edited by Robert Oresko, G. C. Gibbs, and H. M. Scott, 149–87. Cambridge: Cambridge University Press, 1997.

——. *Richelieu's Army: War, Government and Society in France, 1624–1642*. Cambridge: Cambridge University Press, 2001.

Passolunghi, Pier Angelo. *I Collalto: Linee, documenti, genealogie per una storia del casato*. Villorba: B & M edizioni, 1987.

Pazderová, Alena, "Francesco Ottavio Piccolomini in Archival Documents." In *Siena in Prague: History, Art, Society,* edited by Alena Pazderová and Lucia Bonelli Conenna, 26-9eds. . Prague: National Gallery, 2000.

Peball, Kurt. "Raimund Fürst Montecuccoli 1609–1680. Gedanken zum Leben und Werk eines großen österreichischen Feldherrn." *Österreichische Militärische Zeitschrift* 2 (1964): 301–5.

Perjés, Géza. "The Zrínyi-Montecuccoli Controversy." In *From Hunyadi to Rákóczi: War and Society in Late Medieval and Early Modern Hungary: War and Society in Eastern and Central Europe.* Vol. 3, edited by János M. Bak and Béla K. Kiraly, 335–49. New York: Brooklyn College Press, 1982.

Pieraccini, Gaetano. *La stirpe de'Medici di Cafaggiolo: Saggio di ricerche sulla trasmissione ereditaria dei caratteri biologici.* 3 vols. Florence: Vallechi, 1924–25.

Pieri, Piero. *Guerra e politica negli scrittori italiani.* Milan: Riccardo Ricciardi Editore, 1954.

——. *The Thirty Years' War.* Translated by Robert Evans. Berkeley: University of California Press, 1971.

Polišenský, Josef V., and Frederick Lewis Snider. *War and Society in Europe, 1618–1648.* Cambridge: Cambridge University Press, 1978.

Press, Volker. "Österreichische Großmachtbildung und Reichsverfasung: Zur kaiserlichen Stellung nach 1648." *Mitteilungen des Instituts für Österreichische Geschichtsforschung* 98 (1990): 131–54.

Pugliese, Salvatore. *Le prime strette dell'austria in italia.* Milan: Treves, 1932.

Pursell, Brennan C. *The Winter King: Frederick V of the Palatinate and the Coming of the Thirty Years' War.* Aldershot: Ashgate, 2003.

Rebitsch, Robert. *Das werden einer Großmacht. Österreich von 1700 bis 1740.* 4th ed. Vienna: R. M. Rohrer, 1962.

——. *Matthias Gallas (1588–1647): Generalleutnant des Kaisers zur Zeit des Dreissigjährigen Krieges: Eine militärische Biographie.* Münster: Aschendorff, 2006.

——. *Wallenstein: Biografie eines Machtmenschen.* Vienna: Böhlau, 2010.

Rebitsch Robert, Jenny Öhman, and Jan Kilián. *1648: Kriegführung und Friedensverhandlungen: Prag und das Ende des Dreißigjährigen Krieges.* Innsbruck: Innsbruck University Press, 2018.

Redlich, Fritz. "Contributions in the Thirty Years' War." *Economic History Review* 12, no. 2 (1959): 247–54.

——. *The German Military Enterpriser and His Work Force: A Study in European Economic and Social History.* 2 vols. Wiesbaden: F. Steiner, 1964.

——. "Military Entrepreneurship and the Credit System in the 16th and 17th Centuries." *Kyklos* 10 (1957): 186–93.

Reid, W. Stanford. "The Four Monarchies of Daniel in Reformation Historiography." *Historical Reflections/Réflexions Historiques* 8, no. 1 (Spring 1981): 115–23.

Ricci, Lodovico. *Corografia dei territorj di Modena, Reggio e degli altri stati già appartenenti alla Casa d'Este.* Modena: Per gli Eredi di Bartolomaio Soliani, 1806.

Riches, Daniel. "Military Affairs as a Force for Integration across Early Modern Frontiers." Paper presented at the Society for Military History, Ogden, UT, 19 April 2008.

——. *Protestant Cosmopolitanism and Diplomatic Culture: Brandenburg-Swedish Relations in the Seventeenth Century.* Leiden: Brill, 2013.

Richter, Karl. "Die böhmischen Länder von 1471–1740." In *Handbuch der Geschichte der böhmischen Länder,* vol. 2, edited by Karl Bosl, 97–412. Stuttgart: A. Hiersemann, 1974.

Rimondi, Riccardo. *Estensi: Storia e leggende, personaggi e luoghi di una dinastia millenaria.* Ferrara: Cirelli & Zanirato, 2004.

Ritter, Moriz. "Wallensteins Eroberungspläne gegen Venedig 1629." *Historische Zeitschrift* 93 (1904).

Roberts, Michael. *Gustavus Adolphus and the Rise of Sweden.* London: English Universities Press, 1973.

——. "The 'Military Revolution,' 1560–1660." In *The Military Revolution Debate: Readings on the Military Transformation of Early Modern Europe,* edited by Clifford J. Rogers, 13–35. Boulder, CO: Westview Press, 1995.

Rogers, Clifford J, ed. *The Military Revolution Debate: Readings on the Military Transformation of Early Modern Europe.* Boulder: Westview Press, 1995.

Roosen, William. "Early Modern Diplomatic Ceremonial: A Systems Approach." *Journal of Modern History* 52 (September 1980): 452–76.

Rosa, Mario. "The 'World's Theatre': The Court of Rome and Politics in the First Half of the Seventeenth Century." In *Court and Politics in Papal Rome, 1492–1700,* edited by Gianvittorio Signorotto and Maria Antonietta Visceglia, 78–98. Cambridge: Cambridge University Press, 2002.

Rothenberg, Gunther. *The Austrian Military Border in Croatia, 1522–1747.* Urbana: University of Illinois Press, 1960.

——. "Maurice of Nassau, Gustavus Adolphus, Raimondo Montecuccoli, and the 'Military Revolution' of the Seventeenth Century." In *Makers of Modern Strategy from Machiavelli to the Nuclear Age,* edited by Peter Paret, 32–63. Princeton, NJ: Princeton University Press, 1986.

Rowlands, Guy. *Dangerous and Dishonest Men: The International Bankers of Louis XIV's France.* New York: Palgrave Macmillan, 2015.

——. *The Dynastic State and the Army Under Louis XIV: Royal Service and Private Interest, 1661–1701.* Cambridge; New York: Cambridge University Press, 2002.

Sandonnini, Tommaso. *Il Generale Raimondo Montecuccoli e la sua famiglia, note storico-biografico.* Modena: G. Ferraguti, 1913.

Scannell, Paul. *Conflict and Soldiers' Literature in Early Modern Europe: The Reality of War.* London: Bloomsbury Academic, 2015.

Schmidt, Georg. *Die Reiter der Apokalypse. Geschichte des Dreißigjährigen Krieges.* München: C. H. Beck, 2018.

Schnettger, Matthias. "Kaiserinnen und Kardinäle: Wissensbroker(innen) zwischen dem Kaiserhof und Italien im 17. Jahrhundert." In *Transferprozesse zwischen dem Alten Reich und Italien im 17. Jahrhundert,* edited by Sabina Brevaglieri and Matthias Schnettger, 127–60. Bielefeld: Transcript Verlag, 2018.

Schreiber, Georg. *Raimondo Montecuccoli: Feldherr, Schriftsteller und Kavalier: Ein Lebensbild aus dem Barock.* Graz: Styria, 2000.

Schreiber, Renate. *"Ein Galeria nach meinem Humor": Erzherzog Leopold Wilhelm.* Vienna: Kunsthistorisches Museum-Museumsverband, 2004.

——. "Mit Degen und Feder—Erzherzog Leopold Wilhelm als Verfasser italienischer Gedichte." In *Fürst und Fürstin als Künstler,* edited by Annette Cremer, Mathias Müller, and Klaus Pietschmann, 239–59. Munich: DKV, 2018.

Schulze, Winfried. *Landesdefension und Staatsbildung: Studien zum Kriegswesen des innerösterreichischen Territorialstaates (1564–1619).* Vienna: Böhlau, 1973.

Schwarz, Henry F. *The Imperial Privy Council in the Seventeenth Century.* Westport, CT: Greenwood Press, 1972.

Scott, H. M., ed. *The European Nobilities in the Seventeenth and Eighteenth Centuries.* Vol. 2, *Northern, Central and Eastern Europe.* New York: Longman, 1995.

Seifert, Herbert. "Akademien am Wiener Kaiserhof der Barockzeit." In *Akademie und Musik-Erscheinungsweisen und Wirkungen des Akademiegedankens in Kultur- und Musikgeschichte: Institutionem, Veranstaltungen, Schriften: Festschrift für Werner Braun zum 65. Geburtstag,* edited by Wolf Frobenius, Nicole Schwindt-Gross, and Thomas Sick, 215–17. Saarbrücken: SDV, 1993.

Sherer, Idan. *Warriors for a Living: The Experience of the Spanish Infantry in the Italian Wars, 1494–1559.* Boston: Brill, 2017.

Sienell, Stefan. *Die Geheime Konferenz unter Kaiser Leopold I.: Personelle, Strukturen und Methoden zur politischen Entscheidungsfindung am Wiener Hof.* Frankfurt: Lang, 2001.

Signorotto, Gianvittorio. "Guerre spagnoli, ufficiali lombardi." In *I Farnese: Corti, guerra e nobiltà in antico regime: Atti del convegno di studi Piacenza, 24–26 novembre 1994,* edited by Antonella Bilotto, Pietro Del Negro, and Cesare Mozzarelli, 367–96. Rome: Bulzoni editore, 1997.

——. *Milano Spagnola: Guerra, istituzioni, uomini di governo, 1635–1660.* New rev. ed. Florence: Sansoni, 2001.

Simeoni, Luigi. *Francesco I d'Este e la politica italiana del Mazarino.* Bologna: N. Zanichelli, 1921.

Simoni, Anna E. C. "Soldiers' Tales: Observations on Italian Military Books Published at Antwerp in the Early Seventeenth Century." In *The Italian Book, 1465–1800: Studies Presented to Dennis E. Rhodes on His 70th Birthday,* edited by Denis V. Reidy, 255–90. London: British Library, 1993.

Smith, Pamela H. *The Business of Alchemy: Science and Culture in the Holy Roman Empire.* Princeton, NJ: Princeton University Press, 1994.

Snyder, Jon. R., "Mare Magnum: The Arts in the Early Modern Age." In *Early Modern Italy, 1550–1796,* edited by John A. Marino, 143–65. Oxford: Oxford University Press, 2002.

Sodini, Carla. *L'ercole tirreno: Guerra e dinastia medicea nella prima metà del '600.* Florence: Olschki, 2001.

Spagnoletti, Angelantonio. "L'Aristocrazia napoletana nelle guerre del primo seicento: Tra pratica delle armi e integrazione dinastica." In *I Farnese: Corti, guerra e nobiltà in antico regime: Atti del convegno di studi Piacenza, 24–26 novembre 1994,* edited by Antonella Bilotto, Pietro Del Negro, and Cesare Mozzarelli, 445–68. Rome: Bulzoni editore, 1997.

——. *Principi italiani e Spagna nell'eta barocca.* Milan: B. Mondadori, 1996.

——. *Stato, aristocrazie e ordine di Malta nell'Italia moderna.* Roma: École française de Rome; Bari: Universita degli studi, 1988.

Spielman, John P. *Leopold I of Austria.* New Brunswick, NJ: Rutgers University Press, 1977.

Srbik, Heinrich. *Wallensteins Ende: Ursachen, Verlauf und Folgen der Katastrophe.* Salzburg: O. Müller, 1952.

Storrs, Christopher. *The Resilience of the Spanish Monarchy, 1665–1700.* Oxford: Oxford University Press, 2006.

Stoye, John. *Marsigli's Europe, 1680–1730: The Life and Times of Luigi Ferdinando Marsigli, Soldier and Virtuoso*. New Haven, CT: Yale University Press, 1994.

Strohmeyer, Arno. "Das Osmanische Reich—ein Teil des europäischen Staatensystems der Frühen Neuzeit?" In *Das Osmanische Reich und die Habsburgermonarchie: Akten des internationalen Kongresses zum 150-jährigen Bestehen des Instituts für Österreichische Geschichtsforschung, Wien, 22.–25. September 2004*, edited by Marlene Kurz, Martin Scheutz, Karl Vocelka, and Thomas Winkelbauer, 149–65. Vienna: R. Oldenbourg, 2005.

Symcox, Geoffrey. *Victor Amadeus II: Absolutism in the Savoyard State, 1675–1730*. Berkeley: University of California Press, 1983.

Tallett, Frank. *War and Society in Early Modern Europe, 1495–1715*. London: Routledge, 1992.

Tallett, Frank, and D.J.B. Trim, eds. *European Warfare, 1350–1750*. Cambridge: Cambridge University Press, 2010.

Tanner, Marie. *The Last Descendant of Aeneas: The Hapsburgs and the Mythic Image of the Emperor*. New Haven, CT: Yale University Press, 1993.

Thomson, Erik. "Axel Oxenstierna and Books." *Sixteenth Century Journal* 38 (2007): 705–29.

Tiraboschi, Girolamo. *Dizionario topografico-storico degli stati Estensi*. 2 vols. Modena: Tipografia Camerale, 1825.

——. *Memorie storiche modenesi col codice diplomatico*. 5 vols. Modena: Società Tipografica, 1794.

Toifl, Leopold. "Die Schlacht von Mogersdorf, St. Gotthard am 1. August 1664." In *Die Schlacht von Mogersdorf/St. Gotthard und der Friede von Eisenburg/Vasvar 1664: Rahmenbedingungen, Akteure, Auswirkungen und Rezeption eines europäischen Ereignisses*, edited by Karin Sperl, Martin Scheutz, and Arno Strohmeyer, 151–69. Eisenstadt: Amt der Burgenländischen Landesregierung, Hauptreferat Landesarchiv und Landesbibliothek, 2016.

Tomassini, Luciano. *Raimondo Montecuccoli: Capitano e scrittore*. Rome: 1978.

Tóth, Ferenc, and Jean Bérenger, *Saint-Gotthard 1664: Une bataille européenne*. Panazol: Lavauzelle, 2007.

Toulmin, Stephen. *Cosmopolis: The Hidden Agenda of Modernity*. Chicago: University of Chicago Press, 1992.

Trivellato, Francesca. "Renaissance Italy and the Muslim Mediterranean in Recent Historical Work." *Journal of Modern History* 82 (March 2010): 127–55.

Turnbull, Stephen R. *The Ottoman Empire, 1526–1699*. New York: Routledge, 2003.

Turner, Victor W. *The Ritual Process: Structure and Anti-Structure*. Chicago: University of Chicago Press, 1969.

Valensi, Lucette. *The Birth of the Despot: Venice and the Sublime Porte*. Ithaca, NY: Cornell University Press, 2009.

Válka, Josef. *Dějiny Moravy díl 2: Morava Reformace Renesance a Baroka: Vlastivěda moravská země a lid nová řada svazek 6*. Brno: Muzejní a vlastivědná společnost, 1995.

Valleriani, Matteo. *Galileo Engineer*. Dordrecht: Springer, 2010.

Van Gennep, Arnold. *The Rites of Passage*. Chicago: University of Chicago Press, 1960.

Van Horn Melton, James. "The Nobility in the Bohemian and Austrian Lands, 1620–1780." In *The European Nobilities in the Seventeenth and Eighteenth Centuries*. Vol. 2, *Northern and Central Europe*, edited by H. M. Scott, 110–43. New York: Longman, 1995.

Várkonyi, Ágnes R. "Gábor Bethlen and His European Presence." *Hungarian Historical Review* 2, no. 4 (2013): 695–732.

——. "The Preservation of Statehood." In *History of Transylvania*. Vol. 2, *From 1606 to 1830*, edited by Béla Köpeczi et al., 233–64. Boulder, CO: Social Science Monographs, 2002.

Vehse, Eduard. *Memoirs of the Court and Aristocracy of Austria*. 2 vols. London: Nichols, 1896.

Vessely, Kurt. "The Development of the Hungarian Military Frontier until the Middle of the Eighteenth Century." *Austrian History Yearbook* 9–10 (1973–74): 55–110.

Visceglia, Maria Antonietta. "Fazioni e lotta politica nel Sacro Romano Collegio nella prima metà del Seicento." In *La corte di Roma tra Cinque e Seicento: "Teatro" della politica europea*, edited by Gianvittorio Signorotto and Maria Antonietta Visceglia, 37–91. Rome: Bulzoni, 1998.

Von Friedeburg, Robert, "'Lands' and 'Fatherlands': Changes in the Plurality of Allegiances in the Sixteenth-Century Holy Roman Empire." In *Networks, Regions and Nations: Shaping Identities in the Low Countries, 1300–1650*, edited by Judith Pollmann and Robert Stein, 263–82. Leiden: Brill, 2010.

Wagner, Georg. "Die Schlacht von St. Gotthard-Mogersdorf und das Oberkommando Raimund Montecuccolis." In *Atti del convegno di studi su Raimondo Montecuccoli nel terzo centenario della battaglia sulla Raab*, 155–234. Modena: Accademia Nazionale di Scienze, Lettere, e Arti, 1964.

Walton, Stephen A. "State Building through Building for the State: Domestic and Foreign Expertise in Tudor Fortifications." In "Expertise and the Early Modern State," edited by Eric Ash. Special issue, *Osiris* 25 (2010): 66–84.

Weber, Christoph. *Genealogien zur Papstgeschichte*. Vol. 1. Stuttgart: Hiersemann, 1999.

Wheatcroft, Andrew. *The Enemy at the Gate: Habsburgs, Ottomans, and the Battle for Europe*. New York: Basic Books, 2008.

Wilson, Peter. *Absolutism in Central Europe*. London: Routledge, 2000.

——. *Europe's Tragedy: A History of the Thirty Years' War*. London: Allen Lane, 2009.

——. *German Armies: War and German Politics, 1648–1806*. London: UCL Press, 1998.

——. *Heart of Europe: A History of the Holy Roman Empire*. Cambridge, MA: Belknap Press of Harvard University Press, 2016.

——. *The Holy Roman Empire, 1495–1806*. New York: St. Martin's Press, 1999.

Winkelbauer, Thomas. *Fürst und Fürstendiener: Gundaker von Liechtenstein, ein österreichischer Aristokrat des konfessionellen Zeitalters*. Vienna: Oldenbourg, 1999.

Wintroub, Michael. *The Voyage of Thought: Navigating Knowledge across the Sixteenth-Century World*. Cambridge: Cambridge University Press, 2017.

Worthington, David. *Scots in Habsburg Service, 1618–1648*. Leiden: Brill, 2004.

Wrede, Major Alphons Freiherrn von. *Geschichte der k. und k. Wehrmacht*. 5 vols. Vienna: Siedel, 1898–1905.

Zilsel, Edgar. *The Social Origins of Modern Science*. Dordrecht: Kluwer Academic Publishers, 2000.

INDEX

Page numbers in italics denote illustrations. The abbreviation RM denotes Raimondo Montecuccoli.

Printed in the USA
CPSIA information can be obtained
at www.ICGtesting.com
LVHW051645170823
755530LV00014B/270/J